DIFFERENTIAL ABILITY SCALES®

INTRODUCTORY AND TECHNICAL

HANDBOOK

Colin D. Elliott

THE PSYCHOLOGICAL CORPORATION
HARCOURT BRACE JOVANOVICH, INC.
San Antonio, San Diego, Orlando, Chicago, New York, Toronto

About the Author

Colin D. Elliott was born in Ripon, Yorkshire, England. After obtaining his Bachelor's degree in psychology at Hull University, he studied educational (school) psychology, and was awarded his Master of Science and doctoral degrees by the University of Manchester. He began his professional career as a school teacher and was a school psychologist for seven years before becoming a trainer of school psychologists.

In addition to his teaching duties, Dr. Elliott has been involved in research and development on the *Differential Ability Scales* and its predecessor, the *British Ability Scales*, for over seventeen years. For part of his work on the project, he spent nearly a year in the United States. He is currently a Senior Lecturer and tutor to the Masters' course for professional educational psychologists in the Centre for Educational Guidance and Special Needs, School of Education, University of Manchester, England. In addition to the BAS and DAS, Dr. Elliott's research and publications have been concerned with behavior problems in children, the relationship of temperament and personality to learning, the ability profiles of children with learning disabilities, and the measurement of children's developmental stages. He is a Fellow of the British Psychological Society. He is married, has three children, and at the present count in May 1990, has two grandchildren.

Preface

Why? Why should anyone read this preface? After all, most of us skip prefaces without a second thought. And why the DAS? Why another children's cognitive-test battery when there are a range of alternatives available?

With this preface, I intend to answer these questions by giving a brief bird's-eye view of the *Differential Ability Scales* (DAS), its rationale, and its distinctive features. Second, the preface provides a preview of the organization and contents of this **Handbook**. Finally, the preface includes acknowledgment of some of those who contributed significantly to the development of the DAS and particularly to the contents of this **Handbook**.

About seventeen years ago, just after the start of my involvement with the *British Ability Scales*, a colleague of many years said to me, "Why on earth did you ever take that on?" A year ago, I saw him and reminded him of the occasion. He had forgotten the question, and both of us had forgotten my reply. Nevertheless, the question has kept coming back to me over the years, reminding me, through the passage of time, of the frailty of our immediate reasons for doing things, but also emphasizing the solid worth of a vision. In this case, the vision was to produce a cognitive-assessment battery that would provide reliable, interpretable information about children's strengths and weaknesses across a range of cognitive domains. Such information is essential if our assessments are to identify the nature of a child's learning difficulties and consequently lead to what should be the outcome of all assessments: helpful and practical suggestions for teachers, parents, and others concerned about the education and care of the child. The vision, therefore, was to bring to bear a range of psychological theories and advances in test methodology in producing a test battery of direct relevance to psychologists and educators, a battery with characteristics of interpretability and of flexibility of use, and one which offers an exceptional range of measurement resources.

What makes the DAS distinctive?

The DAS was designed primarily as a profile test. That is, it yields reliable, focused, and interpretable scores for a wide range of abilities and at the level of either composites or subtests. To a greater extent than the subtests of many other batteries, the subtests of the DAS have sufficient reliable specificity to make them individually interpretable and to make differences between them meaningful. Thus the battery is designed so that examiners can identify children's cognitive strengths and weaknesses across a range of ability domains.

The terms "intelligence" and "IQ" are not part of the DAS vocabulary, and the DAS does not attempt to yield a global score from heterogeneous components. Its composites derive only from those subtests that are the best measures of conceptual and reasoning abilities, rather than from all subtests.

The DAS emphasizes the concept of "developed ability" in score interpretation. That is, no unwarranted assumptions are made that subtests or composite scores are measures of innate ability.

With its wide range of content, the DAS also includes some measures not found in other batteries. In addition to the subtests that measure conceptual and reasoning abilities, the battery contains a number of "diagnostic" subtests that provide information on varied, independent dimensions of ability, including memory, perception, and speed of information processing.

The DAS covers exceptionally wide age and ability ranges. The subtests were developed to be suitable for the assessment of exceptional children. That is, the many easy and difficult items provide the battery with both a good "floor" and a good "ceiling." The DAS incorporates the concept of "out-of-level" testing by which children may be tested with materials appropriate for their abilities although their performance may well lie outside the normal range for their age.

The DAS also incorporates "tailored testing" to enable examiners to select the most appropriate items for a child. This approach results in both accurate and time-efficient testing.

The DAS is child-centered: It was created from a developmental and educational perspective. It is not a downward extension of an adult battery. The preschool subtests were designed to be attractive and suitable for preschoolers. Similarly, the school-age subtests focus on the abilities that are typically shown by and relevant to school-aged children.

Finally, the DAS has three brief but highly reliable achievement-screening tests co-normed with the cognitive subtests. Therefore, ability–achievement discrepancies can be evaluated quickly and objectively.

What are the purposes of this Handbook?

I anticipate three types of readers of this **Handbook**. First are those who may perhaps not be qualified to use the DAS (such as students, teachers, or lay people) but who wish to know something about its content, background, philosophy, and technical characteristics. Second are those qualified examiners who have not yet decided to use the battery but who wish to evaluate and inform themselves about it. Third are those who have already purchased and decided to use the battery and who are referring to the **Handbook** for technical data and for interpretive guidelines and suggestions.

The first three chapters in this **Handbook** describe the structure, rationale, and history of the DAS. Readers in the third group listed above will no doubt find that the outline description of the DAS in Chapter 1 overlaps considerably with the description given in the *DAS Administration and Scoring Manual* (Elliott, 1990). This description is provided for those readers who do not have the **Manual**. Chapter 2 is important for all readers because it covers a number of issues concerning the rationale, or theoretical underpinning, of the test battery. Chapter 3 outlines the history of the battery over a 25-year period of development.

Chapter 4 focuses on the subtest content and the interpretation of scores obtained on each subtest and ability cluster. The interpretive suggestions regarding the processes underlying high or low scores were designed to be readily accessible to examiners who may wish to refer to them regularly. Chapter 5 presents a systematic procedure for analyzing scores obtained on the DAS, starting at the most general level (that of the General Conceptual Ability score) and working down to the individual subtest level. The first part of Chapter 5 is concerned with the systematic identification of significantly high and low points in the child's score profile. The second part of the chapter discusses the use of this information, and the interpretive suggestions given in Chapter 4, for generating hypotheses about relatively strong or weak underlying cognitive processes. Such hypotheses must always be placed in the context of the child's environmental circumstances and tested against the child's life data. I hope and, indeed, expect that such a systematic approach to test score interpretation will yield useful intervention suggestions tailored to the particular characteristics of the child.

Chapters 6 through 10 present the basic technical information about the DAS: its norm-sample characteristics, the methods of scaling employed, its reliability and validity, and its fairness for different population subgroups.

The **Handbook** concludes with an appendix presenting the basic concepts of the Rasch model of item response theory, a model that has influenced many aspects of the DAS.

Acknowledgments

An unusually large number of people contributed to the development of the DAS. Without many of them, the project would have been the poorer. Without some of them, it would have been impossible. Many of those involved were thanked in the Acknowledgments in the **Manual**. The acknowledgments here are particularly of those who contributed to this **Handbook**.

First and foremost, I wish to thank Dr. Mark Daniel, who did a superlative job in directing the project for its entire duration. Mark's contributions extend beyond the typical responsibilities of a project director. In the early stages, he suggested new subtests and was extensively involved in item writing and development. In later stages, he generated many creative ideas that influenced the final structure and configuration of the battery. Particularly important in the technical area was his concern to find ways of using modern test theory to address the question of efficient, adaptive testing tailored to the child. His work also resulted in advances in sampling methodology and the estimation and reporting of measurement accuracy. Finally, I gratefully acknowledge his many contributions to the writing and careful editing of this **Handbook**.

It has also been a pleasure to work with Drs. Brian Stone and Kathleen Williams. Brian conducted the complex data analyses for the validity studies reported in Chapter 9. He dedicated long hours of work to managing, checking, and analyzing the numerous sets of data that were collected. Kathleen, also a school psychologist, likewise made invaluable contributions to the form and structure of this **Handbook**. She too spent many hours reviewing manuscript and making important, helpful suggestions which, in particular, concerned the description and rationale of the DAS and the interpretive chapters. Apart from these major contributions, I have greatly appreciated the soundness of the comments and criticisms on various aspects of the project from Brian and Kathleen, coming, as they have, from a background of experience in professional school psychology.

I have much appreciated Dr. James Ward's reflections on the early history of the test battery and also Dr. Gale Roid's advice on the content and structure of the appendix on the Rasch model.

Reference to Chapter 6 will indicate that the standardization sample was drawn from all regions of the United States. Assembling this sample required the help and collaboration of many testing coordinators, psychologists, and school districts. The contribution of these individuals and districts, who are listed in Appendix A, is gratefully acknowledged.

Many people contributed to validity studies of the DAS. In particular, I thank Karen Cocco, James Cromer, Dr. Raymond Dean, Nancy deWied, Dr. Elizabeth Doll, Robert Friedle, Larry Gandee, Dr. Betty Gridley, Robert Huzinec, Dr. Susan Jacob, Mark Kelly, Andrew Kercher, Wanda Lillis, David McIntosh, Dr. Nancy McKellar, Janet Muscutt, Jarret Pence, Rocco Persico, Dr. Jonathan Sandoval, Nancy Smith, Dr. Mark Swerdlik, and Dr. Paulette Thomas for their efforts in collecting data and conducting analyses.

I am also grateful to Dr. Joseph Buckhalt, Dr. Jerome Doppelt, Dr. Betty Gridley, Gretchen Guiton, Dr. David Herman, and Dr. Mark Swerdlik for their helpful comments about various portions of this **Handbook**.

Cynthia Halm devoted long hours to editing the hundreds of pages of manuscript; her commitment to ensuring that the presentation not only reads well but also makes sense has been invaluable. I wish to thank Terri Chambers, production editor, for her efforts toward achieving an attractive and consistent presentation. I am grateful to Linda Williams and to the word processing operators under her supervision, particularly Laurel David, for their cheerful and efficient handling of text. Alan Belcher designed the final published form of the DAS, Elizabeth Crawford directed the typesetting operation implemented by Sue Silvers and Deborah Sitler, and production manager Neil Kinch was responsible for coordinating these production activities.

Finally, I turn gratefully to Linda Daniel and Marian Elliott for their unfailing support and encouragement to Mark and me during this project. Test batteries such as the DAS are in a sense very personal. Although as scientists we aim at objectivity, we cannot, and should not, keep our personal qualities, characteristics, and commitments out of the end product. If the battery looks as if it were produced by a computer for the purpose of testing machines, we will have failed. Thus, the interest and support of Linda and Marian have played a part in the shaping of the DAS, which would have been poorer without them. In the Preface to the *British Ability Scales Introductory Handbook*, I noted that Marian had encouraged me to always keep the tests focused on the solution of practical problems. I wrote: "It is human examples which bring technical work to life, for the ultimate justification of technology is its usefulness in helping people. To her, for providing me with 'an ever fixèd mark' through the vicissitudes of nine years (and more), mere words are inadequate to express the gratitude of the heart." Seven years further on, that still sums it up.

Colin D. Elliott
University of Manchester, England
May 1990

Table of Contents

About the Author iii

Preface v

Tables xvii

Figures xxvii

Chapter 1. Introduction   1

An Overview of the DAS   1
    Structure and Components of the DAS   2
    Overview of Administration Procedures   5

Summary   9

Chapter 2. The Assessment of Cognitive Abilities:
Rationale of the DAS **11**

Generalization: The Key Issue in Test Interpretation 11

Basic Rationale of the DAS 12
    Homogeneous, Distinct, and Reliable Subtests 12
    Hierarchical Structure 13
    Broad Theoretical Base 14

The Theoretical Background of the DAS 14

The DAS Assessment Model 18
    Interpretation of the General Conceptual Ability
      Score 19
    The Cluster Scores 20
    The Subtests 23

The Assessment Model in Practice 24

Other Interpretive Issues 26
    The Nature of Ability Scores 26
    Psychometric Tests Versus Behavioral Assessment
      Methods 28

Chapter 3. History **31**

The *British Ability Scales* 31
    First Phase, 1965–1970 32
    Second Phase, 1973–1982 33
    Post-Publication Developments 34

The *Differential Ability Scales* 35

Chapter 4. Description and Interpretation of the DAS Subtests and Clusters 39

General Influences on Test Scores....................... 40

Other Variables to Consider 41

The Nature of the Interpretive Suggestions 42

Preschool Core Subtests................................ 43
    Block Building (Ages 2:6–4:11)..................... 43
    Verbal Comprehension (Ages 2:6–6:11)............... 45
    Picture Similarities (Ages 2:6–7:11)................. 46
    Naming Vocabulary (Ages 2:6–8:11) 47
    Pattern Construction (Ages 3:0–17:11) 48
    Early Number Concepts (Ages 2:6–7:11)............. 51
    Copying (Ages 3:6–7:11) 53

School-Age Core Subtests.............................. 55
    Recall of Designs (Ages 5:0–17:11).................. 55
    Word Definitions (Ages 5:0–17:11) 56
    Pattern Construction (Ages 3:0–17:11) 57
    Matrices (Ages 5:0–17:11)......................... 58
    Similarities (Ages 5:0–17:11) 60
    Sequential and Quantitative Reasoning (5:0–17:11) .. 62

Diagnostic Subtests 64
    Matching Letter-Like Forms (Ages 4:0–7:11) 64
    Recall of Digits (Ages 2:6–17:11) 66
    Recall of Objects—Immediate and Delayed
        (Ages 4:0–17:11) 67
    Recognition of Pictures (Ages 2:6–17:11)............ 69
    Speed of Information Processing (Ages 5:0–17:11).... 70

School Achievement Tests 74
    Basic Number Skills (Ages 6:0–17:11).............. 74
    Spelling (Ages 6:0–17:11) 77
    Word Reading (Ages 5:0–17:11).................... 79

Clusters of the Preschool Level of the Cognitive
Battery (Ages 3:6–5:11) 81
    Verbal Ability..................................... 81
    Nonverbal Ability 82

Clusters of the School-Age Level of the Cognitive Battery
(Ages 6:0–17:11)...................................... 83
    Verbal Ability..................................... 83
    Nonverbal Reasoning Ability 84
    Spatial Ability 85

Chapter 5. Systematic Interpretation of Test Scores 87

Overview 87

Stage One: Identifying High and Low Scores in the DAS
Profile 87
    Descriptive Categories for Scores 88
    Comparing Cluster Scores and the GCA 89
    Comparing Core-Subtest Scores 93
    Comparing Diagnostic-Subtest Scores with the
        Mean of the Core Subtests 94
    Comparison of Scores on Individual Cognitive
        Subtests 95
    Ability–Achievement Comparisons 95

Stage Two: Interpreting Cognitive Strengths and
Weaknesses 98
    Philosophy of Profile Analysis 99
    Analysis of Underlying Processes 100
    Guidelines for Profile Interpretation 104
    Examples of Profile Interpretation 105

Summary 108

Chapter 6. Tryout and Standardization 109

Tryout Phase 109

Standardization Phase 110
    Procedures 111
    Description of the Sample 116
    Sample for Achievement-Test Grade Norms 125

Chapter 7. Scaling and Development of Norms 133

Design of Standardization Data Collection 134

Development of Final Scoring Rules 134

Rasch Scaling 136
    Applications of Rasch Scaling 137
    Special Item-Scaling Decisions 138
    Person Abilities 138
    Item Difficulties 139
    Item Sets Within Subtests 140

Development of Norms 164
    Subtest Norms 164
    Composite Norms 165

Grade Norms for Achievement Tests 165
Age and Grade Equivalents 166
Extended GCA Norms............................. 166

When to Use the Extended GCA Norms 169

Chapter 8. Reliability, Accuracy, and Specificity........ 171

Reliability and Accuracy 171

Internal Reliabilities of Subtests and Composites........ 175
Subtests 175
Constructing Item-Selection Rules for Each Subtest. 177
Composite Scores................................. 180
Standard Errors of Subtest and Composite Scores... 180
Reliability at Different Ability Levels: Out-of-Level
Testing 180

Test–Retest Reliability 184

Interrater Reliability of Four Subtests with Open-Ended
Responses 187

Confidence Intervals 188

Specificity... 190

Comparison of IRT-Based and Traditional Methods of
Estimating Reliability................................ 190

Conclusion 195

Chapter 9. Validity 197

Internal Validity...................................... 197
Intercorrelations of Subtests and Composites 197
Confirmatory Methods of Factor Analysis 198
Exploratory Methods of Factor Analysis 209
Equivalence of the Preschool and School-Age GCA . 213
Equivalence of the Two Versions of the Pattern
Construction Subtest 216

Correlations with Other Cognitive Measures............. 217
Correlations with Other Ability Batteries 217
Correlations with Tests of Specific Cognitive
Abilities 235
Summary of Correlation Studies with Other
Cognitive Measures 240

Correlations with Measures of Academic Achievement.... 242
    Correlations Within the DAS Between Ability and
      Achievement 242
    Correlations with Other Individually Administered
      Achievement Tests............................ 245
    Correlations with Group-Administered,
      Standardized Tests of School Achievement 247
    Correlations with Teacher-Assigned School Grades.. 251
    Summary of Correlation Studies with Measures of
      Academic Achievement 255

DAS Score Profiles of Special Populations 255
    Gifted Students................................. 255
    Educable Mentally Retarded Students............. 257
    Learning-Disabled Students 258

Concluding Comments................................ 262

Chapter 10. Fairness................................. 263

Bias Review Panel 263

Statistical Analyses of Item Bias...................... 264
    Collection of Additional Samples of Black and
      Hispanic Children 265
    Procedure for Item Bias Analysis 266

Fairness of Prediction................................ 266

Conclusion 268

Appendix A. Acknowledgments........................ 271

Field Supervisors and Examiners....................... 272

Schools, Preschools, and Day-Care Centers 280

**Appendix B. Statistical Significance and Frequency
    of Score Differences...................... 289**

**Appendix C. Intercorrelation of Subtests, Composites,
    and Achievement Tests by Age 305**

Appendix D. An Outline of the Rasch Model **331**

An Overview of Item Response Theory Models 331
    The Theory 332
    Features of Item Response Theory Models 332

Mathematical Definition of the Rasch Model 337

Tests of Goodness of Fit to the Model 339

Applications of the Rasch Model to the DAS 340
    Division of Subtests into Item Sets 340
    The Unit of Measurement 340
    Characteristics of Ability Scores 343

Summary 343

References **345**

Tables

Table 2.1. Basic Abilities and Processes Measured by the Preschool DAS Subtests........................... 23

Table 2.2. Basic Abilities and Processes Measured by the School-Age DAS Subtests 24

Table 3.1. Subtest Revisions from BAS to DAS 36

Table 4.1. Content of Basic Number Skills Items.............. 74

Table 5.1. Descriptive Classification Labels for GCA, Cluster and Subtest Scores 89

Table 6.1. Norm Sample: Number of Cases by Age and Sex ... 118

Table 6.2. Norm Sample: Percentages by Age, Sex, and Race.. 119

Table 6.3. Norm Sample: Percentages by Age, Sex, and Parent Education............................... 120

Table 6.4. Norm Sample: Percentages by Age, Sex, and Region... 121

Table 6.5. Norm Sample: Percentages by Age, Race, and Parent Education............................... 122

Table 6.6. Norm Sample: Percentages by Race and Region.... 123

Table 6.7. Norm Sample: Percentages by Community Size 123

Table 6.8. Norm Sample: Percentages of Children Aged 2:6–5:11 Enrolled in Educational Programs 124

Table 6.9. Norm Sample: Percentages by Special Education Category............................. 124

Table 6.10. Overlap of Grade-Norm Sample with Age-Norm Sample... 126

Table 6.11. Grade-Norm Sample: Number of Cases by Grade and Age 127

Table 6.12. Grade-Norm Sample: Number of Cases by Grade and Sex................................. 129

Table 6.13. Grade-Norm Sample: Percentages by Grade and Race 130

Table 6.14. Grade-Norm Sample: Percentages by Grade and Parent Education 131

Table 6.15. Grade-Norm Sample: Percentages by Grade and Region 132

Table 6.16.   Grade-Norm Sample: Percentages by Special
Education Category............................... 132

Table 7.1.   DAS Item Difficulties 141

Table 8.1.   Internal Reliabilities of Subtests and Composites
for the Preschool Level of the Cognitive Battery.... 178

Table 8.2.   Internal Reliabilities of Subtests, Achievement
Tests, and Composites for the School-Age Level..... 179

Table 8.3.   Standard Errors of Measurement of Subtests
and Composites for the Preschool Level of the
Cognitive Battery................................ 181

Table 8.4.   Standard Errors of Measurement of Subtests,
Achievement Tests, and Composites for the
School-Age Level 182

Table 8.5.   Out-of-Level Subtests: Reliability at Different
Levels of Ability................................. 183

Table 8.6.   Test–Retest Reliabilities of Preschool Subtests
and Composites.................................. 185

Table 8.7.   Test–Retest Reliabilities of School-Age Subtests,
Composites and Achievement Tests 186

Table 8.8.   Interrater Reliabilities of Four Subtests 188

Table 8.9.   Specificities of Subtests and Composites for the
Preschool Level of the Cognitive Battery........... 191

Table 8.10.   Specificities of Subtests and Composites for the
School-Age Level of the Cognitive Battery.......... 192

Table 8.11.   Comparison of IRT-Based Reliability Estimates,
Traditional Estimates, and "True" Reliabilities 195

Table 9.1.   Intercorrelation of Subtests and Composites
by Age Range: Ages 2:6–3:5...................... 198

Table 9.2.   Intercorrelation of Subtests and Composites
by Age Range: Ages 3:6–5:11..................... 199

Table 9.3.   Intercorrelation of Subtests and Composites
by Age Range: Ages 6:0–17:11.................... 200

Table 9.4.   Confirmatory Factor Analyses: Ages 2:6–3:5
(Six Subtests)................................... 202

Table 9.5.   Confirmatory Factor Analysis—Subtest Correlations
with the General Factor: Ages 2:6–3:5 202

Table 9.6. Confirmatory Factory Analyses: Ages 4:0–5:11 (Ten Subtests) 203

Table 9.7. Confirmatory Factor Analyses—Subtest Loadings for the One-Factor and Two-Factor Models: Ages 4:0–5:11 204

Table 9.8. Confirmatory Factor Analyses: Ages 3:6–5:11 (Six Core Subtests) 204

Table 9.9. Confirmatory Factor Analyses—Subtest Loadings for the Two-Factor Model (ENC on Both): Ages 3:6–5:11 205

Table 9.10. Confirmatory Factor Analyses: Ages 6:0–17:11 (Ten Subtests) 205

Table 9.11. Confirmatory Factor Analyses—Subtest Loadings for the One-, Two-, and Three-Factor Models: Ages 6:0–17:11 206

Table 9.12. Confirmatory Factor Analyses: Ages 6:0–17:11 (Six Core Subtests) 207

Table 9.13. Confirmatory Factor Analyses—One-, Two-, and Three-Factor Models for School-Aged Subsamples (Six Core Subtests) 208

Table 9.14. Exploratory Principal-Factor Analysis—Promax Factor Pattern: Ages 2:6–3:5 210

Table 9.15. Exploratory Principal-Factor Analyses—Promax Factor Patterns: Ages 4:0–5:11 211

Table 9.16. Exploratory Principal-Factor Analyses—Promax Factor Patterns: Ages 6:0–17:11 212

Table 9.17. Intercorrelation of Preschool and School-Age Core Subtests: Ages 5:0–6:11 214

Table 9.18. Confirmatory Factor Analyses Testing the Equivalence of the Preschool and School-Age GCA Scores 215

Table 9.19. Confirmatory Factor Analyses Comparing the Two Versions of the Pattern Construction Subtest 217

Table 9.20. Correlations of the DAS with the Wechsler Preschool and Primary Scale of Intelligence—Revised (WPPSI–R): 4- and 5-Year Olds 219

Table 9.21.   Selected Correlations Between DAS and WPPSI–R
Subtests 220

Table 9.22.   Correlations of the DAS with the Stanford–Binet
Intelligence Scale, Fourth Edition (SB–IV): 4- and
5-Year Olds 221

Table 9.23.   Selected Correlations Between DAS and SB–IV
Subtests: Preschool 221

Table 9.24.   Correlations of the DAS with the McCarthy Scales
of Children's Abilities (MSCA): British 3-Year-Olds . 223

Table 9.25.   Correlations of the DAS with the Wechsler Preschool
and Primary Scale of Intelligence—Revised
(WPPSI–R), Woodcock–Johnson Psycho-Educational
Battery Preschool Skills Cluster (WJ–PSSC), and
Kaufman Assessment Battery for Children (K–ABC):
3- to 5-Year-Olds................................. 224

Table 9.26.   Correlations of the DAS with the Wechsler
Intelligence Scale for Children—Revised
(WISC–R): 8- to 10-Year-Olds 226

Table 9.27.   Selected Correlations Between DAS and WISC–R
Subtests: Ages 8:0–10:2 227

Table 9.28.   Correlations of the DAS with the Wechsler
Intelligence Scale for Children—Revised (WISC–R):
14- and 15-Year-Olds.............. 228

Table 9.29.   Selected Correlations Between DAS and WISC–R
Subtests: Ages 14:0–15:11 229

Table 9.30.   Correlations of the DAS with the Stanford–Binet
Intelligence Scale, Fourth Edition (SB–IV):
9- and 10-Year-Olds 230

Table 9.31.   Selected Correlations Between DAS and SB–IV
Subtests: School-Age.............................. 231

Table 9.32.   Correlations of the DAS with the Stanford–Binet
Intelligence Scale, Fourth Edition (SB–IV):
7- to 11-Year-Old Gifted Referrals 232

Table 9.33.   Correlations of the DAS with the Kaufman
Assessment Battery for Children (K–ABC): 5- to
7-Year-Olds....................................... 234

Table 9.34. Correlations of Three DAS Subtests with the Peabody Picture Vocabulary Test—Revised (PPVT–R), Test for Auditory Comprehension of Language—Revised (TACL–R), and Columbia Mental Maturity Scale (CMMS): 3- to 5-Year-Olds........................ 235

Table 9.35. Correlations of the DAS with the Peabody Picture Vocabulary Test—Revised (PPVT–R): 1st- and 3rd-Graders 237

Table 9.36. Correlations of Two DAS Subtests with Selected Cognitive and Neuropsychological Tests: Hearing-Impaired 12- to 14-Year-Olds.............. 237

Table 9.37. Correlations of the DAS Cognitive Composites with the DAS Achievement Tests: 6- to 17-Year-Olds from the Norm Sample 242

Table 9.38. Correlations of the DAS Cognitive Composites with the DAS Achievement Tests: Three Age Ranges of the Norm Sample 243

Table 9.39. Correlations of the DAS Preschool and School-Age Cognitive Composites with DAS Achievement Tests: 6-Year-Olds from the Norm Sample................. 244

Table 9.40. Correlations of the DAS Cognitive Composites and Achievement Tests with the Basic Achievement Skills Individual Screener (BASIS)................. 245

Table 9.41. Correlations of the DAS with the Kaufman Test of Educational Achievement (K–TEA): 7- to 11-Year-Old Gifted Referrals 246

Table 9.42. Correlations of Two DAS Subtests with the Woodcock Reading Mastery Test—Revised (WRMT–R): 8- to 11-Year-Olds 247

Table 9.43. Correlations of DAS Cognitive Composites and Achievement Tests with Group Achievement Tests: Grades 1–12 in the Standardization Sample 249

Table 9.44. Correlations of DAS Cognitive Composites and Achievement Tests with Group Achievement Tests: Grades 1–3 in the Standardization Sample 250

Table 9.45. Correlations of DAS Cognitive Composites and Achievement Tests with Group Achievement Tests: Grades 4–7 in the Standardization Sample 251

Table 9.46. Correlations of DAS Cognitive Composites and Achievement Tests with Group Achievement Tests: Grades 8–12 in the Standardization Sample 252

Table 9.47. Correlations of DAS Cognitive Composites and Achievement Tests with School Grades: Grades K–12 in the Standardization Sample 253

Table 9.48. Correlations of DAS Cognitive Composites and Achievement Tests with School Grades: Grades K–3 in the Standardization Sample 253

Table 9.49. Correlations of DAS Cognitive Composites and Achievement Tests with School Grades: Grades 4–7 in the Standardization Sample 254

Table 9.50. Correlations of DAS Cognitive Composites and Achievement Tests with School Grades: Grades 8–12 in the Standardization Sample 254

Table 9.51. DAS Scores of Students Classified as Gifted 256

Table 9.52. DAS Scores of Students Classified as Educable Mentally Retarded 257

Table 9.53. DAS Scores of Students Classified as Learning Disabled 259

Table 9.54. Means and Standard Deviations for Four Clusters of Reading-Disabled Students on DAS Subtests and Composites 260

Table 10.1. Average Number of Black and Hispanic Children Taking Each Item for Item Bias Analysis 265

Table 10.2. Prediction of Academic Achievement from GCA and Race/Ethnicity 269

Table B.1. Between-Cluster and Within-Cluster Score Differences Required for Statistical Significance: Ages 3:6–5:11 290

Table B.2. Between-Cluster and Within-Cluster Score Differences Shown by Various Percentages of the Norm Sample: Ages 3:6–5:11 291

Table B.3. Between-Cluster and Within-Cluster Score Differences Shown by Various Percentages of the Norm Sample: Ages 6:0–17:11 291

Table B.4.   Between-Cluster and Within-Cluster Score Differences Required for Statistical Significance: Ages 6:0–17:11 292

Table B.5.   Differences Between Cognitive-Subtest *T* Scores and the Mean *T* Score on the Core Subtests Required for Statistical Significance 294

Table B.6.   Differences Between Cognitive-Subtest *T* Scores and the Mean *T* Score on the Core Subtests Shown by Various Percentages of the Norm Sample: Ages 2:6–3:5 295

Table B.7.   Differences Between Cognitive-Subtest *T* Scores and the Mean *T* Score on the Core Subtests Shown by Various Percentages of the Norm Sample: Ages 3:6–5:11 296

Table B.8.   Differences Between Cognitive-Subtest *T* Scores and the Mean *T* Score on the Core Subtests Shown by Various Percentages of the Norm Sample: Ages 6:0–17:11 297

Table B.9.   Differences Between Subtest *T* Scores Required for Statistical Significance........................... 298

Table B.10. Differences Between Achievement-Test Standard Scores and GCA or SNC Scores Required for Statistical Significance 300

Table B.11. Achievement-Test Standard Scores Predicted from GCA or Special Nonverbal Composite Scores 301

Table B.12. Differences Between Observed and Predicted Achievement-Test Standard Scores Required for Statistical Significance........................... 303

Table B.13. Differences Between Observed and Predicted Achievement-Test Standard Scores Shown by Various Percentages of the Norm Sample........... 304

Table C.1.   Intercorrelation of Preschool Subtests and Composites by Age: 2:6–2:11 306

Table C.2.   Intercorrelation of Preschool Subtests and Composites by Age: 3:0–3:5 307

Table C.3.   Intercorrelation of Preschool Subtests and Composites by Age: 3:6–3:11 308

Table C.4.   Intercorrelation of Preschool Subtests and Composites by Age: 4:0–4:5 309

Table C.5.   Intercorrelation of Preschool Subtests and
Composites by Age: 4:6–4:11 310

Table C.6.   Intercorrelation of Preschool Subtests and
Composites by Age: 5:0–5:11 311

Table C.7.   Intercorrelation of Preschool Subtests and
Composites by Age: 6:0–6:11 312

Table C.8.   Intercorrelation of Preschool Subtests and
Composites by Age: 7:0–7:11 313

Table C.9.   Intercorrelation of School-Age Subtests, Composites,
and Achievement Tests by Age: 5:0–5:11 314

Table C.10.   Intercorrelation of School-Age Subtests, Composites,
and Achievement Tests by Age: 6:0–6:11 315

Table C.11.   Intercorrelation of School-Age Subtests, Composites,
and Achievement Tests by Age: 7:0–7:11 316

Table C.12.   Intercorrelation of School-Age Subtests, Composites,
and Achievement Tests by Age: 8:0–8:11 317

Table C.13.   Intercorrelation of School-Age Subtests, Composites,
and Achievement Tests by Age: 9:0–9:11 318

Table C.14.   Intercorrelation of School-Age Subtests, Composites,
and Achievement Tests by Age: 10:0–10:11 319

Table C.15.   Intercorrelation of School-Age Subtests, Composites,
and Achievement Tests by Age: 11:0–11:11 320

Table C.16.   Intercorrelation of School-Age Subtests, Composites,
and Achievement Tests by Age: 12:0–12:11 321

Table C.17.   Intercorrelation of School-Age Subtests, Composites,
and Achievement Tests by Age: 13:0–13:11 322

Table C.18.   Intercorrelation of School-Age Subtests, Composites,
and Achievement Tests by Age: 14:0–14:11 323

Table C.19.   Intercorrelation of School-Age Subtests, Composites,
and Achievement Tests by Age: 15:0–15:11 324

Table C.20.   Intercorrelation of School-Age Subtests, Composites,
and Achievement Tests by Age: 16:0–16:11 325

Table C.21.   Intercorrelation of School-Age Subtests, Composites,
and Achievement Tests by Age: 17:0–17:11 326

Table C.22. Correlations of Preschool Subtests and Composites with School-Age Subtests, Composites, and Achievement Tests: Ages 5:0–5:11 327

Table C.23. Correlations of Preschool Subtests and Composites with School-Age Subtests, Composites, and Achievement Tests: Ages 6:0–6:11 328

Table C.24. Correlations of Preschool Subtests and Composites with School-Age Subtests, Composites, and Achievement Tests: Ages 7:0–7:11 329

Table D.1. Probability of a Correct Answer for Various Combinations of Ability and Item Difficulty......... 342

Figures

Figure 1.1.   Ages at Which Each Subtest is Normed 4

Figure 1.2.   Example of Stopping at the Designated Decision
              Point 6

Figure 1.3.   Example of Continuing to the Next Decision Point... 6

Figure 1.4.   Example of Going Back to an Earlier Starting Point . 7

Figure 1.5.   Example of a Raw-Score-to-Ability-Score Table 8

Figure 2.1.   DAS Score Interpretations at Three Levels of
              Generality 11

Figure 2.2.   Cognitive Battery for Ages 2:6–3:5 15

Figure 2.3.   Cognitive Battery for Ages 3:6–5:11 15

Figure 2.4.   Cognitive Battery for Ages 6:0–17:11 16

Figure 2.5.   Developing Structure of the DAS Cognitive Battery.. 21

Figure 4.1.   Sample Matrices Items 58

Figure 4.2A. Example Item from Sequential and Quantitative
              Reasoning, Set A 63

Figure 4.2B. Example Item from Sequential and Quantitative
              Reasoning, Set B 63

Figure 4.3.   Example Item of Matching Letter-Like Forms 65

Figure 4.4.   Example Items of Speed of Information Processing ... 70

Figure 4.5.   Excerpt from the Basic Number Skills Record Form
              Page 75

Figure 5.1A. Record Form Summary Page for Preschool Child..... 90

Figure 5.1B. Record Form Summary Page for School-Aged Child .. 91

Figure 5.2.   Shared Underlying Processes for Each Preschool
              Subtest 101

Figure 5.3.   Shared Underlying Processes for Each School-Age
              Subtest 102

Figure 6.1.   Standardization Testing Sites..................... 111

Figure 6.2.   Demographic Characteristics of the DAS Norm Sample
              Compared with Those of the U.S. Population 117

Figure 6.3.   Demographic Characteristics of the DAS Grade-Norm
              Sample Compared with Those of the General
              Population 128

Figure 7.1. Raw-Score-to-Ability-Score Tables. 149

Figure 7.2. GCA Scores at Ages 6:0–6:2 and 9:0–9:5 That
Correspond to the Same Level of Performance 167

Figure 8.1. Raw-Score Distributions for a Test With and
Without a Ceiling Effect 174

Figure 9.1. Models Used for the Comparison of the GCAs
from the Preschool and School-Age Levels. 215

Figure 10.1. Relationship Between Ability and Achievement for
Different Groups 267

Figure D.1. Item Characteristic Curves for One-, Two-, and
Three-Parameter Models 336

Figure D.2. The Relationship Between Person Ability and Item
Difficulty for a Person with a DAS Ability of 50. 342

Chapter 1

Introduction

As with many endeavors, the *Differential Ability Scales* (DAS) began simply as a vision. In this case, the vision was to create a cognitive-assessment test battery that would provide a much greater degree of flexibility of use and a wider range of measurement possibilities than have existing test batteries.

Why is the DAS necessary? Why do we need yet another individually administered cognitive test battery? It is because the tests used by psychologists generally have not been designed to measure specific abilities. Most traditionally constructed cognitive batteries are aimed more at yielding IQs or other global scores than at providing specific information about children's strengths and weaknesses across a range of cognitive domains. Such information is essential if our assessments are to identify the nature of a child's learning difficulties and consequently to lead to what should be the outcome of all assessments: helpful and practical suggestions for teachers, parents, and others concerned about the education and care of the child. The vision, therefore, was to bring to bear a range of psychological theories and recent advances in test methodology in producing an instrument of direct, practical usefulness to psychologists who assess the cognitive abilities of children.

An Overview of the DAS

The DAS is an individually administered battery of cognitive and achievement tests for children and adolescents aged 2 years, 6 months (2:6) through 17 years, 11 months (17:11). Designed to measure specific, definable abilities, the cognitive subtests permit us to obtain and evaluate profiles of strengths and weaknesses. The achievement tests were co-normed with the cognitive battery to make direct ability–achievement discrepancy analyses possible.

Individually administered ability and achievement test batteries have two major purposes. First is the purpose of classification. We generally use a single, overall score in combination with other data to determine whether or not a child falls into a particular category such as gifted, mentally retarded, or learning disabled. The DAS provides a composite measure of conceptual and reasoning abilities which we may use for classification and placement decisions. The second purpose is diagnostic. A reliable profile of within-person cognitive strengths and weaknesses is necessary for answering questions such as "Why is this child failing to learn?" and "What methods can I use to help this child learn better?" The DAS was developed to serve both purposes.

Information needed to administer, score, and interpret the DAS is provided in two volumes. First, this book, the *Differential Ability Scales Introductory and Technical Handbook* (the **Handbook**), contains information essential for learning to use as well as for evaluating the battery, but it is not needed during actual testing. The first four chapters of the **Handbook** should be read as the first step in learning to use the DAS. Second, the *DAS Administration and Scoring Manual* provides detailed instructions for administering and scoring the battery as well as the tables used in scoring; it will be referred to as the **Manual**.

Any new cognitive-assessment instrument published today is likely to be greeted by a knowledgeable, but skeptical, professional audience. Therefore, a technical handbook should anticipate and address those questions and concerns already on the minds of potential users. This handbook will attempt to satisfy this purpose by providing answers to the following questions:

Briefly, what kind of test is the DAS and how should it be used?   Chapter 1
What is the rationale and theoretical background?   Chapter 2
What is the developmental background?   Chapter 3
What are the tasks (subtests)?   Chapter 4
How can high and low scores on these tasks be interpreted?   Chapter 4
How can a profile of these scores be interpreted?   Chapter 5
Who was in the standardization sample?   Chapter 6
How were the norms developed?   Chapter 7
Is the test reliable?   Chapter 8
Is the test valid?   Chapter 9
Is the test fair?   Chapter 10
What is the Rasch model and how was it used in test development?   Appendix D

An overview, or outline, of the DAS and definitions of its specific terminology are prerequisites for the following chapters. Those who have already obtained this information from the introductory chapters of the **Manual** (Chapters 1, 2, and 3) may wish to skip the following shaded section which introduces the structure and components of the battery and summarizes the administration procedures.

Structure and Components of the DAS

The DAS is suitable for use in any setting where the cognitive abilities of children and adolescents must be evaluated. The cognitive portion of the DAS yields a composite score focused on reasoning and conceptual abilities, called the *General Conceptual Ability* (GCA) score; lower-level composite scores called *cluster* scores; and diverse, specific-ability measures, including the *core* subtests, which compose the GCA, and *diagnostic* subtests. For school-aged children, three achievement screening tests measure basic number skills, spelling skills, and word reading skills. This combination of scores makes the DAS useful for classification and placement decisions that require an index of intellectual ability and for diagnostic testing that may contribute to understanding a child's problems or to designing interventions.

The individual DAS subtests are designed to measure a variety of separate and distinct areas of cognitive functioning; that is, they have a relatively high level of specificity. This specificity enables the DAS to provide a sound basis for diagnostic (or profile) interpretation because differences among many of the subtests are reliable and interpretable.

The **Cognitive Battery** includes 17 cognitive subtests divided into two overlapping levels.

The **Preschool Level** actually comprises two levels. Children aged 2:6–3:5 take four core subtests to obtain the GCA composite and can also take two additional diagnostic subtests. Children aged 3:6–5:11 (the upper Preschool Level) take six core subtests, which contribute to the GCA composite score, and can also take five diagnostic subtests. (Administration time is about 25–65 minutes.)

The **School-Age Level** is for children aged 6:0–17:11 and includes six core subtests, which contribute to the GCA composite score, and three additional diagnostic subtests. (Administration time is about 40–65 minutes.)

The **School Achievement Tests** include three measures of the basic skills of arithmetic, spelling, and word reading. They are generally administered to children aged 6:0–17:11. (Administration time is about 15–25 minutes.)

For the upper Preschool Level and the School-Age Level, the core subtests not only contribute to the GCA score but also yield two or three cluster scores. For children aged 3:6–5:11, these cluster scores represent *Verbal Ability* and *Nonverbal Ability*; for children aged 6:0–17:11, they represent *Verbal Ability*, *Nonverbal Reasoning Ability*, and *Spatial Ability*. A complete discussion of the hierarchical structure of DAS scores (subtests, clusters, and the GCA) is provided in Chapter 2.

The Preschool and School-Age Levels of the Cognitive Battery were actually normed for overlapping age ranges: Both were standardized with children aged 5:0 through 6:11. This overlap provides us with important advantages in terms of out-of-level testing because bright, younger children and less able, older ones can be given subtests appropriate for their abilities. Furthermore, a number of subtests were given and normed throughout a wide age range. Finally, some subtests, mainly appropriate for preschoolers, link very well both statistically and conceptually with school-age subtests whose item content, although somewhat different, targets the same cognitive processes (see the sections on Naming Vocabulary and Word Definitions in Chapter 4 for an example). These links between the Preschool and School-Age Levels of the Cognitive Battery provide us practical and interpretive benefits. Figure 1.1 illustrates both the age ranges at which each subtest is normed and this overlapping structure of the Cognitive Battery.

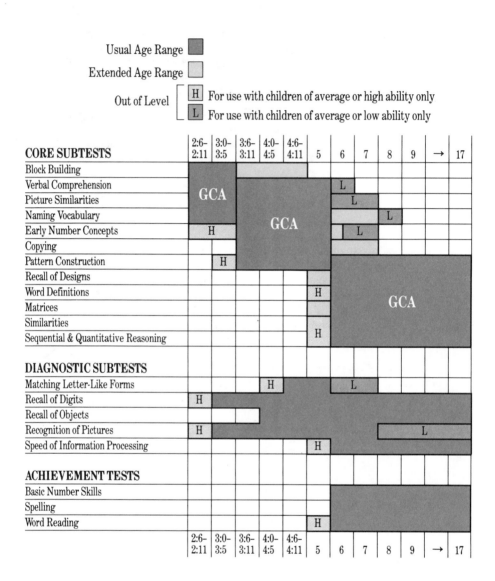

Figure 1.1. Ages at Which Each Subtest Is Normed

Overview of Administration Procedures

The Examiner

An examiner qualified to administer, score, and interpret the DAS is someone who has had formal training in administration and interpretation of individually administered cognitive test batteries for children and adolescents.

Item-Selection Procedures

The objective of the DAS administration procedures is to have most of the testing time devoted to items that are appropriate for the child's level of ability. The DAS uses a form of tailored testing to achieve this objective. We would usually start a subtest with the item indicated for the child's age. These *Starting Points* are designated on the Record Form and in the subtest directions. We would continue to administer items until reaching the normal stopping point for that age, called a *Decision Point*. If the child passed at least three items and failed at least three items, testing for that subtest would end (as shown in Figure 1.2). If the child **did not fail at least three items**, we would continue testing with harder items to the next Decision Point (see Figure 1.3). If the child **did not pass at least three items** at the first Decision Point, we would go back to an earlier Starting Point and administer an easier set of items (see Figure 1.4).

Testing normally stops only at a Decision Point. However, when a child fails a string of items before reaching the Decision Point, an *Alternative Stopping Point* rule may be applied. The Alternative Stopping Point rule varies from subtest to subtest and is printed at the top of each Record Form page and in the subtest directions. For example, for the Naming Vocabulary subtest, the Alternative Stopping Point rule is five consecutive failures. If the child answered three or more items correctly but then failed five items in a row, we would not administer any further items in that set and would score the remaining items as if they had been failed. Because the child passed at least three items, we would have sufficient information for a reliable estimate of the child's ability. If, on the other hand, the child passed only two items, we would go back to an earlier Starting Point and administer an easier set of items.

In summary, except when an Alternative Stopping Point rule is used, every child should take a continuous set of items from a Starting Point to a Decision Point. The procedure for converting raw scores to ability scores (explained below) is based on the assumption that the test has been administered in this way.

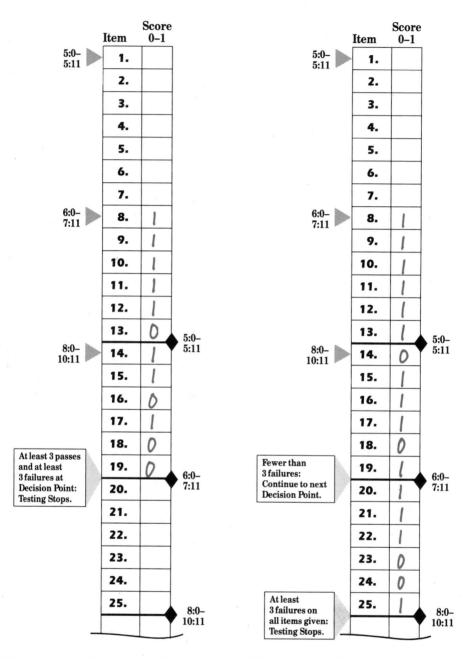

Figure 1.2. Example of Stopping at the Designated Decision Point

Figure 1.3. Example of Continuing to the Next Decision Point

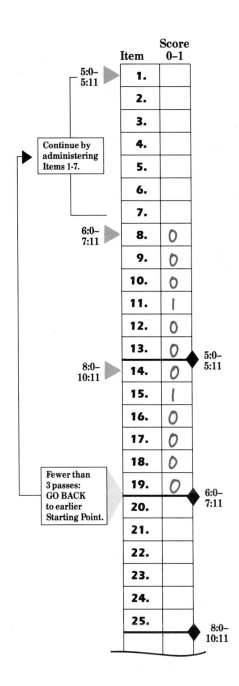

Figure 1.4. Example of Going Back
to an Earlier Starting Point

Calculation of DAS Scores

This section describes the basic steps necessary for converting subtest raw scores to normative scores.

1. The raw score for each subtest is the sum of the item-response scores on a particular range of items administered according to the item-selection procedure described above. We convert this raw score to an *ability score*, using the table provided on the Record Form page for each subtest. The ability score indicates the raw level of performance on the subtest, based on the number of correct responses and the difficulty of the items administered. The figures in parentheses are the standard errors of each of the ability estimates.

Recognition of Pictures
Raw Score to Ability Score

Raw Score	Item Set 1–9	1–13	1–20	5–20
0	10(16)	10(16)	10(16)	
1	19(11)	19(12)	19(11)	48(12)
2	30(9)	29(9)	29(9)	58(9)
3	38(9)	38(9)	38(9)	66(8)
4	46(9)	46(9)	46(9)	72(8)
5	54(9)	54(9)	53(9)	77(7)
6	62(9)	61(8)	60(8)	82(7)
7	71(9)	68(8)	66(8)	87(7)
8	81(11)	74(8)	72(7)	91(6)
9		80(8)	77(7)	95(6)
10		87(8)	82(7)	99(6)
11		94(9)	87(7)	104(7)
12		104(11)	91(6)	108(7)
13			95(6)	113(8)
14			99(6)	120(9)
15			104(7)	129(11)
16			108(7)	138(16)
17			113(8)	
18			120(9)	
19			129(11)	
20			138(16)	

Figure 1.5. Example of a Raw-Score-to-Ability-Score Table

2. The ability score for a subtest is converted to a T score which is an age-based standard score ($M=50$, $SD=10$) with a range from 20 to 80. Performance on an individual subtest can also be expressed as a percentile or an age equivalent. Tables for making these conversions are found in the **Manual**.

3. We then sum the core-subtest T scores and convert the total to a standard score ($M=100$, $SD=15$) for the cluster or composite it represents. For example, we find the GCA for the lower level of the Preschool Battery

by summing the four core-subtest T scores and using the tables in the **Manual** to convert this sum to a standard score. We can also convert cluster and GCA scores to percentiles by using the same tables.

4. We determine achievement-test scores by converting the ability scores to standard scores ($M = 100$, $SD = 15$). Achievement-test scores and cognitive-cluster and GCA scores are in the same metric for direct comparisons of achievement and ability. Tables in the **Manual** also provide the conversion of achievement-test ability scores to age or grade percentiles, age equivalents, normal curve equivalents, and grade equivalents.

Usual, Extended, and Out-of-Level Age Ranges

Most children will take the core and diagnostic subtests prescribed for their age, the *Usual Age Range*, indicated by the dark green shading in Figure 1.1. Many subtests were also normed outside this age range and may be given for the additional diagnostic information they may provide. These wider age ranges, called *Extended Age Ranges*, are indicated by light green shading in Figure 1.1. Some subtests are also appropriate for *out-of-level* testing. An age range denoted with an "H" (for average-to-high) or an "L" (for average-to-low) in Figure 1.1 indicates that the subtest is appropriate for most but not all children at that age.

The DAS Record Forms

The DAS includes two Record Forms corresponding to the two levels of the Cognitive Battery. Each of the forms contains all of the subtests that are usually given at that age level. Thus, the Preschool Level Record Form includes core and diagnostic subtests, and the School-Age Level Record Form includes core and diagnostic subtests and achievement tests. The last page of each Record Form is a tear-off summary page which provides a record of demographic information and observations of the child's test-taking behaviors as well as a summary of subtest, cluster, composite, and achievement scores.

Summary

The diversity of the DAS structure and components and the flexibility in subtest and item selection make possible detailed information about the abilities of children across a range of cognitive domains. The core and diagnostic subtests describe patterns of strengths and weaknesses, information useful for designating appropriate placement and for providing important diagnostic information to parents, teachers, and other professionals who work with children. The cognitive and achievement measures of the DAS were developed and normed together so that ability-achievement differences can be interpreted in terms of both statistical significance and unusualness. Thus, with a single instrument, we will be able to address a wide variety of referral questions for a broad age range of children in school and clinical settings and in research.

Chapter 2

The Assessment of Cognitive Abilities: Rationale of the DAS

When we set out to assess an individual's cognitive abilities, we always apply some theory or model of ability to the evaluation. Often because we do not make the theory or model explicit, it must be inferred from the tests and the scores that we employ. Do we emphasize the overall composite score? If so, we are assigning significance to the construct of intelligence, if only implicitly. Do we place more emphasis on subtest scatter? If so, we are giving weight to a componential theory.

The DAS was developed to accommodate users with various theoretical perspectives by providing interpretable scores at various levels of generality. Figure 2.1 illustrates these levels. This chapter explains the major issues and the rationale of the DAS approach to evaluating cognitive abilities and discusses the theoretical framework for the measures. The chapter also provides an outline of the DAS assessment model and of aspects of interpretation, which are elaborated more fully in later chapters.

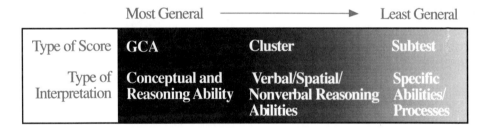

	Most General ⟶ Least General		
Type of Score	GCA	Cluster	Subtest
Type of Interpretation	Conceptual and Reasoning Ability	Verbal/Spatial/ Nonverbal Reasoning Abilities	Specific Abilities/ Processes

Figure 2.1. DAS Score Interpretations at Three Levels of Generality

Generalization: The Key Issue in Test Interpretation

A test battery such as the DAS is a means of quickly, economically, and objectively assessing children's abilities. Such information could, of course, be obtained through observation of a child in various settings and from talking to teachers and parents. Although these methods offer several benefits, such as reduced effects of the observer, they are more time consuming and less objective than testing. With a psychometric test, the child is presented a sample of items from a particular domain. Based on the child's performance, we can generalize about the child's ability in that domain and in other related domains.

Generalization is the key feature upon which all tests are based. Tests are useful because much of human behavior is not specific to a particular time or action but reflects more lasting and general characteristics of the individual. A vocabulary test can be used to illustrate this point. First, the test would be of no use to us if the person's performance applied only to a particular occasion and particular set of testing circumstances, that is, if the test were not *reliable*. Second, the test would be useless if it measured only the person's knowledge of the particular words in the test and did not indicate the person's knowledge of a larger domain of words; the test should have *content validity*. Third, the scope of generalization may be so broad that a vocabulary score might be viewed as an index of general language skills, or even of general intelligence; this view concerns the issues of *criterion-related* and *construct validity*.

The broader the domain to which we wish to generalize our interpretation, the more cautious we must be and the more supporting evidence we need to bring to bear in forming a judgment.

Issues related to generalization are addressed in several chapters of this **Handbook**. In examining the detailed evidence on reliability and validity, we can sometimes lose sight of the key concept that cements everything together: generalization. Likewise in the school or clinic, when we are faced with an array of test scores for a child we may forget the importance of generalization. The key questions for test interpretation are "What evidence do I now have of general cognitive strengths and weaknesses of this person? Are these test results, obtained after an hour or so of testing, related to behaviors in other settings?" To begin to address the issue of generalization, this chapter outlines the theoretical framework of the DAS.

Basic Rationale of the DAS

Three features underlie the rationale of the DAS:
* homogeneous, distinct, and reliable subtests;
* a hierarchical structure; and
* a broad theoretical base

Homogeneous, Distinct, and Reliable Subtests

At the most specific level of measurement, the greatest priority was given to developing subtests that are homogeneous in content, that measure distinct and identifiable abilities, and that are sufficiently reliable to support separate interpretation.

Homogeneity is an essential prerequisite for interpretability. If a subtest score is to be interpreted as a measure of a specific, identifiable ability, the items within that subtest must be of similar content and must require the examinee to perform similar operations. For example, in the Naming Vocabulary subtest, a child is shown a picture and asked to name the object depicted. All items have the same form and include concepts that are part of general knowledge. The items, which are graded in difficulty, vary only in terms of the specific objects. From an interpretive viewpoint, the subtest would be unsatisfactory if it consisted of a mixture of item types, if it contained pictures drawn from domains of specialized knowledge, or if the pictures themselves were obscure.

While each subtest's content should be homogeneous, that content should also be distinct from that of other subtests if the subtest is to be interpreted as a measure of a different ability. Furthermore, each subtest should be designed to focus on the ability of interest and to minimize the influence of extraneous variables. Thus, only two of the DAS subtests are speeded: one is a measure of speed (Speed of Information Processing), and the other, Pattern Construction (which measures spatial ability), offers an alternative, unspeeded administration and scoring procedure for children for whom a speeded score might be invalid. Similarly, the Recall of Digits subtest focuses on auditory memory by presenting only forward-recall trials (backward-recall trials call on higher-order cognitive processing). As a third example, the Verbal Comprehension subtest for preschoolers does not require the child to speak, but allows the child to demonstrate understanding of the oral instructions by making simple motor movements.

In addition to having homogeneous content that focuses on a distinct ability, a subtest should be reliable. Because the DAS emphasizes the identification of cognitive strengths and weaknesses, subtests must have a sufficient amount of reliable specificity to be separately interpretable. Differences in scores between subtests should not be subject to extreme measurement error, nor should different subtests overlap to such an extent that they can be interpreted only as measuring the same ability.

Hierarchical Structure

As already outlined in Chapter 1 and as illustrated in Figure 2.1, the DAS provides score interpretations at three levels of generality: GCA, cluster, and subtest scores. This configuration implies a hierarchical view of mental abilities, with the most specific ability measures, the subtests, providing the base or foundation of the structure. Some of these subtests tend to cluster into groupings at the second level, and these groupings are themselves interrelated and yield an index of psychometric g at the apex. Because only those subtests that intercorrelate reasonably highly contribute to the computation of these composite scores, the interpretability of the GCA and clusters is maximized.

As well as having a hierarchical structure, the DAS reflects the developmental trend of the differentiation of abilities. At the youngest age level (below age 3:6) there are no cluster scores; the individual subtests contribute only toward a single composite GCA score (see Figure 2.2). From ages 3:6 to 5:11, the subtests yield two cluster scores in addition to the GCA, and for older children the subtests yield three cluster scores and the GCA (see Figures 2.3 and 2.4). This developing hierarchical differentiation is consistent with observations of the cognitive development of young children.

Broad Theoretical Base

Although its structure is primarily hierarchical, the DAS is not based on any single theory of human ability. Instead, it is built on a collection of subtests that sample a range of abilities thought to be useful in assessing children, particularly children with learning difficulties. The selection of the abilities sampled was influenced by a variety of theoretical points of view. Moreover, empirical results as well as theoretical considerations guided the organization of these components. Because the DAS structure comprises small, interpretable units (the individual diagnostic subtests and the clusters of two or three subtests), the battery is relatively flexible and lends itself to interpretation from various theoretical perspectives.

The Theoretical Background of the DAS

The DAS is the outcome of research spanning two decades. During that time, developments in the theory of intelligence and abilities continued apace. The battery is inevitably a product of its historical context and was developed with a variety of evolving theories in view. Chapter 3 describes in more detail the work of the research team who developed the *British Ability Scales* (BAS; Elliott, Murray, & Pearson, 1979), the forerunner of the DAS, and the particular theoretical and pragmatic influences which guided that research. A brief review of theoretical developments and approaches to the assessment of intelligence and cognitive abilities will provide a backdrop for various interpretive approaches to the DAS.

It has been the nature of intelligence, rather than the nature of abilities in somewhat narrower domains, that has most engaged theorists and researchers past and present. Accordingly, the following discussion focuses on broad general- and group-ability factors, even though the DAS places a major emphasis on the measurement of specific abilities. Chapter 4 will consider in detail the nature and interpretation of the individual subtests.

Since his publication of two major texts in 1923 and 1927, Spearman has had a major influence on this field. Central to his concept of the nature of intelligence are two aspects of performance: the eduction of relations and the eduction of correlates. (*Eduction* means developing or inferring a principle from data.) These are complex mental functions, and many tests that measure some aspect of the eduction of relations and of correlates have since been devised (for example, tests of analogies, similarities, and matrices).

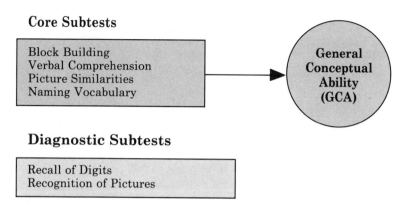

Core Subtests

> Block Building
> Verbal Comprehension
> Picture Similarities
> Naming Vocabulary

→ General Conceptual Ability (GCA)

Diagnostic Subtests

> Recall of Digits
> Recognition of Pictures

Figure 2.2. Cognitive Battery for Ages 2:6–3:5

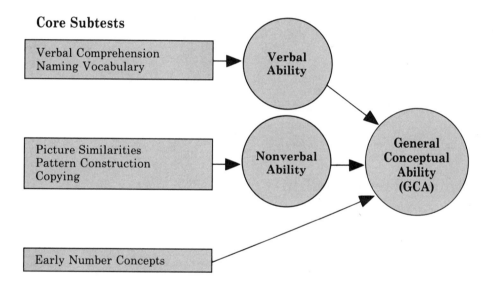

Core Subtests

> Verbal Comprehension
> Naming Vocabulary

→ Verbal Ability

> Picture Similarities
> Pattern Construction
> Copying

→ Nonverbal Ability

> Early Number Concepts

→ General Conceptual Ability (GCA)

Diagnostic Subtests

> Block Building*
> Matching Letter-Like Forms**
> Recall of Digits
> Recall of Objects**
> Recognition of Pictures

* 3:6–4:11 only
** 4:0–5:11 only

Figure 2.3. Cognitive Battery for Ages 3:6–5:11

Core Subtests

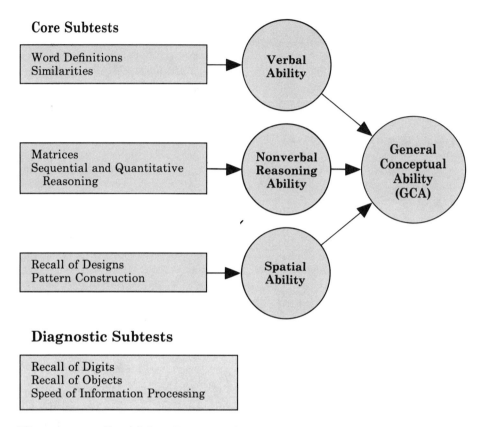

Diagnostic Subtests

Figure 2.4. Cognitive Battery for Ages 6:0–17:11

Since Spearman's time many test constructors have incorporated such tests into their batteries, a trend that has resulted in the similarity of content of many of these instruments. Also in the years since Spearman, many theorists, including a large number working in the broad psychometric and factor analytic tradition, have expanded our understanding of the nature of human abilities. Carroll (1982), Sternberg and Salter (1982), and Sternberg and Powell (1982) provide reviews of concepts, measurement, and theories of intelligence.

Two psychologists are notable among early developers of the theory and measurement of abilities. Thurstone (1938) produced a battery of tests that measure the seven "primary mental abilities" of number, word fluency, verbal meaning, memory, reasoning, space, and perceptual speed. Wechsler (1939) took a somewhat different approach which focuses on overall intelligence rather than on distinct abilities. He defined intelligence as "the aggregate or global capacity of the individual to act purposefully, to think rationally and to deal effectively with his environment" (p. 3). This definition goes beyond Spearman's description of the nature of intelligence in terms of the three principles of the apprehension of experience, the eduction of relations, and the eduction of correlates, a description that more appropriately refers to psychometric g. Wechsler's belief that intelligence is more than the sum of intellectual abilities led him to include subtests that are not good measures of g in his widely-used intelligence batteries.

Vernon (1950) factor-analyzed Thurstone's primary mental-ability tests and found that the tests intercorrelated and yielded two group factors, which he labeled $v{:}ed$ (a verbal–educational factor) and $k{:}m$ (a spatial–mechanical factor). Vernon produced a hierarchical model of cognitive abilities that develops from first-order (lower-level) primary abilities to second-order group factors which in turn yield a general factor such as the one that Spearman had originally suggested.

Later theorists include Cattell (1971), who suggested two broad group factors to replace Vernon's $v{:}ed$ and $k{:}m$, namely "fluid" and "crystallized" general intelligence. With Horn (1978), Cattell identified additional group factors, and this work influenced the development of the fourth edition of the *Stanford–Binet Intelligence Scale* (Thorndike, Hagen, & Sattler, 1986) and the *Woodcock–Johnson Psycho-Educational Battery—Revised* (Woodcock & Johnson, 1989). Other major theorists include Guilford (1967), who produced a highly complex three-dimensional taxonomy of cognitive abilities; Jensen (1970), who developed a hierarchical theory of Level I abilities, typically characterized by immediate-memory tests, and Level II abilities, chiefly characterized by reasoning tasks; and Das, Kirby, and Jarman (1975), who suggested two group factors related to Luria's theory of simultaneous and successive information processing. This latter theory provided the basis for the development of the *Kaufman Assessment Battery for Children* (Kaufman & Kaufman, 1983).

In the 1980s, important contributions to intelligence theory were made by Gardner and Sternberg. Gardner (1983) outlined a theory of multiple intelligences. Three of these categories—linguistic, spatial, and logical-mathematical—are well represented in ability tests and theories. The other three intelligences—musical, bodily, and personal—are probably less well supported in the literature. Sternberg (1984, 1985) elaborated an ambitious and comprehensive triarchic theory of human intelligence, which comprises contextual, componential, and two-facet (novelty–automatization) subtheories.

In the last several decades, experimental cognitive psychologists have extended their research into cognitive components of intelligence. Much of this work focused on various types and contents of memory and on the development of information-processing models of intelligent behavior (see for example, Carroll & Maxwell, 1979; Hunt, 1980; Sternberg, 1977, 1979). Accounts of a number of such studies conducted in the early 1970s were collected by Resnick (1976).

Considerable subsequent research focused on chronometric measurement (that is, speed of information processing). Some interesting early work along these latter lines was conducted by Furneaux (1960), who analyzed the patterns of people's responses on intelligence-test items to estimate parameters of mental speed, accuracy, and continuance (persistence). Eysenck (1967) continued with this theme, and the research literature continues to report many studies on chronometric measurement (such as Frearson & Eysenck, 1986; Jensen, 1982; Larson & Saccuzzo, 1989). Chapter 4 briefly reviews a number of these studies in relation to the development of the DAS Speed of Information Processing subtest.

Theoretical developments and controversies in the area of human abilities continue. Despite this activity, or perhaps because of it, no single theory or model has or is likely to have universal acceptance. Therefore, it is probably a mistake to base a cognitive test battery on any single theory. Rather, the tasks and score interpretations of a battery should reflect a wide range of theories to accommodate users who have varying theoretical views. Applied psychologists tend to be eclectic in their theoretical stances, drawing upon various theories that appear to have relevance to the particular problems they encounter. Consistent with such a deliberately eclectic approach, the DAS represents to varying degrees many of the theoretical developments reviewed.

The DAS Assessment Model

As outlined above, the DAS structure reflects a hierarchy of abilities. The way we view human ability is important not only for the structure of a test battery such as the DAS but also for the way we use the battery and interpret its scores. This section considers the meaning of the scores obtained at each of the three levels of generality in the DAS: the GCA score, the cluster scores, and the individual subtest scores. This order is followed in the chapter on score-interpretation and sequential-assessment procedures (Chapter 5) and is also reflected in the recommended procedure for score interpretation incorporated in the DAS Record Form.

Interpretation of the General Conceptual Ability Score

To be interpretable, each cluster score and the GCA score must be derived from a set of subtests that measure a common dimension of ability. Each DAS subtest is homogeneous—and therefore interpretable—in terms of content. An entire battery of mental tests that cover diverse processes and knowledge, however, cannot be homogeneous in content. Instead, the subtests that contribute to a composite score should be similar in the sense that they correlate highly with a common group factor or with psychometric g.

In contrast to the composite scores of many other individually administered test batteries, which give equal weighting to all subtests, the GCA score of the DAS is derived from only those subtests with high g loadings. With this feature, we can efficiently obtain a valid and focused measure of a central component of intellectual ability.

A question now arises: What is the nature of psychometric g? It is usually operationally defined by the first component in a principal-component analysis, the first factor in a common-factor analysis, or the most general factor in a hierarchical-factor analysis (Jensen, 1980, 1987). (In this **Handbook**, the term g will refer to this operational definition rather than to any more general concept, such as intelligence, which may convey a variety of meanings.) Those tests with the highest g loadings are the ones that best define the nature of the underlying variable. Many studies of various batteries of mental tests indicate that the tests with the highest g loadings also measure the most complex mental functions. Several authors have concluded, on the basis of such findings, that g is essentially a mental-complexity factor (Jensen, 1979, 1987; Larson, Merritt, & Williams, 1988; Marshalek, Lohman, & Snow, 1983; Vernon, 1985). Larson and Saccuzzo (1989) somewhat elaborated this concept by concluding that g "is related to the agility of symbol manipulation during dynamic cognitive processing" (p. 23). These conjectures help in the interpretation of the composite GCA score of the DAS, which consists of subtests that load highest on the first common factor.

In view of the focus of the DAS composite on g, why is the composite not labeled "intelligence" or "IQ"? One reason is that the term intelligence is subject to numerous definitions. The essence of the problem was expressed many years ago by Spearman (1927) who wrote that "in truth, 'intelligence' has become a mere vocal sound, a word with so many meanings that finally it has none" (p. 14). Sixty years later, Jensen (1987) repeated that sentiment: "For scientific purposes, then, 'intelligence' can best be thrown out altogether" (p. 196). From the 14 experts who contributed their views on the nature and definition of intelligence to an issue of the *Journal of Educational Psychology* in 1921, through a notable essay by Miles (1951), to a more recent symposium of 25 experts (Sternberg & Detterman, 1986), there seem to be almost as many conceptualizations and definitions of intelligence as there are experts to write about them.

Second, the notions of intelligence and IQ have become very popular with the general public but have also been subject to widespread misunderstanding. The terms have provoked such violent social, political, and ideological debates, with all the surplus baggage from such debates, that it may be useful to avoid the terms in careful, objective descriptions of individuals.

A third reason for avoiding the terms intelligence and IQ is that the GCA score of the DAS is defined somewhat differently than are the global scores of the well-known Wechsler and Stanford–Binet scales, which use the term intelligence in their titles. Those instruments adopt a relatively broad definition of intelligence, as reflected in Wechsler's (1939) statement: "One of the greatest contributions of Binet was his intuitive assumption that in the selection of tests, it made little difference what sort of tasks you used, provided that in some way it was a measure of the child's general intelligence" (p. 6). Wechsler's method of obtaining IQs from a diverse collection of tasks, some of which have low g loadings, has been used in many individually administered mental-ability tests. The DAS departs from this tradition by focusing the GCA score more closely on g. For all ages, the DAS uses a relatively small number of core subtests that have high g loadings for the calculations of the GCA score. Consequently, the GCA score is a purer, more homogeneous and, therefore, more interpretable measure.

Abandoning the terms intelligence and IQ necessitates defining and naming the DAS overall composite score that reflects psychometric g. The definition is as follows:

> **Psychometric g is the general ability of an individual to perform complex mental processing that involves conceptualization and the transformation of information.**

The name for the overall composite score is a descriptor of that definition: General Conceptual Ability (GCA).

The Cluster Scores

As described earlier, the DAS provides scores for clusters of subtests that are at a higher level of generality than the subtest scores but that are less general than the GCA. An important characteristic of the DAS is the developmental trend in the number of such clusters that can be identified. For ages 2:6–3:5 there is no evidence for clustering of subtests except in terms of g. For 3:6–5:11 there are two clusters, and for ages 6:0 and over there are three. For children aged 3:6–5:11, the core subtests form the Verbal Ability and Nonverbal Ability cluster.

For children aged 6:0–17:11, the Nonverbal Ability cluster further differentiates into Nonverbal Reasoning Ability and Spatial Ability clusters. Figure 2.5 illustrates this structure for each level.

Just as the major principle in forming the GCA score is that the component subtests should correlate relatively highly with g, the subtests composing each cluster score should correlate highly with the group factor that measures the ability targeted by the cluster. Because the cluster scores are derived only from the core subtests (that is, those that contribute to the GCA), the clusters represent

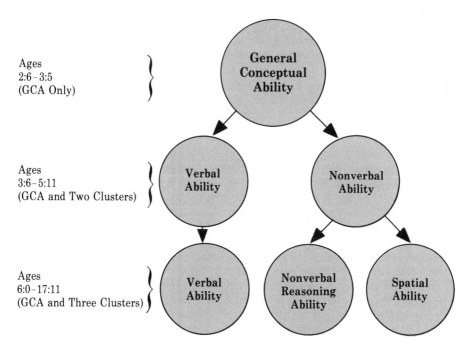

Figure 2.5. Developing Structure of the DAS Cognitive Battery

relatively complex mental processing and intercorrelate fairly highly. Nevertheless, a series of confirmatory factor analyses to evaluate the fit of various models to the entire set of cognitive subtests indicated that these clusters have sufficient specific variance to be interpretable. There is no evidence of significant clustering of the diagnostic subtests, that is, those not included in GCA estimation. In particular, there is no support for a memory factor. The memory subtests (other than Recall of Designs) and the Speed of Information Processing subtest have low correlations with *g* and do not contribute to group factors. As a result, they tend to have a high degree of reliable specificity; that is, they measure relatively independent abilities.

What is the nature of the distinctions between verbal, nonverbal reasoning, and spatial abilities? The distinctions obviously resemble the "Verbal–Performance" distinction in the Wechsler scales. The content of the clusters suggests that the Nonverbal Reasoning and Spatial clusters would be subsumed by Wechsler's Performance classification. However, the DAS goes beyond Wechsler's system by distinguishing between nonverbal subtests that primarily measure spatial ability and those that measure inductive reasoning and therefore allow for verbal mediation in the solution of the problems.

Evidence from exploratory factor analyses of the School-Age Level of the DAS (described in Chapter 9) helps to clarify the interpretation of these factors. When only two common factors are indicated for extraction, the factors are principally defined by the verbal and the spatial subtests, respectively; the two nonverbal reasoning subtests load moderately on both factors (but with somewhat higher loadings on the spatial factor). This pattern of loadings possibly indicates that nonverbal reasoning is associated with both visual–spatial ability and verbal ability. Presumably the reason for the latter association is that verbal mediation is often useful in the solution of "nonverbal" reasoning problems.

The three cluster scores at the School-Age Level strongly resemble group factors identified in many studies. In a review of research on cognitive abilities, Carroll and Maxwell (1979, p. 613) observed that psychometric studies had identified a substantial number of primary abilities in domains that are reasonably distinct. Three of these domains—verbal, reasoning, and spatial abilities—strongly resemble the DAS clusters. The Verbal Ability cluster is clearly similar to Thurstone's (1938) primary mental ability of "verbal meaning" (*V*). It is probably also similar to the Cattell-Horn second-stratum factor of "crystallized general intelligence" (*Gc*), although it may be argued that the DAS Similarities subtest, which contributes to the Verbal Ability cluster, also has a component of "fluid general intelligence" (*Gf*). The Nonverbal Reasoning Ability cluster is similar to Thurstone's primary mental ability of "general reasoning" (*R*). The inclusion of the Sequential and Quantitative Reasoning subtest in this cluster is consistent with the fact that the "general reasoning" tests in the ETS *Kit of Factor Referenced & Cognitive Tests* (Ekstrom, French, & Harman, 1976) have strong elements of reasoning about quantitative concepts. Carroll and Maxwell make the point that tests of analogical reasoning relate to the Cattell-Horn second-stratum *Gf* factor, of which the series-completion tests and DAS Matrices subtest are good measures. The Spatial Ability cluster is obviously similar to Thurstone's "spatial" (*S*) factor and also to the Cattell-Horn second-stratum "power of visualization" factor (*Gv*). According to Cattell (1971, p. 107), this factor includes all kinds of performance that is aided by visualization ability, including spatial-orientation and visual- motor tasks. Such a description applies to the tasks required of children in the DAS subtests of this cluster—Recall of Designs and Pattern Construction.

Thus the DAS two- and three-cluster structure not only is supported by statistical, factor analytic evidence, but also is consistent with many previous findings on the organization of abilities.

The Subtests

The DAS subtests were developed so that they incorporate a number of desirable features. These features, together with the chapters which provide information on each, are listed below.

Homogeneity of item content and interpretability of scores	Chapter 4
Reliability and specificity	Chapter 8
Fairness	Chapter 10

Chapter 4 fully describes the content of the DAS subtests and discusses interpretive aspects of high and low scores on each subtest. Tables 2.1 and 2.2 list the subtests along with the basic ability each measures, and indicate whether the subtest contributes to the GCA, a cluster score, or neither.

The subtests cover a range of abilities and processes, including a number of types of verbal and nonverbal reasoning, visual and auditory memory, language expression and comprehension, perceptual-motor skills, speed of information processing, and school achievement in essential areas.

Table 2. Basic Abilities and Processes Measured by the Preschool DAS Subtests

Subtest	GCA	Cluster[a]	Ability/Process
Naming Vocabulary	✓	V	Verbal knowledge (expressive)
Verbal Comprehension	✓	V	Verbal knowledge (receptive)
Early Number Concepts	✓	[b]	Nonverbal and verbal knowledge
Picture Similarities	✓	NV	Nonverbal reasoning
Pattern Construction	✓	NV	Nonverbal (spatial) reasoning
Block Building	✓	—	Perceptual-motor ability
Copying	✓	NV	Perceptual-motor ability
Matching Letter-Like Forms	—	—	Visual-perceptual matching
Recall of Digits	—	—	Short-term auditory memory
Recall of Objects	—	—	Short- and intermediate-term verbal memory
Recognition of Pictures	—	—	Short-term visual memory

[a]V = Verbal Ability; NV = Nonverbal Ability
[b]Early Number Concepts loads on both the Verbal and Nonverbal clusters. To maintain interpretability of clusters, it is not included in either cluster.

Table 2.2. Basic Abilities and Processes Measured by the School-Age DAS Subtests

Subtest	GCA	Cluster[a]	Ability/Process
Word Definitions	✓	V	Verbal knowledge (expressive)
Similarities	✓	V	Verbal reasoning
Matrices	✓	NVR	Nonverbal reasoning
Sequential and Quantitative Reasoning	✓	NVR	Sequential and quantitative reasoning
Pattern Construction	✓	S	Spatial reasoning
Recall of Designs	✓	S	Short-term visual–spatial memory
Recall of Digits	—	—	Short-term auditory memory
Recall of Objects	—	—	Short- and intermediate-term verbal memory
Speed of Information Processing	—	—	Speed of information processing
Basic Number Skills	—	—	School knowledge–numerical computation
Spelling	—	—	School knowledge–spelling
Word Reading	—	—	School knowledge–reading

[a]V =Verbal Ability; NVR = Nonverbal Reasoning Ability; S = Spatial Ability

The Assessment Model in Practice

Given that the DAS has a range of subtests which measure various abilities and also has cluster scores and a measure of General Conceptual Ability, we might well ask how the battery should be used in practice. Chapter 5 provides some possible answers that use an approach similar to Kaufman's (1979) which he labeled "intelligent testing." Although Kaufman focused on the WISC–R, his method of using information from an individually administered test battery is readily generalizable. A brief outline of the approach is given here as an overview.

The recommended approach to interpreting DAS scores consists of certain stages. The approach assumes that we must sort through the evidence provided by the test results, together with data from the school, the home, and other sources, in order to form a judgment about the child's mental abilities. Although the DAS has a composite GCA estimate and may also have two or three cluster scores (depending on the child's age), the approach assumes that virtually no child's abilities can be fully summarized with such a small number of scores. The detective work to be performed starts at the apex of the ability hierarchy and systematically sifts through the information down to the subtest level.

The following stages summarize the sequence of steps for analyzing the child's profile of scores on the DAS. The stages include the analysis of intra-cognitive discrepancies which provide evidence of relative strengths and weaknesses in abilities. Chapter 5 fully describes and illustrates the stages, their rationale, and their systematic use.

Stage 1: Comparison of Cluster Standard Scores and the GCA Score. This comparison identifies any cluster that is a strength or weakness relative to the rest of the GCA.

Stage 2: Comparison of Cluster Standard Scores with One Another. A significant difference between two cluster scores means that the child is stronger in one ability area than in the other.

Stage 3: Comparison of Within-Cluster Subtest T Scores with One Another. A significant difference between subtest scores within a cluster may give useful information about specific skills and may affect interpretation of the cluster score.

Stage 4: Comparison of Subtest T Scores with the Mean T Score of the Core Subtests. We can identify significantly high or low points in the subtest profile by comparing individual subtest scores with the child's mean score on the core subtests.

Stage 5: Comparisons Between Ability and Achievement. Comparisons would normally be made between the GCA score and the achievement tests. For exceptional children (for example, a dysphasic child), the comparison may be made between the Special Nonverbal Composite score and the achievement-test scores.

Having identified the significant high and low points in DAS scores, we can then interpret the scores in light of additional information about the child's abilities, school performance, and behavior. Are the cognitive strengths and weaknesses shown by the DAS profile consistent with other observations of the child's behavior? Is the profile similar to any of the profiles that characterize special groups of children? How can the strengths and weaknesses of the child be reconciled with what is known of the child's history? Even if the profile does not match other commonly found profiles, do the child's strengths and weaknesses form a meaningful, interpretable pattern? Answers to these and other questions related to the context within which the child lives and is educated will naturally form the background to the evaluation of the DAS profile. These answers will also help us to determine essential, additional information which may be used together with the test information as a basis for the development of intervention programs.

Other Interpretive Issues

A complete discussion of the DAS rationale must include a brief consideration of two additional issues. These are issues which have been the subject of much discussion in recent years but about which there continues to be a good deal of misunderstanding. The problems surround the questions of (a) the nature of ability scores and (b) the utility of psychometric test scores compared to curriculum-based measures or observational data.

The Nature of Ability Scores

There has been much controversy about the acceptability and fairness of measuring intelligence or cognitive abilities, particularly with minorities and the disadvantaged. This concern has even led to prohibition in some areas of certain applications of general ability testing. (For reviews see R. Elliott, 1987, and Reschly, Kicklighter, & McKee, 1988a, 1988b, 1988c.)

To a large extent, the controversy arises from differing assumptions about what cognitive-ability tests measure or are supposed to measure. The central issue is the extent to which test scores are thought to represent *innate* ability as opposed to *developed* ability. Are test scores measures of the genotype, which refers to the genetic basis for the growth and efficiency of the organism? Or are they measures of the phenotype, which refers to developed abilities that arise from the interaction between the person's genetic predispositions and the environment?

Although it is generally accepted that physical characteristics of the neurological system (its structures and chemistry) affect cognitive performance and that there is some genetic influence on neurological development, ability tests do not measure this underlying neurophysiology. Instead, cognitive-ability tests measure the problem-solving and other skills that result from the interaction between the person's neurophysiology and the environment. Even neurophysiological characteristics are not genetically fixed because they are subject to external influences such as nutrition, injury, and exposure to toxins. Therefore, cognitive-ability tests do not measure innate ability as they are sometimes thought to do, for three reasons: Ability tests do not measure the physical characteristics of the nervous system, those characteristics may themselves change, and the performance that the tests do measure reflect skills developed through experience.

Another criticism of ability tests is that they do not measure all of the person's abilities that may be useful in dealing successfully with the environment (see Gardner, 1983). No cognitive-test battery could claim to measure all such abilities. Developers of ability tests usually have in mind some area of application when they design their instruments, and this restriction affects their choice of domains to be measured. Thus, Binet developed the first widely used individual ability test for educational applications. Wechsler was more concerned with the clinical use of ability tests and developed his first battery for adults (no doubt this application is one reason that his definition of intelligence—discussed earlier in this chapter—emphasizes non-intellective factors). The DAS was developed with educational applications as the foremost goal, but also with neuropsycholog-ical applications in mind. It was assumed that the DAS would be used primarily in the evaluation of children who, in a broad sense, were demonstrating learning problems. Hence, the DAS content represents a number of areas within the cog-nitive domain but does not attempt to measure noncognitive domains such as personality, interpersonal skills, or motor ability. If we are evaluating a child be-cause of concerns related to noncognitive domains, other instruments that mea-sure these domains are available to us.

Although culture-*fair* testing has been a major objective over the years, it is im-possible to develop culture-*free* tests. Because performance on psychometric tests is conditioned by environmental experience, tests reflect the relative level of an individual's cognitive development in a given cultural setting. One of the objec-tives of the DAS was the incorporation of content that is fair in a variety of lit-erate, industrial societies, in which language and communication, reasoning, and memory functions are likely to be widely relevant. For this reason the test does not include country-specific content or questions about social values.

Given that test scores represent the child's current level of development, how should we interpret the test-score profile of a child's high and low scores? We can have more confidence in the interpretation of high scores than in that of low scores. High scores indicate that both the neurophysiology and the prior experi-ence necessary for developing the skill are at least adequate. Even when a child obtains a high score, we should not assume that the child is unable to develop further in this area. Low scores present a greater interpretive problem. If the motivation and rapport are satisfactory, we can assume that either the portions of the nervous system relevant to the task are inadequate or the child's prior ex-perience is limited, or both. Again, in neither case should we assume that further development is not possible. The psychologist's task is to identify the most likely reasons for the low level of performance. Intervention strategies and suggestions may focus on a compensatory approach that uses the child's strengths to bypass the weaknesses, or an approach aimed at remediating the weaknesses, or an approach that involves both. These issues are considered in Chapter 5.

Finally the word "potential" deserves mention. This term is sometimes used in a positive sense to indicate that the individual may develop stronger skills than he or she presently demonstrates. Yet, in truth, all individuals have potential, a prin-ciple on which much of the work of psychologists and teachers rests. There may, however, be a problem in inferring finite potential from cognitive-test scores. As discussed above, cognitive-ability tests do not measure innate capacity. Conse-quently, ability-test scores cannot be appropriately interpreted as setting the upper limit, or ceiling, of a child's future performance. Such negative usage of the term potential is unjustified and may be harmful.

To conclude, test scores represent the current status of an individual. They should not be interpreted as indicating an upper limit of development beyond which a child cannot move. Rather, cognitive-test scores should indicate to us that, at the present time, the child's cognitive abilities have developed to a partic-ular level relative to those of other children of the same age.

Psychometric Tests Versus Behavioral Assessment Methods

Over the years many authors have strongly criticized existing intelligence tests for failing to provide information that can be used to design intervention programs (for example, Gillham, 1978; Gresham, 1987; Ysseldyke & Salvia, 1974). Although much of this criticism is directed specifically toward intelligence tests (see for example, "Debate over Usefulness of IQ," NASP, 1988), the critics often generalize their argument to all norm-referenced ability tests. The criticisms often imply that norm-referenced tests of psychometric abilities should provide *complete and sufficient information* on which to base intervention programs. This assumption reflects a misconception of the function of cognitive-ability tests. Certainly these tests can provide information on general strengths and weaknesses in cognitive domains (such as memory or visual–perceptual abilities) that may well have considerable relevance to a child's learning in school. Because they provide samples of tasks from general cognitive domains, however, cognitive tests do not address themselves to the specifics of school curricula. Nevertheless, strengths and weaknesses in a particular domain or area may have very important implications for the child's ability to learn material presented by a teacher. Tests of cognitive abilities, therefore, provide evidence which is necessary but which may not be sufficient for designing specific intervention programs.

Partly in reaction to this alleged failure of psychometric instruments, a number of psychologists have developed theories and models to link assessment to intervention (for two extensive reviews, see the special sections of *School Psychology Review*, 1986, 1989). Broadly termed, these models take a *behavioral* approach to assessment, rather than a *cognitive* approach of analyzing strengths and weaknesses with psychometric tests. Early examples of this approach include applied behavioral analysis (for example, Lovitt, 1975), task and curriculum analysis (for example, Ainscow & Tweddle, 1979; Cameron, 1981; Siegel, 1972), and precision teaching (for example, Alper & White, 1971; White & Liberty, 1976). Later developments in the 1980s generally came under the heading of "curriculum-based assessment" (Blankenship, 1985; Deno, 1985; Gickling, Shane, & Croskery, 1989; Hargis, 1987; Howell & Morehead, 1987; Shinn, 1989). Shinn, Rosenfield, and Knutson (1989) reviewed various developments in this area.

Behavioral-assessment models may be applied most readily to learning difficulties in the early school years and particularly to hierarchies of basic skills. The approach is limited by the lack of defined school curricula and by the difficulty of performing task analyses of complex academic skills, which presumably may be acquired through any of a number of possible instructional sequences. Again, although methods of assessment involving observation and criterion-referenced testing linked to the school curriculum are necessary for developing appropriate instructional programs, they are not in themselves sufficient. Behavioral-assessment models do not take into account cognitive deficits which may be generalized and which may cause the child not to learn specific academic skills. Knowledge about the child's cognitive strengths and weaknesses relates to the selection of both an appropriate instructional hierarchy and an appropriate teaching method.

The rationale for the individual assessment of a child's needs must assume that neither the cognitive, psychometric approach nor the behavioral, task-analysis approach is in itself sufficient for designing an intervention program and that both are usually necessary. A cognitive approach focuses on the assessment of generalized skills and abilities, whereas a behavioral approach focuses on the assessment of specific skills and abilities.

After intervention, such as remedial teaching, we can use either approach to assess the intervention. With the cognitive approach we can determine whether or not the child has developed generalized skills; with the behavioral approach we can determine if the child has acquired additional, specific skills.

The cognitive approach implies that a problem may in part be associated with a generalized difficulty in some area of cognition. The behavioral approach implies that the problem may be basically contextual or environmental and that by manipulating the conditions under which the child learns or by arranging the material to be learned into small and tightly defined hierarchical steps, the child will learn. Both implications clearly may have considerable validity. Knowledge of the specific skills that the child does or does not possess is clearly important as a starting point for developing a program of remediation. Knowledge of the child's generalized difficulties in one or more cognitive areas may be important in deciding the best way of presenting the material to be learned.

Cognitive methods of assessment typically use norm-referenced, psychometric tests. Although psychometric tests are not the only method of assessing a child's cognitive abilities, they are commonly used because they offer efficiency, objectivity, and interpretability. In contrast to the cognitive approach, behavioral methods of assessment typically use criterion-referenced tests and usually measure a relatively narrow range of specific achievements. In addition, behavioral methods commonly feature observational procedures that are linked to a curriculum-based hierarchy of skills.

If only one assessment approach is used, there is a tendency for the resulting report to be limited in its prescriptions. With the cognitive approach, the report often recommends a teaching method but seldom addresses the content to be taught. In contrast, the behavioral-approach report often specifies the content to be taught and the sequence of presentation but seldom addresses the method of instruction. If the report does recommend a teaching method, the method is usually based on behavioral principles such as giving appropriate reinforcement and feedback and providing opportunities for overlearning. Such recommended techniques, although helpful, are not the outcome of a method of assessment. Rather, they are based on generally accepted teaching principles which do not tailor the presentation of materials to the individual strengths and weaknesses of the child.

Although it is possible to find psychologists and teachers who almost exclusively follow either the cognitive or the behavioral approach to assessment, in practice most people will use a mixture of the two. Thus, in addition to carrying out some form of cognitive profile analysis of a child who, for example, is failing in reading, psychologists and teachers will administer criterion-referenced tests and will observe the child's performance. From all of this information, the psychologist and teacher will have a good idea of the most appropriate point at which to start intervention. Although authors sometimes seem to suggest that the approaches are mutually exclusive, a mixture of the two approaches is arguably the best possible form of practice.

Chapter 3

History

The *British Ability Scales*

The DAS is a revision and extension of the *British Ability Scales* (BAS; Elliott et al., 1979), an earlier instrument published in Great Britain. For this reason even a brief history of the DAS must begin with an account of the parent instrument's development.

By the 1960s, British psychologists and educators had long felt the need for an individually administered intelligence scale for school-aged children, developed in the context of British culture and standardized on a British population. For many years psychologists in Great Britain had used adaptations of scales published in the United States, such as the various Wechsler scales or editions of the Stanford–Binet. These instruments met many of the needs of British users, yielding credible estimates of general ability and useful predictions of school achievement. At the same time, however, these scales were criticized along several lines. For example, some test questions with specifically American content were considered unsuitable for use in Great Britain. The lack of British norms was also an important issue (although the results of a Scottish standardization of the WISC in the mid-1960s were extremely close to the U.S. norms) (Scottish Council for Research in Education, 1967).

Psychologists also criticized the available intelligence scales in more general terms. Concerns over ethnic and social-class bias in test scores fueled research and provoked controversy. Some test users were dissatisfied with scales whose purposes were primarily to produce a summary score (IQ) and only secondarily to yield multiple subscores with known diagnostic implications. Furthermore, in the 1960s, researchers inspired by Piagetian theory were exploring several dimensions of early cognitive development that were not measured by existing ability-test batteries.

All of these concerns amplified the need for a new intelligence battery constructed and standardized in Great Britain. In the late 1950s the British Psychological Society convened a committee of specialists to produce a plan for such a battery. Following some preliminary discussions, the committee generated a broad outline for a new test. The British Department of Education and Science provided a substantial grant to the British Psychological Society to support the development of the new scale. In turn this grant made possible the establishment of a research unit at the University of Manchester, which began its work in 1965 under the direction of Professor F. W. Warburton.

First Phase, 1965–1970

Initially the research team focused on preparing a "British Intelligence Scale" (BIS), as it was then called, that would measure the "educability" of children aged 5-12 years, the typical age range of primary school children. The concept of educability was linked to the provisions of the 1944 Education Act and had wide currency in the 1960s.

The research team first reviewed the extensive literature in the field and consulted with psychologists who were researching concepts of intelligence and the development of children's thinking. With this general background, the team drafted preliminary versions of several subtests. The draft materials were critically reviewed by groups of school psychologists who informally tried out and modified the items. The research team then administered the revised collection of subtests to a sample of school-aged children and explored the statistical properties of the items.

At about the same time, the research team redefined the BIS to include children aged 2-18 years and to give more emphasis to measuring the abilities of young, handicapped children and gifted, older students. The team also decided to model the test's content on six of Thurstone's (1938) seven "primary mental abilities" (omitting the perceptual–speed factor) and to include an index of general mental ability. In the mid-1960s while this developmental work was proceeding, considerable interest in the possibility of measuring divergent thinking, or more loosely, "creativity," was also growing. Thus, the project team added tests thought to measure aspects of this domain. Additionally, the team included some items derived from Piagetian theory, hoping that the test scores would thus indicate qualitative aspects of children's thinking.

Two articles (Warburton, 1970; Warburton, Fitzpatrick, Ward, & Ritchie, 1970) explain the rationale of early versions of the subtests and indicate the types of items developed. More detailed accounts of specific aspects of item development are given by Ward (1972) and Ward and Fitzpatrick (1970, 1973).

The result of this preparatory work was a rather long tryout version of the BIS. Examiners were especially trained in the administration of the materials, and by 1970, the tests had been administered to about 1,200 children. Ostensibly the necessary data analyses and test revisions could therefore begin and the standardization testing kits could be produced.

Several difficulties, however, had become apparent. The original project director, F. W. Warburton, had died in 1969, and some members of the research group had taken other positions. Problems related to the size and complexity of the tryout version had possibly delayed the collection of test data. Perhaps the most fundamental difficulty was that the overall plan was too ambitious for the resources available—the original funding for the project was depleted. The research team was also finding that some of the experimental tests were not sufficiently long or reliable and that some of the innovative tests designed to measure divergent thinking or derived from Piagetian theory were difficult to analyze and scale.

Evidently more developmental work was required before standardization could proceed. Compounding these difficulties was growing skepticism among psychologists as well as the general public about the usefulness of the construct of intelligence in general and of intelligence tests in particular.

In response to these problems, the British Department of Education and Science deliberated with the University of Manchester and the British Psychological Society on the future of the project. In 1972 the government decided to provide the funding necessary to continue work on the scale, and the project restarted in early 1973 with Dr. Colin Elliott as Director. The funding continued until 1978.

Second Phase, 1973–1982

After reviewing the existing test materials and scanning the literature, the new team made two major decisions that significantly changed the goals and course of the project. First, the major emphasis of the battery would be on providing a profile of meaningful and distinct subtest scores, with the consequent possibility of differential diagnosis. IQ estimation would be a concurrent but secondary function of the battery. This change of emphasis eventually led to a change in the battery's name from the British Intelligence Scale to the *British Ability Scales*.

The other major decision made by the team stemmed from new developments in test theory. These new theoretical developments provided an alternative to classical test theory—namely, item response theory. The one-parameter Rasch model was particularly prominent in this work. Consequently, the second major decision that guided the project team from this point was to develop subtests of the new scale that fit the Rasch model. Because the Rasch model is unidimensional, this decision meant that the content of each resulting subtest should be homogeneous. Factor analysis was relegated to a secondary role of describing the structure of the battery, whereas formerly it had guided the battery's content and structure.

The research team, therefore, set out to produce a battery consisting of a wide range of homogeneous, unidimensional subtests whose content and interrelationships would be compatible with a number of theoretical models. The items already developed for the scale were reexamined according to their scaling characteristics—that is, whether or not they would likely form homogeneous scales. At this point, the project team abandoned some of the earlier items. In other cases, the team prepared new items to supplement item sets that inadequately covered their intended ability ranges. Some subtests were found during tryout to be unsatisfactory for various reasons, but several of these subtests were deemed worthwhile and were extensively rewritten. Finally, the team drafted a few entirely new subtests to represent cognitive abilities that are relevant to common learning difficulties but that were not yet reflected by the item materials. Notable among these new subtests was Speed of Information Processing, a measure related to the only one of Thurstone's primary mental abilities not already represented in the battery.

The team administered the new items and subtests to suitable groups of children and further refined the subtests on the basis of the results. The outcome of this work was the standardization edition of what was still called the British Intelligence Scale. The standardization testing took place between October 1975 and July 1976. Analysis of the data on the 3,435 children of the norm sample began in the summer of 1976 and concluded in mid-1978.

The first edition of the *British Ability Scales* was published in 1979, but without a technical manual because of delays in data processing. The Project Director immediately undertook to complete the analytic work as well as to further develop a few of the subtests. The project team had found weaknesses in some subtests such as a lack of sufficient items at particular age levels or problems with scoring procedures. After this work was completed in 1982, a revised edition of the BAS that incorporated these changes and that included the technical manual was published in early 1983. The revised edition comprises 21 subtests and covers an age range of 2 1/2 to 17 1/2 years. Its subtests represent six major process areas: speed, reasoning, spatial imagery, perceptual matching, short-term memory, and retrieval and application of knowledge.

Post-Publication Developments

A considerable body of research with the BAS has been published since its appearance. Although much of the research is rather specialized, a few of the findings that have more general implications are of interest to us.

An important goal of the test development project, mentioned earlier, was that each BAS subtest should have diagnostic significance. This goal is achieved by ensuring, at the least, that a large proportion of each subtest's reliable variance should be *specific variance*—that is, variance not shared in common with other subtests. Studies by Wallbrown, McLoughlin, Elliott, and Blaha (1984) and by Elliott (1986) reported high levels of specificity among the BAS subtests. This specificity enables us to compare subtest scores and thus to profile a child's cognitive strengths and weaknesses.

Attempts to isolate a distinctive test profile that would help in the diagnosis of reading disability have been historically disappointing. Patterns of relative strengths and weaknesses that at first seemed promising either proved difficult to distinguish from "normal" profiles or were not found in subsequent studies. Research with the BAS, however, did reveal distinguishable test profiles (Elliott & Tyler, 1986; Tyler & Elliott, 1988). In these studies, the score profiles of reading-disabled children clustered into three distinctive groups. Moreover, these subgroups corresponded significantly to clinically defined varieties of reading disability. This research indicated that dyslexia was not a single syndrome and suggested that this lack of homogeneity within reading-disabled populations may have accounted for the inconclusiveness of earlier research with other instruments.

A more detailed history of the BAS and a review of post-publication research are given by Ward and Elliott (1990) and Elliott, Pearson, Daniel, and Ward (1990).

The *Differential Ability Scales*

The development of the DAS began in 1984 with Colin Elliott as the author. Through interviews with educational and clinical psychologists who used the test in England and Scotland, the perceived strengths and weaknesses of the BAS were determined. At the same time, prominent school, clinical, and cognitive psychologists in the United States reviewed the test's coverage of abilities and the quality and appropriateness of its content and recommended additions, deletions, and revisions that would improve the battery. Psychologists who specialized in assessing special populations such as the retarded, the gifted, and the perceptually handicapped also reviewed the battery. They suggested ways of modifying the test to better suit their needs. Reviews published in Great Britain (Blinkhorn, 1984) and in the United States (Childs, 1984; Embretson, 1985; Wright & Stone, 1985) supplemented these activities.

These various sources agreed on many points, including the need to delete certain subtests. The reasons for deleting subtests were lack of clarity about the ability being measured (leading to difficulties in interpretation) and practical problems in administration and objective scoring. Six BAS subtests were not retained in the DAS: Formal Operational Thinking, Visualization of Cubes, Rotation of Letter-Like Forms, Verbal Fluency, Social Reasoning, and Verbal-Tactile Matching.

The decision to drop these six subtests was later supported by an independent survey. In 1986, the authors and publisher of the BAS conducted a survey of British users to identify areas for special attention in a possible British revision. The tallied results of several related questions indicated consistently that six of the subtests were used least often and were most often recommended for deletion. These least popular subtests were the same ones that had already been eliminated from the DAS.

The second point on which the reviewers agreed was the need to add new content in several areas. Four new subtests were therefore added to the battery. Decisions to add subtests were guided by the goal to create a battery that would measure relatively diverse abilities, especially those that are related to learning problems. Two of the new subtests were nonverbal subtests for preschool children: Picture Similarities and Block Building were designed to better balance the verbal and nonverbal content of the preschool battery. The Sequential and Quantitative Reasoning subtest augmented the group of reasoning tests, and Spelling complemented the measurement of achievement.

The third area of revision was to make several of the retained subtests more efficient and reliable. New items were added, particularly at the lower and upper difficulty levels, to most of the retained subtests. Table 3.1 summarizes the changes and additions incorporated in the revision from the BAS to the DAS.

In 1985 and 1986, examiners administered the new test materials to various samples in the United States. The standardization edition of the DAS was normed during 1987-1989. In addition to the content decisions described above, the standardization edition of the DAS reflected efforts to improve the instrument's attractiveness and ease of use. Chapter 6 describes the tryout and standardization activities in detail.

Table 3.1. Subtest Revisions from BAS to DAS

Process[a]/Subtest	New Items Included	Age Range BAS	DAS	Comments
Speed				
Speed of Information Processing	Yes	6:0–17:5	5:0–17:11	Number of items reduced. Format modified. Multi-point scoring used.
Reasoning				
Matrices	Yes	5:0–17:5	5:0–17:11	Converted to multiple–choice.
Picture Similarities	—	—	2:6–7:11	New subtest.
Sequential and Quantitative Reasoning	—	—	5:0–17:11	New subtest.
Similarities	Yes	5:0–17:5	5:0–17:11	Revised presentation—fourth category member not required.
Spatial Imagery				
Pattern Construction	Yes	4:0–17:5	3:0–17:11	Called Block Design in the BAS. Multi-point scoring used. Flat pieces for younger children.
Perceptual Matching				
Block Building	—	—	2:6–4:11	New subtest.
Copying	Yes	3:6–7:11	3:6–7:11	
Matching Letter-Like Forms	Yes	4:0–8:11	4:0–7:11	
Short–Term Memory				
Recognition of Pictures	Yes	2:6–7:11	2:6–17:11	Formerly Visual Recognition in the BAS. Greatly extended item range. Abstract designs deleted.
Recall of Designs	Yes	5:0–17:5	5:0–17:11	
Recall of Digits	No	2:6–17:5	2:6–17:11	
Recall of Objects—Immediate and Delayed	No	5:0–17:5	4:0–17:11	Formerly Immediate and Delayed Visual Recall in the BAS. Shortened and completely revised presentation to include three immediate-recall trials.

[a]As categorized in the BAS.

Process[a]/Subtest	New Items Included	Age Range		Comments
		BAS	DAS	
Retrieval and Application of Knowledge				
Early Number Concepts	Yes	—	2:6–7:11	Derived from early pictorial items in BAS Basic Number Skills. Easier items added.
Naming Vocabulary	Yes	2:6–7:11	2:6–8:11	
Verbal Comprehension	Yes	2:6–4:11	2:6–6:11	New items to extend upper end.
Word Definitions	Yes	5:0–17:5	5:0–17:11	
Basic Number Skills	Yes	2:6–14:5	6:0–17:11	Derived from later worksheet items in BAS Basic Number Skills. New items to extend upper end.
Spelling	—	—	6:0–17:11	New subtest.
Word Reading	Yes	5:0–14:5	5:0–17:11	

[a]As categorized in the BAS.

37

Chapter 4

Description and Interpretation of the DAS Subtests and Clusters

Chapter 2 presented the rationale and the nature of DAS composite scores. In order to get to know a test, however, we also need to explore the content and nature of the individual subtests. What is it that the child will have to do? What are the tasks? How will we be able to talk about the child's performance on these tasks? What do high and low scores mean? This chapter provides more detailed descriptions of the individual subtests and the clusters.

The 17 cognitive subtests and 3 school achievement tests are described first. Each description includes a brief rationale for the subtest and some proposals about the component skills and processes which underlie performance on that subtest. Brief, global descriptions of the five clusters are presented after the subtest descriptions. Each of these descriptive sections concludes with a list of possible interpretive statements about the score on that particular subtest or cluster. The subtests and clusters are described in the following sequence:

- Preschool Core Subtests
  - Block Building
  - Verbal Comprehension
  - Picture Similarities
  - Naming Vocabulary
  - Pattern Construction
  - Early Number Concepts
  - Copying
- School-Age Core Subtests
  - Recall of Designs
  - Word Definitions
  - Pattern Construction
  - Matrices
  - Similarities
  - Sequential and Quantitative Reasoning

- Diagnostic Subtests (Preschool and School-Age)
  - Matching Letter-Like Forms
  - Recall of Digits
  - Recall of Objects—Immediate and Delayed
  - Recognition of Pictures
  - Speed of Information Processing
- School Achievement Tests
  - Basic Number Skills
  - Spelling
  - Word Reading
- Preschool Clusters
  - Verbal Ability
  - Nonverbal Ability
- School-Age Clusters
  - Verbal Ability
  - Nonverbal Reasoning Ability
  - Spatial Ability

General Influences on Test Scores

One of the major reasons we give a test battery designed to provide a cognitive profile is to interpret relatively high and low scores as indicators of particular strengths and weaknesses in abilities. Having established that there is a pattern of strengths and weaknesses, we will then often wish to formulate hypotheses about the possible reasons for this pattern.

Before deciding that a particular profile pattern is interpretable, we must satisfy ourselves that there were no extraneous factors that might invalidate these interpretations. We should consider the following questions when deciding whether or not to interpret the scores as valid:

- Was the test administered according to the standardized instructions?
- Were the child's responses scored more leniently or more severely than the standardized scoring rules specify?
- Did noise, distraction, or interruption interfere with the test administration?
- Was the child extremely distractible, have a poor attention span, or have great difficulty concentrating?
- Did the child appear anxious to the degree that concentration or flexibility of thought seemed impaired?

- Did the child have a sensory impairment (particularly a vision or hearing impairment)?
- Did the child have a motor handicap (either permanent or temporary such as from an injury)?
- Was the child hesitant or reluctant to respond?
- Did the child refuse to persist on more difficult items?
- Was rapport with the child difficult to establish?
- Was the child on medication?
- Was the child ill or fatigued?

The first two of these influences may, of course, be associated with invalidly high scores as well as with invalidly low scores. The other influences are usually associated with low scores.

Other Variables to Consider

Let us assume that we have obtained a profile of cognitive strengths and weaknesses and that we are reasonably confident that the profile is valid. As a next step in the analysis of the data, we will often wish to draw some conclusions about the factors underlying the child's strengths and weaknesses and will probably focus on possible causes of the weaknesses. In order to draw such conclusions, we will need to relate the profile to contextual information about the child. That is, we must generate our hypotheses within the framework of other sources of data about the child such as teacher observations, other test scores, and parental interviews. Moreover, we need to consider the following types of variables:

- environmental, cultural, or economic disadvantage;
- visual, hearing, or motor handicaps;
- educational history including preschools and schools attended, record of school absences, and reasons for absences;
- educational curriculum and teaching methods used;
- the language(s) used in the home;
- family structure;
- temporary family trauma (such as death or divorce);
- developmental history including any birth complications, medical problems, effects of drugs or surgery, and dates of developmental milestones; and
- any factors contributing to educational disadvantage such as lack of community resources.

The Nature of the Interpretive Suggestions

The suggested interpretations are appropriate not only for consideration of normatively high or low scores, but also for interpreting scores relative to the individual child's profile. That is, a high or low score may be interpreted as a strength or weakness relative to the performance of other children of the same age (a normative interpretation). A high or low score may also be interpreted relative to the other scores made by that child (a within-child interpretation). We will want to use both approaches when generating hypotheses about the child, and the interpretive suggestions are appropriate in either case. For many of the subtests, the list of interpretive statements concludes with one or more factors that are specifically related to low scores.

The interpretations in this chapter are hypotheses. They are meant to provide us suggestions about how the child's performance might be explained or described. A child's performance on a subtest or cluster would not indicate that *all* of the interpretive statements are applicable. In the tradition of scientific methodology, we should seek further evidence that will support or refute any given hypothesis. We should view the lists of interpretive statements as options to consider and should apply those statements to the child's performance in light of other information. Chapter 5 will continue with a more global approach to interpreting the overall pattern of test scores.

Preschool Core Subtests

Block Building (Ages 2:6–4:11)

Block Building is a core subtest which contributes to the measurement of GCA only at the youngest preschool ages, 2:6–3:5. For children aged 3:6–4:11, it may be used as a diagnostic subtest.

Tower building with wooden blocks has been used for many years in young children's cognitive test batteries. Block Building measures the child's ability to copy a design with wooden blocks. Some of the items in this subtest were included in the standardization edition of the BAS, but the number of items was insufficient to produce a reliable subtest. The items were therefore shelved until the development of the DAS.

Block Building was created to measure the same abilities measured by the Copying subtest for young children not yet able to manipulate a pencil. On the first item the child is required to build a tower, using eight blocks, each 1 5/8 by 1 5/8 by 3/4 inches. The response score of 0, 1, or 2 points depends on the number of blocks the child uses in the construction. For the remaining 11 items, the examiner constructs a two-dimensional or three-dimensional design with four of the blocks and leaves the design in view while the child attempts to copy it, using the other four blocks. These item responses are scored 1 or 0 points based on the orientation and relative position of the blocks. The last 5 of the 12 items present "flat" (two-dimensional) designs which are more challenging than the preceding three-dimensional items because they emphasize orientation and sequence. The rotation and reversal errors made on the flat Block Building items are like those made on the drawing items of the Copying subtest.

Performance on this subtest requires motor skills and visual–perceptual encoding. It also requires the child to have developed the notion of copying models. As with many so-called nonverbal tests, performance on this subtest may be enhanced if the child has begun to develop efficient verbal-encoding strategies. In addition to these factors, performance may be affected by idiosyncratic tendencies in young children to make designs that they like rather than designs required by the test.

Scores on the Block Building subtest may reflect the child's

- nonverbal problem solving,
- visual–perceptual matching,
- eye–hand coordination,
- perception of spatial orientation (the preservation of relative position and angles in different aspects of the design),
- use of verbal mediation strategies,
- visual–motor skills, and
- ability to follow verbal instructions and visual cues.

In addition, low scores on this subtest may reflect the child's

- egocentricity (paying insufficient attention to the examiner's instructions).

Verbal Comprehension (Ages 2:6–6:11)

Verbal Comprehension is a verbal subtest which contributes to the measurement of GCA for children aged 2:6–5:11 and to the Verbal Ability cluster for children aged 3:6–5:11. It can be administered to children aged 6:0–6:11 of average or low ability.

The Verbal Comprehension subtest assesses understanding of language. Tests such as this are common in batteries for preschool children. In the DAS, the first items use a picture of a teddy bear; the child is asked to point to several features named by the examiner. The child is shown an array of toys for the next set of items, which sample the child's understanding of object names, of commands to do certain manipulations with the objects (for example, "Put the cat in the box"), and of the functions of the objects (for example, "Give me the one that goes on your coat"). The next set of items uses wooden objects such as a bridge, houses, and a car. The instructions generally sample the child's understanding of prepositions (for example, "Put the child *under* the bridge"). For the most difficult items the child uses red, blue, and yellow chips of different shapes to demonstrate understanding of more complex instructions (for example, "Give me all of the blue chips except the triangle").

Verbal Comprehension measures language comprehension through a receptive mode. None of the items requires the child to respond orally, and only the most physically handicapped child would be unable to perform the requisite operations on the toys and other materials.

> Scores on the Verbal Comprehension subtest may reflect the child's
> - understanding of spoken language, including
>   - understanding of syntax,
>   - knowledge of prepositional and relational concepts, and
>   - vocabulary knowledge;
> - ability to formulate and test alternative hypotheses (items with chips);
> - ability to follow verbal instructions; and
> - short-term auditory memory of sentences.
>
> In addition, low scores on this subtest may reflect the child's
> - egocentricity (paying insufficient attention to the examiner's instructions),
> - distractibility (playing with the objects instead of following the examiner's instructions), or
> - impulsiveness (responding to only the first part of a spoken command).

Picture Similarities (Ages 2:6–7:11)

Picture Similarities is a nonverbal subtest which contributes to the measurement of GCA for children aged 2:6–5:11 and to the Nonverbal Ability cluster for children aged 3:6–5:11. For children 6:0–7:11 of low ability, this subtest can be administered as a diagnostic subtest.

Picture Similarities measures the reasoning ability of preschool children. Similarities items have had a long history in mental-ability testing as measures of reasoning. Spearman (1927) considered them to be excellent measures of the eduction of relations, one of the major characteristics of psychometric g (see Chapter 2). Although many similarities tests are verbal, the DAS subtest was designed to be entirely nonverbal. The task does not require any oral response from the child.

For each item the child is shown a row of four pictures or designs in a booklet. The child places a fifth card with a single picture or design below the stimulus picture that it best goes with. The nature of the task is demonstrated for the child in the first two items which require the child to match identical pictures. The increasingly difficult items require the child to recognize a relationship based on a common concept or element. For example, the child would match a picture of a hand with one of four pictures of clothing, including a picture of a glove. Thus, to perform the task the child must perceive various, possibly relevant features of the drawings. The child must engage in hypothesis testing to select a feature that the target picture shares with one and only one of the four drawings.

Most of the item content is representational rather than abstract. Although speech is not required, good verbal-encoding strategies may well help the child solve the problems. The test does not require fine motor coordination because the child must only place or push the response card near the correct stimulus picture; the orientation or exact placement of the card does not affect scoring.

Scores on the Picture Similarities subtest may reflect the child's
- ability to solve nonverbal problems (inductive reasoning),
- ability to identify features of pictures,
- ability to formulate and test hypotheses about common features,
- ability to perceive and analyze visual information,
- use of verbal mediation strategies,
- ability to attach meaning to pictures, and
- level of the general knowledge base.

In addition, low scores on this subtest may reflect the child's
- impulsiveness (responding without checking the response).

Naming Vocabulary (Ages 2:6–8:11)

Naming Vocabulary is a verbal subtest which contributes to the measurement of GCA for children aged 2:6–5:11 and to the Verbal Ability cluster for children aged 3:6–5:11. It can be used as a diagnostic subtest for children aged 6:0–7:11 of all ability levels and for children aged 8:0–8:11 of average or low ability.

This subtest assesses the spoken vocabulary of young children. Such tests have long been a common feature of cognitive ability batteries. The test items consist of two objects and a booklet of colored pictures of objects which the child is shown one at a time and is asked to name.

This subtest measures expressive-language ability, in contrast to the receptive-language ability measured by the Verbal Comprehension subtest. Successful performance on this subtest depends on the child's previous development of a vocabulary of nouns. Picture recognition is also crucial; however, the pictures are large and brightly colored and are unlikely to cause problems except for children with major visual impairments or with no experience with picture books. The items require the child to recall words from long-term memory rather than to recognize or to understand the meaning of words, as comprehension tests do. The task is also more convergent and more highly structured than the task in the Word Definitions subtest, which involves more open-ended responses.

Scores on the Naming Vocabulary subtest may reflect the child's

- expressive language skills,
- vocabulary knowledge of nouns,
- ability to attach verbal labels to pictures,
- level of the general knowledge base,
- general language development,
- ability to retrieve names from long-term memory, and
- level of language stimulation.

In addition, low scores on this subtest may reflect the child's

- reluctance to speak.

47

Pattern Construction (Ages 3:0–17:11)

Pattern Construction is a nonverbal subtest which contributes to the measurement of GCA for children aged 3:6–17:11, to the Nonverbal Ability cluster for preschool children aged 3:6–5:11, and to the Spatial Ability cluster for children aged 6:0–17:11. It may also be given to children aged 3:0–3:5 of average or high ability for additional diagnostic information.

Since the publication of *Kohs' Block Design Test* (Kohs, 1919), a number of cognitive test batteries have included block-design items. Such items measure spatial ability and are also highly related to overall cognitive ability. In general, a block-design item requires a child to copy a two-dimensional pattern, usually of two colors, by arranging three-dimensional blocks whose sides are of different colors and patterns. The task requires the child to analyze and synthesize the sample design (usually presented in a picture).

The initial items in the DAS Pattern Construction subtest, intended for young children, require the child to construct patterns with crepe foam squares approximately 1/4 inch thick, with each side either solid yellow or solid black. For the first item, the child duplicates a model provided by the examiner. Pictures in the test booklet are then introduced as the target designs. The procedures of modeling, teaching, demonstration, and often a second trial help children to understand the nature of the task.

Later items, for older children, require the child to construct patterns with plastic blocks. Each side of a block may be black, yellow, black and yellow divided diagonally, or black and yellow divided vertically. The block items begin with easy two-block patterns and increase in complexity to nine-block patterns.

The BAS version of this subtest used only blocks. Although it was normed down to age 4 years, the test was too difficult for many 4- and 5-year-olds and only began to function accurately across the full range of ability at about age 6½ years. Young children have difficulty understanding that they are to use only the top surfaces of the blocks to create a pattern. The flat-square items were developed to extend the age range downward. Because the patterns for all items are two-dimensional, the flat-square items should measure the same ability. During the tryout phase of DAS development, a study conducted with sixth-grade children showed that items measure the same construct whether they use blocks or flat squares (Daniel, 1986).

Unlike similar tests in other batteries, the Pattern Construction subtest can be administered and scored in either of two ways. The *Standard Procedure* yields a score based on accuracy and speed; the child earns from 0 to 5 points for each item, depending on the time taken to construct a correct design. With the *Alternative Procedure*, the score is based solely on accuracy within very liberal time limits, and a few extra items are administered at the end to increase reliability. Except for its additional items, the Alternative Procedure is administered in exactly the same way as the Standard Procedure. Therefore, at the end of the Standard administration, the examiner may decide to give more items and to score the subtest with the Alternative method.

The two versions of Pattern Construction appear to measure the same construct. An analysis, described in Chapter 9, demonstrated that scores from the two procedures have the same patterns of correlations with the rest of the DAS battery. Research with the BAS showed that the speed of children's responses to relatively easy Pattern Construction items measured the same ability as the accuracy of their responses to difficult items (Elliott & Murray, 1977). An Alternative Procedure score can be used interchangeably with a Standard Procedure score for deriving cluster or GCA scores and for identifying strengths and weaknesses.

The Alternative Procedure should be particularly useful whenever we believe that speed of response may not be a valid measure for the particular child being tested, such as a child with a physical handicap or an attentional problem or one who takes an extremely deliberate approach to the task. Both the Standard and Alternative Procedures are appropriate for children across the full range of ability up to about age 12. At older ages, Alternative Procedure scores encounter a ceiling that makes the procedure inappropriate for examinees of high ability.

Pattern Construction requires visual–spatial skills for successful solution. The patterns in the booklet are two-dimensional, whereas the blocks themselves are three-dimensional. The task therefore requires the child to make a two-dimensional construction and to ignore the third dimension. Poor scores may indicate poor visual–spatial ability which may be reflected in a number of ways, such as the child's rotating the designs, the child's being distracted by the sides of the blocks, or the child's inability to perceive the correspondence between the pattern on the blocks and the pattern in the booklet. With the Standard Procedure a number of other factors may contribute to the child's poor performance: The child may be noticeably clumsy and have difficulty manipulating the squares or blocks; a distractible child may have to be reminded frequently to continue with the task; or the child may have a cautious cognitive style and opt for accurate rather than speedy performance.

Scores on the Pattern Construction subtest may reflect the child's

- spatial visualization ability, including
  - perception of spatial orientation (the preservation of relative position, size, and angles in different aspects of the design),
  - the ability to reproduce designs with objects, and
  - the ability to perceive and analyze visual information; and
- nonverbal reasoning ability, including
  - the use of systematic strategies (for example, sequential assembly, hypothesis testing, or trial and error) and
  - the ability to analyze (to see the components of the whole) and to synthesize (to reconstruct the whole from the components).

In addition, low scores on this subtest may reflect the child's

- poor motor control,
- anxiety from a timed task (Standard Procedure),
- clumsiness (Standard Procedure), or
- excessive cautiousness (Standard Procedure).

Early Number Concepts (Ages 2:6–7:11)

Early Number Concepts is a subtest with both verbal and quantitative content which contributes to the measurement of GCA for children aged 3:6–5:11. As a diagnostic subtest, it can be used with children aged 6:0–6:5 at all ability levels, with children aged 2:6–3:5 of average or high ability, and with children aged 6:6–7:11 of average or low ability.

The subtest assesses the following number concepts and skills:

- reciting by rote numbers up to ten,
- counting up to ten objects in one-to-one correspondence with pointing,
- matching and classifying according to qualitative attributes,
- matching and classifying by number,
- making comparisons of sets by concepts such as more, less, same/equal,
- recognizing number names and numerals,
- recognizing ordinal relationships such as first, second, or last,
- understanding numerical order shown by identifying larger or smaller numbers,
- solving basic addition and subtraction word problems, and
- counting by tens and recognizing place value of tens and ones.

The first item in the Early Number Concepts subtest requires the child to count a set of ten chips; the subsequent items ask questions about colored pictures in a booklet. Most of the questions require the child to respond by pointing, although a few items require the child's counting aloud or saying a number. None of the items requires extended verbal responses.

Scores on this subtest represent the child's acquired knowledge of concepts of number and quantity. Because it focuses particularly on the child's knowledge of number concepts, the subtest should not be considered a complete assessment of general mathematical concepts (for example, it does not include concepts of measurement). However, because there is a fundamental relationship between conceptual knowledge and verbal knowledge, scores on the subtest also reflect more general aspects of language development. Low scores on this subtest may reflect relatively poor general cognitive or verbal development. Poor performance may also result from disadvantage or a lack of experience in using language about number or quantity.

The analysis of failures on specific subtest items may reveal particular concepts that the child has not yet mastered. Such information about gaps in the child's conceptual knowledge may be useful for teachers in planning early learning activities. For example, the child may have missed an item that asks the child to "point to the cake with one more candle than this one." The concept of "more" or "one more" is basic to many primary instructional activities. Informing the primary teacher that the child may not understand this concept can help the teacher to tailor lessons to the individual needs of the child.

This subtest is not part of any cluster because it has high loadings on both the Verbal Ability and Nonverbal Ability clusters. Because of its high g loading, however, it does contribute to the General Conceptual Ability score.

Scores on the Early Number Concepts subtest may reflect the child's
- knowledge of numerical and prenumerical concepts,
- verbal comprehension,
- knowledge of basic language concepts, and
- visual perception and analysis of pictures.

In addition, a low score on Item 1 (counting) may reflect the child's
- problems in verbal expression (including reluctance to speak).

Copying (Ages 3:6–7:11)

Copying is a nonverbal subtest which contributes to the measurement of GCA and to the Nonverbal Ability cluster for children aged 3:6–5:11. It may also be given as a diagnostic subtest to children aged 6:0–7:11.

Copying items are popular in tests of cognitive ability, particularly in those for young children. The development of copying skills has a place of some importance in the educational curriculum for young children, having implications for the development of skills in writing and perceptual matching. Learning the alphabetic and numeric symbols, for example, and learning to reproduce and visually discriminate these symbols demand a great amount of the curriculum time in primary education.

The items in the subtest cover a wide range of difficulty. The initial items are very simple figures, such as a straight line or a circle; later items include letter shapes which commonly cause reversal difficulties for young children; and the final items are more complex geometric figures. For each item, the child is presented with a line drawing printed in a booklet. The drawing remains in view while the child attempts to reproduce it.

Scoring criteria address the accuracy of position, proportion, and detail. Scoring templates are provided to objectify the scoring of many aspects of the children's drawings. Drawings are given 0, 1, 2, or 3 points according to the scoring criteria.

The copying of designs appears to require, along with some motor ability, the ability to perceive similarities between a standard figure and the figure being drawn. Poor performance may be a function of the child's poor experience or lack of opportunity in copying activities at home and in school, or may indicate poor development of matching skills or poor motor control.

Scores on the Copying subtest may reflect the child's

- ability to match visual shapes by paper-and-pencil response,
- fine motor coordination,
- perception of spatial orientation (the preservation of relative position, size, and angles in different aspects of the design), and
- pencil control.

In addition, low scores on this subtest may be associated with the child's

- poor posture and hand position in relation to the paper or
- poor pencil grasp and high pencil pressure.

We should also recognize that

- the child's difficulty is more likely to be perceptual if the design is copied easily but incorrectly,
- motor difficulties are indicated by slow drawing, arduous drawing, or both, and
- many erasures may indicate compulsivity (drawing has to be exactly right).

School-Age Core Subtests

Recall of Designs (Ages 5:0–17:11)

Recall of Designs is a nonverbal subtest which contributes to the measurement of GCA and to the Spatial Ability cluster for children aged 6:0–17:11. It can also be administered to children aged 5:0–5:11.

This subtest has a number of features that are similar to those of previously published recall of designs tests, such as those by Graham and Kendall (1960) and Benton (1974). Each item is a non-pictorial line drawing which is presented to the child for 5 seconds. The design is then removed and the child is asked to draw it from memory. The child's drawings receive from 0 to 3 points according to quality. Scoring criteria address factors such as the presence or absence of a component of the design, distortions, and correctness of spatial relationships between and within components. For example, intentionally added lines that are not part of the stimulus figure result in a score of 0. Including the parts of a design but reversing their relative positions may result in a score of 1 rather than 2 points. Accuracy of details, however, does not play a major role in scoring.

Performance on the Recall of Designs subtest requires not only visual–spatial encoding and retention but also an adequate level of motor skills. The drawings, however, are such that they should not cause difficulty for children with normal motor development.

Scores on the Recall of Designs subtest may reflect the child's

- short-term visual recall,
- perception of spatial orientation (the preservation of relative position, size, and angles in different aspects of the design), and
- drawing skills.

In addition, low scores on this subtest may reflect the child's

- poor retention or poor retrieval (or both) of whole visual images and
- interference in recall from previous designs (for example, perseveration).

We should also recognize that

- low scores are more likely to reflect memory or visual–spatial difficulties if the design is copied easily but incorrectly,
- motor difficulties are indicated by slow drawing, arduous drawing, or both, and
- many erasures may indicate compulsivity (drawing has to be exactly right).

Word Definitions (Ages 5:0–17:11)

Word Definitions is a verbal subtest which contributes to the measurement of GCA and to the Verbal Ability cluster for children aged 6:0–17:11. It may also be administered to children aged 5:0–5:11 of average or high ability.

This subtest is similar to the vocabulary subtests found in many cognitive-test batteries. Generally considered to be good measures of crystallized mental abilities, such tests correlate highly with performance on many other cognitive tasks.

For each item in the subtest, a word is orally presented to the child who is asked what the word means. An important feature of the DAS Word Definitions subtest is that it requires the child to give the meaning of the word rather than merely to use it correctly in context. Responses to the Word Definitions items are scored as correct or incorrect according to whether or not the child expresses key concepts of the word's meaning. This task contrasts with the task of the Naming Vocabulary subtest, which is far less open-ended and which assesses a child's acquired knowledge of object names.

The Word Definitions subtest measures acquired verbal knowledge. A child's comprehension of words and fluency in expressing definitions may depend on experience as well as on education. Low scores may be generally attributable to poor verbal development. Because of the influence of experience on language acquisition, low scores may be associated with disadvantaged environmental circumstances. Children who are very inhibited, who lack fluency, or who lack confidence may also score poorly on this subtest, and we need to be alert for signs of such response styles.

Scores on the Word Definitions subtest may reflect the child's
- vocabulary knowledge,
- ability to formulate definitions of words,
- expressive language skills, including verbal fluency,
- level of the general knowledge base,
- verbal conceptualization,
- abstract thinking, and
- long-term information retrieval.

In addition, low scores on this subtest may reflect the child's
- verbal inhibition, that is, unwillingness to give open-ended verbal responses when uncertain.

Pattern Construction (Ages 3:0–17:11)

The rationale and description of the Pattern Construction subtest have already been presented on pages 48-50, within the sequence of the Preschool Core subtests. Score interpretations are repeated here for ease of reference.

Scores on the Pattern Construction subtest may reflect the child's

- spatial visualization ability, including
    - perception of spatial orientation (the preservation of relative position, size, and angles in different aspects of the design),
    - the ability to reproduce designs with objects, and
    - the ability to perceive and analyze visual information; and
- nonverbal reasoning ability, including
    - the use of systematic strategies (for example, sequential assembly, hypothesis testing, or trial and error) and
    - the ability to analyze (to see the components of the whole) and to synthesize (to reconstruct the whole from the components).

In addition, low scores on this subtest may reflect the child's

- poor motor control,
- anxiety from a timed task (Standard Procedure),
- clumsiness (Standard Procedure), or
- excessive cautiousness (Standard Procedure).

Matrices (Ages 5:0–17:11)

Matrices is a nonverbal subtest which contributes to the measurement of GCA and to the Nonverbal Reasoning Ability cluster for children aged 6:0–17:11. It can also be administered to children aged 5:0–5:11.

Matrices items have been used frequently in measures of cognitive abilities. They are very good examples of Spearman's eduction of relations and correlates (1927). By far the most well-known of these tests is *Raven's Progressive Matrices* (Raven, 1958). Matrix items were probably originally designed by Burt (see Keir, 1949).

The DAS Matrices subtest presents matrix problems in a multiple-choice format. Each matrix is a square consisting of four or nine cells (see Figure 4.1). A blank cell is in the lower right corner of each matrix. From among four or six alternatives, the child chooses the design that correctly completes the matrix.

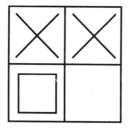

A Partly Symmetrical
Identity Item

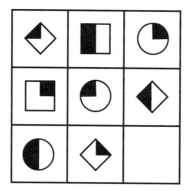

A Symmetrical Latin-
Square Item

Figure 4.1. Sample Matrices Items

According to Ward and Fitzpatrick (1973), each matrices item can be classified as symmetrical or nonsymmetrical. A symmetrical item may have columns or rows containing identical shapes or may have identical patterns running horizontally and vertically. The symmetrical category also includes Latin-square items which have symmetry of order; that is, the cell contents are varied or balanced systematically (see Figure 4.1). Items in the nonsymmetrical category may use horizontal or vertical summation of attributes, and a considerable range of item difficulty may be achieved through altering the size, number, shape, and position of attributes within the cells.

In the BAS, the Matrices subtest was presented in a self-completion format in which the child drew the correct design in the blank cell. This format was changed in the DAS to a multiple-choice format for three reasons. First, although the drawing skills required were not demanding, children with motor difficulties could be penalized. Second, the draw-in format introduced subjectivity into the scoring. Third, the self-completion format took more time to administer and score.

Matrices is a measure of reasoning ability. Although the items are nonverbal, verbal mediation of the problems will often help the child devise appropriate solutions. Initially the child must educe the relationship between the figures in the cells of the matrix and then, on the basis of that relationship, must select an appropriate correlate from among the answer choices. Poor performance on the Matrices subtest may indicate poor reasoning ability. For example, the child may not be able to independently rationalize the pattern of the first two rows and to apply this pattern to the third row in order to supply the missing element. Specific visual–spatial difficulties may also possibly cause poor performance on this subtest.

Scores on the Matrices subtest may reflect the child's

- nonverbal, inductive reasoning, including
  - the ability to identify rules governing features or variables in abstract figures and
  - the ability to formulate and test hypotheses about relationships;
- use of verbal mediation strategies involving labeling of diagrams; and
- perception of visual detail and spatial orientation in drawings.

In addition, low scores on this subtest may reflect the child's

- poor understanding of verbal instructions or visual cues,
- impulsivity (responding too rapidly), or
- inflexibility in choosing solution strategies.

Similarities (Ages 5:0–17:11)

Similarities is a verbal subtest which contributes to the measurement of GCA and to the Verbal Ability cluster for children aged 6:0-17:11. It can also be administered to children aged 5:0-5:11 of average or high ability.

Similarities is a measure of verbal reasoning. The items are good examples of Spearman's eduction of relations (1927), a central feature of psychometric g (see Chapter 2). As in the case of matrices items, similarities items have long been used in individually administered ability tests. Traditionally, items in similarities tests present two words, and the child explains how those words are similar.

In some other tests, responses that differ in quality of expression are assigned different quantitative values. For example, when asked how an apple and orange are alike, a child may say that they are both fruits (a superordinate response) or that they both have skins (a subordinate response). Usually the superordinate response is assumed to indicate more ability than does a subordinate response; superordinates thus receive a higher score, and subordinates, a lower score. This procedure may be an unsatisfactory way of handling qualitative differences in responses. It makes the assumption, for example, that the child who makes four superordinate responses could be of the same ability as a child who makes eight subordinate responses (if superordinates are awarded 2 points and subordinates 1 point). This procedure is **not** followed in the DAS Similarities subtest. Generally, subordinate responses are scored as incorrect, and all items require the child to name a superordinate class for the stimulus words in order to earn credit.

The work of Bruner and his colleagues (Bruner, Olver, & Greenfield, 1966) further influenced the development of the present DAS items. In particular, Olver and Hornsby (1966) found that children of about 6 years of age tend to give subordinate definitions of similarity, often in terms of surface properties such as the colors, sizes, shapes, and places of things, or in terms of their common possession of minor features (as in the above example, "skins"). With increasing age and language development, children shift from giving such perceptually influenced definitions to giving ones that are superordinate, often in terms of the functions of things. By early adolescence, children have generally mastered the rules for forming superordinate classes. This mastery, however, is seldom complete, and the ability to apply the rules varies widely among children. The transition from giving subordinate to giving superordinate classifications is gradual rather than sudden and can be viewed as a process of skill acquisition. This view influenced the selection of the stimulus words for the DAS items.

Another consideration in developing items for the DAS Similarities subtest was to reduce ambiguity by the use of three rather than two stimulus words. For example, the child may be given "orange, strawberry, banana" and be asked to name the class to which all the examples belong. A child who gives an over-general or under-general response is encouraged to try again. Acceptable class names are generally scored 1 point, although six of the more difficult items have two levels of correct responses, scored 1 or 2 points. The two levels reflect differences in the quality of the concept rather than in the quality of expression.

At first glance, we might believe that superordinate definitions that summarize a similarity with a single word are superior to superordinate definitions that take several words to convey the idea. However, placing a premium on relatively low-frequency, abstract words makes the subtest a test much more of vocabulary than of verbal reasoning. For example, in response to the question, "How are sausage, orange, and potato chips alike?" the response "nourishment" is certainly briefer than "You eat them for dinner." However, it is dubious that the single word better conveys the essential similarity. Statistical analyses confirmed that the more extended responses usually discriminate just as well between more and less able children.

Scores on the Similarities subtest may reflect the child's
- verbal, inductive reasoning ability, including
    - the ability to relate words to superordinate categories and
    - the ability to formulate and test hypotheses about common features;
- vocabulary and general verbal development;
- level of the general knowledge base;
- logical and abstract thinking abilities; and
- ability to distinguish between essential and superficial features.

In addition, low scores on this subtest may reflect the child's
- verbal inhibition (unwillingness to make verbal responses when uncertain) or
- failure to consider all three stimulus words.

Sequential and Quantitative Reasoning (Ages 5:0–17:11)

Sequential and Quantitative Reasoning is a nonverbal subtest which contributes to the measurement of GCA and to the Nonverbal Reasoning Ability cluster for children aged 6:0–17:11. It can also be administered to children aged 5:0–5:11 of average or high ability.

This subtest provides a measure of nonverbal reasoning. The problems are presented visually, with little verbal instruction. Responses to the initial items have no oral component (the child draws the response), and the later items require only short oral responses (which can be avoided entirely by having the child write the responses). Grouped into two sets, the items in each set are linked in terms of the strategies and processes required for solving.

The first 15 items (Set A) are presented in a consumable booklet. Each item is a series of simple abstract figures with one part of the series missing. The missing element may be at the end or somewhere in the middle of the series, as shown in Figure 4.2(A). The child is asked to draw the missing figure in the appropriate place. Each of the final 24 items (Set B), presented in a stimulus booklet, consists of three pairs of numbers. The second number of the third pair is missing, as shown in Figure 4.2(B). The child must determine the rule that relates the numbers in each of the first two pairs and then apply that rule to the incomplete third pair. The child says the number that should go in the blank space. In the first example of Figure 4.2(B), the child must determine in each of the first two pairs of numbers that the second number is 11 more than the first number. The child must then apply that rule to the first number in the third pair (9) in order to arrive at the answer (20).

The rules in Set B (simple addition, subtraction, multiplication, and division) are very easy for the ages at which they are given. A few of the hardest items involve simple fractions, negative numbers, or compound operations. The difficulty of the subtest derives from the variation of operations from item to item, which requires the child to be flexible in generating hypotheses.

Sequential and Quantitative Reasoning measures the ability to perceive sequential patterns in geometric figures or common rules in numerical relationships. Like the Matrices subtest, this subtest provides another measure of the eduction of relations and correlates. The early items are suitable for primary school children who have had limited exposure to mathematics. Poor performance on these items may reflect low nonverbal reasoning ability or weak sequential information-processing ability. On the later items, poor performance may also be due to poor basic arithmetic skills or the child's inflexibility in selecting solution strategies.

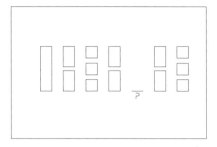

Figure 4.2(A). Example Item from Sequential and
Quantitative Reasoning, Set A

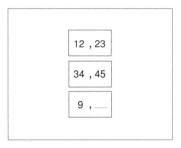

Figure 4.2(B). Example Item from Sequential and
Quantitative Reasoning, Set B

Scores on the Sequential and Quantitative Reasoning subtest may
reflect the child's

- ability to perceive sequential patterns or relationships in
  figures or numbers,
- ability to draw conclusions from known facts or principles
  (inductive reasoning),
- analytical reasoning ability (the process of separating a problem or
  situation into its components),
- ability to formulate and test hypotheses,
- perception and attachment of meaning to pictures (for Set A), and
- long-term information retrieval (for Set B).

In addition, low scores on this subtest may reflect the child's

- lack of knowledge of numerals, basic number facts, and basic
  arithmetic operations (for Set B) or
- inflexibility in choosing solution strategies.

Diagnostic Subtests

Matching Letter-Like Forms (Ages 4:0–7:11)

Matching Letter-Like Forms, which measures visual discrimination and aware-ness of the spatial orientation of asymmetric letter-like figures, is a diagnostic subtest for children aged 4:6–5:11. It can also be administered to children aged 4:0–4:5 of average or high ability and to children aged 6:0–7:11 of average or low ability.

This subtest is based on a study reported by Gibson (1969) of children's ability to discriminate between letter-like forms. Gibson and her co-workers used symmetric and asymmetric letter-like figures with both straight and curved lines. They trans-posed each standard figure in various ways and asked children, aged 4–9 years, to indicate the figure that was identical to the standard figure. They found that reversed and rotated forms were often selected by young children who had not started formal schooling. The children appeared to perceive the figures as con-stant, despite changes in orientation. Although children aged 4 years made many errors with rotations and reversals, this error rate dropped steeply by age 7 years. The task appears to be highly relevant to young children's development of visual discrimination skills, which in turn are relevant to the acquisition of reading and writing skills.

The DAS subtest consists of a number of asymmetric letter-like forms similar to the figures used by Gibson and which look like letters of our alphabet or of the Greek alphabet (see Figure 4.3). For each item, the stimulus figure appears both on the upper page of the booklet and among five transpositions on the lower fac-ing page. The transpositions include a reversal, a 180° rotation, a 180° rotation and reversal, a 45° rotation, and a 315° rotation. The child must select the one figure that is identical to the stimulus figure.

The task requires relatively fine discriminations to be made between the orienta-tions of similar figures. Poor performance may indicate the child's general diffi-culties in distinguishing between letter-like shapes or a lack of development of visual discrimination skills.

Scores on the Matching Letter-Like Forms subtest may reflect the child's

- ability to make visual discriminations among similar figures,
- perception and discrimination of the spatial orientation of letter-like figures,
- strategies for scanning and making visual comparisons, and
- ability to follow verbal instructions and visual cues.

Low scores on this subtest may reflect the child's

- impulsiveness (responding without checking the response),
- lack of experience in visual matching activities, or
- normal developmental pattern (the child is simply not ready to understand the task).

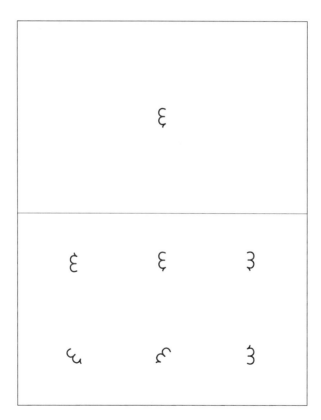

Figure 4.3. Example Item of Matching Letter-Like Forms

Recall of Digits (Ages 2:6–17:11)

Recall of Digits, which measures short-term auditory–sequential recall of digits, is a diagnostic subtest for children aged 3:0–17:11. It can also be administered to children aged 2:6–2:11 of average or high ability.

Many cognitive-test batteries have tests involving the recall of digits. Items typically start with two digits and increase to several digits. In many previous tests this arrangement yielded a measure of "digit span," that is, the number of digits that a child could recall correctly in sequence. Some tests include some items for which the child recalls the digits in the order in which they were presented and other items for which the child recalls the digits in reverse order. The total score derived from the two types of items produces a composite that is difficult to interpret because the skills required for forward- and reverse-digit recall are different. Forward-digit recall requires a basic short-term memory process. Reverse-digit recall requires deeper processing of the stimulus because the child must both remember and manipulate (reverse the sequence of) the information.

The items in the DAS Recall of Digits subtest are presented to the child at the rate of *two digits per second*. Faster than the usual presentation rate in digit-recall subtests, this speed was chosen because it prevents the child's use of verbal rehearsal strategies during the presentation, thus making the subtest a purer measure of short-term auditory memory. The rapid presentation rate has the added advantage of allowing more items to be given in the same amount of time. These features and the subtest's homogeneity of content contribute to its high level of reliability.

Early items in the Recall of Digits subtest consist of sequences of two digits; the sequences gradually increase to nine digits. After the digits are presented in a monotone, with a slight drop in tone on the last digit to indicate the end of the sequence, the child immediately recalls the sequence aloud.

Although scores on this subtest may be affected by anxiety or by inattention, under normal circumstances the scores may reasonably be taken as measures of immediate auditory recall.

Scores on the Recall of Digits subtest may reflect the child's

- short-term auditory memory,
- oral recall of sequences of numbers (non-meaningful memory), and
- concentration and attention.

In addition, low scores on this subtest may reflect the child's

- use of inappropriate strategies for storage or retrieval of numbers (for example, attempting to start rehearsal or recall before the examiner has finished presenting the digit sequence),
- distractibility and inattention, or
- anxiety, poor rapport, or both.

Recall of Objects—Immediate and Delayed (Ages 4:0–17:11)

Recall of Objects, which measures short-term and intermediate-term verbal recall, is a diagnostic subtest for children aged 4:0–17:11.

The task requires verbal recall of the names of 20 common objects pictured on a single card. On the first of three trials, the card is shown to the child and the objects are named by the examiner. The child is told to look carefully because he or she will be required to remember as many of the pictures as possible. After one minute the card is withdrawn, and the child is asked to recall the objects. One point is awarded for each correctly recalled object. For the second and third trials, the child is shown the card again, but for only 20 seconds per trial. The child again recalls as many objects as possible and receives 1 point for each correct answer. The sum of the scores on the three trials makes up the *Immediate Recall* score.

After two nonverbal subtests have been given (taking about 10–30 minutes), and without prior warning or being shown the picture card again, the child is asked to recall the objects on the card. The score from this trial is the *Delayed Recall* score. If the child's normative scores on the Immediate and Delayed recalls are reliably different, both scores are reported, compared, and interpreted. (A difference of 14 or more *T*-score points is significant at $p < .10$.) Otherwise, only the Immediate Recall score is reported and interpreted. Although the Delayed Recall trial measures, to a considerable extent, the same ability as the Immediate Recall trials, it consists of only one trial and, thus, is less reliable. A statistically significant difference between the normative scores indicates that the child performed differently on the Delayed Recall trial than expected from performance on the Immediate Recall trials. This difference, then, may be interpreted for its possible implications for memory processes.

The Recall of Objects subtest is a test of short-term and intermediate-term verbal memory, with an added visual component. Verbal encoding, rehearsal, and retrieval strategies are important in the performance of these tasks. Tyler and Elliott (1988) and Elliott (1989) report that the BAS version of this subtest appears to discriminate between two subgroups of reading-disabled children of average to above-average intelligence. One of these subgroups had low scores on Recall of Objects, Recall of Digits, and Speed of Information Processing, scores which suggest a memory problem in sequential information processing. The other subgroup had relatively high scores on these three subtests but low scores on Recall of Designs and Word Definitions, scores which suggest problems of holistic information retrieval. Poor performance on Recall of Objects may therefore be associated with general memory problems or, more specifically, with problems in short-term auditory memory or short-term visual memory. It may also be indicative of a general problem with attention and concentration.

Scores on the Recall of Objects subtest may reflect the child's

- short-term and immediate-term verbal recall,
- ability to remember a number of pieces of information presented both visually and verbally,
- use of strategies for storage and retrieval of information, and
- concentration and attention.

In addition, low scores on this subtest may reflect the child's

- poor imagery for visual information,
- difficulty in integrating visual and verbal information,
- low rates of learning with repeated trials, or
- lack of understanding of instructions (not naming the same objects on later trials).

A Delayed score significantly lower than the Immediate score may reflect the child's

- use of a superficial encoding strategy on the immediate trials,
- relatively rapid loss of memory trace, and
- interference effects from intervening activities.

A Delayed score significantly higher than the Immediate score may reflect the child's

- efficient consolidation of memory trace or
- use of "deep" encoding and rehearsal strategies on immediate trials.

Recognition of Pictures (Ages 2:6–17:11)

Recognition of Pictures is a diagnostic subtest for children aged 3:0–7:11. It can also be administered to children aged 2:6–2:11 of average or high ability and to children aged 8:0–17:11 of average or low ability.

This memory subtest measures short-term visual recognition rather than visual recall (which is measured by the Recall of Designs subtest). Each item consists of one or more pictures of familiar objects, presented for either 5 seconds (for most of the items) or 10 seconds (for the five most difficult items). The stimulus page is then turned, and the child is presented with an array of drawings including the original object or objects. The child's task is to point to the pictures that were originally shown.

The subtest is nonverbal. The examiner does not name the pictures, and the child responds by pointing. Pictures are presented with little verbal instruction, although there is provision for teaching if the child fails to understand the nature of the task. Successful performance requires the abilities of remembering and recognizing visual images, both of which may entail some detailed discrimination. For example, one item presents three horses, and the child must identify these from an illustration of six horses.

The objects within an item reflect a limited number of categories in order to reduce the possibility of the child's verbally encoding the target objects. Nevertheless, performance on some of the items in the subtest may be aided by verbal mediation and rehearsal strategies. Poor performance on this subtest may indicate poor short-term visual recognition, general visual–perceptual problems, anxiety, or inattention.

Scores on the Recognition of Pictures subtest may reflect the child's

- short-term visual memory,
- recognition memory for pictures,
- memory for picture detail,
- memory for picture orientation, and
- use of verbal mediation strategies (shown by verbal rehearsal of names or use of verbal labels on recall).

In addition, low scores on this subtest may reflect the child's

- tendency to be distracted by competing visual information,
- use of inappropriate strategies (for example, wanting to name all of the pictures aloud),
- lack of understanding of instructions (as shown, for example, by the child's pointing to all of the drawings on the second page), or
- problems with attention and concentration.

Speed of Information Processing (Ages 5:0–17:11)

Speed of Information Processing, which measures mental speed, is a diagnostic subtest for children aged 6:0–17:11. It can also be administered to children aged 5:0–5:11 of average or high ability.

The basic task of Speed of Information Processing is relatively easy, and almost all children can solve the items correctly. The variation in performance lies in the time the child takes to complete the task.

Figure 4.4 is an example of the item content of the subtest. For each of the first six items the child must determine and mark the circle with the greatest number of squares in each row. In these first six items the number of squares within each circle never exceeds four. The child's working time for a page is measured from the moment the child **makes a mark** in the top row to the moment he or she marks a circle in the last row. Thus, the time the child spends looking at the top row is not included in the total time for the page; this technique eliminates inter-examiner variability in starting times.

In Items 7–18 the child's task is very similar, but the items use numbers instead of squares. The child marks the highest number in each row. Items 7–12, usually given to children aged 9:0–13:11, use one-digit numbers. The numbers in Items 13–18, appropriate for older children, have two or three digits.

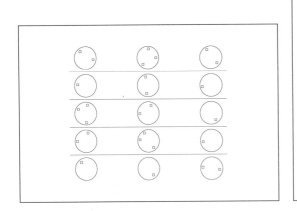

Figure 4.4. Example Items of Speed of Information Processing

Because the subtest is designed to measure speed of **accurate** information processing, item responses that have more than two errors are scored 0. Very few children above age 6 make more than a very small number of errors. If a child does make numerous errors, the subtest is not measuring the ability it was designed to measure, and we should interpret the score with appropriate caution or disregard it entirely.

The inclusion of this subtest may surprise some psychologists because such scales have not been a feature of previously published, individually administered tests of cognitive ability. Nevertheless, in some other batteries, quick problem-solving is recognized as a feature of intelligence and yields higher scores on a number of scales.

The inclusion of speed as a factor in the BAS and consequently in the DAS was spurred by a report by Eysenck (1967) and the work of Furneaux (1960). Furneaux analyzed the patterns of people's responses on intelligence test items to estimate parameters of mental speed, accuracy, and continuance (persistence). As part of the developmental work on the BAS, Elliott and Murray (1977) conducted research that showed that speed of completing very easy block-design items was significantly related to children's age and to performance on non-speeded, more difficult block-design items. Work on the "chronometry of mental performance" (Jensen, 1982) burgeoned in the 1980s. Nearly all of the large number of studies now available show a small but significant, positive relationship between speed of information processing and a range of measures of psychometric g (for example, Jensen & Vernon, 1986; Longstreth, 1984; Widaman & Carlson, 1989). Although such statistically significant relationships are commonly found, it is rare for speed measures to account for more than 10% of the variance in g (that is, to correlate higher than about .3 with g). The research therefore suggests that measures of speed of information processing have a high level of specificity independent of g.

The name of this subtest implies that it measures a general speed of processing information regardless of domain or task content. What is the justification for this general interpretive view as opposed to a narrower interpretation as, for example, of a measure of clerical speed or speed of making quantitative comparisons?

First, measures of speed of processing show small but significant correlations with complex cognitive tests across a wide range of content domains. Virtually all of the research on chronometric aspects of intelligence reports that such correlations occur regardless of the paradigm or the stimulus materials used to measure speed of information processing. Experiments using the Hick paradigm (Jensen, 1982, 1987; Roberts, Beh, & Stankov, 1988), the inspection-time paradigm (Brand & Deary, 1982; Eysenck, 1986; Irwin, 1984), the "odd-man-out" procedure (Frearson & Eysenck, 1986), the stimulus-identification paradigm (Hunt, Lunneborg, & Lewis, 1975; Posner & Mitchell, 1967), the sentence-verification paradigm (Clark & Chase, 1972; Hunt, 1980), and the competing-task paradigm (Stankov, 1983) all showed low but significant relationships with various cognitive measures across a range of domains.

The second source of justification for a general interpretive view is a study specifically relating the BAS Speed of Information Processing subtest to chronometric measures. Using a range of reaction-time measures that had no quantitative content at all, Buckhalt and Jensen (1989) still found considerable construct validity for the Speed of Information Processing subtest. That study and the *BAS Technical Handbook* (Elliott, 1983) both report that Speed of Information Processing correlated with a wide range of cognitive tests, mostly unspeeded and nonquantitative. Buckhalt and Jensen (1989) concluded that the subtest "is a credible indicator of speed of performing very simple cognitive operations. [The] results are highly consistent with the findings and theoretical interpretation by Lindley, Smith, and Thomas (1988) regarding the basis of the correlation between speeded coding tests and psychometric *g*" (p. 105). Thus, this study supported the interpretation of the Speed of Information Processing subtest as a measure of general cognitive speed.

Third, the following correlational results from the DAS standardization sample (presented in more detail in Chapter 9) also support such an interpretation:

- Speed of Information Processing has positive but low (approximately .2) correlations with other cognitive subtests. The correlation with Sequential and Quantitative Reasoning is similar to correlations with other subtests and is not notably higher, as would be expected if Speed of Information Processing were primarily a measure of quantitative speed.

- The correlation of Speed of Information Processing with the speeded score on Pattern Construction is very similar to its correlations with other core subtests and not notably higher, as might at first be expected. However, in contrast with Speed of Information Processing, in which all items are easy, Pattern Construction presents the child with a range of more challenging problems. The speed with which these nontrivial problems are solved provides additional evidence of good spatial ability rather than evidence of speed of more generalized cognitive problem solving.

- Speed of Information Processing correlates higher (about .3) with the three DAS achievement tests than with any cognitive subtests or even with the cognitive composites. If Speed of Information Processing had a major quantitative component, we would expect it to correlate higher with Basic Number Skills than with Spelling and Word Reading. In fact, the correlation with Spelling is the highest.

To summarize, (1) experimental measures of cognitive speed are related to complex cognitive performance across a wide range of domains; (2) Speed of Information Processing is significantly related to experimental measures and also to a wide range of cognitive performances; and (3) Speed of Information Processing does not have a stronger relationship with quantitative measures than with measures in other domains. The evidence therefore supports the interpretation of the subtest as a general measure of cognitive speed.

Recent research suggests that one explanation of the relationship between cognitive speed measures and ability measures lies in the concept of "attentional resource allocation" (Hunt, 1980; Roberts, Beh, & Stankov, 1988; Stankov, 1983).

Rapid encoding, storage, and retrieval of information would enable attentional resources to be switched rapidly and to be devoted to incoming information from various sources. Because information is processed faster, the mind should be able to handle more information and thus to develop a larger store of information over time. This process may account for the finding that Speed of Information Processing correlates more highly with the DAS school achievement tests than with any cognitive subtests or composites.

In addition to requiring rapid information processing, the test items require basic perceptual skills. Different sequential scanning strategies may affect the solution times, although there is no specific evidence for this theory. All items require very basic ordinal-number concepts. Items 7–18 require knowledge of numerals. Items 13–18 additionally require knowledge of place values. Therefore, children who have difficulty with reading or who lack number skills should be given Items 1–6. Poor performance on this subtest may not always be due to poor speed of information processing. Individual differences in cognitive style may result in a large number of careless errors or, at the other extreme, in an obsessive overemphasis on accuracy at the expense of speed.

Scores on the Speed of Information Processing subtest may reflect the child's

- speed in performing simple mental operations,
- ability to work fast under time pressure,
- ability to make quantitative comparisons rapidly,
- sequential strategies for making comparisons,
- short-term, numerical memory,
- basic understanding of ordinal-number concepts, and
- recognition of single- and multi-digit numbers and their place values (for items using numerals).

In addition, low scores on this subtest may reflect the child's

- inefficient balance between speed and accuracy—either overly cautious, sacrificing speed for the sake of accuracy, or overly impulsive, sacrificing accuracy for the sake of speed,
- poor motivation for tasks involving numbers, or
- problems with attention and concentration.

School Achievement Tests

Because we frequently must compare scores on achievement and ability tests, the DAS includes measures of three areas of academic achievement: basic number skills, spelling, and word reading. The common norm sample and the availability of reliable information on intercorrelations enhance the interpretability of these comparisons.

Basic Number Skills (Ages 6:0–17:11)

Basic Number Skills is an achievement test for children aged 6:0-17:11.

This test focuses particularly on the concepts and skills that underlie basic competence in arithmetic calculation. Such skills clearly form the core of any mathematics curriculum and are recognized as important in everyday life. The areas covered in the test may be summarized as follows:

- recognition of printed numbers, including knowledge of place value notation;

- understanding of the four arithmetic operations (addition, subtraction, multiplication, and division); and

- ability to perform numerical calculations using whole numbers, decimals, fractions, and percentages.

The initial sets of items require the child to recognize and read aloud printed numbers. Most of the remaining items require the child to perform basic arithmetic operations with whole numbers, common fractions, and decimal fractions, and to convert fractions and percentages. The final few items are word problems, which are printed on the worksheet and also read aloud by the examiner.

The items are arranged primarily according to their empirical order of difficulty. However, consideration was also given to the sequence in which specific skills tend to be introduced in school curricula. The test includes at least one item requiring each of the basic operations (addition, subtraction, multiplication, and division) for one-digit integers, whole numbers with two or more digits, common fractions, and decimal fractions. Table 4.1 shows the distribution of the Basic Number Skills items by content.

Table 4.1. Content of Basic Number Skills Items

| | Operations | | | |
| | Addition | Subtraction | Multiplication | Division |
			(Number of Items)	
Whole Numbers				
One-digit	1	1	1	1
Two-digit+	4	4	4	4
Fractions	2	2	2	2
Decimals	1	1	5	5

Each item can be analyzed behaviorally in terms of specific skills taught in the classroom. For example, the item

$$\begin{array}{r} 52 \\ -19 \\ \hline \end{array}$$

could be described as, "Subtract a two-digit number from a two-digit number, regrouping once." Such performance descriptions of all items are provided in the **Manual** and are summarized on the Record Form (see Figure 4.5). An inspection of those items that the child passes and fails can give clues to the child's particular strengths and weaknesses in number skills and the particular aspects of this part of the mathematics curriculum that may need attention. Samples of the child's classroom work and further diagnostic testing are required before we draw conclusions about the child's mathematical skills.

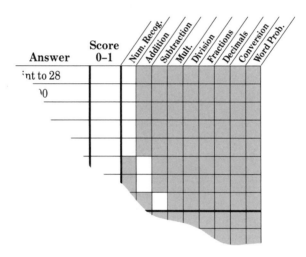

Figure 4.5. Excerpt from the Basic Number Skills Record Form Page

Scores on this test provide a measure of the child's acquired computational skills. While such a measure might well be related to progress in mathematics in general, the test should not be regarded as a measure of more general mathematics achievement. Poor scores probably indicate poor skills in basic numerical calculation. Severe attentional or motivational problems could also have a depressing effect on performance.

We must consider performance in relation to the mathematics curriculum available to the child. For example, percentages may not be taught until a specific grade level. If we detect a certain error pattern in the performance analysis, we should first determine if the child has been taught the material before we formulate hypotheses about specific skill deficits.

Scores on the Basic Number Skills subtest may reflect the child's
- skill in applying a range of arithmetic operations and
- ability to recognize and express the names of numerals.

In addition, low scores on this subtest may reflect the child's
- poor understanding of the meaning of the operands $(+, -, \times, \div)$,
- non-mastery of basic number concepts, or
- poor attention or motivation.

Spelling (Ages 6:0–17:11)

Spelling is an achievement test for children aged 6:0–17:11.

The test focuses on the child's ability to produce correct spellings and includes a range of phonetically regular and irregular words. Young children (aged 6:0–8:11) are also asked to write their names. For each item the examiner says the word in isolation, embeds the word in a sentence to provide suitable contextual clues, and finally repeats the word in isolation. The child writes the word on a worksheet. The test is, therefore, a test of spelling recall.

Items were selected according to several criteria. Early items represent a good proportion of words that occur frequently in children's written work and in primary books. A wide range of phonetic rules are represented. Many of the more difficult items are polysyllabic. A number of items are words that are often misspelled, such as words requiring knowledge of when to use single or double consonants.

As well as providing a measure of spelling achievement, the test includes a diagnostic performance analysis which is presented in the **Manual** and summarized on the Record Form. A number of models of spelling error analysis were reviewed for the development of the DAS diagnostic system. Particularly influential were the models of Gentry (1982, 1984) and Frith (1985). Both models assume that errors in spelling reveal much about the processes and strategies children use to solve spelling problems and that these processes and strategies show a developmental progression.

The DAS takes a whole-word approach to error analysis. Incorrect spellings can be classified into one of five strategy categories:

- Prespelling Strategy
- Rudimentary Strategy
- Semiphonetic Strategy
- Basic Phonetic Strategy
- Plausible Phonetic Strategy

The **Manual** describes and illustrates these strategies.

Scores on the Spelling subtest may reflect the child's

- knowledge and recall of correct spellings,
- retention of facts (the conventional spelling of words), and
- knowledge of spelling rules.

In addition, low scores on this subtest may reflect the child's

- poor visual memory (often shown in difficulties in recall of letters or whole words),
- poor auditory-sequential memory (often shown in inadequate skills in the phonetic spelling of regular words),
- poor skills in phonological segmentation of words into component sounds or syllables,
- poor knowledge of letters, letter sounds, or letter combinations, or
- poor auditory discrimination of sound.

Word Reading (Ages 5:0–17:11)

Word Reading is an achievement test for children aged 6:0–17:11. It can also be administered to children aged 5:0–5:11 of above-average reading skill.

Word Reading is a test of the recognition and oral reading of single words. Such word-reading tests are sometimes criticized for not measuring the child's comprehension of what is read and for not presenting the words in sentences or in context. The principal purpose of word-reading tests, however, is to assess word-decoding ability. The influence of reading comprehension is deliberately excluded. As Mook (1983) and Stanovich (1988) have pointed out, variables in the "real world" are always intercorrelated, and it is the purpose of well-controlled experimental research to break apart these naturally correlated variables in a controlled manner. Although this procedure is often done in an "artificial" way, the results contribute to our understanding of how things work. In the same way, a word-reading test is ecologically invalid in that it does not reflect real-world reading tasks. Yet a word-reading test gives us valuable information on decoding skills *in the absence* of reading comprehension, and these skills are generally recognized as vital to the reading process (for example, Carroll, 1976; Miller, 1976).

The score obtained from a test with words in context is determined partly by decoding skills and partly by more general linguistic abilities. For some children, the lack of contextual clues exposes their difficulties in decoding the printed word. These children may perform better on a test that uses prose passages to assess reading achievement; such tests allow children to utilize their general language and reasoning skills to increase their probability of reading words correctly. The functional literacy level of such children, whose general linguistic abilities are relatively strong, but whose decoding skills are relatively weak, may be higher than that indicated by the DAS Word Reading test. For diagnostic purposes, it is most important to distinguish between the various contributory factors, which are likely related to "real life" performances. The Word Reading test score highlights difficulties the child may have in the systematic decoding of single words.

Word-reading tests are good indicators of a child's familiarity with the words presented, and this familiarity is a fundamental factor in reading comprehension. As stated earlier, there may be discrepancies for some individuals between word-reading and prose-reading performance. Nevertheless, across the population, word-reading tests correlate highly with other measures of reading achievement, such as measures of reading comprehension or of reading rate and accuracy obtained from the presentation of prose passages. Such evidence may be seen, for example, in the correlations of word reading (WR) with a range of other reading measures, detailed in Chapter 9.

The Word Reading test provides a measure of a child's word reading achievement. In view of the previous discussion, however, this test obviously does not pretend to yield scores related to every aspect of the reading curriculum. Rather, the Word Reading test provides a sample of single words ranging from those most commonly found in children's reading materials (Burroughs, 1957; Gates, 1937;

McNally & Murray, 1962; Vernon, 1948) to words encountered far less frequently. The test also samples a wide range of the phonic rules which are taught to children when phonic teaching methods are used. The words in the test are reasonably evenly distributed across a wide range of difficulty. Words related to specialized areas of knowledge as well as words spelled differently in different English-speaking countries are excluded.

Scores on the Word Reading subtest may reflect the child's
- recognition of printed words,
- visual and auditory working memory,
- skills in word analysis without additional contextual cues, and
- vocabulary knowledge.

In addition, low scores on this subtest may reflect the child's
- poor visual memory (often shown in a limited whole-word sight vocabulary and which may also be associated with an over-dependence on basic phonetic strategies),
- poor auditory–sequential memory (often shown in inadequate skills in the phonetic analysis of regular words),
- poor skills in phonetic segmentation of words into component sounds or syllables,
- poor skills in sound blending, and
- poor knowledge of letters, letter sounds, or letter combinations.

Clusters of the Preschool Level of the Cognitive Battery (Ages 3:6–5:11)

Verbal Ability

This cluster measures acquired verbal concepts and knowledge. The subtests contributing to this cluster score (Verbal Comprehension and Naming Vocabulary) are both verbal: One measures language comprehension, requiring listening skills but no verbal response; the other measures language expression. Both of the component subtests involve the visual presentation of pictures or objects.

> Scores on the Verbal Ability cluster may reflect the child's
>
> - knowledge of verbal concepts,
> - language comprehension and expression,
> - level of vocabulary development, and
> - general knowledge base.
>
> In addition, low scores on this cluster may reflect the child's
>
> - problems with processing auditory cues,
> - problems with verbal memory,
> - lack of language stimulation from experiences and educational opportunities, and
> - undiagnosed hearing loss or history of hearing difficulties not conveyed prior to testing.

Nonverbal Ability

This cluster score represents complex, nonverbal mental processing. The contributing subtests (Picture Similarities, Pattern Construction, and Copying) require no verbal responding and use only simple verbal instructions to the child. The subtests represent a range of nonverbal content. One requires the identification of conceptual similarities between pictures; the others require the construction of designs by copying either with a pencil or with colored squares and blocks.

Scores on the Nonverbal Ability cluster may reflect the child's

- perception of spatial orientation (the preservation of relative position, size, and angles in different aspects of the design),
- nonverbal reasoning ability,
- perceptual–motor skills (the ability to see, understand, and respond with a motor action as an organized unit or pattern of functioning),
- understanding of simple verbal instructions and visual cues, and
- ability to identify important elements of a visual stimulus.

In addition, low scores on this cluster may reflect the child's

- overdependence on verbal instructions or auditory cues or
- inability to use verbal mediation strategies.

Clusters of the School-Age Level of the Cognitive Battery (Ages 6:0–17:11)

Verbal Ability

This cluster is a measure of complex, verbal mental processing including acquired verbal concepts, verbal knowledge, and reasoning. Both subtests (Word Definitions and Similarities) contributing to this cluster score require verbal responses. Word Definitions measures word knowledge and language expression. Similarities measures verbal, inductive reasoning which is dependent upon verbal concepts, vocabulary, and the ability to relate words to superordinate categories. The questions in both of the component subtests are verbally presented.

Scores on the Verbal Ability cluster reflect the child's

- knowledge of verbal concepts,
- level of vocabulary development,
- expressive-language ability,
- general knowledge base, and
- retrieval of factual information from long-term memory.

In addition, low scores on this cluster may reflect the child's

- verbal inhibition (unwillingness to make verbal responses when uncertain) and
- undiagnosed hearing loss or history of hearing difficulties not conveyed prior to testing.

Nonverbal Reasoning Ability

This cluster score is a measure of nonverbal, inductive reasoning and requires complex mental processing. The subtests contributing to this cluster score (Matrices and Sequential and Quantitative Reasoning) require the child to identify important elements of stimuli, to formulate and test hypotheses about relationships among those stimuli, and to apply the relationship to new stimuli. The subtests are nonverbal in the sense that they require only minimal verbal instructions to the child and either minimal or no verbal response from the child. These nonverbal problems, however, almost certainly allow for verbal mediation in their solution.

Scores on the Nonverbal Reasoning Ability cluster may reflect the child's

- inductive reasoning, including
  - an ability to identify rules that govern features or variables in abstract, visual problems and
  - an ability to formulate and test hypotheses;
- understanding of simple verbal instructions and visual cues; and
- use of verbal mediation strategies.

In addition, low scores on this cluster may reflect the child's

- overdependence on verbal instructions or auditory cues,
- inflexibility in choosing alternative solutions, or
- impulsiveness (responding without checking the response).

Spatial Ability

This cluster score is a measure of complex visual–spatial processing. Recall of Designs and Pattern Construction, the subtests contributing to this cluster score, are nonverbal and require only simple verbal instructions to the child about the nature of the tasks. The subtests require the abilities to perceive and to remember spatial relationships and shapes. Responses require a modest amount of eye–hand coordination for drawing or for constructing block patterns but do not require verbalization. Pattern Construction may also require inductive reasoning for forming hypotheses about how to synthesize a pattern. These visual–spatial problems do not permit as much verbal mediation in their solutions as do the subtests in the Nonverbal Reasoning cluster.

Scores on the Spatial Ability cluster may reflect

- ability in spatial imagery and visualization,
- perception of spatial orientation (the preservation of relative position, size, and angles in different aspects of the design),
- analytic thinking (the separation of the whole into its component parts), and
- attention to visual detail.

In addition, low scores on this cluster may reflect the child's

- poor understanding of simple verbal instructions or
- poor eye–hand coordination.

Chapter 5

Systematic Interpretation of Test Scores

Overview

Having considered interpretive aspects of subtest and cluster scores in Chapter 4, we now turn to the issue of the specific interpretation of a child's performance. Specific interpretation is a two-stage procedure. The *first* stage concerns the analysis of DAS composite and subtest scores. We must decide whether composite scores or individual subtest scores are more appropriate for describing a child's performance. At this stage of analysis, significantly high or low scores are identified among the various cognitive and achievement measures. The *second* stage concerns the task of interpreting the profile, that is, of drawing inferences from and formulating hypotheses about the nature of the underlying processes that may best explain the score profile.

Stage One: Identifying High and Low Scores in the DAS Profile

It is, perhaps, platitudinous to state that every child is special, that there are no two children with the same appearance, experience, gifts, problems, personality, or pattern of intellectual strengths and weaknesses. And yet in mental testing we have the paradox that the most reliable, and often the most used, scores are global, with the implication, unless carefully avoided, that a child's ability can be encapsulated in a single score. It is fortunately only a paradox and is readily resolvable, if we use information from test scores and other sources sensitively and with a view to emphasizing the diversity of the child's abilities.

This discussion starts with the assumption that *the DAS profile presents us with the challenge of describing individuality*. Of course, we can make general statements about the child's ability in terms of psychometric *g*, as measured by the GCA score. We know that abilities are interrelated. Such statements, however, are always generalizations, and the most satisfactory description of a child's abilities is nearly always at the level of profile analysis. The task, then, is to detect patterns and to interpret those patterns.

The philosophy for identifying cognitive strengths and weaknesses is to start at the most general score, the GCA, and to work down the hierarchy to the most specific score. Nearly always we will find evidence that the child's ability profile cannot be summarized by a single score or even by two or three cluster scores. This prospect of finding evidence of individuality makes the task a challenging and exciting one.

A test battery such as the DAS provides a picture of an individual's cognitive strengths and weaknesses. This type of evaluation is essentially *ipsative*, or within-individual. Consequently, in the evaluation of the test profile, the **relative** level of a subtest score, rather than its absolute level, is of the greatest interest. The procedures of Stage 1, described below, explain how to compare a cluster or a subtest score with the child's own mean level of ability on the core subtests. Strengths and weaknesses so identified are therefore **relative** to the child's own performance.

The approach begins with a description of the GCA score and evaluates whether or not this composite provides an adequate picture of the child's conceptual and reasoning abilities. If its contributing cluster scores are significantly diverse, we would conclude that the GCA alone provides an incomplete description of the child's cognitive abilities as measured by the subtests. Next, we turn our attention to the cluster scores and ask a similar question: Do the component subtest scores within each cluster vary so much that the cluster score does not adequately summarize the child's pattern of abilities? Significant differences between the subtest scores within a cluster constrain the interpretation of that cluster score: The cluster score provides an incomplete or misleading description of the child's ability. Finally we compare the diagnostic-subtest scores with the **mean** of the core-subtest scores in order to determine whether they are significantly higher or lower than the child's average score on the more highly g-loaded subtests. We then compare the achievement-test scores with the GCA score in order to discover any significant discrepancies between achievement and level of ability.

On the lower half of the Summary Page of the Record Form, significant discrepancies at the .05 level for these various comparisons are printed beneath the scores to which they refer. The most commonly used levels of significance, .01 and .05, are provided in the **Manual**. Additional levels of significance are given in Appendix B of this **Handbook**. All values have been adjusted for multiple, simultaneous comparisons. Appendix B also provides information on the frequency of differences for many of these score comparisons. For the purposes of presenting and illustrating the interpretive approach described here in Stage 1, the .05 level of significance is used.

Descriptive Categories for Scores

Sometimes in describing a child's abilities, we may wish to use verbal labels that reflect in a broad way the unusualness of the child's score. Based on a table of descriptive category labels for GCA scores provided in the **Manual**, Table 5.1 shows the same descriptive labels also applied to cluster and subtest scores.

Table 5.1. Descriptive Classification Labels for GCA, Cluster and Subtest Scores

Subtest Scores ($M = 50; SD = 10$)	GCA and Cluster Scores ($M = 100; SD = 15$)	Category	Percentiles
70 and above	130 and above	Very High	98–99
63–69	120–129	High	91–97
57–62	110–119	Above Average	75–90
43–56	90–109	Average	25–74
37–42	80–89	Below Average	9–24
30–36	70–79	Low	3–8
29 and below	69 and below	Very Low	1–2

Comparing Cluster Scores and the GCA

The nature of the GCA composite score has been discussed in Chapter 2. To summarize, the GCA score measures higher mental processing, or conceptual and reasoning abilities, as its name implies, and derives from subtests that have relatively high, homogeneous loadings on psychometric g. It is the most general of the DAS measures. Our task is to start at this point and, as Kaufman (1979) puts it, to use it as a target at which to take careful aim. Carefully uncovering the underlying peaks and dips in the child's abilities will significantly add to the information provided by the GCA alone.

The first step in the systematic analysis of a test-score profile is to examine differences between the cluster scores that contribute to the GCA composite score. In the case of young children aged 2:6–3:5, the structure of abilities is insufficiently differentiated to yield cluster scores, so for them the analysis starts at the level of identifying high and low core-subtest scores. For children aged 3:6 and above, however, we begin the examination with cluster scores. The process of systematic score analysis is illustrated by two case examples. The scores are summarized on the completed Record Form Summary Pages shown in Figures 5.1(A) and 5.1(B); Child A is a preschool child and Child B is a school-aged child.

Child A obtained a GCA score of 85. The chances that the range of scores from 79 to 91 includes the true GCA are about 90 in 100. Child A's overall performance is classified in the "below average" range according to the classification ratings of the DAS. At a lower level of generality the child obtained a Nonverbal Ability score of 93 and a Verbal Ability score of 78. Nonverbal Ability is in the "average" range, but Verbal Ability is categorized as "low." As indicated on the Summary Page of the Record Form, a difference of 9 points between the Verbal Ability cluster score and the GCA standard score and a difference of 8 points between the Nonverbal Ability cluster score and the GCA score are significant at the .05 probability level. We may therefore conclude that, for this child, Nonverbal Ability is a *relative* strength compared with the GCA, although "average" when compared with the general population. The Verbal Ability score is not significantly discrepant from the GCA.

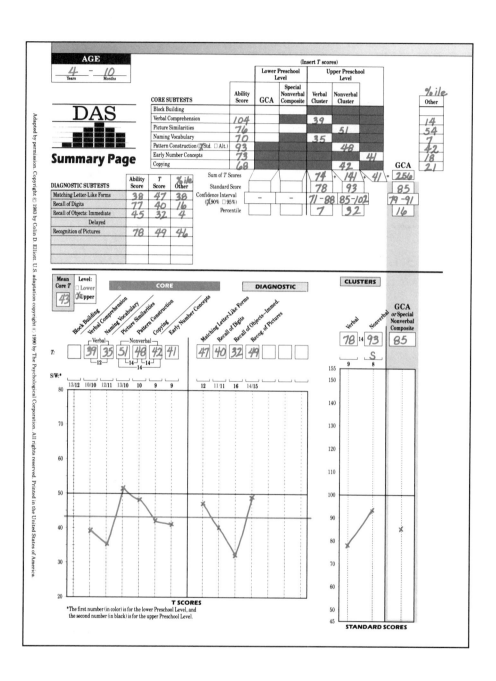

Figure 5.1(A). Record Form Summary Page for Preschool Child

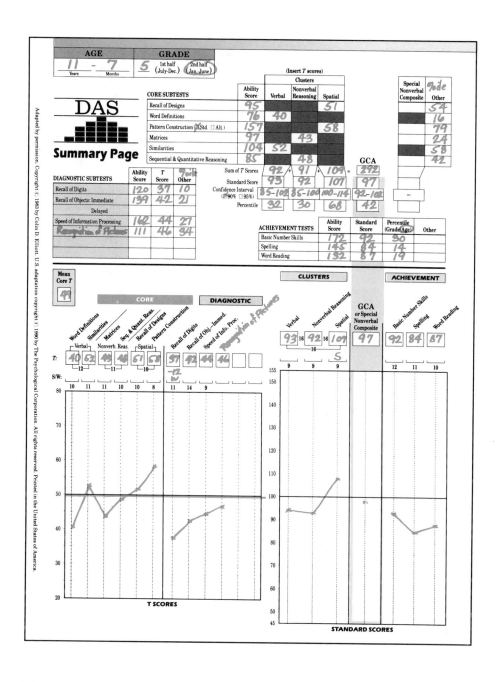

Figure 5.1(B). Record Form Summary Page for School-Aged Child

We can also compare the cluster scores with each other. This step confirms the analysis. The difference of 15 points between the cluster scores represents a real difference ($p < .05$) between the nonverbal and verbal abilities of this child. The child's nonverbal ability is significantly higher than his or her verbal ability. Thus, we may conclude that the below-average GCA, while being an indication of global conceptual ability, does not adequately express all of the reliable information contained in the core-subtest scores.

As well as evaluating the statistical significance of discrepancies between cluster scores, we may also evaluate their relative frequency in the population. In general, a difference of 17 or more standard-score points between the Verbal and Nonverbal cluster scores is found in approximately 1 in 4 cases, and a difference of 25 points occurs in approximately 1 in 10 cases (see Appendix B). Although reliable, the observed discrepancy of 15 points is thus relatively common, occurring in more than 25% of children.

Child B obtained a GCA score of 97. Overall performance is classified in the "average" range. The child's scores on the Verbal Ability and Nonverbal Reasoning Ability clusters are almost the same, 93 and 92, respectively. These scores are still categorized as "average," but they are at the lower end of that score range. The child's score of 107 on the Spatial Ability cluster is also within the "average" range but is higher than the scores of the other two clusters. The Record Form indicates that a difference of 9 points between the GCA standard score and any of the cluster scores is significant at the .05 level. The difference of 10 standard-score points between the GCA and Spatial Ability scores is therefore significant, and we may interpret the child's spatial ability as *relatively* higher than his or her verbal and nonverbal reasoning abilities. While the GCA indicates that the child's general conceptual abilities are "average," this general score does not express the full range of reliable variation in the core-subtest scores. It presents us with a limited, insufficient summary of the child's cognitive abilities.

Once again we can evaluate the frequency, or unusualness, of the differences between the Spatial Ability cluster score and the other two scores. A difference of 16 or more points between school-age cluster scores is found in about 1 in 4 cases. The observed differences of 14 and 15 points between the Spatial Ability cluster and the Verbal Ability and Nonverbal Reasoning Ability clusters, respectively, are relatively common, occurring in more than 25% of cases.

The examples illustrate that statistically significant differences between scores may be common in the population. The fact that a particular, statistically significant discrepancy occurs relatively frequently, however, does not make the discrepancy unimportant in the assessment of an individual. For example, in the area of physical measurement, individual adults may commonly weigh, say, 10 or 20 pounds more than the average weight for their age and height. The discrepancy between actual and predicted weight is significant (that is, reliable and replicable, not attributable to measurement error), but it is also common. Nevertheless, it may well have importance for the individual, depending on that person's attitude, health, and other individual variables.

Having examined differences between the GCA and the cluster scores, we turn our attention next to the analysis of differences between subtests.

Comparing Core-Subtest Scores

The clusters and the core subtests are fairly homogeneous in that they all, in various ways, measure conceptualization. However, while their scores are related, they differ in item content, and this difference causes their scores to vary. In statistical terms, the scores each have components of shared variance along with a proportion of specific, reliable variance. Hence, they can, and often do, show differences. The next step in the score analysis focuses on these differences between subtest scores within the core subtests.

The analysis of core-subtest scores is a two-part procedure:

1. First, differences between subtest scores within each cluster are examined for significance. If any score within a cluster significantly differs from the other(s), we would conclude that the cluster score is insufficient to describe the information contained in the subtest scores. If, and only if, the discrepancy between scores within a cluster is significant, we proceed to the second part of analysis.

2. Second, we evaluate whether one of the scores is significantly higher or lower than the *mean of all the core-subtest scores*. If it is, we may characterize that subtest score as indicating an overall strength or weakness. If the score is neither, our interpretation is restricted to the subtest's being relatively strong or weak *within its cluster*.

For Child A, we conduct the first stage of analysis by evaluating differences between subtest scores within each cluster. The largest difference between any pair of subtest T scores within a cluster is the 9-point difference between Copying and Picture Similarities. The Summary Page of the Record Form indicates that in the Nonverbal Ability cluster, a difference of 14 points between subtest scores is required at the .05 level of significance. The observed difference of 9 points is less than that, so we may conclude that the cluster score of 94 is a reliable summary of the child's performance. Similarly, the difference of 4 points between the two verbal subtests does not reach the level required for the .05 level of significance, 12 points. For Child A, therefore, the cluster scores provide an adequate summary of the child's performance on the core subtests. Because there are no significant discrepancies between scores within clusters, our analysis of differences between the core subtests stops here.

Similarly for Child B, the first part of analysis is to evaluate differences between subtest scores within each cluster. Reference to the Summary Page of the Record Form indicates that subtest T-score differences of 12, 11, and 10 are required for significance at the .05 level within the Verbal Ability, Nonverbal Reasoning Ability, and Spatial Ability clusters, respectively. The small differences between the Nonverbal Reasoning Ability subtest scores and between the Spatial Ability subtest scores are not significant at the .05 level, but the 12-point difference between the scores of the Verbal Ability subtests (Similarities and Word Definitions) meets this significance criterion. We would therefore use the Nonverbal Reasoning

Ability and Spatial Ability cluster scores, rather than their component-subtest scores, to interpret the child's performance in those ability areas. Assuming that there is no firm evidence that one of the verbal subtest scores is invalidly high or low, the Verbal Ability Cluster score is our best estimate of the child's overall ability in this area; however, it would not sufficiently summarize the information contained in its two component subtests.

Having found a significant discrepancy between the Verbal Ability cluster subtest scores, we now proceed to the second step of the analysis. The Word Definitions score in this case apparently indicates a weakness relative to the Similarities score, and also appears to be lower than all other core-subtest T scores. Can we characterize the Word Definitions score as an indication of an overall weakness? We must determine if it is significantly lower than the average of all the other scores by comparing it with the mean T score of all of the core subtests. The Record Form indicates that a difference of 10 points between the Word Definitions score and the core-subtest mean score is significant at the .05 level. The child's core-subtest mean T score is 49, so the discrepancy of 9 falls just short of being significantly different at the .05 level.

Comparing Diagnostic-Subtest Scores with the Mean of the Core Subtests

The diagnostic subtests are intended to be interpreted individually. Although they correlate positively with all cognitive subtests, the correlations tend to be low. Statistically, they have high levels of reliable, specific variance.

For the purpose of identifying within-person strengths and weaknesses, we use the mean T score obtained by a child on the core subtests as the baseline against which to compare performance on the diagnostic subtests. As in the case of the core subtests, we are evaluating high and low scores relative to mean performance on the core. Because of the relative independence of the diagnostic subtests, interpreting these scores with reference to the normative sample, as well as with reference to the within-examinee mean level, will often be helpful. Once again, reference to the two examples in Figure 5.1 will serve to clarify the procedures.

For Child A, three of the diagnostic subtests have T scores that are relatively near the mean of 43 for the core subtests. The child has a low score on Recall of Objects, however, and this score is the lowest score recorded for any subtest. The score of 32 on this subtest places the child at the 4th percentile. The Summary Page of the Record Form indicates that a discrepancy of 16 points between this subtest score and the child's mean T score on the core subtests is required for significance at the .05 level. Therefore, at this first stage in the analysis of composite and subtest scores, none of the diagnostic subtests provides additional evidence of strengths or weaknesses. The major finding for Child A is that the child exhibits a significant difference between verbal and nonverbal abilities.

For Child B, all of the diagnostic subtests have scores below 49, the core-subtest mean T score. The lowest of these is the Recall of Digits score of 37, which places the child at the 10th percentile. The Record Form indicates that a discrepancy of

11 points between the Recall of Digits score and the core-subtest mean T score is required for significance at the .05 level. The observed discrepancy of 12 points meets this criterion, so we may conclude that Recall of Digits score is significantly low, relative to the child's performance on the core subtests.

Comparison of Scores on Individual Cognitive Subtests

We may have an interest in comparing scores on two diagnostic subtests or in comparing the scores of a diagnostic subtest and a core subtest. For example, a frequent comparison may be between Recall of Digits, a diagnostic subtest measuring short-term auditory recall and attention, and Recall of Designs, a core subtest measuring short-term visual recall as well as spatial ability. In such a case, we probably have a hypothesis that the child's memory in one modality is better than that in the other. Using Table B.9 in Appendix B in this **Handbook** (or Table 13 in the **Manual**), we may test such hypotheses at the .05 or .15 levels of significance. Child B's scores on Recall of Designs and Recall of Digits differ by 14 points, a difference that is significant at the .05 level and that suggests a difference between the child's abilities in short-term visual and auditory memory.

Because of the very large number of possible pairings among the cognitive subtests,. the values found in these significant-differences tables are not adjusted for multiple, simultaneous comparisons. It is not recommended that we make these comparisons as a matter of course. We are warned against taking the largest difference between subtest scores and systematically working through differences in order of size, because in doing so, we take a high risk of selecting a chance difference. Rather, we should use these tables only when we have a specific hypothesis about an observed difference between two subtests.

Ability–Achievement Comparisons

When assessing children who may be learning disabled, we often need to determine if a child shows a significant or important discrepancy between ability and achievement. For this comparison, we should generally use the GCA score as the measure of ability because the GCA includes only subtests that are strong and valid measures of general reasoning and conceptual abilities. Because the GCA score is a focused index, it is less likely than the composite scores of other test batteries to be affected by disabilities in specific cognitive dimensions such as memory, perception, and speed of information processing.

For some children the Special Nonverbal Composite may be more appropriate than the GCA for making ability–achievement comparisons. For example, if a child has an expressive-language disability or is an elective mute, the Verbal Ability core subtests may reduce the validity of the GCA in predicting school achievement. In such cases the Special Nonverbal Composite is useful because as a subset of the GCA it still focuses on reasoning and conceptual abilities.

The DAS offers two approaches to the comparison of ability and achievement, and these are illustrated by reference to Child B. First, we may evaluate the statistical significance of a difference in the same way as we evaluate a difference between cluster scores. This method is called the *simple difference approach* and it asks the question: Does the child's level of achievement differ reliably from the child's level of cognitive ability? To evaluate a discrepancy between the GCA score and an achievement-test score, we refer to the Record Form, which provides the differences that are statistically significant at the .05 level of confidence. The **Manual** and Appendix B of this **Handbook** provide a range of differences at various significance levels. Child B's GCA score of 97 is not significantly different at the .05 level from the score of 92 on the Basic Number Skills subtest, because a difference of 12 points is required for significance. The respective scores of 84 and 87 on the Spelling and Word Reading subtests are both significantly discrepant from the GCA, however, because differences of 11 and 10 points, respectively, are required for significance at the .05 level. Using the simple difference approach, we may interpret a significant difference between the GCA score and an achievement-test score as reliable and not likely to have been caused by measurement error.

Contrasting to the simple difference approach is the *regression approach*. This approach asks the question: Does the child's level of achievement differ reliably from what we would expect for a child with this ability level? This question differs from the one asked by the simple difference approach, and as we will see, the answers may sometimes differ. With the regression approach, we compare the child's observed score on an achievement test with the achievement score that would be predicted on the basis of the GCA score (or the score on the Special Nonverbal Composite). Listed in Table B.11 in Appendix B (and in the **Manual**), these predicted scores are based on the correlations of the GCA and Special Nonverbal Composite scores with the achievement measures observed in the standardization sample. One of the advantages of the regression approach is that the percentage of children showing a particular size of discrepancy is expected to be the same at all ability levels. We can evaluate the difference between the observed and predicted achievement scores in two ways: by *statistical significance* and by *frequency*. Thus, just as we can evaluate discrepancies between cluster scores for unusualness, so can we evaluate discrepancies between observed and predicted achievement.

The use of the regression approach is also illustrated with reference to Child B. Table 14 in the **Manual** indicates that, with a GCA score of 97, Child B would be predicted to have the following achievement test scores: Basic Number Skills, 99; Spelling, 99; Word Reading, 98. The difference of 7 points between the obtained and predicted scores on Basic Number Skills is not significant at the .05 level. On the other hand, the discrepancies of 15 and 11 points for Spelling and Word Reading, respectively, are both significant at the .01 level of confidence. Using the regression approach, we may interpret such significant differences as indicating that Child B's achievement in spelling and word reading is significantly lower than would be expected for a child at this GCA level.

We may also evaluate the relative frequency of the discrepancies by referring to Table 3.6 of the **Manual** or to the more detailed table of frequency of discrepancies in Appendix B. The tables show only those differences for which the observed achievement score is *lower* than the predicted score, because these are the differences that concern us in the investigation of learning disability. These tables indicate that observed achievement scores 9 points lower than predicted achievement scores were found in 25% of the standardization sample, a difference of 13 points was found in 15% of cases, and 10% of the sample had a difference of 16 points or more. The difference of 15 points between the observed and predicted scores for Spelling is therefore likely to be found in just over 10% of the population, while the discrepancy of 11 points for Word Reading is found in around 20% of cases.

In the example just given, the simple difference approach and the regression approach yielded very similar results in the evaluation of discrepancies between GCA and achievement scores. The reason for this similarity is the nearness of Child B's GCA score to the population mean of 100, so the predicted achievement scores were very close to the GCA score. The farther the GCA score is from 100, the greater the difference between the results of the simple difference and regression approaches is likely to be.

To illustrate, let us consider the case of a child with a GCA score of 115 and a Basic Number Skills score of 100. The simple difference approach indicates that the difference of 15 points between these scores is reliable ($p < .05$): The difference is not likely due to chance or measurement error. We may therefore conclude that the child's level of reasoning and conceptual ability is higher than his or her level of arithmetic achievement. Using the regression approach, we may ask the somewhat different question of whether or not the child's mathematics achievement is reliably lower than expected for a child of this ability. Table B.11 (Table 14 in the **Manual**) indicates that for a child with a GCA score of 115, the predicted score on Basic Number Skills is 110. Table 3.5 in the **Manual** indicates that the difference of 10 points between the child's observed and predicted scores is not statistically significant at the .05 level: This child's achievement in mathematical calculation is not reliably different than expected for children with a GCA score of 115. Furthermore, such a discrepancy is found in about 20% of individuals. What we have learned, then, is that although the child's conceptual and reasoning ability is higher than his or her skill in arithmetic computation, the level of mathematics achievement is not very different from what we would expect for a child of that ability, and that almost a quarter of children have achievement-test scores that are this far below their predicted values.

Let us consider a child at the other extreme of the GCA range, one with a GCA score of 80 and a Word Reading score of 75. The difference between the child's ability and achievement scores is very small. We may be tempted to conclude erroneously that the child is functioning in Word Reading at about the level that we might expect from the GCA score. However, Table B.11 (Table 14 in the **Manual**) indicates that a child with a GCA score of 80 is predicted to have a Word Reading score of 89. A discrepancy of 14 points between the observed and predicted Word Reading scores is statistically significant ($p < .01$): The child's word-reading achievement is lower than expected. Furthermore, such a discrepancy is found in about 15% of the population. In this case, ability and achievement are both very low, and achievement is reliably lower than expected for a child at that ability level.

Stage Two: Interpreting Cognitive Strengths and Weaknesses

Interpreting a test battery such as the DAS clearly relies on statistical analyses. This reliance is true both for obtaining ability estimates and for comparing subtest scores for an individual child. Such procedures yield so-called hard data. They enable us to make statements about a child's abilities in relation to others of the same age and also to make statements about significant differences between scores in the individual's test profile. Stage One of score interpretation focused on such *statistical* procedures.

We have now reached Stage Two in the analysis, at which we wish to develop and test hypotheses about strengths and weaknesses in the cognitive processes underlying the peaks and dips in scores. Such a task is essentially *rational*, based upon an analysis of the content of each of the subtests and the cluster scores. Finally, we must test our hypotheses against a range of additional information about the child, information usually drawn from school and home. This process is often aimed at drawing causal inferences about the pattern of the cognitive profile, which may have implications for intervention strategies. Such interpretations are essentially *clinical*.

Clearly we are using our statistical analyses to provide a firm base for these somewhat more speculative, but still systematic, interpretations. Without this firm base, our interpretations can be no more than speculation. With it, they become informed judgments. We should always remember that profile interpretations are hypotheses and judgments; they are not facts.

The nature of profile interpretation may therefore be summarized as follows.

Profile interpretation is

- clinical rather than statistical,

- suggestive rather than definitive, and

- concerned with hypothesis generation.

Because of these considerations, the .05 criterion used in Stage One of this interpretation may be too restrictive. For the purposes of profile interpretation, differences that are significant at the .15 level may also be used as a starting point for generating hypotheses. Profile interpretations at Stage Two follow three steps:

1. Subtest scores are identified as high or low relative to the mean T score of the core subtests.

2. Features common to low subtest scores and to high subtest scores are identified for generating hypotheses about underlying processes.

3. Hypotheses about strengths and weaknesses in underlying processes are linked to life information, observations, and other test results.

A brief discussion of the philosophy of profile analysis and interpretation is presented first and is followed by the details of this process.

Philosophy of Profile Analysis

Let us assume that we have identified at least one subtest score obtained by a child as significantly high or low. Our task is to identify the underlying ability or psychological process that has resulted in that discrepant score.

Clearly, the performance of individuals on all psychometric tests is determined by a complex range of psychological processes. The aim of the test constructor is to produce subtests that are homogeneous in content. Even then, when homogeneity has been achieved, scores on the test may be determined and affected by a range of variables which will be different from individual to individual. For example, the DAS Word Definitions subtest is homogeneous in that its items are all similarly presented and always require the same type of response from the child. There may be, however, a number of determinants of performance. Scores may be influenced by individual differences in conceptual ability, verbal fluency of expression, or efficiency of retrieval of verbal information from long-term memory, as well as language exposure and experience.

An individual who scores low on any subtest is unlikely to be weak in all of the component ability areas. Likewise, a high score on a subtest may be associated with strength in some, but not all, component variables.

Each subtest has a varying number of underlying processes in common with other subtests. By comparing a subtest with a distinctly high (or low) score with other subtests with above- (or below-) average scores, we attempt to identify the processes which underlie consistently high (or low) scores. We try to answer the question: Why does the child score higher on some subtests and lower on others?

An example may illustrate the logic of the approach. On the Naming Vocabulary subtest, a preschool child receives a score that is nearly the average of the core-subtest scores, and on Early Number Concepts, a score that is significantly below that average. We might hypothesize that the processes underlying the two subtests are as follows:

	Naming Vocabulary	Early Number Concepts
Verbal Conceptualization	Yes	Yes
Verbal Comprehension	No	Yes
Verbal Expression	Yes	Yes (Item 1)
Verbal Information Retrieval from Long-Term Memory	Yes	No
Knowledge of Quantitative Concepts	No	Yes

In formulating our hypothesis, we assume that a child is not likely to be relatively weak in a process that underlies a high score. This occurrence is not impossible, since weaknesses may be compensated for by strengths, but it is unlikely. It seems more likely that a significantly low score on a subtest is largely determined by processes that are not common to subtests on which the child has higher scores. In our example, two processes are apparently unique to performance on the Early Number Concepts subtest—verbal comprehension and knowledge of quantitative concepts. At this stage, we would generate hypotheses about weaknesses on tasks that require these two processes. By similarly comparing other subtests, we can restrict the possibilities and test our hypotheses about relatively strong and weak processes.

Analysis of Underlying Processes

The processes that are considered to underlie subtests and clusters (as presented in Chapter 4) and that are **common to two or more subtests** are listed in Figures 5.2 and 5.3 for the DAS Preschool and School-Age Levels, respectively, of the Cognitive Battery. Each process area is as conceptually distinct and as specific as possible. These process categories are suggestive rather than definitive; they are provided for the purpose of hypothesis generation.

Some processes, such as the comprehension of verbal instructions, are somewhat required for most subtests, but for clarity, the tables indicate only those subtests for which the process is a major determinant. Thus, the coverage of the tables is not exhaustive, but is intended to be helpful in highlighting some of the major processes that subtests have in common. The following brief descriptions of the process areas are followed by suggestions for their use.

- Processes Related to Conceptual Abilities

  Because the core subtests are measures of conceptual ability in various domains, these domains are listed as higher-order process categories. Thus, both the preschool and the school-age subtests include the categories "nonverbal problem solving" and "verbal conceptualization." These processes are intended to represent the g component of the core subtests. Some, but not all, of the core subtests are concerned with problem solving, which involves the process of "formulation and testing of hypotheses."

- Processes Related to Visual–Spatial Abilities

  Subtests that involve the presentation of pictures or abstract figures to the child clearly require the process of "visual discrimination of figures or designs." In addition, a number of visual–motor tasks require the child to employ processes of "spatial visualization and orientation."

- Processes Concerned with Verbal Abilities

  Subtests that either involve the understanding of verbal instructions or require a verbal response from the child reflect this process area. The Verbal Comprehension subtest for preschool children, for example, requires the child to demonstrate comprehension of commands without giving a verbal response. The Recall of Digits subtest, on the other hand, requires the child to respond verbally but with very little comprehension. Thus, a distinction is made between the processes of "verbal comprehension" and "verbal expression."

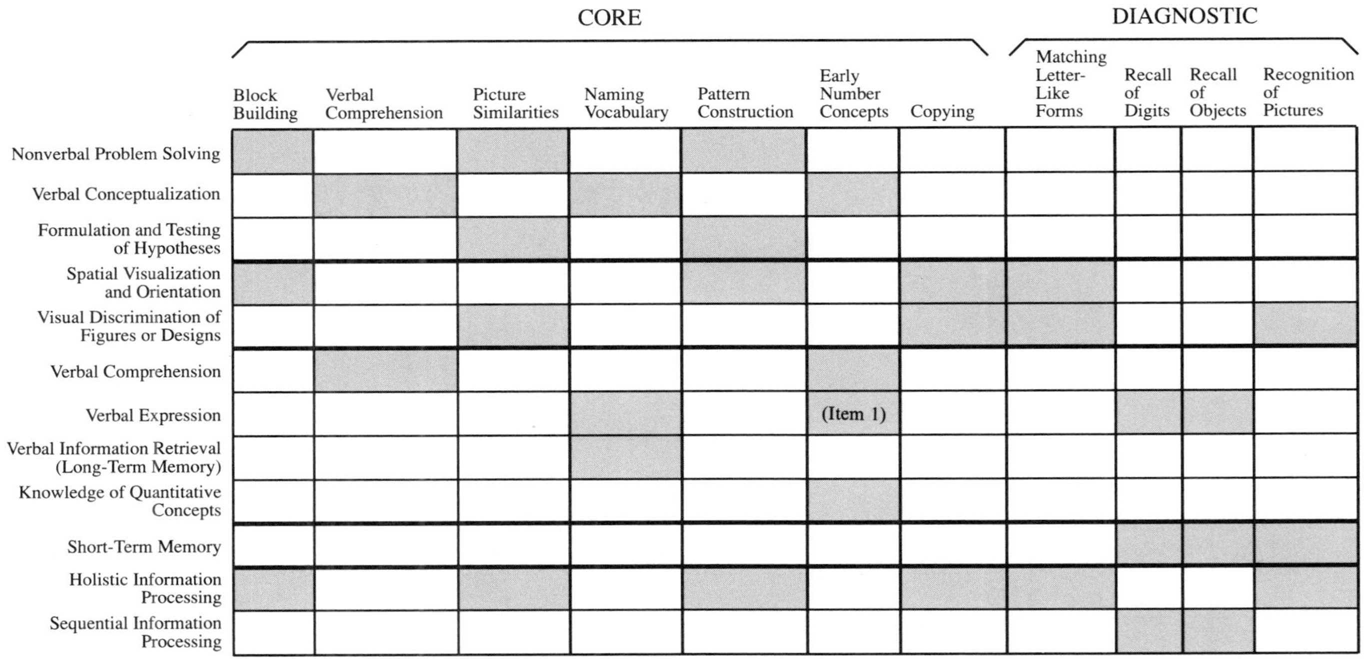

Process	CORE							DIAGNOSTIC			
	Block Building	Verbal Comprehension	Picture Similarities	Naming Vocabulary	Pattern Construction	Early Number Concepts	Copying	Matching Letter-Like Forms	Recall of Digits	Recall of Objects	Recognition of Pictures
Nonverbal Problem Solving	■		■		■						
Verbal Conceptualization		■				■					
Formulation and Testing of Hypotheses			■		■						
Spatial Visualization and Orientation	■						■	■			
Visual Discrimination of Figures or Designs							■	■			■
Verbal Comprehension		■	■								
Verbal Expression				■		(Item 1)				■	
Verbal Information Retrieval (Long-Term Memory)		■		■							
Knowledge of Quantitative Concepts						■					
Short-Term Memory									■	■	■
Holistic Information Processing	■		■		■		■	■			■
Sequential Information Processing									■	■	

Figure 5.2. Shared Underlying Processes for Each Preschool Subtest

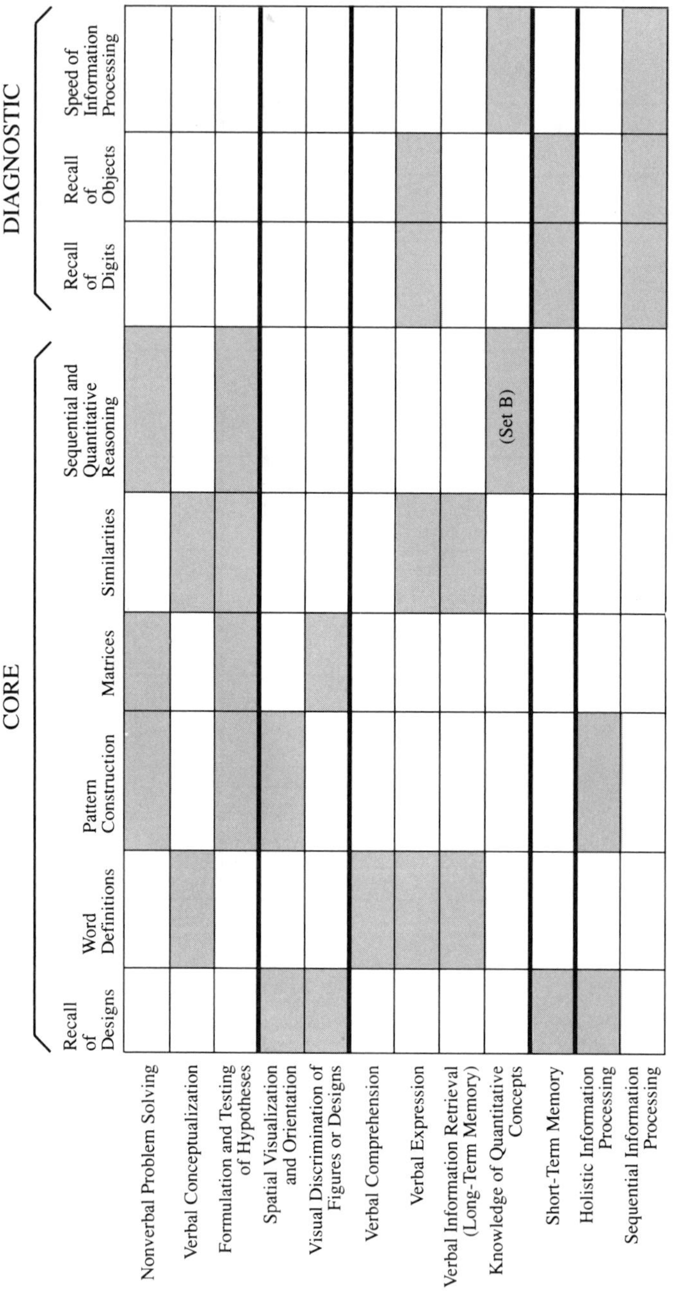

	CORE						DIAGNOSTIC		
	Recall of Designs	Word Definitions	Pattern Construction	Matrices	Similarities	Sequential and Quantitative Reasoning	Recall of Digits	Recall of Objects	Speed of Information Processing
Nonverbal Problem Solving			■	■		■			
Verbal Conceptualization		■			■				
Formulation and Testing of Hypotheses			■		■	■			
Spatial Visualization and Orientation	■		■						
Visual Discrimination of Figures or Designs				■					
Verbal Comprehension		■							
Verbal Expression		■			■			■	
Verbal Information Retrieval (Long-Term Memory)		■			■				
Knowledge of Quantitative Concepts						(Set B)			
Short-Term Memory	■						■	■	
Holistic Information Processing	■		■						
Sequential Information Processing	■							■	■

Figure 5.3. Shared Underlying Processes for Each School-Age Subtest

The two school-age verbal subtests may illustrate how the underlying cognitive processes were identified. Only the Word Definitions subtest includes verbal comprehension as an underlying process. Similarities, the other subtest in the verbal cluster, does not. Failure on Similarities items is seldom attributable to a lack of understanding of the meaning of the stimulus words themselves (that is, to a failure in comprehension). Occasionally, failure on a Similarities item may be attributable to a word unfamiliar to the child (for example, "Hexagon" in the first half of the subtest; "Drought," "Vaccine," "Generation," or "Compassion" in the second half). Failure on this subtest, however, is far more likely to be due to the child's inability to state the similarity among the three stimulus words (that is, to a failure to conceptualize). Thus, because comprehension plays a relatively minor role in Similarities, it is not included as a major underlying process component (see Figure 5.3). In cases where failure has clearly been due to the child's lack of word knowledge, we would no doubt have noted this observation and would relate it to other data on the child.

The verbal process area includes two other processes, "verbal information retrieval" and "knowledge of quantitative concepts." The first is related to long-term memory of word meanings. The second involves concepts of quantity and number, which may be incidentally acquired through experience or which may be more formally taught in school.

- Short-Term Memory

"Short-term memory" is not subdivided into auditory and visual aspects because these are part of the specific interpretations of the various memory subtests.

- Holistic Versus Sequential Information Processing

The process areas of "holistic information processing" and "sequential information processing" are often major features of cognitive ability tests. There appears to be good empirical support for separating sequential and holistic information processing systems (Das, Kirby, & Jarman, 1979). There is a tendency to oversimplify the distinction, that is, to characterize verbal tests as sequential because of the sequential nature of spoken language and to characterize nonverbal tests as holistic because visual information is usually perceived as a whole.

A subtest has been assigned either to the holistic or to the sequential category if it appears to utilize primarily one of these modes of information processing. Since a number of subtests appear to have major components of both, they have not been assigned to either. For example, the early items of the Matrices subtest are largely solvable by holistic processing, whereas many of the later items require a sequential approach to problem solving. Likewise, Set A of the Sequential and Quantitative Reasoning subtest presents tasks that are largely sequential in nature, whereas the items of Set B may have elements of both sequential and holistic processing.

In addition to these general aspects of the processes and subtests in Figures 5.2 and 5.3, some specific comments can be made.

- Knowledge of quantitative concepts is represented in only one subtest in the Preschool Level of the Cognitive Battery. If only that battery were given to a child, that process would be specific to that subtest. However, if the child were of suitable age and ability to also be given the Basic Number Skills achievement test, we would have additional evidence of the child's knowledge of quantitative concepts.

- Similarly, the process of verbal comprehension is measured by only one subtest in the School-Age Level of the Cognitive Battery. For younger children of suitable ability, two subtests from the Preschool Level of the battery, Verbal Comprehension and Early Number Concepts, include the process of verbal comprehension as a major component.

Guidelines for Profile Interpretation

In Stage One of the analysis, one or more of the composite and subtest scores may have been identified as significantly high or low. The .05 significance criterion at the first stage is intended to provide a reasonably firm basis for confidence in our evaluations of strengths and weaknesses in abilities. Such significantly high or low scores provide the starting point for Stage Two of the profile interpretation.

The .05 level of significance is a conservative criterion that is designed to minimize the likelihood of our interpreting a difference that has arisen by chance. In clinical practice, however, we must also be concerned about the danger of failing to notice and interpret real differences. For this reason, we may decide to employ instead the .15 significance level as a starting point for hypothesis generation, particularly if no significantly high or low scores at the .05 level have been identified. Even for some relatively high or low points in the profile that do not reach the .15 level, we may still wish to examine the profile for consistent patterns. Clearly we will have less confidence in the reliability of the conclusions or hypotheses so generated.

The steps in profile analysis are as follows:

1. **Identifying from Stage One those cluster or subtest scores that are significantly high or low at the .05 level:** If no high or low scores are significant at the .05 level (or for generating further hypotheses), we may select high or low scores significant at the .15 level. The less conservative is the probability level of the starting point, the greater is the caution necessary in interpretation.

2. **Identifying from Figures 5.2 or 5.3 those subtests that share underlying processes with the significantly high or low composite or subtest.**

3. **For a significantly high score, checking each underlying process:** If the other subtests with the same underlying process have scores higher than the mean T score of the core subtests, the process may be a cognitive strength.

4. **For a significantly low score, checking each underlying process:** If the other subtests with the same underlying process have scores lower than the mean T score of the core subtests, the process may be a cognitive weakness.

5. **Checking the hypotheses:** Hypotheses about cognitive strengths and weaknesses generated from Steps 3 and 4 may be supported or refuted by life information, observations, or other test results.

The example cases from Figures 5.1(A) and 5.1(B) illustrate the use of these guidelines and the use of Figures 5.2 and 5.3.

Examples of Profile Interpretation

Child A

As described above, the first step of profile interpretation requires the identification of cluster or subtest scores that are significantly high or low. Because Child A's high Nonverbal Ability cluster score is significantly different from the low Verbal Ability cluster score, these scores are the starting points for interpretation. We then proceed to the next steps in the interpretation:

1. We must check those subtests that share underlying processes with Verbal Comprehension and Naming Vocabulary (the subtests forming the Verbal Ability cluster). If all have scores lower than the core-subtest mean T score, the process may be a cognitive weakness.

2. We next check those subtests that share underlying processes with Picture Similarities, Pattern Construction, and Copying (the subtests forming the Nonverbal Ability cluster). If all have scores higher than the core-subtest mean T score, the process may be a cognitive strength.

We now have the following results of these analyses:

- Verbal conceptualization may be a relative weakness because all three subtests that include this process as a component (Verbal Comprehension, Naming Vocabulary, and Early Number Concepts) have scores below the core-subtest mean T score and below the average for children of this age.

- We may also hypothesize that verbal expression, verbal comprehension, and verbal information retrieval are relative weaknesses, because the subtests with the same underlying processes (Naming Vocabulary, Verbal Comprehension, Recall of Digits, and Recall of Objects) all have scores lower than the mean T score of the core subtests.

- Scores on the two subtests for which nonverbal problem solving and hypothesis formulation are underlying processes (Picture Similarities and Pattern Construction) are both above the core-subtest mean T score. These processes may be relative strengths.

Drawing together the evidence from the initial analysis of the GCA and cluster scores and the results of the subtest-profile analysis, we can summarize the following findings about Child A:

- The child has a below-average GCA.

- The child's nonverbal ability is average and is a relative strength.

- The analysis of shared processes underlying the subtest profile clearly links with the findings of significant differences between the verbal and nonverbal clusters. Nonverbal problem solving and the formulation and testing of hypotheses may represent relative cognitive strengths. Both of these processes underlie the Nonverbal Ability cluster. Possible cognitive weaknesses center on the verbal abilities of conceptualization, expression, comprehension, and information retrieval. We would need to test and verify such hypotheses by referring to other tests and life data.

Because we have only an example and not a real case, we have no life data or contextual evidence to add to this analysis. Such information, of course, is essential to profile analysis (see Chapter 4). If Child A were a real case, we might consider further testing in the areas of expressive- and receptive-language skills. We would have already interviewed the parent (and the teacher if the child were attending preschool). Samples of the child's cutting and coloring activities would augment information about nonverbal and fine motor skills observed during the nonverbal subtests. Such external sources of data would provide additional evidence for the acceptance or rejection of the hypotheses generated from the test scores and testing observations.

Child B

Once again, the first step of profile interpretation is the identification of significantly high or low scores. We identified the Spatial Ability cluster score of 107 as a significantly high score relative to the child's GCA score. The two component subtests, Recall of Designs and Pattern Construction, will therefore form a starting point for possible interpretation. The score on the Recall of Digits subtest is significantly low, and the score on the Word Definitions subtest, while falling just short of significance at the .05 level, is significantly low at the .15 level. These two subtests will therefore provide additional starting points for the interpretation of low scores.

With these starting points we proceed to the next steps in the profile interpretation:

1. We must check those subtests that share underlying processes with Recall of Designs and Pattern Construction (the subtests forming the Spatial Ability cluster). If all have scores higher than the mean T score of the core subtests, the process may be a cognitive strength.

2. We next check those subtests that share underlying processes with the Recall of Digits and Word Definitions subtests. If all have scores lower than the core-subtest mean T score, the process may be a cognitive weakness.

We now have the following results of these analyses:

- Spatial visualization and orientation appear to be relative processing strengths.

- The child's high Spatial Ability cluster score may also reflect an underlying strength in holistic information processing.

- The child's low score on the Word Definitions subtest ($p < .15$) may be associated with poor verbal fluency or with verbal inhibition. This specific interpretation would be supported by observations of the child's giving only one- or two-word responses or the child's unwillingness to say anything, particularly when uncertain about the answer. The reason for the low score is not likely to be poor vocabulary knowledge or a lack of verbal concepts, because the child's score on the Similarities subtest, which also has these underlying requirements, is high. Further evidence of a problem associated with certain aspects of verbal expression is available in the scores on the Recall of Digits and Recall of Objects subtests, which are also below the core-subtest mean T score.

- Sequential information processing may be a relative cognitive weakness. This interpretation is supported by low scores on the Recall of Digits, Recall of Objects, and Speed of Information Processing subtests. We may formulate an alternative (and related) hypothesis that the child has a relative weakness in short-term verbal memory.

Drawing together the evidence from the initial analysis of the GCA and cluster scores and the results of the subtest-profile analysis, we can summarize the following findings about Child B:

- The child has an average GCA.

- The child's spatial ability is a strength relative to verbal and nonverbal reasoning abilities.

- The child's Verbal Ability cluster score is qualified by a significant difference between the Similarities and Word Definitions subtest scores.

- The Recall of Digits subtest score is significantly lower than the mean T score of the core subtests and suggests a possible weakness in short-term auditory memory.

- The child's spelling and word-reading achievement is significantly lower than would be expected for a child at this GCA level. (See the discussion of the regression approach to ability–achievement discrepancies presented in the first half of this chapter.)

- The analysis of shared processes underlying the subtest profile clearly links with the findings of significant differences between clusters and subtests. Analysis of the subtest profile further supports the hypothesis that spatial visualization and orientation are relative cognitive strengths. The significant difference between the child's low score on the Word Definitions subtest and the score on the other verbal subtest, Similarities, may be associated with poor verbal fluency or with verbal inhibition. Finally, the profile pattern suggests a relative strength in holistic information processing and a weakness in sequential processing.

As in the case of Child A, because this is an example and not a real case, we have no additional contextual or life evidence against which to evaluate our test findings. If Child B were a real case, we would consider further expressive-language testing. The low score on the Word Definitions subtest may reflect a problem in the child's formulating verbal responses. Comparisons of Child B's abilities in oral and written expression would be informative. Classroom observation could focus on the child's expressive-language behaviors in that setting. In class, does the child respond to the teacher's questions? Does the child take part in group discussions? An interview with the parent(s) and teacher(s) could address questions about short-term auditory memory. Do oral requests or directions have to be repeated? Can the child remember things better if they are written? Do the child's reading and spelling errors show evidence of difficulties with the use of phonetic strategies (sequentially based)? And does the child show evidence of knowing some words well (good visual–holistic memory) but of having few strategies for reading or spelling unfamiliar words? Samples of the child's work and further testing in the areas of spelling and reading would help us to plan appropriate intervention strategies. Again, such contextual evidence would be necessary for acceptance or rejection of the hypotheses generated from the test scores.

Summary

This chapter has offered a systematic approach to the sifting of evidence about a child's cognitive abilities that is provided by the DAS. Starting with the GCA and cluster scores, we identify relatively high and low scores among clusters and subtests and also ability-achievement discrepancies. The final stage in the analysis is the identification of score patterns which enable us to hypothesize about strengths and weaknesses in shared processes that underlie the cluster and subtest scores. We should always relate these hypotheses about strengths and weaknesses in underlying processes to life information, observations, and other test results obtained from school and home.

Chapter 6

Tryout and Standardization

Chapter 3 describes the stages in the development of the DAS content. Those subtests that were completely new to the battery required pilot testing and tryout. The entire battery was then administered to a large, carefully selected, nationwide sample to establish norms and to examine reliability and validity. This chapter describes the methods used for tryout and standardization.

Tryout Phase

Tryouts of the DAS subtests were designed to provide information about administration procedures (such as clarity of instructions and time requirements) and the statistical properties of individual items so that the standardization edition could be administered smoothly with the items in their approximate order of difficulty. Although items cannot be analyzed as accurately in the tryout phase as in the standardization phase, seriously problematic items can be identified and either modified or discarded. Also, new administration procedures can be evaluated objectively in terms of their effects on reliability and on children's performance. Just as important are the children's reactions to the test materials. Examiners provided their subjective impressions of the children's comprehension of the directions, degree of interest in the task, confusions or misunderstandings, and so on. During tryout, examiners were encouraged to probe for the examinees' evaluations of the subtests.

Seven of the DAS subtests did not require tryout in the United States because they changed little from the BAS versions and the BAS standardization data was judged sufficient to guide the design of the DAS standardization edition. The subtests not tried out included Basic Number Skills, Copying, Early Number Concepts, Matching Letter-Like Forms, Recall of Digits, Speed of Information Processing, and Word Reading. The other 13 subtests underwent various stages of tryout between spring 1985 and summer 1986. The specific purposes of the tryouts were

- to test new items that had been developed to replace existing items, to extend the age range of a subtest, or to increase reliability at certain ability levels. The subtests involved were Matrices, Naming Vocabulary, Pattern Construction, Recall of Designs, Similarities, Verbal Comprehension, and Word Definitions.
- to evaluate changes in administration procedures. The Matrices, Recall of Objects, and Recognition of Pictures subtests were tried out for this purpose.

- to develop entirely new subtests. Block Building, Picture Similarities, and Sequential and Quantitative Reasoning were piloted and then tried out on U.S. samples. The other new subtest, Spelling, had been extensively researched in England and those findings were used to design the U.S. standardization edition.

Chapter 4 provides more detailed information on the development of each subtest during the tryout phase.

Tryouts were conducted in Ohio and Texas with the cooperation of several public and parochial school districts and preschools. Particular ages and grade levels appropriate to the material were selected for tryout. The major objective of sample selection was to approximate the distribution of socioeconomic status (SES) in the U.S. population. Published references provided SES indexes for school districts, and preschool administrators were asked to describe the SES levels of their student populations. Within participating institutions, parents of all children in selected classrooms and of all preschool children in the targeted age range received consent forms. Only those children whose parents gave consent were tested.

In addition to the tryout testing, in early 1986 a bias review panel evaluated the final version of the tryout materials. (See Chapter 10 for a discussion of the panel's work.)

Standardization Phase

Using the panel's findings and results of the tryout testing, the project team finalized the content of the DAS standardization edition and distributed the edition in early fall 1986. The team's three primary objectives for the standardization program were

- to construct a norm sample that accurately represented the target population of U.S. children aged 2:6 through 17:11 according to major demographic variables;

- to analyze item difficulty and discrimination, subtest reliability and unidimensionality, and the factor structure of the entire battery; and

- to evaluate each item for possible bias according to race/ethnicity, sex, and (for some subtests) geographic region by using large samples from each subgroup for each item. Approximately 600 additional cases of Black and Hispanic children were therefore collected to supplement the norm sample.

In addition, the standardization process yielded a variety of criterion data to use in validity studies and to guide the structuring of the final battery. Careful selection of examiners, the composition of the sample, and the data collection procedures ensured that the standardization would meet its major objectives and would yield additional, necessary analytical data.

Procedures

Examiners

The DAS examiners were carefully selected. All had prior formal training in the individual assessment of cognitive ability and were independently qualified to administer such tests or were under appropriate supervision. The majority were graduate students in school psychology programs; some clinical psychology students and practicing clinical or school psychologists also served as examiners or field supervisors.

Project staff members trained most of the examiners at workshops conducted at various sites during the fall of 1986. Others, who joined the project later, were trained by an examiner or field supervisor who had gained experience in administering the DAS and who had demonstrated proper administration procedures. Regardless of the method of training, all examiners submitted two satisfactory practice cases before being authorized to begin actual testing. Throughout the project the central project staff monitored the quality of administration by reviewing all cases as they were received and by dealing promptly with any problems that arose.

Approximately 225 examiners and 80 field supervisors contributed standardization data. The geographically diverse testing sites (shown in Figure 6.1) were in or near approximately 70 metropolitan areas. By traveling to rural areas to collect cases, examiners further increased the geographic diversity of the sample. Appendix A lists the names and affiliations of all examiners and field supervisors and the names of all participating school districts, preschools, and other institutions.

Figure 6.1. Standardization Testing Sites

Construction of the Sample

Demographic Characteristics

The representativeness of the norm sample is crucial to an instrument, such as the DAS, that measures cognitive ability. The ultimate goal of sampling is to assemble a reference, or norm, group that has the same distribution of abilities as the population to which we want to generalize. A second purpose for controlling the demographic makeup of a sample is to include examinees from different backgrounds so that the suitability of test content for various groups can be evaluated through item analysis.

One way to construct a sample that represents the distribution of abilities of the population is to match the demographic characteristics of the sample to those of the population. The demographic variables must be ones that are related to the abilities being measured and that are objectively measurable. For the DAS, the sample population was defined as all noninstitutionalized, English-proficient children aged 2:6–17:11 living in the United States during the period of data collection (spring 1987 through spring 1989). Furthermore, the target population did not include severely handicapped children for whom the DAS and similar instruments would be inappropriate. This restriction, however, did not exclude children with mild perceptual, speech, or motor impairments, if the examiner judged that the impairment would not prevent valid assessment.

In addition to these general restrictions, the sampling plan for the DAS was constructed around the following stratification variables.

- **Age.** The norm sample of 3,475 children included 175 cases for each six-month age group from ages 2:6 through 4:11, and 200 cases per year from ages 5:0 through 17:11. Each year or half-year group had an approximately even distribution of cases by month of age.

- **Sex.** Each age group was evenly divided between males and females.

- **Race/Ethnicity.** Four categories were used: Black, Hispanic (including all children of Spanish origin, regardless of race), White, and Other (including Asian, Pacific Islander, American Indian, Eskimo, and Aleut).

- **Parent Education.** The average educational level of the parent(s) or guardian(s) living with the child was chosen to represent SES because it is a variable that has a plausible causal link to the child's developed cognitive abilities, it is information that parents are likely to be willing to provide, and it is relatively objective and easy to code. To maximize its validity, the index was based on both parents rather than on only one. For a child living in a single-parent household, the educational level of that parent was used.

- **Geographic Region.** The sample was stratified according to the four regions defined by the U.S. Bureau of the Census: Northeast, North Central, South, and West.

- **Educational Preschool Enrollment.** Because preschool-aged children who attend an educational program are exposed to learning and social situations that may affect their performance on a test such as the DAS, this variable was used as a stratification criterion at preschool ages.

Three additional variables were monitored but not used as selection criteria. First, the size of the community, which was based on the child's home address, was measured according to the Metropolitan Statistical Area (MSA) classifications. Second, the sample included 16- and 17-year-old school dropouts as well as currently enrolled students. Third, after the DAS testing, information about special-education status for most of the school-aged children was obtained directly from the schools. The random procedure (described below) used to select the school-aged children resulted in an appropriate representation in the sample of most of the special education categories except the mentally-retarded category. To obtain appropriate representation of children in this category, educable mentally retarded children were sought and included in the sample.

As the sample was collected, its correspondence to the population target figures was tracked at the level of joint frequencies of the demographic variables. That is, the sample was matched to the population not only at the level of one demographic variable at a time, but also at the level of combined variables. Thus, for example, the sample's distribution of SES among White female children living in the Northeast resembled the corresponding distribution in the population.

For each sex and year of age (or half-year at the preschool level), the target matrix represented the joint distribution of SES, race/ethnicity, and region. This matrix could not have been designed accurately without access to raw Census data: Published tables do not provide the needed information. Consequently, computer tapes of Census data were obtained from the Bureau of the Census to enable targets to be estimated accurately. Initially the targets were based on data from the *Current Population Survey, March 1986* (U.S. Bureau of the Census, 1986). When March 1988 data became available, the targets were updated, and the final sample was matched to those more current targets. Thus, the DAS sample was matched to Census data collected approximately midway through the period of DAS standardization.

The Census data tape offered several important advantages. First, it permitted calculation of the joint distributions of demographic variables, as described above. Second, it provided up-to-date information for variables that were possibly changing relatively rapidly. An example of such a variable is the proportion of children who are of Spanish origin. The 1980 Census showed that 8.7% of children were of Spanish origin, but that figure increased to 10.3% in March 1986, and to 10.9% in March 1988.

Third, the data tape made possible the creation of demographic variables that were well suited to the needs of the project. For example, the single dimension of race/ethnicity was created from the two independent Census dimensions of race (Black, White, and Other) and Spanish origin. All children in the data-tape sample who were of Spanish origin were assigned to the Hispanic category on the

113

race/ethnicity dimension, and all other children were assigned to an appropriate race category (Black, White, and Other). This consolidation of race and Spanish origin into a single dimension made it feasible to calculate the joint distributions of race/ethnicity with other variables. Another example is the variable for SES which was created by averaging the educational levels of the parents of each child in the Census data-tape sample. With the raw data, then, the SES levels of the *children* in the DAS sample could be matched to the SES distribution of children in the population. Without access to raw data, it would have been necessary to use the SES distribution of adults as the target because that is the information available from published tables.

Although information on race (Black, White, or Other) was available for all children in the Census sample, for a small percentage of children the separate question about Spanish origin had not been answered. These children were not representative of the overall Census sample on the demographic variables of SES, race, and region, and so could not be omitted without biasing the target figures. The missing data were filled in by applying the relationship between Spanish origin and the other demographic variables to the cases with the missing information.

Sampling Procedures

Because demographic variables are indirect indicators of the representativeness of the sample rather than ends in themselves, the sampling procedure must incorporate random selection whenever possible so that the sample will approximate a random subset of the target population. For the DAS, random selection was implemented through a multistage process. First, institutions (public and private schools, preschools, day-care centers, churches, social service agencies, YMCAs, etc.) were recruited for participation. From among those responding positively, the project staff selected institutions whose populations appeared likely to exhibit the desired range of demographic characteristics. Some potential sources of cases were excluded at this stage if they served children who were unlikely to meet sampling requirements (for example, the physically disabled) or if they preselected children for high or low ability (for example, a school for the gifted).

The second step was to send letters with consent forms and demographic information sheets to the parents of all children in each institution (or, in the case of schools, of all children in representative classrooms). The demographic form requested the following information: the child's birth date, sex, and race/ethnicity; whether or not the child attended an educational program (for preschool-aged children); and the number of years of education of each parent living with the child. The form also requested information on other preschool-aged children living in the home who might be available to participate. (No more than one child from any family actually participated.)

The central project staff randomly selected children from among those whose parents had given consent and whose demographic characteristics fit the requirements of the sampling plan. The staff then notified the institution, the examiner, and the parents.

The preschool sample required some special techniques so that the sample would include representative numbers of children who were not in educational programs. One source was younger siblings of school-aged children for whom consent forms had been returned but who had not been selected for testing. Other children were recruited through churches and welfare agencies. Still others were found through directories of at-home day-care centers.

Bias Oversample

Additional cases of Black and Hispanic children beyond those in the norm sample were collected for statistical analyses of item bias (as described in Chapter 10). Selected age groups were oversampled to ensure that every item would be administered to at least a minimum number of Black and Hispanic children. Once the numbers of additional cases were determined, they were built into the sampling plan for those ages, and those cases were selected and assigned for testing in exactly the same way as the cases intended to be used in the norm sample.

Representation of Special Education Students

The DAS sampling procedure drew children from public- and private-school populations without respect to special education status. As a result, children receiving various special educational services were represented in the norm sample in roughly the proportions that occur in the U.S. school population (see Table 6.9). The sample excluded only children institutionalized for severe intellectual deficiency or emotional problems.

There are several reasons for including special-education children in a norm sample. Perhaps the most important reason is to maintain continuity with previous instruments, such as the WISC–R (Wechsler, 1974) and the Stanford–Binet, Fourth Edition (Thorndike, Hagen, & Sattler, 1986), that utilized inclusion criteria similar to those of the DAS. A second and related reason is that special-education categories and criteria are affected by legislation, district and state policies, budgets, and developments in psychological knowledge—and are thus changeable. Today's regular-education child may be tomorrow's special-education student, and vice versa. These temporal variations influence the makeup of samples that include special-education status as a selection variable; samples formed by random selection without regard to special-education status are not so affected.

The third reason for including special-education children in a norm sample has to do with the intended function of the sample. The DAS norm group is not intended to be a "normal" group, that is, one consisting only of children with no deficits or gifts, that is to be contrasted with exceptional children. Rather, the DAS norm group is to be considered a *comprehensive* group within which all school-attending children are arrayed. In this way, we can know the status of a child within this broadly defined population. Distinctions between normal and exceptional children are made within this range.

A test's appropriateness and accuracy for any individual child, including an exceptional child, depend much more on the test's content and level of difficulty than on the makeup of its norm sample. To differentiate accurately between children or groups, a test must contain a sufficient number of items whose difficulties are in the vicinity of the abilities of those children or groups. The mere inclusion of exceptional children in a norm sample does not make the instrument appropriate for use with such children, nor does their exclusion make the test inappropriate. During item and subtest development, the DAS team sought to create tasks that would be suitable in content, format, and difficulty for many exceptional children. The success of these efforts, like those of any other test development project, can be determined only through research that focuses on how the test works with such children.

Description of the Sample

Figure 6.2 and Tables 6.1–6.9 portray the characteristics of the DAS norm sample. The figure summarizes the distributions of SES, race/ethnicity, and region across age. The tables specify the distributions of these characteristics by age and sex, the joint (or crossed) distributions of race/ethnicity with SES and with region, and the distributions of community size, educational enrollment, and special-education status. The data show a very close fit to population distributions for the major demographic variables.

Data are based on the complete norm sample for all variables except special-education status. That information was requested from participating schools after testing; it was obtained from the majority of schools and is assumed to be representative of the overall sample of schools. The percentages in Table 6.9 are therefore calculated on the cases for which data were available. Data on mentally retarded children were tabulated somewhat differently because, as previously mentioned, virtually no such children were accessed through the general sampling procedures. Children classified as educable mentally retarded were located and added to the sample near the end of the standardization period; therefore, the percentage shown in Table 6.9 is based on the entire standardization sample.

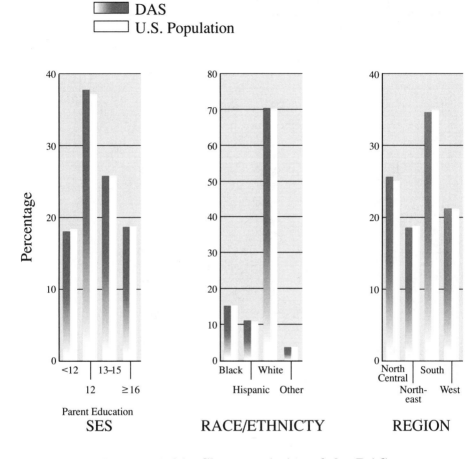

Figure 6.2. Demographic Characteristics of the DAS
Norm Sample Compared with Those of the
U.S. Population

Table 6.1. Norm Sample: Number of Cases by Age and Sex

Age	Male	Female	Total
2:6–2:11	87	88	175
3:0–3:5	88	87	175
3:6–3:11	87	88	175
4:0–4:5	87	88	175
4:6–4:11	88	87	175
5	100	100	200
6	100	100	200
7	100	100	200
8	100	100	200
9	100	100	200
10	100	100	200
11	100	100	200
12	100	100	200
13	100	100	200
14	100	100	200
15	100	100	200
16	100	100	200
17	100	100	200
Total	**1737**	**1738**	**3475**

Table 6.2. Norm Sample: Percentages by Age, Sex, and Race

Age	N	Male					Female					Total				
		Black	His-panic	White	Other[a]	Total	Black	His-panic	White	Other[a]	Total	Black	His-panic	White	Other[a]	Total
2:6-2:11	175	8.6	5.7	34.8	0.6	49.7	6.9	3.4	38.3	1.7	50.3	15.4	9.2	73.1	2.3	100.0
3:0-3:5	175	9.1	6.3	34.3	0.6	50.3	8.0	6.9	33.7	1.1	49.7	17.1	13.2	68.0	1.7	100.0
3:6-3:11	175	7.4	6.3	34.9	1.1	49.7	8.0	5.7	34.9	1.7	50.3	15.4	12.0	69.7	2.9	100.0
4:0-4:5	175	8.0	3.4	36.6	1.7	49.7	8.0	6.3	33.7	2.3	50.3	16.0	9.7	70.3	4.0	100.0
4:6-4:11	175	6.9	6.3	35.4	1.7	50.3	6.9	2.9	36.6	3.4	49.7	13.7	9.1	72.0	5.1	100.0
5	200	8.0	6.0	34.0	2.0	50.0	8.5	6.0	33.0	2.5	50.0	16.5	12.0	67.0	4.5	100.0
6	200	7.5	4.5	35.0	3.0	50.0	8.0	5.0	35.0	2.0	50.0	15.5	9.5	70.0	5.0	100.0
7	200	7.0	5.0	36.0	2.0	50.0	8.5	5.5	34.5	1.5	50.0	15.5	10.5	70.5	3.5	100.0
8	200	7.5	5.0	36.0	1.5	50.0	8.5	6.0	34.0	1.5	50.0	16.0	11.0	70.0	3.0	100.0
9	200	6.5	6.0	36.0	1.5	50.0	7.5	5.5	35.0	2.0	50.0	14.0	11.5	71.0	3.5	100.0
10	200	8.5	5.5	35.5	0.5	50.0	7.5	5.5	35.0	2.0	50.0	16.0	11.0	70.5	2.5	100.0
11	200	6.0	5.0	35.5	3.5	50.0	7.0	6.0	35.5	1.5	50.0	13.0	11.0	71.0	5.0	100.0
12	200	6.0	6.0	36.0	2.0	50.0	8.0	4.5	35.0	2.5	50.0	14.0	10.5	71.0	4.5	100.0
13	200	6.5	6.0	34.5	3.0	50.0	7.5	6.0	35.0	1.5	50.0	14.0	12.0	69.5	4.5	100.0
14	200	8.0	6.0	34.5	1.5	50.0	8.0	5.5	34.0	2.5	50.0	16.0	11.5	68.5	4.0	100.0
15	200	8.0	5.5	35.5	1.0	50.0	7.0	6.0	35.0	2.0	50.0	15.0	11.5	70.5	3.0	100.0
16	200	6.5	6.0	36.0	1.5	50.0	8.5	5.0	35.5	1.0	50.0	15.0	11.0	71.5	2.5	100.0
17	200	6.5	6.0	35.5	2.0	50.0	6.5	6.0	36.5	1.0	50.0	13.0	12.0	72.0	3.0	100.0
Total	**3475**	**7.4**	**5.6**	**35.3**	**1.7**	**50.0**	**7.7**	**5.4**	**35.0**	**1.9**	**50.0**	**15.1**	**11.0**	**70.3**	**3.6**	**100.0**
U.S. Population[b]		*7.6*	*5.5*	*35.0*	*1.9*	*50.0*	*7.6*	*5.5*	*35.0*	*1.9*	*50.0*	*15.2*	*10.9*	*70.1*	*3.8*	*100.0*

[a]Within the "Other" category the DAS sample includes 1.8% Asian children and 0.7% Native American children.
[b]Percentages for each sex are half of the percentages for the total. U.S. population data for children aged 2–17 is from *Current Population Survey, March 1988* [Machine-readable data file] by U.S. Bureau of the Census, 1988, Washington, DC: U.S. Bureau of the Census (Producer/Distributor).

Table 6.3. Norm Sample: Percentages by Age, Sex, and Parent Education

Age	N	Male					Female					Total				
		<12 Years	12 Years	13-15 Years	≥16 Years	Total	<12 Years	12 Years	13-15 Years	≥16 Years	Total	<12 Years	12 Years	13-15 Years	≥16 Years	Total
2:6–2:11	175	6.3	19.4	13.1	10.9	49.7	8.6	20.0	13.1	8.6	50.3	14.9	39.4	26.3	19.4	100.0
3:0–3:5	175	9.7	17.7	14.9	8.0	50.3	7.4	20.0	11.4	10.9	49.7	17.1	37.7	26.3	18.9	100.0
3:6–3:11	175	9.7	18.3	12.6	9.1	49.7	8.6	19.4	12.0	10.3	50.3	18.3	37.7	24.6	19.4	100.0
4:0–4:5	175	6.9	18.8	14.3	9.7	49.7	8.6	19.5	13.1	9.1	50.3	15.5	38.2	27.4	18.9	100.0
4:6–4:11	175	8.6	19.4	12.6	9.7	50.3	6.3	17.7	14.3	11.4	49.7	14.8	37.2	26.9	21.1	100.0
5	200	8.0	21.0	12.5	8.5	50.0	8.0	20.0	13.5	8.5	50.0	16.0	41.0	26.0	17.0	100.0
6	200	10.0	16.0	14.0	10.0	50.0	9.5	18.5	12.0	10.0	50.0	19.5	34.5	26.0	20.0	100.0
7	200	9.5	17.0	13.0	10.5	50.0	11.5	18.5	11.0	9.0	50.0	21.0	35.5	24.0	19.5	100.0
8	200	7.0	19.0	14.5	9.5	50.0	9.0	19.5	12.0	9.5	50.0	16.0	38.5	26.5	19.0	100.0
9	200	9.0	20.0	10.5	10.5	50.0	9.0	18.5	13.5	9.0	50.0	18.0	38.5	24.0	19.5	100.0
10	200	9.5	18.5	13.5	8.5	50.0	10.0	18.5	12.0	9.5	50.0	19.5	37.0	25.5	18.0	100.0
11	200	9.0	16.0	13.5	11.5	50.0	8.5	18.0	15.0	8.5	50.0	17.5	34.0	28.5	20.0	100.0
12	200	9.0	19.0	13.5	8.5	50.0	9.0	19.0	12.5	9.5	50.0	18.0	38.0	26.0	18.0	100.0
13	200	9.0	19.5	12.5	9.0	50.0	11.0	19.5	11.5	8.0	50.0	20.0	39.0	24.0	17.0	100.0
14	200	9.0	20.0	11.5	9.5	50.0	10.5	17.5	12.5	9.5	50.0	19.5	37.5	24.0	19.0	100.0
15	200	9.5	18.0	13.0	9.5	50.0	9.5	19.0	13.5	8.0	50.0	19.0	37.0	26.5	17.5	100.0
16	200	9.0	19.5	12.0	9.5	50.0	10.5	19.5	13.0	7.0	50.0	19.5	39.0	25.0	16.5	100.0
17	200	10.0	19.0	11.0	10.0	50.0	10.0	20.0	11.5	8.5	50.0	20.0	39.0	22.5	18.5	100.0
Total	**3475**	**8.8**	**18.7**	**12.9**	**9.6**	**50.0**	**9.2**	**19.0**	**12.6**	**9.2**	**50.0**	**18.0**	**37.7**	**25.6**	**18.7**	**100.0**
U.S. Population[a]		*9.2*	*18.5*	*12.9*	*9.4*	*50.0*	*9.2*	*18.5*	*12.9*	*9.4*	*50.0*	*18.4*	*37.1*	*25.7*	*18.8*	*100.0*

Note. Parent Education is the average number of years of school completed by the parent or parents living with the child.
[a]Percentages for each sex are half of the percentages for the total. U.S. population data for children aged 2–17 is from *Current Population Survey, March 1988* [Machine-readable data file] by U.S. Bureau of the Census, 1988, Washington, DC: U.S. Bureau of the Census (Producer/Distributor).

Table 6.4. Norm Sample: Percentages by Age, Sex, and Region

Age	N	Male					Female					Total				
		North Central	North-east	South	West	Total	North Central	North-east	South	West	Total	North Central	North-east	South	West	Total
2:6–2:11	175	13.1	5.7	20.6	10.3	49.7	13.1	9.7	16.6	10.9	50.3	26.3	15.4	37.1	21.2	100.0
3:0–3:5	175	11.4	9.1	21.2	8.6	50.3	16.6	6.9	18.2	8.0	49.7	28.0	16.0	39.4	16.6	100.0
3:6–3:11	175	14.3	11.4	17.1	6.9	49.7	11.4	10.9	18.9	9.1	50.3	25.7	22.3	36.0	16.0	100.0
4:0–4:5	175	12.0	9.7	18.3	9.7	49.7	10.3	12.6	14.3	13.1	50.3	22.3	22.3	32.5	22.9	100.0
4:6–4:11	175	12.6	9.1	18.9	9.7	50.3	11.4	11.4	18.3	8.6	49.7	24.0	20.6	37.1	18.3	100.0
5	200	12.0	8.5	19.5	10.0	50.0	13.5	8.5	19.0	9.0	50.0	25.5	17.0	38.5	19.0	100.0
6	200	13.5	9.5	15.0	12.0	50.0	13.5	10.0	12.0	14.5	50.0	27.0	19.5	27.0	26.5	100.0
7	200	12.5	11.0	14.0	12.5	50.0	13.0	10.0	20.0	7.0	50.0	25.5	21.0	34.0	19.5	100.0
8	200	12.0	8.0	19.5	10.5	50.0	13.0	8.5	17.0	11.5	50.0	25.0	16.5	36.5	22.0	100.0
9	200	14.0	7.5	16.5	12.0	50.0	14.5	9.0	15.5	11.0	50.0	28.5	16.5	32.0	23.0	100.0
10	200	13.0	7.0	16.0	14.0	50.0	14.5	9.5	18.0	8.0	50.0	27.5	16.5	34.0	22.0	100.0
11	200	11.0	11.5	16.0	11.5	50.0	16.5	8.0	17.0	8.5	50.0	27.5	19.5	33.0	20.0	100.0
12	200	13.0	8.0	16.5	12.5	50.0	14.0	10.5	16.5	9.0	50.0	27.0	18.5	33.0	21.5	100.0
13	200	12.0	10.0	16.0	12.0	50.0	12.5	9.5	16.5	11.5	50.0	24.5	19.5	32.5	23.5	100.0
14	200	11.0	9.5	16.0	13.5	50.0	13.5	11.0	15.0	10.5	50.0	24.5	20.5	31.0	24.0	100.0
15	200	15.5	8.5	18.5	7.5	50.0	9.0	10.5	17.0	13.5	50.0	24.5	19.0	35.5	21.0	100.0
16	200	12.0	9.0	18.0	11.0	50.0	11.5	9.5	18.5	10.5	50.0	23.5	18.5	36.5	21.5	100.0
17	200	11.5	8.0	19.0	11.5	50.0	12.0	9.0	18.5	10.5	50.0	23.5	17.0	37.5	22.0	100.0
Total	**3475**	**12.6**	**9.0**	**17.5**	**10.9**	**50.0**	**13.0**	**9.7**	**17.0**	**10.3**	**50.0**	**25.6**	**18.6**	**34.6**	**21.2**	**100.0**
U.S. Population[a]		_12.6_	_9.4_	_17.4_	_10.6_	_50.0_	_12.6_	_9.4_	_17.4_	_10.6_	_50.0_	_25.1_	_18.8_	_34.9_	_21.2_	_100.0_

[a]Percentages for each sex are half of the percentages for the total. U.S. population data for children aged 2-17 is from *Current Population Survey, March 1988* [Machine-readable data file] by U.S. Bureau of the Census, 1988, Washington, DC: U.S. Bureau of the Census (Producer/Distributor).

Table 6.5. Norm Sample: Percentages by Age, Race, and Parent Education

Age	N	Black				Hispanic				White				Other				Total
		<12 Years	12 Years	13-15 Years	≥16 Years	<12 Years	12 Years	13-15 Years	≥16 Years	<12 Years	12 Years	13-15 Years	≥16 Years	<12 Years	12 Years	13-15 Years	≥16 Years	
2:6-2:11	175	4.6	6.3	2.9	1.7	4.4	2.3	1.7	0.6	5.1	30.3	21.1	16.6	0.6	0.6	0.6	0.6	100.0
3:0-3:5	175	5.2	8.0	2.9	1.1	7.3	2.9	1.7	1.1	4.0	26.3	21.1	16.6	0.6	0.6	0.6	0.0	100.0
3:6-3:11	175	5.7	5.7	2.9	1.1	6.9	3.4	1.7	0.0	5.7	28.6	18.9	16.6	0.0	0.0	1.1	1.7	100.0
4:0-4:5	175	5.1	6.9	2.3	1.7	4.1	2.9	2.3	0.6	6.3	27.4	21.1	15.4	0.0	1.1	1.7	1.1	100.0
4:6-4:11	175	2.9	6.3	2.9	1.7	2.8	4.0	1.7	0.6	9.1	25.7	20.6	16.6	0.0	1.1	1.7	2.3	100.0
5	200	3.5	7.5	4.5	1.0	5.0	4.5	2.0	0.5	6.5	27.5	19.0	14.0	1.0	1.5	0.5	1.5	100.0
6	200	5.5	6.5	2.5	1.0	6.0	2.0	1.0	0.5	7.5	25.0	21.0	16.5	0.5	1.0	1.5	2.0	100.0
7	200	6.5	5.5	1.5	2.0	7.5	2.5	0.0	0.5	7.0	26.5	21.0	16.0	0.0	1.0	1.5	1.0	100.0
8	200	4.5	6.0	4.0	1.5	3.5	4.0	3.0	0.5	8.0	27.5	18.5	16.0	0.0	1.0	1.0	1.0	100.0
9	200	3.5	6.0	3.5	1.0	5.5	3.0	2.0	1.0	8.0	27.5	18.5	17.0	1.0	2.0	0.0	0.5	100.0
10	200	4.0	6.5	3.5	2.0	6.5	3.0	1.0	0.5	8.5	27.5	20.5	14.0	0.5	0.0	0.5	1.5	100.0
11	200	3.5	4.0	3.5	2.0	5.5	3.5	1.5	0.5	7.5	25.5	22.0	16.0	1.0	1.0	1.5	1.5	100.0
12	200	2.5	7.0	3.0	1.5	6.0	2.5	1.0	1.0	8.5	28.0	20.5	14.0	1.0	0.5	1.5	1.5	100.0
13	200	4.0	6.5	2.0	1.5	7.0	3.5	1.5	0.0	7.5	27.5	20.0	14.5	1.5	1.5	0.5	1.0	100.0
14	200	4.0	7.0	3.0	2.0	6.0	3.0	1.5	1.0	8.5	26.5	18.5	15.0	1.0	1.0	1.0	1.0	100.0
15	200	4.5	6.0	4.0	0.5	6.5	2.5	1.0	1.5	6.5	28.0	21.0	15.0	1.5	0.5	0.5	0.5	100.0
16	200	4.5	7.0	3.0	0.5	6.5	3.0	1.0	0.5	8.0	28.0	20.5	15.0	0.5	1.0	0.5	0.5	100.0
17	200	5.0	6.0	1.5	0.5	6.5	3.5	1.5	0.5	7.5	29.0	19.0	16.5	1.0	0.5	0.5	1.0	100.0
Total	**3475**	**4.4**	**6.4**	**3.0**	**1.4**	**5.8**	**3.1**	**1.5**	**0.6**	**7.3**	**27.3**	**20.1**	**15.6**	**0.6**	**0.9**	**0.9**	**1.1**	**100.0**
U.S. Population[a]		*4.6*	*6.4*	*2.9*	*1.3*	*5.8*	*3.1*	*1.5*	*0.5*	*7.1*	*26.7*	*20.5*	*15.8*	*0.9*	*0.9*	*0.9*	*1.1*	*100.0*

Note. Parent Education is the average number of years of school completed by the parent or parents living with the child.
[a] U.S. population data for children aged 2-17 is from *Current Population Survey, March 1988* [Machine-readable data file] by U.S. Bureau of the Census, 1988, Washington, DC: U.S. Bureau of the Census (Producer/Distributor).

Table 6.6. Norm Sample: Percentages by Race and Region

Race/ Ethnicity	Region							
	North Central		Northeast		South		West	
	DAS Sample	U.S. Pop.	DAS Sample	U.S. Pop.	DAS Sample	U.S. Pop.	DAS Sample	U.S. Pop.
Black	2.9	*3.0*	2.2	*2.2*	8.6	*8.8*	1.4	*1.2*
Hispanic	0.8	*0.8*	1.6	*1.9*	3.4	*3.4*	5.2	*4.8*
White	21.1	*20.7*	14.4	*14.2*	21.8	*22.0*	13.0	*13.2*
Other	0.8	*0.6*	0.4	*0.6*	0.7	*0.6*	1.7	*2.0*

Note. U.S. population data for children aged 2-17 is from *Current Population Survey, March 1988* [Machine-readable data file] by U.S. Bureau of the Census, 1988, Washington, DC: U.S. Bureau of the Census (Producer/Distributor).

Table 6.7. Norm Sample: Percentages by Community Size

Community Size	DAS Sample	U.S. Population
Metropolitan Statistical Area (MSA):		
Over 1,000,000	40.8	*43.5*
250,000–999,999	21.3	*17.7*
100,000–249,999	16.2	*6.8*
Under 100,000	1.7	*5.7*
Non-MSA	20.0	*26.3*
Total	**100.0**	***100.0***

Note. U.S. population data for children aged 2-17 is from *Current Population Survey, March 1988* [Machine-readable data file] by U.S. Bureau of the Census, 1988, Washington, DC: U.S. Bureau of the Census (Producer/Distributor).

Table 6.8. Norm Sample: Percentages of Children
Aged 2:6–5:11 Enrolled in Educational Programs

Age	DAS Sample	U.S. Population[a]
2:6–3:11	29.7	*28.9*[b]
4:0–4:11	47.1	*49.0*
5:0–5:11	75.5	*86.7*

[a]U.S. Population data from *Current Population Survey, October 1986* [Machine-readable data file] by U.S. Bureau of the Census, 1986, Washington, DC: U.S. Bureau of the Census (Producer/Distributor).
[b]Ages 3:0–3:11

Table 6.9. Norm Sample: Percentages
by Special Education Category

Special Education Category	DAS Sample	U.S. Population[a]
Learning Disabled	3.9	*4.7*
Speech Impaired	2.4	*2.9*
Emotionally Disturbed	0.3	*1.0*
Physically Impaired	0.4	*0.8*
Mentally Retarded	1.5	*1.8*
Gifted/Talented	6.3	*4.2*[b]

[a]U.S. Population data from *Eighth annual report to Congress on the implementation of the Education of the Handicapped Act* by U.S. Department of Education, Office of Special Education and Rehabilatative Services, 1986.
[b]Data from *Elementary and secondary civil rights survey* by U.S. Department of Education, Office for Civil Rights, 1978 and 1984, unpublished tabulations.

Sample for Achievement-Test Grade Norms

A useful feature of the DAS is the provision of achievement tests normed on the same sample as the ability measures. With a common norm group, accurate comparisons can be made between ability and achievement. In general, the age-based standard scores, based on the entire DAS norm sample, will be the most useful achievement test scores for this purpose. Because academic achievement depends on the curriculum that the child has experienced, however, grade-based norms are also useful in evaluating a child's acquired skills. The DAS therefore provides percentiles and normal curve equivalents (NCEs), along with grade equivalents, for the first and second halves of each grade from the second half of kindergarten through grade 12.

The project team was able to collect information on grade placement for almost all school-aged children in the DAS standardization sample. Because academic performance grows during the school year, the available cases were divided into two groups, those tested in the first half of the school year (July–December) and those tested in the second half (January–June). Substantially more cases were tested in the second half than in the first half. For that reason, cases tested in the first half of the year were omitted from the grade-norm sample. The grade norms were based only on cases tested between January and June, and norms for the first half of the school year were interpolated.

Almost all (86%) of the grade-norm sample is a subset of the age-norm sample. A small number of cases not used for age norms were added to the grade-norm sample to achieve the desired demographic characteristics. Table 6.10 reports the percentages by grade of grade-norm cases that are from the age-norm sample. Table 6.10 also shows the means and standard deviations of the GCA scores for all members of the grade-norm sample by grade. The grade-norm sample clearly is comparable in ability to the full age-norm sample.

Table 6.11 shows the joint distribution of grade and age for the grade-norm sample. There is some restriction in the age ranges of the sample at the lowest and highest grades. For the Basic Number Skills and Spelling tests there are no 5-year-olds in the kindergarten sample, and for all three achievement tests, students 18 years and older are omitted from the norms for the upper grades.

Figure 6.3 shows the distributions of SES, race/ethnicity, and region for the entire sample used for the grade norms. Tables 6.12–6.15 provide specific information on the distributions of sex, race/ethnicity, SES, and region at each grade, and Table 6.16 shows the sample proportions of various special-education categories. Because the sample used for grade norms was primarily a subset of the overall DAS norm sample and was selected only by having been tested in the second half of the school year, the oversample corresponds closely to the demographic characteristics of the national population. The slight deviations from target percentages within particular grades are random fluctuations whose effects were minimized through smoothing.

Table 6.10. Overlap of Grade-Norm Sample
with Age-Norm Sample

Grade	N (Grade Norms)	Percent Overlap[b]	GCA[a] Mean	SD
K	186	80.1	100.0	14.1
1	169	71.0	99.7	13.8
2	169	75.7	99.8	14.5
3	158	88.0	100.4	14.3
4	169	89.3	99.9	14.3
5	152	87.5	100.2	13.6
6	159	90.6	101.6	16.7
7	159	90.6	97.6	14.2
8	140	89.3	101.5	15.6
9	131	86.3	101.9	15.7
10	129	93.8	98.7	16.8
11	80	90.0	100.6	15.9
12	86	94.2	102.7	14.7
Total	1887	85.9	100.2	14.9

[a]GCA from the upper Preschool Level of the Cognitive Battery for ages 5:0–5:11 and from the School-Age Level for ages 6:0–17:11

[b]Percentage of cases in the grade-norm sample that are from the age-norm sample.

Table 6.11. Grade-Norm Sample: Number of Cases by Grade and Age

Grade	Age													Total
	5	6	7	8	9	10	11	12	13	14	15	16	17	
K	85	100	1	0	0	0	0	0	0	0	0	0	0	186
1	1	79	82	7	0	0	0	0	0	0	0	0	0	169
2	0	3	84	77	5	0	0	0	0	0	0	0	0	169
3	0	0	2	66	82	8	0	0	0	0	0	0	0	158
4	0	0	0	0	65	92	12	0	0	0	0	0	0	169
5	0	0	0	0	1	58	76	14	3	0	0	0	0	152
6	0	0	0	0	0	1	67	81	10	0	0	0	0	159
7	0	0	0	0	0	0	1	57	82	16	3	0	0	159
8	0	0	0	0	0	0	0	0	54	78	7	1	0	140
9	0	0	0	0	0	0	0	0	1	47	69	12	2	131
10	0	0	0	0	0	0	0	0	0	2	50	70	7	129
11	0	0	0	0	0	0	0	0	0	0	0	46	34	80
12	0	0	0	0	0	0	0	0	0	0	0	2	84	86
Total	86	182	169	150	153	159	156	152	150	143	129	131	127	1887

Note. Norms for the Basic Number Skills and Spelling subtests are based on scores for children aged 6:0–17:11.

127

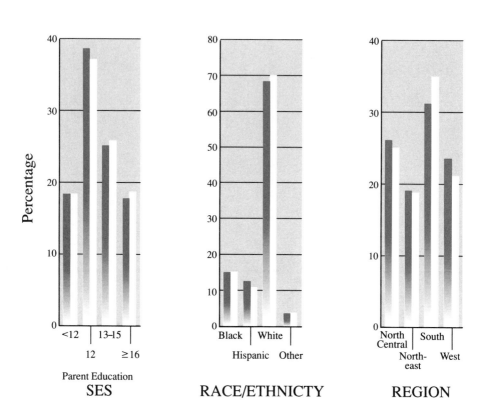

Figure 6.3. Demographic Characteristics of the DAS
Grade-Norm Sample Compared with
Those of the General Population

Table 6.12. Grade-Norm Sample:
Number of Cases by Grade and Sex

Grade	Male N	Male %	Female N	Female %	Total N	Total %
K	97	52.2	89	47.9	186	100.0
1	79	46.8	90	53.3	169	100.0
2	82	48.5	87	51.5	169	100.0
3	81	51.3	77	48.7	158	100.0
4	84	49.7	85	50.3	169	100.0
5	79	52.0	73	48.0	152	100.0
6	84	52.8	75	47.2	159	100.0
7	82	51.6	77	48.4	159	100.0
8	62	44.3	78	55.7	140	100.0
9	71	54.2	60	45.8	131	100.0
10	65	50.4	64	49.6	129	100.0
11	45	56.3	35	43.8	80	100.0
12	34	39.5	52	60.5	86	100.0
Total	942	49.9	945	50.1	1887	100.0

Table 6.13. Grade-Norm Sample:
Percentages by Grade and Race

Grade	N	Race/Ethnicity				Total
		Black	Hispanic	White	Other	
K	186	12.9	13.4	68.8	4.8	100.0
1	169	18.3	13.6	63.9	4.1	100.0
2	169	22.5	13.6	62.7	1.2	100.0
3	158	8.9	12.7	74.7	3.8	100.0
4	169	19.5	12.4	63.9	4.1	100.0
5	152	11.8	11.8	74.4	2.0	100.0
6	159	10.1	11.4	72.8	5.7	100.0
7	159	15.2	13.3	68.4	3.2	100.0
8	140	11.4	13.6	68.6	6.4	100.0
9	131	19.1	13.0	64.9	3.1	100.0
10	129	17.1	10.1	70.5	2.3	100.0
11	80	17.5	12.5	70.0	0.0	100.0
12	86	9.3	12.8	74.4	3.5	100.0
Total	**1887**	**15.0**	**12.7**	**68.7**	**3.6**	**100.0**
U.S. Population[a]		*15.2*	*10.9*	*70.1*	*3.8*	*100.0*

[a]U.S. population data for children aged 2–17 is from *Current Population Survey, March 1988* [Machine-readable data file] by U.S. Bureau of the Census, 1988, Washington, DC: U.S. Bureau of the Census (Producer/Distributor).

Table 6.14. Grade-Norm Sample:
Percentages by Grade and Parent Education

		Parent Education				
Grade	N	<12 Years	12 Years	13–15 Years	≥16 Years	Total
K	186	18.8	39.3	26.3	15.6	100.0
1	169	17.8	43.2	25.4	13.6	100.0
2	169	22.5	35.5	22.5	19.5	100.0
3	158	12.0	41.8	26.6	19.6	100.0
4	169	18.4	34.3	24.3	23.1	100.0
5	152	20.4	39.5	29.0	11.2	100.0
6	159	15.1	34.0	30.8	20.1	100.0
7	159	15.7	42.1	24.5	17.6	100.0
8	140	22.1	35.0	23.6	19.3	100.0
9	131	19.1	42.0	22.1	16.8	100.0
10	129	19.4	45.7	22.5	12.4	100.0
11	80	23.8	32.5	21.3	22.5	100.0
12	86	17.4	34.9	26.7	20.9	100.0
Total	1887	18.4	38.7	25.2	17.7	100.0
U.S. Population[a]		18.4	37.1	25.7	18.8	100.0

[a]U.S. population data for children aged 2–17 is from *Current Population Survey, March 1988* [Machine-readable data file] by U.S. Bureau of the Census, 1988, Washington, DC: U.S. Bureau of the Census (Producer/Distributor).

Table 6.15. Grade-Norm Sample:
Percentages by Grade and Region

Grade	N	North Central	North-east	South	West	Total
K	186	32.3	14.0	30.7	23.1	100.0
1	169	29.6	23.1	25.4	21.9	100.0
2	169	26.0	18.3	34.9	20.7	100.0
3	158	31.7	19.6	24.7	24.1	100.0
4	169	25.4	20.1	31.4	23.1	100.0
5	152	24.3	17.8	31.6	26.3	100.0
6	159	28.9	17.0	27.7	26.4	100.0
7	159	18.4	18.4	41.8	21.5	100.0
8	140	29.3	20.7	23.6	26.4	100.0
9	131	22.9	19.1	29.0	29.0	100.0
10	129	20.9	22.5	38.8	17.8	100.0
11	80	27.5	15.0	38.8	18.8	100.0
12	86	15.1	24.4	32.6	27.9	100.0
Total	**1887**	**26.1**	**19.1**	**31.2**	**23.6**	**100.0**
U.S. Population[a]		*25.1*	*18.8*	*34.9*	*21.2*	*100.0*

[a]U.S. population data for children aged 2-17 is from *Current Population Survey, March 1988* [Machine-readable data file] by U.S. Bureau of the Census, 1988, Washington, DC: U.S. Bureau of the Census (Producer/Distributor).

Table 6.16. Grade-Norm Sample: Percentages by
Special Education Category

Special Education Category	DAS Sample	U.S. Population[a]
Learning Disabled	3.7	*4.7*
Speech Impaired	3.9	*2.9*
Emotionally Disturbed	1.0	*1.0*
Physically Impaired	0.3	*0.8*
Mentally Retarded	0.7	*1.8*
Gifted/Talented	6.2	*4.2*[b]

[a]U.S. Population data from *Eighth annual report to Congress on the implementation of the Education of the Handicapped Act* by U.S. Department of Education, Office of Special Education and Rehabilitative Services, 1986.
[b]Data from *Elementary and secondary civil rights survey* by U.S. Department of Education, Office for Civil Rights, 1978 and 1984, unpublished tabulations.

Chapter 7

Scaling and Development of Norms

This chapter describes the procedures used to score the raw data, calibrate the item-difficulty values, obtain an ability score for each person on each subtest, and compute the norms for the subtest and composite scores. Because the DAS uses some advanced methods in test development and analysis, portions of this chapter and the following chapter on reliability must necessarily be somewhat technical. However, it is not necessary for the examiner to read these more technical sections in order to obtain the fundamental information that is important for using the test appropriately. Because some familiarity with the Rasch model is helpful in understanding these chapters, some of its key features are presented below. Appendix D fully explains the model along with some of its applications.

The following are some of the concepts basic to the use of the Rasch model.

Adaptive Testing. An adaptive (or "tailored") testing procedure is one that allows us to match item difficulty to the child's ability by selecting items according to the child's performance on previous items. A form of adaptive testing was used in the standardization edition of the DAS and was further refined to produce the time-efficient and reliable procedures that are incorporated in the final edition.

The Rasch Model. The Rasch model is the simplest member of the family of item response theory (IRT) models. It is based on the concept that the only variables that determine whether a person will solve an item correctly are the *difficulty of the item* and the *ability of the person*. The model permits the calibration of the difficulty values for each subtest item and the estimation of the ability values for each person who took some of the items in the subtest. The item difficulties and the person abilities are placed on the same measurement scale, which is a non-normative scale. This procedure of converting raw scores to ability scores is called subtest scaling.

Goodness of Fit to the Rasch Model. No model, and particularly not a very simple one, such as the Rasch model, can be expected to represent complex human behavior perfectly. As a reasonable approximation, however, such a model can provide many practical benefits. Item-difficulty and person-ability values are initially estimated on the assumption that the model is correct. An examination of the data reveals whether or not the model satisfactorily predicts each person's actual pattern of item passes and failures. The goodness-of-fit statistic, based on discrepancies between predicted and observed item responses, identifies items that fail to "fit the model." Dropping such items helps to create a homogeneous item set.

Design of Standardization Data Collection

The DAS standardization edition incorporated a form of adaptive testing that helped ensure that children would take items appropriate for their ability levels. The items of each subtest were first arranged in order of estimated difficulty according to data from the BAS and from the DAS tryouts. The items were then subdivided into overlapping sets, with at least five items shared by adjacent sets. An age range was assigned to each item set. For each subtest, the child started with the item set for his or her age.

On most subtests, examiners scored the items as they were given, using tentative scoring rules for those subtests with open-ended responses, such as Copying and Word Definitions. At the completion of the item set, the examiner applied Decision Point rules to decide whether to stop or to give additional items. Generally if the child had passed at least three items and had failed at least three items, testing stopped. If the child had failed fewer than three items, the child took an additional set of more difficult items (up to the Decision Point for the next older age group). If the child had passed fewer than three items, he or she took a set of easier items. The examiner could stop testing before a Decision Point if the examinee failed a number of items in succession. The required number of consecutive failures, however, was purposely high so that the child would not stop too soon.

Development of Final Scoring Rules

Examiners scored cases during administration solely for the purpose of making item-selection decisions. They recorded children's responses to the verbal subtests verbatim and the responses and response times on the other subtests. The central project staff later rescored all of the cases.

The development of item-scoring rules incorporated all of the cases collected in standardization for which that particular subtest had been administered correctly, including cases not used for norms construction. These cases included bias-oversample cases and cases that were unusable because one or more of the other subtests were spoiled. About a third of the cases used in scoring-rule development were Black and Hispanic children.

For several of the subtests, the project staff developed scoring rules based on a combination of content and statistical considerations. For the *verbal* subtests (Naming Vocabulary, Similarities, and Word Definitions) the actual responses were assigned code numbers which were entered into a computer database. An initial, tentative set of scoring rules was established and used to assign a raw score to each case. This tentative raw score served as the criterion for evaluating the detailed scoring rules for each item. The project staff statistically analyzed each coded response for its correlation with the total raw score. Then, using different combinations of scoring criteria, the staff evaluated the statistical behavior of each item as a whole. They used this information in conjunction with content analysis to create the final scoring criteria for each item.

For some of the more difficult items in the Similarities subtest, two-point scoring was used to improve discrimination at the top of the scale. The addition of the second score point was based on two considerations: (1) the additional point reflected a difference in the quality of the concept embodied in the response rather than a difference in the quality of expression; and (2) the additional point was supported statistically through its item–total correlation and evidence of good fit to the Rasch model. According to these criteria, several of the most difficult Similarities items did not lend themselves to two-point scoring.

The project team followed a similar sequence of steps to develop scoring rules for the two *drawing* subtests, Copying and Recall of Designs. First, a tentative set of criteria was created for each item. Each criterion of the set applied to one distinct feature of the drawing. The criteria were then divided into two or more score-point levels. To receive the score for a given level, the child's drawing had to pass all of the criteria of that level. The child's item score was the highest point level at which the drawing passed all of the criteria. The total of these tentative item scores functioned as the standard for evaluating the scoring rules. Individual criteria were deleted, added, modified, or assigned to higher or lower point levels as a result of these analyses. The decision on the number of score points (1, 2, or 3) to allow on each item was determined by (1) item–total correlations, (2) the difficulty and goodness of fit of each criterion, and (3) qualitative evaluation of content. Final score-point levels contained criteria of similar difficulty, so that no single, more difficult criterion would dominate a level.

The time-based point scales for Speed of Information Processing and Pattern Construction were also based on standardization data. Each item (page) of Speed of Information Processing had multi-point scoring based on completion time, so that each item could discriminate at multiple levels of ability. Point scales based on time, rather than raw completion times, were used because response-time distributions often are extremely skewed, and a very slow time on one item can outweigh very good performance on several items.

A crucial issue in developing the Speed of Information Processing score scales was how to handle uncorrected errors. The purpose of the subtest is to measure the speed of accurate performance on a task that is so easy that almost all examinees can attain nearly perfect accuracy. It was assumed that a highly accurate performance would indicate that the examinee was attempting to be accurate and that the response time would therefore be a valid measure of information-processing speed. Because distributions of errors on each item (page) showed that errors were very infrequent, the project team decided that two or fewer errors on an item response would be disregarded in scoring, but that an item response with three or more errors would be scored 0. For those responses with two or fewer errors, a score ranging from 0 to 6 points was assigned according to the response time. The point scale for each item was created by first dividing the distribution of response times into seven intervals with approximately equal numbers of cases.

The scales were then adjusted so that, of the six items administered to a child, the first two would have relatively lenient time limits (to discriminate among the lower-ability examinees) and the last two would have stringent limits (to discriminate among the higher-ability children).

The Pattern Construction subtest was scaled in much the same way as was the Speed of Information Processing subtest. For each item, the project staff constructed point scales based on the distribution of response times for correct responses. The number of time intervals increases with item difficulty, from three or four intervals for the easy items, to six for the hardest items. There are two reasons for this variation. First, children respond very quickly to easy items, and little differentiation is possible among the majority of cases. Second, the team suspected that speed would be a less valid indicator of ability for younger children than for older children. This expectation was indeed supported by the poor statistical fit of points corresponding to relatively fast response times on the easy items.

Rasch Scaling

Item and subtest scaling through Rasch model analysis influenced the development of item-scoring rules. The project team used the MSTEPS computer program (Wright, Congdon, & Rossner, 1987) to scale all subtests except the delayed trial of Recall of Objects, for which the program could not be used. MSTEPS, a variation of the earlier, simpler Rasch program BICAL (Wright & Mead, 1976), has two notable features: It scales polychotomously-scored items (that is, items with three or more score values, as opposed to dichotomous, right-or-wrong items), and it permits cases with missing item-response data to be included in the analysis. With the DAS, most examinees take only a subset of a subtest's items and, in effect, have incomplete data. This second feature of the MSTEPS program was therefore used extensively because it allowed an entire subtest to be scaled in a single run. MSTEPS accomplished in one analysis what otherwise would have required separate scalings and vertical linking of item subsets. Furthermore, MSTEPS utilizes all of the available data even for those cases with missing scores within an item set (such as might result from accidentally skipped items or illegible, unscorable responses).

The first feature of MSTEPS mentioned above, the ability to scale polychotomously-scored items, was not used in DAS scaling for reasons discussed in Appendix D. Instead, an alternative approach to scaling polychotomously-scored items, the one previously used with the BAS, was adopted for the DAS. This adaptation of the Rasch model treats each item as if it were two or more dichotomously-scored "dummy" items. For example, an item with three possible score values (0, 1, and 2) would be represented as two dummy items, each with score values of 0–1. If a child obtained an item score of 2, both of the dummy items would be scored 1. If the item score were 1, the first dummy item would be scored 1 and the second would be scored 0. An item score of 0 would be represented by scores of 0 on both dummy items.

This type of scoring assumes that differences between score levels within an item are quantitative, such that a higher item score reflects a higher level of ability on a single dimension. For polychotomous scales based on response time, this assumption is highly plausible. For the verbal and drawing subtests, the validity of the assumption is in part tested by the information on goodness of fit of the individual dummy items. On occasion, one score level of an item would fit poorly or would be biased against a demographic group, but the remaining score levels would work well. In such instances, it was often possible to omit that score level from the scoring rules for that item. In the Similarities, Copying, Pattern Construction, and Recall of Designs subtests, the number of well-fitting score points varied from item to item.

The information on goodness of fit tended to support the dummy-item method of scaling polychotomous items. Nevertheless, the method probably violates the Rasch-model assumption of local independence, because a score of 1 point on the dummy item that represents the high point score means that the examinee will have scored 1 point on all of the easier dummy items corresponding to that test item. The effect of this violation on the applicability of the Rasch model is not fully known, although the practical consequences are not likely serious. Chapter 8 discusses the effect on the estimation of reliability.

Applications of Rasch Scaling

As in the scoring-rule development, the analysis of each subtest for item fit and item bias incorporated all of the cases collected in standardization, including bias-oversample cases and cases in which one or more of the other subtests were spoiled. Only actual item responses were analyzed; no assumptions were made about how examinees would have performed on easier or more difficult items that were not administered.

At the beginning of the item-analysis phase, the project team extensively compared the results of two methods of scaling: the MSTEPS one-pass method in which all cases are scaled simultaneously and the more traditional method in which each overlapping item set is scaled separately and the resulting item difficulties are placed on a single scale through vertical linking. Because these comparisons demonstrated nearly identical results and because the MSTEPS method is much simpler and makes use of all of the available item-response data, the MSTEPS method was applied to all subtests.

Each analysis produced information on the fit of the Rasch model to individual item data and to the subtest as a whole (see Appendix D). In addition to numerical indexes of item fit, the program provided for each item a table comparing the actual and expected performance of examinees at different ability levels. To construct the table, the program subdivided the cases into approximately 14 ability levels according to their ability scores on the subtest. Traditional item–total correlations, often used as indexes of item discrimination, were also calculated and used to check item-fit statistics.

Some items were deleted (or retained as unscored sample items) if they were judged to fit poorly on the bases of poor fit values, large differences between expected and observed performance at different ability levels, and (for some subtests) low item–total correlations. The numerical fit indexes and item–total correlations agreed closely with each other in identifying items that discriminated poorly between high-ability and low-ability examinees. After any items had been deleted, the remaining items were reanalyzed by the Rasch model to identify any other misfitting items. The project team repeated this process until it was unnecessary to delete additional items.

Special Item-Scaling Decisions

The results of the MSTEPS one-pass scaling indicated that for two subtests the structure or the method of analysis needed modification. The standardization edition of one of these subtests, Basic Number Skills, included all of the items that later became the items of the Early Number Concepts subtest as well as those of the Basic Number Skills test. Because the subtest included two distinct types of items (orally administered questions and paper-and-pencil computation), the results of the single scaling of all of the items was compared with the results of separate scalings of the two subsets of items. The separate scalings yielded a much wider range of item difficulties within each of the two sets than did the single scaling of the total set. These results suggested that the overall set of items was less homogeneous than each separate subset. The project team therefore decided that the two sets of items should compose separate subtests.

The other subtest subjected to more detailed analysis was Speed of Information Processing. Here, perhaps because of the change from figural to numerical stimuli (described in Chapter 4), the scalings within narrow item subsets produced wider ranges of item difficulties than the single, overall scaling. For this subtest, the within-level scaling results were linked and were used for all further analyses.

Scaling of the Recall of Objects subtest also required special attention. The score for each of the three immediate-recall trials ranged from 0 to 20 points according to the number of objects recalled. Although there is some variability in the frequency with which each of the 20 objects is recalled (attributable to factors such as familiarity and serial position), these differences are not strongly related to the number of items recalled on each trial. The ability is measured not on the basis of the "hardest" objects recalled, but rather on the basis of the *number* of objects recalled. Therefore, Recall of Objects—Immediate was scaled as a subtest with three 20-point items. Because the delayed-recall trial, being a single "item," cannot be scaled by the Rasch model, the raw score, rather than a Rasch ability score, is used in the norm tables.

Person Abilities

All individuals in the standardization sample received a Rasch ability score on each subtest taken. Because the final item sequences and Starting and Decision Points are different from those used in standardization, examinees in the standardization sample could not be scored on exactly the same set of items that they would have taken in the final version. To maximize the accuracy of ability scores, the project staff based each standardization examinee's score on his or her performance on all of the attempted items that were retained in the final edition.

For each examinee who neither passed nor failed all of the items attempted, these ability estimates were automatically generated by the MSTEPS program. For purposes of norming, ability scores were also assigned for examinees who did pass all or fail all of the items they attempted. Although Rasch methodology considers the ability of an examinee with a zero or perfect raw score to be unmeasurable, it would be impractical and inappropriate for us to treat such an examinee as if the subtest had not been administered. Moreover, if we intend to use the subtest score in a composite score, we must assign some numerical value to the child's ability. Therefore, ability scores corresponding to zero and perfect raw scores were extrapolated. The difference in ability scores between raw scores of 1 and 2 was used to determine the difference between raw scores of 0 and 1, and a similar method was used for perfect scores. The typical size of this difference was about 10 ability-score points. The standard error of the ability score corresponding to a zero or perfect raw score is, of course, very high, because the subtest is inappropriate in difficulty for the examinee. The **Manual** emphasizes that a child who obtains such a score should be given an easier or a more difficult subtest that measures the same domain of ability, if one is available.

The DAS scale values for abilities and difficulties are expressed as positive integers. The values are Rasch difficulty and ability scores transformed by multiplying by 10, rounding, and adding a constant to remove negative values. The constant for each subtest was selected so that an ability score of 10 corresponds to a raw score of 0 on the entire set of items of that subtest. The same constant is applied to that subtest's item difficulties.

Item Difficulties

Table 7.1 reports the difficulties of all items for each subtest. As explained in the above section on person abilities, these are linear transformations of the obtained Rasch item difficulties, such that all values are expressed as positive integers. Because the item difficulties are on the same scale as the person abilities, we can make predictions about the performance of examinees of known abilities on an individual item.

It is important to note that item difficulty and person ability values are comparable only *within subtests*—they are not comparable between subtests. Thus, for example, a difficulty value of 60 on an item of one subtest does not indicate that the item is of the same difficulty for a given group of people as an item with a difficulty value of 60 on a different subtest. Appendix D gives interpretive suggestions about differences between item difficulty and person ability.

Item Sets Within Subtests

After item difficulties and person abilities had been estimated for a subtest, the final item sequence and the Starting and Decision Points for each age were established. Generally, items were arranged in ascending order of difficulty. Polychotomously-scored items were usually arranged according to the difficulty associated with an item score of 1. There were two exceptions to these general rules: when a group of items used the same materials and had to be kept together (as in the Verbal Comprehension subtest), or when changing the standardization sequence might have affected item difficulties because of practice effects (as on the Matrices subtest).

The DAS takes advantage of item response theory by allowing the examinee's ability to be estimated from a subset of items in the subtest. ***The goal is to administer a set of items that are appropriate in difficulty to the child's ability level.*** Item selection is governed by Starting Points that are tailored to the examinee's age and Decision Points at which the examiner decides whether or not additional items must be given to obtain an accurate score. (Chapter 1 discusses the item-selection rules.)

With this goal in mind, the Starting and Decision Points that define each subtest's item sets were developed after the items had been scaled and the distribution of ability scores at each age was known. Computer simulation was used to model the performance of examinees at each ability level under various assumed Starting Points, Decision Points, and Decision Point rules. The expected reliability was calculated for each set of assumptions. The final item sets are designed to yield high reliability from efficient item-selection procedures and to allow as much of the testing time as possible to be spent on items near the child's level of ability. (Chapter 8 describes in detail the procedure of constructing item sets.)

After the examinee has been given an appropriate set of items, the raw score is converted to an ability score by means of the tables printed on the Record Form and also presented in Figure 7.1.

Table 7.1. DAS Item Difficulties

Core Subtests: Preschool

Block Building

Item[a]	Difficulty	Item	Difficulty	Item	Difficulty	Item	Difficulty
1A	24	4	114	7	128	10	155
1B	54	5	120	8	141	11	158
2	81	6	116	9	151	12	175
3	99						

Verbal Comprehension

Item	Difficulty	Item	Difficulty	Item	Difficulty	Item	Difficulty
1	27	10	48	19	80	28	117
2	33	11	65	20	81	29	126
3	40	12	55	21	87	30	98
4	41	13	84	22	91	31	112
5	33	14	85	23	90	32	114
6	71	15	102	24	92	33	119
7	35	16	116	25	103	34	144
8	37	17	117	26	117	35	149
9	48	18	117	27	122	36	164

Picture Similarities

Item	Difficulty	Item	Difficulty	Item	Difficulty	Item	Difficulty
1	23	9	47	17	56	25	77
2	35	10	48	18	64	26	78
3	29	11	52	19	61	27	78
4	32	12	53	20	64	28	79
5	38	13	54	21	67	29	85
6	44	14	54	22	67	30	93
7	44	15	55	23	68	31	94
8	46	16	56	24	68	32	96

[a]Letters next to item numbers refer to score levels within the item (A = 1 point, B = 2 points, etc.).

Table 7.1. DAS Item Difficulties *(Continued)*

Naming Vocabulary

Item	Difficulty	Item	Difficulty	Item	Difficulty	Item	Difficulty
1	42	8	66	15	83	21	114
2	60	9	67	16	85	22	116
3	19	10	70	17	97	23	122
4	31	11	70	18	101	24	133
5	34	12	74	19	108	25	152
6	48	13	76	20	109	26	152
7	49	14	75				

Early Number Concepts

Item	Difficulty	Item	Difficulty	Item	Difficulty	Item	Difficulty
1A	20	5	71	13	78	21	100
1B	40	6	60	14	84	22	102
1C	54	7	86	15	86	23	116
1D	40	8	81	16	106	24	112
1E	53	9	78	17	94	25	118
1F	62	10	77	18	107	26	126
2	49	11	90	19	112	27	138
3	41	12	68	20	95	28	137
4	52						

Copying

Item	Difficulty	Item	Difficulty	Item	Difficulty	Item	Difficulty
1	19	7B	91	12C	114	17A	106
2	30	8A	68	13A	99	17B	122
3A	44	8B	82	13B	111	17C	139
3B	64	9A	72	14A	101	18A	106
4A	53	9B	90	14B	129	18B	132
4B	69	10A	70	15A	105	18C	149
5A	63	10B	99	15B	113	19A	115
5B	74	11A	79	15C	131	19B	127
6A	66	11B	87	16A	107	20A	125
6B	87	12A	86	16B	113	20B	147
7A	66	12B	108	16C	139		

Table 7.1. DAS Item Difficulties *(Continued)*

Core Subtests: School-Age

Recall of Designs

Item	Difficulty	Item	Difficulty	Item	Difficulty	Item	Difficulty
1A	18	7A	64	13A	88	18A	103
1B	51	7B	82	13B	111	18B	114
2A	39	8A	70	14A	94	18C	121
2B	80	8B	100	14B	107	19A	107
3A	45	9A	69	15A	98	19B	135
3B	66	9B	94	15B	110	19C	148
4A	55	10A	75	16A	102	20A	109
4B	84	10B	93	16B	119	20B	127
5A	55	11A	72	17A	98	20C	136
5B	79	11B	87	17B	126	21A	113
6A	64	12A	78	17C	137	21B	123
6B	71	12B	105			21C	145

Word Definitions

Item	Difficulty	Item	Difficulty	Item	Difficulty	Item	Difficulty
1	21	12	67	23	86	33	120
2	28	13	70	24	86	34	124
3	43	14	71	25	87	35	134
4	49	15	71	26	94	36	140
5	50	16	72	27	105	37	141
6	53	17	73	28	106	38	140
7	57	18	75	29	107	39	152
8	60	19	78	30	109	40	160
9	60	20	78	31	112	41	162
10	62	21	79	32	116	42	168
11	62	22	83				

Pattern Construction (Alternative)

Item	Difficulty	Item	Difficulty	Item	Difficulty	Item	Difficulty
1A	12	7	110	13	98	19	126
1B	40	8A	61	14A	101	20	133
2A	56	8B	69	14B	113	21	140
2B	71	9A	79	15A	104	22	147
3	77	9B	95	15B	116	23	158
4A	65	10	87	16	118	24	159
4B	75	11	96	17	124	25	155
5	87	12	93	18	128	26	162
6	83						

Table 7.1. DAS Item Difficulties *(Continued)*

Pattern Construction (Standard Administration)

Item	Difficulty	Item	Difficulty	Item	Difficulty	Item	Difficulty
1A	11	8A	52	14A	94	19A	124
1B	44	8B	66	14B	109	19B	132
1C	44	8C	85	14C	126	19C	143
2A	55	8D	107	14D	139	19D	155
2B	70	9A	75	14E	157	19E	171
2C	100	9B	95	15A	99	20A	131
3A	79	9C	114	15B	113	20B	143
3B	93	9D	140	15C	123	20C	158
3C	112	10A	90	15D	139	20D	173
4A	62	10B	97	15E	158	20E	192
4B	74	10C	107	16A	118	21A	137
4C	107	10D	133	16B	126	21B	143
5A	87	11A	98	16C	139	21C	154
5B	95	11B	105	16D	153	21D	163
5C	106	11C	116	16E	170	21E	177
5D	117	11D	143	17A	123	22A	144
6A	82	12A	95	17B	131	22B	150
6B	92	12B	109	17C	145	22C	160
6C	103	12C	120	17D	160	22D	170
6D	116	12D	146	17E	178	22E	188
7A	106	13A	99	18A	127	23A	154
7B	112	13B	115	18B	136	23B	162
7C	124	13C	125	18C	150	23C	174
7D	143	13D	150	18D	166	23D	184
				18E	183	23E	207

Matrices

Item	Difficulty	Item	Difficulty	Item	Difficulty	Item	Difficulty
1	32	10	68	18	98	26	114
2	25	11	80	19	100	27	121
3	31	12	84	20	105	28	120
4	35	13	81	21	103	29	119
5	50	14	85	22	107	30	110
6	57	15	91	23	105	31	135
7	53	16	90	24	116	32	135
8	75	17	96	25	119	33	129
9	85						

Table 7.1. DAS Item Difficulties *(Continued)*

Similarities

Item	Difficulty	Item	Difficulty	Item	Difficulty	Item	Difficulty
1	42	11	72	21	99	28B	115
2	26	12	72	22	99	29	115
3	38	13	75	23	99	30	120
4	38	14	77	24	102	31	123
5	42	15	79	25A	93	32A	121
6	43	16	80	25B	117	32B	146
7	44	17	80	26A	100	33A	123
8	45	18	92	26B	113	33B	141
9	56	19	94	27	108	34A	126
10	62	20	128	28A	107	34B	136

Sequential and Quantitative Reasoning

Item	Difficulty	Item	Difficulty	Item	Difficulty	Item	Difficulty
1	31	11	60	21	72	31	107
2	26	12	62	22	80	32	104
3	27	13	64	23	72	33	112
4	38	14	65	24	94	34	97
5	33	15	64	25	79	35	121
6	32	16	56	26	86	36	117
7	36	17	64	27	91	37	141
8	56	18	62	28	84	38	121
9	52	19	74	29	82	39	116
10	58	20	67	30	92		

Table 7.1. DAS Item Difficulties *(Continued)*

Diagnostic Subtests

Matching Letter-Like Forms

Item	Difficulty	Item	Difficulty	Item	Difficulty	Item	Difficulty
1	24	8	42	15	49	22	59
2	31	9	44	16	50	23	60
3	32	10	46	17	51	24	63
4	36	11	47	18	51	25	64
5	34	12	48	19	51	26	64
6	36	13	48	20	52	27	70
7	38	14	50	21	56		

Recall of Digits

Item	Difficulty	Item	Difficulty	Item	Difficulty	Item	Difficulty
1	35	10	62	19	119	28	165
2	35	11	89	20	119	29	162
3	32	12	98	21	143	30	156
4	29	13	88	22	130	31	177
5	33	14	94	23	139	32	187
6	63	15	103	24	149	33	183
7	68	16	121	25	152	34	171
8	58	17	117	26	163	35	184
9	62	18	131	27	154	36	195

Recognition of Pictures

Item	Difficulty	Item	Difficulty	Item	Difficulty	Item	Difficulty
1	25	6	64	11	92	16	103
2	36	7	67	12	92	17	101
3	29	8	73	13	94	18	99
4	36	9	70	14	97	19	113
5	50	10	86	15	117	20	120

Table 7.1. DAS Item Difficulties (Continued)

Speed of Information Processing

Item	Difficulty	Item	Difficulty	Item	Difficulty	Item	Difficulty
1A	21	5D	133	10A	106	14D	196
1B	49	5E	152	10B	139	14E	216
1C	69	5F	167	10C	161	14F	236
1D	82	6A	74	10D	182	15A	164
1E	97	6B	98	10E	205	15B	183
1F	117	6C	113	10F	234	15C	197
2A	30	6D	129	11A	117	15D	214
2B	50	6E	150	11B	153	15E	231
2C	68	6F	181	11C	171	15F	249
2D	81	7A	75	11D	192	16A	160
2E	95	7B	95	11E	224	16B	188
2F	113	7C	119	11F	269	16C	203
3A	55	7D	137	12A	130	16D	220
3B	73	7E	163	12B	165	16E	240
3C	92	7F	180	12C	182	16F	262
3D	108	8A	73	12D	204	17A	179
3E	130	8B	95	12E	233	17B	204
3F	156	8C	119	12F	269	17C	226
4A	49	8D	134	13A	137	17D	254
4B	69	8E	159	13B	159	17E	275
4C	90	8F	180	13C	181	17F	300
4D	105	9A	99	13D	194	18A	177
4E	125	9B	127	13E	212	18B	206
4F	151	9C	152	13F	232	18C	229
5A	79	9D	171	14A	143	18D	247
5B	97	9E	196	14B	163	18E	269
5C	116	9F	227	14C	183	18F	303

Achievement Tests

Basic Number Skills

1	29	13	98	25	168	37	193
2	27	14	113	26	172	38	193
3	38	15	113	27	175	39	196
4	35	16	113	28	174	40	201
5	50	17	128	29	171	41	203
6	64	18	130	30	178	42	205
7	85	19	135	31	185	43	214
8	69	20	133	32	187	44	215
9	86	21	146	33	184	45	214
10	84	22	155	34	189	46	237
11	111	23	159	35	183	47	225
12	108	24	163	36	191	48	232

Table 7.1. DAS Item Difficulties *(Continued)*

Spelling

Item	Difficulty	Item	Difficulty	Item	Difficulty	Item	Difficulty
N1	16	17	104	36	143	54	177
N2	42	18	106	37	143	55	179
N3	64	19	105	38	144	56	179
1	80	20	107	39	141	57	180
2	83	21	110	40	150	58	185
3	82	22	112	41	151	59	188
4	84	23	111	42	153	60	194
5	88	24	113	43	154	61	196
6	89	25	112	44	155	62	200
7	92	26	114	45	153	63	201
8	94	27	116	46	160	64	202
9	94	28	114	47	163	65	208
10	99	29	126	48	164	66	211
11	100	30	118	49	166	67	223
12	100	31	127	50	173	68	233
13	101	32	130	51	174	69	235
14	102	33	131	52	167	70	248
15	104	34	133	53	175		
16	105	35	136				

Word Reading

Item	Difficulty	Item	Difficulty	Item	Difficulty	Item	Difficulty
1	27	24	73	47	96	69	135
2	34	25	71	48	97	70	137
3	37	26	73	49	97	71	138
4	43	27	73	50	98	72	143
5	44	28	74	51	102	73	146
6	42	29	74	52	102	74	152
7	44	30	75	53	105	75	154
8	46	31	77	54	105	76	155
9	49	32	77	55	107	77	157
10	51	33	79	56	107	78	157
11	56	34	80	57	108	79	160
12	61	35	81	58	108	80	162
13	60	36	81	59	111	81	165
14	63	37	81	60	111	82	163
15	69	38	83	61	111	83	165
16	62	39	84	62	112	84	170
17	64	40	88	63	112	85	173
18	66	41	84	64	112	86	175
19	66	42	88	65	113	87	175
20	68	43	88	66	118	88	178
21	69	44	94	67	123	89	191
22	68	45	95	68	124	90	194
23	69	46	94				

Block Building
Raw Score to Ability Score

Raw Score	Item Set 1–13
0	10(18)
1	38(18)
2	66(16)
3	87(13)
4	100(11)
5	111(9)
6	119(9)
7	127(9)
8	135(9)
9	144(9)
10	152(9)
11	161(10)
12	174(12)
13	186(16)

Recognition of Pictures
Raw Score to Ability Score

Raw Score	1–9	1–13	1–20	5–20
0	10(16)	10(16)	10(16)	
1	19(11)	19(12)	19(11)	48(12)
2	30(9)	29(9)	29(9)	58(9)
3	38(9)	38(9)	38(9)	66(8)
4	46(9)	46(9)	46(9)	72(8)
5	54(9)	54(9)	53(9)	77(7)
6	62(9)	61(8)	60(8)	82(7)
7	71(9)	68(8)	66(8)	87(7)
8	81(11)	74(8)	72(7)	91(6)
9		80(8)	77(7)	95(6)
10		87(8)	82(7)	99(6)
11		94(9)	87(7)	104(7)
12		104(11)	91(6)	108(7)
13			95(6)	113(8)
14			99(6)	120(9)
15			104(7)	129(11)
16			108(7)	138(16)
17			113(8)	
18			120(9)	
19			129(11)	
20			138(16)	

Copying
Raw Score to Ability Score

Raw Score	1–12	1–15	5–15	5–20	11–20
0	10(12)	10(12)			
1	20(12)	20(12)	48(11)	48(11)	71(11)
2	32(10)	32(10)	56(8)	56(8)	80(8)
3	41(9)	41(9)	61(7)	61(7)	86(7)
4	48(8)	48(8)	66(6)	65(6)	91(6)
5	53(7)	53(7)	69(6)	69(6)	94(6)
6	57(6)	57(6)	73(6)	72(6)	98(6)
7	61(6)	61(6)	76(6)	75(5)	101(5)
8	64(6)	64(6)	79(5)	78(5)	104(5)
9	67(5)	67(5)	82(5)	81(5)	107(5)
10	70(5)	70(5)	85(5)	83(5)	109(5)
11	73(5)	72(5)	88(5)	86(5)	112(5)
12	76(5)	75(5)	90(5)	88(5)	114(5)
13	79(5)	78(5)	93(5)	91(5)	117(5)
14	82(5)	80(5)	96(5)	93(5)	119(5)
15	85(6)	83(5)	99(6)	96(5)	122(5)
16	88(6)	86(5)	103(6)	98(5)	125(5)
17	91(6)	88(5)	106(6)	100(5)	128(5)
18	95(6)	91(5)	109(6)	102(5)	131(6)
19	99(7)	94(5)	113(6)	104(5)	134(6)
20	104(7)	97(5)	118(7)	107(5)	137(6)
21	111(9)	100(5)	123(7)	109(5)	141(6)
22	120(11)	103(6)	129(9)	111(5)	146(7)
23		106(6)	138(11)	113(5)	151(8)
24		109(6)		115(5)	160(11)
25		113(6)		118(5)	170(12)
26		118(7)		120(5)	
27		123(7)		123(5)	
28		129(9)		125(5)	
29		139(11)		128(5)	
30				131(5)	
31				134(6)	
32				137(6)	
33				141(6)	
34				146(7)	
35				152(8)	
36				160(11)	
37				170(12)	

Figure 7.1. Raw-Score-to-Ability-Score Tables

Verbal Comprehension
Raw Score to Ability Score

Raw Score	Item Set 1-12	1-29	1-36	13-36
0	10(12)	10(12)	10(12)	
1	15(11)	15(11)	15(11)	
2	24(8)	24(8)	24(8)	
3	30(7)	29(7)	29(7)	78(7)
4	34(7)	34(7)	34(7)	83(6)
5	39(7)	39(7)	39(7)	86(6)
6	43(7)	43(6)	43(6)	90(6)
7	48(7)	47(7)	47(7)	93(6)
8	53(7)	51(7)	51(7)	96(6)
9	59(8)	56(7)	56(7)	99(5)
10		61(7)	61(7)	102(5)
11		66(7)	65(7)	105(5)
12		70(7)	70(7)	108(5)
13		74(6)	74(6)	111(5)
14		78(6)	78(6)	114(5)
15		82(6)	81(6)	117(6)
16		86(6)	84(6)	120(6)
17		89(6)	88(6)	123(6)
18		93(6)	91(6)	127(6)
19		96(6)	94(5)	131(7)
20		100(6)	97(5)	136(7)
21		104(6)	100(5)	143(8)
22		107(6)	102(5)	151(10)
23		111(6)	105(5)	163(12)
24		115(6)	108(5)	174(16)
25		120(7)	111(5)	
26		124(7)	114(5)	
27			117(5)	
28			120(6)	
29			123(6)	
30			127(6)	
31			131(7)	
32			136(7)	
33			143(8)	
34			151(10)	
35			163(12)	
36			174(16)	

Picture Similarities
Raw Score to Ability Score

Raw Score	Item Set 1-24	1-28	1-32	11-32
0	10(13)	10(13)	10(13)	
1	18(11)	18(11)	18(11)	
2	26(8)	26(8)	26(8)	
3	29(7)	29(7)	29(7)	45(7)
4	32(6)	31(6)	31(6)	49(6)
5	34(6)	33(6)	33(6)	52(6)
6	37(5)	37(5)	37(5)	55(5)
7	40(5)	39(5)	39(5)	58(5)
8	42(5)	42(5)	42(5)	61(5)
9	45(5)	44(5)	44(5)	63(5)
10	47(5)	47(5)	47(5)	66(5)
11	49(5)	49(5)	49(5)	68(5)
12	52(5)	51(5)	51(5)	71(5)
13	54(5)	53(5)	53(5)	73(5)
14	56(5)	55(5)	55(4)	76(5)
15	58(5)	57(5)	57(4)	79(5)
16	61(5)	59(5)	59(4)	82(6)
17	63(5)	61(5)	61(5)	86(6)
18	66(5)	64(5)	63(5)	90(6)
19	68(5)	66(5)	65(5)	94(7)
20	72(6)	68(5)	67(5)	100(8)
21	75(7)	71(5)	70(5)	108(11)
22		73(5)	72(5)	118(16)
23		76(6)	74(5)	
24		79(6)	77(5)	
25		83(7)	80(5)	
26			83(6)	
27			86(6)	
28			90(6)	
29			94(7)	
30			100(8)	
31			108(11)	
32			118(16)	

Figure 7.1. Raw-Score-to-Ability-Score Tables *(Continued)*

Pattern Construction
Raw Score to Ability Score

Raw Score	1-7	1-10	1-16	8-16	8-20	8-23	14-20	14-23
0	10(18)	10(18)	10(18)					
1	21(15)	20(14)	20(14)	53(12)	53(12)	53(12)	87(11)	87(11)
2	38(11)	35(10)	35(10)	64(9)	64(9)	64(9)	96(8)	96(8)
3	48(9)	43(8)	43(8)	71(8)	71(8)	71(8)	102(7)	102(7)
4	55(8)	50(8)	49(7)	77(7)	77(7)	77(7)	107(7)	107(6)
5	62(8)	55(7)	54(7)	81(6)	81(6)	81(6)	111(6)	110(6)
6	68(7)	60(7)	59(6)	85(6)	85(6)	85(6)	115(6)	114(6)
7	73(7)	64(6)	63(6)	88(6)	88(5)	88(5)	118(5)	116(5)
8	77(7)	67(6)	66(6)	91(5)	91(5)	91(5)	120(5)	119(5)
9	82(6)	71(6)	69(5)	94(5)	93(5)	93(5)	123(5)	121(5)
10	86(6)	74(6)	72(5)	96(5)	96(5)	95(5)	125(5)	124(5)
11	89(6)	77(5)	75(5)	99(5)	98(5)	98(5)	128(5)	126(4)
12	93(6)	80(5)	77(5)	101(5)	100(5)	100(4)	130(5)	128(4)
13	96(6)	82(5)	79(5)	103(5)	102(4)	102(4)	132(5)	130(4)
14	99(6)	85(5)	81(4)	105(5)	104(4)	104(4)	134(5)	131(4)
15	103(6)	87(5)	83(4)	107(5)	106(4)	105(4)	136(5)	133(4)
16	106(6)	90(5)	85(4)	109(5)	107(4)	107(4)	139(5)	135(4)
17	109(6)	92(5)	87(4)	111(4)	109(4)	109(4)	141(5)	137(4)
18	113(6)	94(5)	89(4)	113(4)	111(4)	110(4)	143(5)	138(4)
19	116(6)	96(5)	90(4)	115(5)	112(4)	112(4)	145(5)	140(4)
20	121(7)	98(5)	92(4)	117(5)	114(4)	114(4)	147(5)	141(4)
21	126(8)	101(5)	93(4)	119(5)	116(4)	115(4)	150(5)	143(4)
22	133(9)	103(5)	95(4)	121(5)	117(4)	117(4)	152(5)	144(4)
23	143(12)	105(5)	96(4)	124(5)	119(4)	118(4)	154(5)	146(4)
24		107(5)	98(4)	126(5)	120(4)	120(4)	157(5)	148(4)
25		109(5)	99(4)	128(5)	122(4)	121(4)	159(5)	149(4)
26		112(5)	100(4)	130(5)	123(4)	122(4)	162(5)	151(4)
27		114(5)	102(4)	133(5)	125(4)	124(4)	165(5)	152(4)
28		117(5)	103(4)	135(5)	126(4)	125(4)	168(6)	154(4)
29		120(5)	104(4)	138(5)	128(4)	127(4)	171(6)	155(4)
30		123(6)	105(4)	141(5)	129(4)	128(4)	174(6)	157(4)
31		126(6)	107(4)	143(5)	131(4)	129(4)	178(7)	158(4)
32		130(7)	108(4)	146(6)	132(4)	130(4)	183(7)	160(4)
33		135(7)	109(4)	149(6)	134(4)	132(4)	189(8)	162(4)
34		142(9)	110(4)	153(6)	135(4)	133(4)	198(11)	163(4)
35		151(11)	112(4)	157(7)	137(4)	134(4)		165(4)
36			113(4)	162(7)	138(4)	136(4)		167(4)
37			114(4)	167(8)	140(4)	137(4)		168(4)
38			116(4)	176(11)	141(4)	138(4)		170(4)
39			117(4)		143(4)	139(4)		172(4)
40			118(4)		145(4)	140(4)		174(5)

Figure 7.1. Raw-Score-to-Ability-Score Tables *(Continued)*

Pattern Construction *(Continued)*
Raw Score to Ability Score

Raw Score	Item Set							
	1–7	1–10	1–16	8–16	8–20	8–23	14–20	14–23
41			120(4)		146(4)	142(4)		177(5)
42			121(4)		148(4)	143(4)		179(5)
43			123(4)		150(4)	144(4)		182(5)
44			124(4)		151(4)	145(4)		184(5)
45			126(4)		153(4)	147(4)		187(6)
46			127(4)		155(4)	148(4)		191(6)
47			129(4)		157(5)	149(4)		196(7)
48			131(4)		159(5)	150(4)		202(8)
49			133(4)		161(5)	152(4)		211(11)
50			135(4)		164(5)	153(4)		231(23)
51			137(5)		166(5)	154(4)		
52			139(5)		169(5)	156(4)		
53			141(5)		172(6)	157(4)		
54			143(5)		175(6)	158(4)		
55			146(5)		179(6)	160(4)		
56			148(5)		184(7)	161(4)		
57			151(6)		190(8)	163(4)		
58			155(6)		198(11)	164(4)		
59			158(6)			166(4)		
60			163(7)			168(4)		
61		168(8)				169(4)		
62		177(11)				171(4)		
63						173(4)		
64						175(5)		
65						177(5)		
66						179(5)		
67						182(5)		
68						185(5)		
69						188(6)		
70						191(6)		
71						196(7)		
72						202(8)		
73						211(11)		
74						231(23)		

Figure 7.1. Raw-Score-to-Ability-Score Tables *(Continued)*

Pattern Construction (Alternative)
Raw Score to Ability Score

Raw Score	Item Set							
	1–7	1–13	1–20	8–20	8–23	8–26	14–23	14–26
0	10(16)	10(16)	10(16)					
1	23(16)	22(15)	22(15)	57(11)	57(11)	57(11)	91(11)	91(11)
2	42(12)	39(11)	39(11)	67(9)	67(9)	67(9)	99(8)	99(8)
3	53(9)	48(9)	48(9)	73(8)	73(8)	73(8)	105(7)	105(7)
4	61(8)	55(7)	55(7)	78(7)	78(7)	78(7)	109(6)	109(6)
5	67(7)	60(7)	59(7)	83(6)	82(6)	82(6)	113(6)	113(6)
6	72(7)	63(6)	63(6)	86(6)	86(6)	86(6)	117(6)	116(6)
7	76(7)	67(6)	67(6)	89(6)	89(6)	89(6)	120(6)	119(5)
8	81(7)	70(5)	70(5)	92(5)	92(5)	92(5)	123(5)	122(5)
9	85(7)	73(5)	72(5)	95(5)	95(5)	95(5)	126(5)	125(5)
10	91(7)	75(5)	75(5)	98(5)	98(5)	98(5)	129(5)	128(5)
11	97(8)	78(5)	77(5)	101(5)	101(5)	101(5)	131(5)	130(5)
12	104(9)	80(5)	80(5)	104(5)	103(5)	103(5)	134(6)	133(5)
13	115(12)	83(5)	82(5)	106(5)	106(5)	106(5)	138(6)	136(5)
14		85(5)	84(5)	109(5)	109(5)	109(5)	141(6)	138(5)
15		87(5)	86(5)	112(5)	111(5)	111(5)	145(6)	141(5)
16		90(5)	88(4)	114(5)	114(5)	114(5)	149(7)	144(5)
17		92(5)	90(4)	117(5)	116(5)	116(5)	154(7)	147(5)
18		94(5)	92(4)	120(5)	119(5)	119(5)	160(8)	150(5)
19		97(5)	94(4)	123(5)	122(5)	121(5)	169(11)	153(6)
20		100(5)	96(4)	126(6)	124(5)	124(5)		156(6)
21		103(6)	98(4)	129(6)	127(5)	126(5)		159(6)
22		106(6)	100(4)	133(6)	129(5)	129(5)		163(6)
23		110(7)	102(5)	137(7)	132(5)	131(5)		167(7)
24		115(8)	104(5)	142(8)	135(5)	134(5)		172(8)
25		124(11)	106(5)	150(11)	138(6)	136(5)		180(11)
26			108(5)		141(6)	139(5)		191(16)
27			110(5)		145(6)	141(5)		
28			112(5)		149(7)	144(5)		
29			115(5)		154(7)	147(5)		
30			117(5)		160(8)	150(5)		
31			119(5)		169(11)	153(5)		
32			122(5)			156(6)		
33			124(5)			159(6)		
34			127(5)			163(6)		
35			130(6)			167(7)		
36			133(6)			172(8)		
37			137(7)			180(11)		
38			142(8)			191(16)		
39			150(10)					

Figure 7.1. Raw-Score-to-Ability-Score Tables *(Continued)*

Naming Vocabulary
Raw Score to Ability Score

Raw Score	Item Set		
	1–16	1–26	8–26
0	10(13)	10(13)	
1	20(12)	20(12)	52(11)
2	28(9)	28(9)	60(8)
3	35(8)	35(8)	66(7)
4	42(8)	42(8)	71(7)
5	47(7)	47(7)	75(7)
6	52(7)	52(7)	79(7)
7	57(7)	57(7)	84(7)
8	61(7)	61(6)	88(7)
9	66(6)	65(6)	93(7)
10	70(6)	69(6)	98(7)
11	74(6)	73(6)	103(7)
12	78(7)	76(6)	108(7)
13	83(7)	80(6)	113(7)
14	88(8)	84(6)	119(8)
15	97(11)	89(7)	125(8)
16		93(7)	133(9)
17		98(7)	143(10)
18		103(7)	156(12)
19		108(7)	169(16)
20		113(7)	
21		119(8)	
22		125(8)	
23		133(9)	
24		143(10)	
25		156(12)	
26		169(16)	

Early Number Concepts
Raw Score to Ability Score

Raw Score	Item Set					
	1–6	1–15	1–22	2–22	2–28	16–28
0	10(14)	10(14)	10(14)			
1	19(12)	19(12)	19(12)	36(11)	36(11)	82(11)
2	30(9)	29(9)	29(9)	46(9)	46(9)	90(8)
3	37(8)	36(8)	36(8)	53(8)	53(8)	96(7)
4	42(7)	41(7)	41(7)	58(7)	58(7)	101(7)
5	47(7)	46(7)	46(7)	63(7)	63(7)	105(7)
6	52(7)	50(6)	50(6)	68(6)	67(6)	110(6)
7	57(7)	54(6)	54(6)	71(6)	71(6)	114(7)
8	62(8)	57(6)	57(6)	75(6)	75(6)	118(7)
9	69(9)	61(6)	61(6)	78(6)	78(6)	123(7)
10	78(11)	65(6)	64(6)	81(6)	81(6)	129(8)
11		68(6)	67(6)	84(6)	84(5)	136(9)
12		71(6)	70(6)	88(6)	87(5)	145(11)
13		75(6)	73(5)	91(6)	90(5)	154(16)
14		78(6)	76(5)	94(6)	93(5)	
15		82(6)	79(5)	97(6)	96(5)	
16		86(6)	82(5)	101(6)	99(5)	
17		90(7)	85(5)	105(6)	102(6)	
18		96(8)	88(5)	109(7)	105(6)	
19		104(11)	91(6)	115(8)	108(6)	
20			94(6)	123(11)	112(6)	
21			97(6)		115(6)	
22			101(6)		119(7)	
23			105(6)		124(7)	
24			109(7)		129(8)	
25			115(8)		136(9)	
26			123(11)		146(11)	
27					154(16)	

Figure 7.1. Raw-Score-to-Ability-Score Tables *(Continued)*

Recall of Digits
Raw Score to
Ability Score

Raw Score	Item Set 1–36
0	10(15)
1	18(11)
2	27(9)
3	34(8)
4	41(8)
5	47(8)
6	54(8)
7	60(8)
8	66(8)
9	72(8)
10	78(8)
11	84(8)
12	90(8)
13	96(7)
14	102(7)
15	107(7)
16	112(7)
17	117(7)
18	122(7)
19	126(7)
20	131(7)
21	135(7)
22	139(7)
23	143(6)
24	147(6)
25	151(6)
26	155(6)
27	159(6)
28	163(6)
29	167(6)
30	171(7)
31	176(7)
32	181(7)
33	186(8)
34	193(9)
35	202(11)
36	211(16)

Recall of Objects—Immediate
Raw Score to Ability Score

Raw Score	Item Set 1–60	Raw Score	Item Set 1–60
0	10(27)	31	139(6)
1	19(11)	32	143(6)
2	28(8)	33	146(6)
3	34(8)	34	150(6)
4	40(7)	35	154(6)
5	44(7)	36	158(6)
6	49(7)	37	162(6)
7	53(6)	38	165(6)
8	57(6)	39	169(6)
9	61(6)	40	173(6)
10	66(6)	41	177(6)
11	69(6)	42	181(6)
12	73(6)	43	185(6)
13	77(6)	44	189(6)
14	81(6)	45	193(6)
15	85(6)	46	197(6)
16	88(6)	47	201(6)
17	92(6)	48	205(7)
18	95(6)	49	209(7)
19	99(6)	50	214(7)
20	102(6)	51	219(7)
21	106(6)	52	223(7)
22	109(6)	53	229(7)
23	112(6)	54	234(8)
24	115(6)	55	240(8)
25	119(6)	56	247(8)
26	122(6)	57	255(9)
27	125(6)	58	264(10)
28	129(6)	59	275(12)
29	132(6)	60	285(14)
30	136(6)		

Figure 7.1. Raw-Score-to-Ability-Score Tables *(Continued)*

Matching Letter-Like Forms
Raw Score to Ability Score

Raw Score	Item Set 1–20	1–27	10–27
0	10(12)	10(12)	
1	18(10)	18(10)	24(10)
2	24(8)	24(8)	32(8)
3	27(7)	26(7)	37(6)
4	29(6)	28(6)	41(6)
5	31(6)	30(5)	44(5)
6	34(5)	33(5)	47(5)
7	36(5)	35(5)	49(5)
8	39(5)	37(5)	52(5)
9	41(5)	39(5)	54(5)
10	43(5)	41(4)	57(5)
11	46(5)	43(4)	59(5)
12	48(5)	45(4)	62(5)
13	50(5)	47(4)	65(6)
14	53(5)	49(4)	68(6)
15	56(5)	51(4)	72(7)
16	59(6)	53(4)	77(8)
17	62(6)	55(4)	85(10)
18	67(8)	57(5)	93(16)
19	75(10)	59(5)	
20		61(5)	
21		64(5)	
22		66(5)	
23		69(6)	
24		73(6)	
25		78(8)	
26		86(10)	
27		93(16)	

Recall of Designs
Raw Score to Ability Score

Raw Score	Item Set 1–12	1–16	4–16	4–21	9–21
0	10(15)	10(15)			
1	21(13)	21(13)	42(11)	42(11)	58(11)
2	33(9)	33(9)	50(8)	50(8)	66(8)
3	40(8)	40(8)	56(7)	55(7)	72(7)
4	46(7)	46(7)	60(6)	60(6)	77(6)
5	50(6)	50(6)	64(6)	63(6)	81(6)
6	54(6)	54(6)	67(6)	66(5)	84(6)
7	58(6)	57(6)	70(5)	69(5)	87(5)
8	61(6)	60(5)	73(5)	72(5)	90(5)
9	64(5)	63(5)	75(5)	75(5)	93(5)
10	67(5)	66(5)	78(5)	77(5)	95(5)
11	69(5)	68(5)	81(5)	79(5)	98(5)
12	72(5)	71(5)	83(5)	82(5)	100(5)
13	74(5)	73(5)	86(5)	84(5)	102(5)
14	77(5)	75(5)	88(5)	86(5)	104(5)
15	80(5)	78(5)	91(5)	88(5)	107(5)
16	82(5)	80(5)	93(5)	90(5)	109(5)
17	85(5)	82(5)	96(5)	92(4)	111(5)
18	88(6)	85(5)	99(5)	94(4)	113(5)
19	92(6)	87(5)	101(5)	96(4)	116(5)
20	96(6)	89(5)	104(6)	98(4)	118(5)
21	100(7)	92(5)	108(6)	100(4)	120(5)
22	106(8)	94(5)	111(6)	102(4)	123(5)
23	114(11)	96(5)	116(7)	104(4)	126(5)
24		99(5)	121(8)	106(4)	129(5)
25		102(5)	130(11)	108(4)	132(6)
26		105(6)		110(4)	135(6)
27		108(6)		112(5)	139(6)
28		112(6)		114(5)	144(7)
29		116(7)		116(5)	150(8)
30		121(8)		119(5)	158(11)
31		130(11)		121(5)	169(15)
32				123(5)	
33				126(5)	
34				129(5)	
35				132(6)	
36				135(6)	
37				139(6)	
38				144(7)	
39				150(8)	
40				158(11)	
41				169(15)	

Figure 7.1. Raw-Score-to-Ability-Score Tables *(Continued)*

Word Definitions
Raw Score to Ability Score

Raw Score	Item Set 1–21	1–25	4–25	4–34	12–34	12–42
0	10(15)	10(15)				
1	18(12)	18(12)	33(11)	33(11)	49(10)	49(10)
2	29(9)	28(9)	41(8)	41(8)	57(8)	57(8)
3	36(8)	35(8)	47(7)	47(7)	62(7)	62(7)
4	41(7)	41(7)	51(6)	51(6)	66(6)	66(6)
5	45(6)	45(6)	54(6)	54(6)	70(6)	70(6)
6	49(6)	49(6)	57(5)	57(5)	73(5)	73(5)
7	53(6)	52(6)	60(5)	60(5)	76(5)	76(5)
8	56(5)	55(5)	62(5)	62(5)	78(5)	78(5)
9	59(5)	58(5)	65(5)	65(5)	81(5)	81(5)
10	61(5)	60(5)	67(5)	67(5)	84(5)	84(5)
11	64(5)	63(5)	70(5)	69(5)	87(5)	87(5)
12	67(5)	65(5)	72(5)	71(5)	90(5)	90(5)
13	69(5)	68(5)	74(5)	74(5)	93(6)	93(6)
14	72(5)	70(5)	77(5)	76(5)	96(6)	96(6)
15	75(5)	72(5)	79(5)	78(5)	99(6)	99(6)
16	78(6)	75(5)	82(6)	81(5)	103(6)	103(6)
17	81(6)	77(5)	85(6)	83(5)	107(6)	106(6)
18	85(7)	80(5)	88(6)	85(5)	111(6)	110(6)
19	90(8)	82(5)	92(7)	88(5)	115(7)	113(6)
20	98(10)	85(6)	97(8)	91(5)	120(7)	117(6)
21		88(6)	105(10)	94(5)	126(8)	121(6)
22		92(7)		97(6)	134(11)	126(7)
23		97(8)		100(6)		130(7)
24		105(10)		103(6)		135(7)
25				107(6)		140(7)
26				111(6)		145(7)
27				115(7)		151(8)
28				120(7)		157(8)
29				126(8)		164(9)
30				134(11)		174(11)
31						185(15)

Matrices
Raw Score to Ability Score

Raw Score	Item Set 1–14	1–23	5–23	5–33	15–33
0	10(15)	10(15)			
1	18(11)	18(11)	43(11)	42(11)	76(11)
2	28(9)	28(9)	52(9)	52(9)	84(8)
3	36(8)	36(8)	59(8)	59(8)	89(7)
4	43(8)	42(8)	65(7)	65(7)	94(6)
5	49(8)	49(8)	70(7)	70(7)	97(6)
6	56(8)	55(8)	74(6)	74(6)	101(6)
7	62(8)	60(7)	78(6)	77(6)	104(5)
8	68(8)	66(7)	82(6)	81(6)	107(5)
9	73(7)	70(7)	85(6)	84(6)	110(5)
10	78(7)	74(6)	88(6)	87(5)	112(5)
11	84(8)	78(6)	91(6)	90(5)	115(5)
12	90(8)	82(6)	95(6)	92(5)	118(6)
13	99(11)	85(6)	98(6)	95(5)	122(6)
14		88(6)	101(6)	98(5)	125(6)
15		91(6)	105(6)	100(5)	129(6)
16		95(6)	109(7)	103(5)	133(7)
17		98(6)	115(8)	105(5)	139(8)
18		101(6)	123(11)	108(5)	148(11)
19		105(6)		111(5)	156(17)
20		109(7)		113(5)	
21		115(8)		116(5)	
22		123(11)		119(5)	
23				122(6)	
24				125(6)	
25				129(6)	
26				134(7)	
27				139(8)	
28				148(11)	
29				156(17)	

Figure 7.1. Raw-Score-to-Ability-Score Tables *(Continued)*

157

Sequential and Quantitative Reasoning
Raw Score to Ability Score

Raw Score	Item Set								
	1–15	1–23	1–30	8–23	8–30	8–39	16–30	16–39	24–39
0	10(13)	10(13)	10(13)						
1	13(11)	12(11)	12(11)						
2	21(8)	21(8)	20(8)						
3	27(7)	26(7)	26(7)	48(7)	47(7)	47(7)	60(7)	59(7)	81(7)
4	32(7)	31(7)	31(7)	52(6)	51(6)	51(6)	64(7)	64(6)	86(7)
5	37(7)	35(6)	35(6)	55(6)	54(5)	54(5)	68(6)	68(6)	90(6)
6	41(7)	39(6)	38(6)	58(5)	57(5)	57(5)	72(6)	71(6)	94(6)
7	45(6)	42(6)	42(6)	61(5)	60(5)	60(5)	75(6)	74(6)	98(6)
8	49(6)	46(6)	45(6)	64(5)	62(5)	62(5)	79(6)	78(6)	102(6)
9	53(6)	49(5)	48(5)	67(5)	65(5)	65(5)	82(6)	81(6)	106(6)
10	58(6)	52(5)	51(5)	70(5)	67(5)	67(5)	86(6)	84(5)	110(7)
11	62(7)	54(5)	54(5)	73(6)	69(5)	69(5)	90(6)	87(6)	114(7)
12	67(7)	57(5)	56(5)	76(6)	72(5)	71(5)	94(7)	90(6)	119(7)
13		60(5)	59(5)	80(7)	74(5)	74(5)		93(6)	124(8)
14		62(5)	61(5)		77(5)	76(5)		96(6)	131(9)
15		65(5)	63(5)		79(5)	78(5)		99(6)	142(12)
16		67(5)	65(5)		82(5)	81(5)		103(6)	152(16)
17		70(5)	68(5)		85(5)	83(5)		107(6)	
18		73(6)	70(5)		88(6)	86(5)		111(6)	
19		77(6)	72(5)		91(6)	88(5)		115(7)	
20		81(7)	74(5)		95(7)	91(5)		119(7)	
21			77(5)			94(5)		125(8)	
22			79(5)			97(6)		132(9)	
23			82(5)			100(6)		142(12)	
24			85(5)			103(6)		152(16)	
25			88(6)			107(6)			
26			91(6)			111(6)			
27			96(7)			115(7)			
28						119(7)			
29						125(8)			
30						132(9)			
31						142(12)			
32						152(16)			

Figure 7.1. Raw-Score-to-Ability-Score Tables *(Continued)*

Similarities
Raw Score to Ability Score

Raw Score	1–17	1–27	8–27	8–34	13–34
0	10(15)	10(15)			
1	19(11)	19(11)	42(11)	42(11)	61(11)
2	26(8)	26(8)	52(9)	52(9)	69(8)
3	32(7)	32(7)	58(8)	58(8)	74(7)
4	37(7)	37(7)	64(7)	64(7)	79(6)
5	42(7)	41(7)	68(6)	68(6)	83(6)
6	46(7)	46(6)	72(6)	72(6)	86(6)
7	50(7)	50(6)	76(6)	75(6)	89(5)
8	54(7)	54(6)	79(6)	79(6)	92(5)
9	59(7)	58(6)	83(6)	82(5)	95(5)
10	63(7)	62(6)	86(6)	85(5)	98(5)
11	68(7)	66(6)	89(6)	88(5)	100(5)
12	72(7)	70(6)	92(6)	90(5)	103(5)
13	76(7)	73(6)	95(6)	93(5)	105(5)
14	81(7)	76(6)	98(6)	96(5)	108(5)
15	87(8)	80(6)	101(6)	98(5)	110(5)
16	96(11)	83(6)	105(6)	100(5)	112(5)
17		86(6)	108(6)	103(5)	115(5)
18		89(6)	113(7)	105(5)	117(5)
19		92(6)	117(7)	108(5)	120(5)
20		95(6)	124(8)	110(5)	123(5)
21		98(6)	133(11)	113(5)	126(5)
22		101(6)		115(5)	129(6)
23		105(6)		117(5)	132(6)
24		108(6)		120(5)	136(6)
25		113(7)		123(5)	140(7)
26		117(7)		126(5)	146(8)
27		124(8)		129(6)	155(11)
28		133(11)		132(6)	165(15)
29				136(6)	
30				140(7)	
31				146(8)	
32				155(11)	
33				165(15)	

Speed of Information Processing
Raw Score to Ability Score

Raw Score	1–6	7–12	13–18
0	10(15)	56(17)	124(15)
1	20(12)	69(12)	134(12)
2	32(10)	80(10)	144(9)
3	40(9)	89(9)	152(8)
4	47(8)	96(8)	158(7)
5	52(7)	102(8)	163(7)
6	57(7)	108(7)	168(7)
7	61(6)	113(7)	172(6)
8	65(6)	118(7)	176(6)
9	69(6)	123(7)	180(6)
10	73(6)	127(7)	183(6)
11	76(6)	132(7)	187(6)
12	79(6)	136(7)	190(6)
13	82(6)	140(7)	193(6)
14	86(6)	145(7)	197(6)
15	89(6)	149(6)	200(6)
16	92(6)	153(6)	203(6)
17	95(6)	157(6)	207(6)
18	98(6)	161(6)	210(6)
19	101(6)	165(6)	213(6)
20	104(6)	168(6)	216(6)
21	107(6)	172(6)	220(6)
22	110(6)	176(6)	223(6)
23	114(6)	179(6)	227(6)
24	117(6)	183(6)	230(6)
25	121(6)	188(7)	234(6)
26	124(6)	192(7)	238(6)
27	128(6)	197(7)	242(6)
28	133(7)	203(8)	246(7)
29	137(7)	209(8)	251(7)
30	142(7)	216(9)	256(7)
31	148(8)	224(9)	262(8)
32	154(8)	231(9)	269(9)
33	160(8)	241(10)	278(10)
34	169(10)	254(13)	289(11)
35	180(12)	271(13)	304(13)
36	191(18)	285(19)	325(26)

Figure 7.1. Raw-Score-to-Ability-Score Tables *(Continued)*

Word Reading
Raw Score to Ability Score

Raw Score	Item Set 1–90	21–90	41–90	51–90
0	10(14)			
1	16(11)	44(10)	67(10)	81(10)
2	24(8)	52(7)	75(8)	88(8)
3	29(7)	57(6)	79(6)	93(6)
4	33(6)	60(6)	83(6)	97(6)
5	37(6)	63(5)	86(5)	100(5)
6	40(5)	65(5)	89(5)	102(5)
7	42(5)	67(5)	91(5)	105(5)
8	45(5)	69(4)	93(5)	107(5)
9	47(5)	71(4)	95(4)	110(5)
10	49(4)	73(4)	97(4)	112(5)
11	51(4)	74(4)	99(4)	114(5)
12	53(4)	76(4)	101(4)	116(5)
13	54(4)	77(4)	102(4)	119(5)
14	56(4)	79(4)	104(4)	121(5)
15	58(4)	80(4)	106(4)	123(5)
16	59(4)	82(4)	107(4)	126(5)
17	61(4)	83(4)	109(4)	129(5)
18	62(4)	84(4)	111(4)	131(5)
19	63(4)	86(4)	113(4)	134(5)
20	65(4)	87(4)	114(4)	137(5)
21	66(4)	88(4)	116(4)	140(5)
22	67(4)	90(4)	118(4)	143(5)
23	68(4)	91(4)	120(5)	145(5)
24	70(3)	92(4)	122(5)	148(5)
25	71(3)	94(4)	124(5)	151(5)
26	72(3)	95(4)	127(5)	153(5)
27	73(3)	96(4)	129(5)	156(5)
28	74(3)	98(4)	132(5)	158(5)
29	76(3)	99(4)	135(5)	161(5)
30	77(3)	100(4)	137(5)	164(5)
31	78(3)	102(4)	140(5)	166(5)
32	79(3)	103(4)	143(5)	169(5)
33	80(3)	105(4)	146(5)	172(5)
34	81(3)	106(4)	148(5)	175(6)
35	82(3)	107(4)	151(5)	178(6)
36	84(3)	109(4)	153(5)	182(7)
37	85(3)	110(4)	156(5)	187(7)
38	86(3)	112(4)	158(5)	193(8)
39	87(3)	114(4)	161(5)	202(11)
40	88(3)	115(4)	164(5)	212(15)
41	89(3)	117(4)	166(5)	
42	91(3)	119(4)	169(5)	
43	92(3)	121(4)	172(5)	
44	93(4)	123(5)	175(6)	
45	94(4)	125(5)	178(6)	
46	96(4)	127(5)	182(7)	
47	97(4)	130(5)	187(7)	
48	98(4)	132(5)	193(8)	
49	99(4)	135(5)	202(11)	
50	101(4)	137(5)	212(15)	
51	102(4)	140(5)		
52	103(4)	143(5)		
53	105(4)	146(5)		
54	106(4)	148(5)		
55	108(4)	151(5)		
56	109(4)	153(5)		
57	111(4)	156(5)		
58	112(4)	159(5)		
59	114(4)	161(5)		
60	115(4)	164(5)		
61	117(4)	166(5)		
62	119(4)	169(5)		
63	121(4)	172(5)		
64	123(5)	175(6)		
65	125(5)	178(6)		
66	127(5)	182(7)		
67	130(5)	187(7)		
68	132(5)	193(8)		
69	135(5)	202(11)		
70	137(5)	212(15)		
71	140(5)			
72	143(5)			
73	146(5)			
74	148(5)			
75	151(5)			
76	153(5)			
77	156(5)			
78	159(5)			
79	161(5)			
80	164(5)			
81	166(5)			
82	169(5)			
83	172(5)			
84	175(6)			
85	178(6)			
86	182(7)			
87	187(7)			
88	193(8)			
89	202(11)			
90	212(15)			

Figure 7.1. Raw-Score-to-Ability-Score Tables (*Continued*)

Basic Number Skills
Raw Score to Ability Score

Raw Score								Item Set						
	1-8	1-16	1-24	1-32	9-24	9-32	9-40	17-32	17-40	17-48	25-40	25-48	33-48	41-48
0	10(16)	10(16)	10(16)	10(16)	78(12)	78(12)	78(12)	118(11)	118(11)	118(11)	153(11)	153(11)	170(11)	194(11)
1	20(11)	20(11)	20(11)	20(11)	89(9)	89(9)	89(9)	128(9)	128(9)	128(9)	161(8)	161(8)	178(8)	204(9)
2	31(9)	30(9)	30(9)	30(9)	96(8)	96(8)	96(8)	135(8)	135(8)	135(8)	167(7)	166(7)	184(7)	211(8)
3	39(9)	39(9)	39(9)	39(9)	103(8)	103(8)	103(8)	141(8)	141(8)	141(8)	171(6)	170(6)	188(7)	218(8)
4	48(10)	47(9)	47(9)	47(9)	108(7)	108(7)	108(7)	147(7)	146(7)	146(7)	174(6)	174(6)	192(6)	224(8)
5	58(10)	56(9)	56(9)	56(9)	113(7)	113(7)	113(7)	152(7)	152(7)	151(7)	178(6)	177(5)	196(6)	232(9)
6	68(11)	65(9)	65(9)	65(9)	118(7)	118(7)	118(7)	157(7)	156(7)	156(7)	181(6)	180(5)	200(6)	242(11)
7	82(13)	73(9)	73(9)	73(9)	123(7)	123(7)	123(7)	162(7)	160(6)	160(6)	184(6)	183(5)	204(6)	253(16)
8		80(8)	80(8)	80(8)	128(7)	127(7)	127(7)	166(6)	164(6)	164(6)	187(6)	186(5)	207(6)	
9		87(8)	87(8)	87(8)	133(7)	132(7)	132(7)	170(6)	167(6)	167(6)	190(6)	188(5)	212(6)	
10		93(8)	93(8)	93(8)	139(8)	137(7)	137(7)	174(6)	170(5)	170(5)	193(6)	191(5)	216(7)	
11		99(8)	98(7)	98(7)	145(8)	143(7)	142(7)	179(7)	173(5)	173(5)	197(7)	194(5)	221(7)	
12		105(8)	104(7)	104(7)	151(8)	148(7)	147(7)	184(7)	176(5)	176(5)	201(7)	196(5)	226(8)	
13		111(8)	109(7)	109(7)	159(9)	153(7)	152(7)	189(8)	179(5)	178(5)	207(8)	199(5)	233(9)	
14		118(9)	113(7)	113(7)	169(11)	158(7)	156(6)	198(11)	182(5)	181(5)	215(11)	202(6)	243(11)	
15		127(11)	118(7)	118(7)		162(7)	160(6)		185(5)	184(5)		205(6)	253(16)	
16			123(7)	123(7)		166(6)	164(6)		188(5)	186(5)		209(6)		
17			128(7)	128(7)		170(6)	167(6)		191(6)	189(5)		213(6)		
18			133(7)	132(7)		174(6)	170(6)		194(5)	191(5)		217(7)		
19			139(8)	138(7)		179(7)	173(5)		197(6)	194(5)		221(7)		
20			145(8)	143(7)		184(7)	176(5)		201(7)	197(5)		227(8)		
21			151(8)	148(7)		189(8)	179(5)		207(8)	199(5)		234(9)		
22			159(9)	153(7)		198(11)	182(5)		215(11)	202(6)		243(11)		
23			169(11)	158(7)			185(5)			206(6)		253(16)		
24				162(7)			188(5)			209(6)				
25				166(6)			191(6)			213(6)				
26				170(6)			194(6)			217(7)				
27				174(6)			197(6)			221(7)				
28				179(7)			201(7)			227(8)				
29				184(7)			207(8)			234(9)				
30				189(8)			215(11)			243(11)				
31				198(11)						253(16)				
32														

Figure 7.1. Raw-Score-to-Ability-Score Tables (*Continued*)

Spelling
Raw Score to Ability Score

Raw Score					Item Set												Raw Score
	1-7*	1-14*	1-21*	1-28*	8-21	8-28	8-35	8-42	15-28	15-35	15-42	15-49	22-35	22-42	22-49	22-56	
0	10(17)	10(17)	10(17)	10(17)	76(10)	74(10)	74(10)	74(10)	83(10)	82(10)	82(10)	82(10)	92(11)	92(11)	92(10)	92(10)	0
1	27(16)	27(16)	27(16)	27(16)	84(8)	82(8)	81(8)	81(8)	91(8)	90(8)	90(8)	90(8)	101(8)	100(8)	100(8)	100(8)	1
2	49(13)	48(13)	48(12)	48(12)	89(7)	87(6)	86(6)	86(6)	96(7)	95(6)	95(6)	95(6)	106(7)	105(7)	105(7)	105(7)	2
3	62(10)	60(10)	60(10)	60(10)	93(6)	90(6)	90(6)	90(6)	100(6)	99(6)	98(6)	98(6)	110(6)	109(6)	109(6)	109(6)	3
4	71(9)	68(8)	67(8)	67(8)	96(6)	93(5)	93(5)	93(5)	104(6)	102(5)	102(5)	102(5)	114(6)	113(6)	113(6)	113(6)	4
5	77(8)	74(7)	73(7)	72(7)	99(6)	96(5)	95(5)	95(5)	107(5)	105(5)	104(5)	104(5)	117(6)	116(6)	116(5)	116(5)	5
6	83(7)	78(6)	77(6)	76(6)	102(5)	98(5)	98(5)	97(5)	110(5)	107(5)	107(5)	107(5)	121(6)	119(5)	119(5)	119(5)	6
7	89(8)	82(6)	80(6)	79(6)	105(6)	101(5)	100(5)	100(5)	113(6)	110(5)	109(5)	109(5)	124(6)	122(5)	122(5)	121(5)	7
8	95(8)	86(6)	83(5)	82(5)	108(6)	103(5)	102(4)	102(4)	116(6)	112(5)	111(5)	111(5)	128(6)	125(6)	124(5)	124(5)	8
9	104(11)	89(6)	86(5)	85(5)	112(6)	105(5)	104(4)	103(4)	119(7)	114(5)	114(5)	114(5)	132(6)	128(5)	127(5)	127(5)	9
10		92(6)	89(5)	87(5)	116(7)	107(5)	106(4)	105(4)	123(7)	117(5)	116(5)	116(5)	136(7)	131(5)	130(5)	129(5)	10
11		95(6)	91(5)	90(5)	121(8)	109(5)	107(4)	107(4)	128(8)	119(5)	118(5)	118(5)	142(8)	133(5)	132(5)	132(5)	11
12		99(6)	93(5)	92(5)	129(10)	111(5)	109(4)	109(4)	136(10)	122(5)	120(5)	120(5)	150(11)	136(5)	135(5)	134(5)	12
13		102(6)	96(5)	94(4)		114(5)	111(4)	111(4)		124(5)	123(5)	122(5)		139(6)	137(5)	137(5)	13
14		106(7)	98(5)	96(4)		116(5)	113(4)	112(4)		127(5)	125(5)	124(5)		142(6)	140(5)	139(5)	14
15		112(8)	100(5)	98(4)		119(5)	115(4)	114(4)		130(5)	127(5)	127(5)		146(6)	142(5)	141(5)	15
16		120(11)	103(5)	99(4)		122(6)	117(4)	116(4)		133(6)	130(5)	129(5)		150(6)	145(5)	144(5)	16
17			105(5)	101(4)		125(6)	119(5)	118(4)		138(7)	132(5)	131(5)		154(7)	147(5)	146(5)	17
18			108(5)	103(4)		130(8)	121(5)	120(4)		143(8)	135(5)	133(5)		159(8)	150(5)	148(5)	18
19			110(5)	105(4)		138(10)	123(5)	122(4)		151(11)	137(5)	136(5)		168(11)	152(5)	151(5)	19
20			113(6)	107(4)			125(5)	124(5)			140(5)	138(5)			155(5)	153(5)	20
21			117(6)	108(4)			128(5)	126(5)			143(6)	140(5)			158(5)	155(5)	21
22			122(8)	110(4)			131(6)	128(5)			146(6)	143(5)			161(6)	158(5)	22
23			130(10)	112(5)			134(6)	130(5)			150(6)	145(5)			164(6)	160(5)	23
24				114(5)			138(7)	133(5)			154(7)	148(5)			168(7)	162(5)	24
25				117(5)			143(8)	135(5)			159(8)	150(5)			174(8)	165(5)	25
26				119(5)			151(10)	138(5)			168(11)	153(5)			182(11)	167(5)	26
27				122(6)				140(5)				156(5)				170(5)	27
28				126(6)				143(6)				159(6)				173(5)	28
29				130(8)				146(6)				162(6)				176(6)	29
30				138(10)				150(6)				166(7)				179(6)	30
31								154(7)				171(8)				183(7)	31
32								160(8)				178(9)				189(8)	32
33								168(11)				191(13)				197(10)	33
34																	34
35																	35

Figure 7.1. Raw-Score-to-Ability-Score Tables (*Continued*)

Raw Score	Item Set															Raw Score
	29-42	29-49	29-56	29-63	36-49	36-56	36-63	36-70	43-56	43-63	43-70	50-63	50-70	57-70	64-70	
0																0
1	108(11)	107(11)	107(11)	107(11)	125(11)	124(10)	124(10)	124(10)	138(11)	138(11)	138(11)	154(11)	154(11)	171(11)	198(12)	1
2	116(8)	116(8)	115(8)	115(8)	133(8)	132(8)	132(8)	132(8)	146(8)	146(8)	146(8)	162(8)	162(8)	180(8)	209(10)	2
3	122(7)	121(7)	121(7)	121(7)	138(7)	137(7)	137(7)	137(7)	152(7)	151(7)	151(7)	168(7)	167(7)	186(7)	218(9)	3
4	126(6)	126(6)	126(6)	125(6)	142(6)	141(6)	141(6)	141(6)	156(6)	156(6)	155(6)	172(6)	172(6)	191(7)	227(10)	4
5	130(6)	129(6)	129(6)	129(6)	146(6)	145(6)	145(6)	145(6)	160(6)	159(6)	159(6)	176(6)	175(6)	196(7)	236(10)	5
6	134(6)	132(6)	132(6)	132(6)	150(6)	148(5)	148(5)	148(5)	164(6)	162(6)	162(6)	180(6)	179(6)	201(7)	248(12)	6
7	138(6)	135(5)	135(5)	135(5)	153(6)	151(5)	150(5)	150(5)	167(6)	165(5)	165(5)	183(6)	182(6)	205(7)	260(16)	7
8	141(6)	138(5)	138(5)	138(5)	156(6)	154(5)	153(5)	153(5)	171(6)	168(5)	168(5)	187(6)	185(6)	210(7)		8
9	145(6)	141(5)	140(5)	140(5)	160(6)	156(5)	156(5)	156(5)	174(6)	171(5)	171(5)	190(6)	189(6)	216(8)		9
10	149(6)	144(5)	143(5)	143(5)	163(6)	159(5)	158(5)	158(5)	178(6)	174(5)	173(5)	195(7)	192(6)	222(8)		10
11	153(7)	146(5)	145(5)	145(5)	168(7)	161(5)	161(5)	160(5)	182(7)	176(5)	176(5)	199(7)	195(6)	229(9)		11
12	159(8)	149(5)	148(5)	148(5)	173(8)	164(5)	163(5)	163(5)	188(8)	179(5)	179(5)	205(8)	199(6)	237(10)		12
13	167(11)	152(5)	150(5)	150(5)	181(11)	167(5)	165(5)	165(5)	196(11)	182(5)	181(5)	214(11)	203(6)	249(12)		13
14		155(5)	153(5)	152(5)		170(5)	168(5)	167(5)		185(5)	184(5)		207(7)	260(16)		14
15		158(6)	155(5)	154(5)		172(5)	170(5)	170(5)		188(6)	187(5)		211(7)			15
16		161(6)	157(5)	157(5)		176(6)	172(5)	172(5)		192(6)	190(5)		216(7)			16
17		164(6)	160(5)	159(5)		179(6)	175(5)	175(5)		196(7)	193(6)		222(8)			17
18		168(7)	162(5)	161(5)		183(7)	177(5)	177(5)		200(7)	196(6)		229(9)			18
19		174(8)	165(5)	163(5)		188(8)	180(5)	179(5)		206(8)	199(6)		238(10)			19
20		182(11)	167(5)	166(5)		196(10)	183(5)	182(5)		214(11)	203(6)		249(12)			20
21			170(5)	168(5)			186(5)	185(5)			207(6)		260(16)			21
22			173(5)	170(5)			189(6)	187(5)			211(7)					22
23			176(6)	173(5)			192(6)	190(5)			216(7)					23
24			179(6)	175(5)			196(6)	193(6)			222(8)					24
25			183(7)	178(5)			200(7)	196(6)			229(9)					25
26			188(8)	180(5)			206(8)	199(6)			238(10)					26
27			197(11)	183(5)			214(11)	203(6)			249(12)					27
28				186(5)				207(6)			260(16)					28
29				189(6)				211(7)								29
30				192(6)				216(7)								30
31				196(6)				222(8)								31
32				200(7)				229(9)								32
33				206(8)				238(10)								33
34				214(11)				249(12)								34
35								260(16)								35

*Includes Name Item

Figure 7.1. Raw-Score-to-Ability-Score Tables *(Continued)*

163

The tables also provide the standard error of each ability score. The standard error is relatively small for raw scores near the middle of the range because an examinee at that level of ability has encountered many items that are near his or her ability level. If the examinee's ability is near either end of the raw-score range, then few appropriately difficult items were administered, and the standard error is high.

Portions of each raw-score-to-ability-score table are shaded, and some cells that represent possible raw scores are blank. The scores in the shaded areas are relatively inaccurate because they reflect improper item selection during administration. If the Decision Point rules are followed, a perfect or nearly perfect score should occur only if the child has taken the hardest items of the subtest, and a score near 0 should occur only if the child has been given the easiest items. Blank cells occur for raw scores of 0 if easier items could have been administered, or for maximum raw scores if harder items could have been given; ability estimates for such raw scores would be much less accurate than for scores obtained from correct item selection.

Development of Norms

Age norms for all of the subtests (including the achievement tests) and for the composite scores are based on a sample of 3,475 children who had valid scores on all of the subtests, with one exception. A small number of children (about 6%) were included for whom the delayed trial of the Recall of Objects subtest could not be used because the length of the delay was outside acceptable limits. These cases were retained because the delayed-trial score is a secondary measure in the battery.

Subtest Norms

The first step in norms development was to convert cognitive subtest ability scores to normalized standard T scores. A parallel procedure was followed to develop standard-score age norms for the achievement tests. For each half-year (ages 2:6–4:11) or one-year (ages 5:0–17:11) age group, mid-interval percentile values were computed for each ability score and were transformed to the T scores corresponding to that area under the normal curve. The ability scores corresponding to every fifth value of T, from 25 to 75, were then plotted against the midpoint of each of these six-month or one-year age ranges, and the growth curves were smoothed. From these smoothed curves, the T scores corresponding to the midpoints of each of the final three-month or six-month age ranges were obtained. A graph of T scores versus ability scores was then constructed for each of these final age groups, and these within-age curves were again smoothed and the T scores of 20 and 80 extrapolated. Finally, T-score equivalents of ability scores were read from these smoothed curves. The project team then scored the standardization cases with these norms and calculated the means and standard deviations of T scores at each age. Some age-to-age variability in the T score distributions was expected as a result of sampling error. The team examined any large deviations from the expected mean of 50 and standard deviation of 10 and, if necessary, revised the norms through further smoothing.

Composite Norms

Norms for each composite (clusters, GCA, and Special Nonverbal scale) are based on the distribution of the sums of T scores on the component subtests. The analyses used only cases from the usual age range for each composite (2:6–3:5, 3:6–5:11, or 6:0–17:11). Even though complete data for each composite were available at some ages outside these ranges, the analyses did not include those ages because those distributions might have caused floor or ceiling effects. Before calculating norms for each composite, the project team statistically tested the equality of variances of the sums of T scores at the ages within the usual age range. No statistically significant inequalities appeared. The sums of T scores for all ages within the usual age range were then combined into a single distribution for each composite. A test for normality of distribution shape showed that there were no statistically significant departures from normality. Mid-interval percentiles were then computed for the combined distribution of sums of T scores, and the percentiles were transformed to their corresponding normalized standard scores. The project team plotted these values against the sums of T scores and graphically smoothed deviations from linearity at the extreme tails of the distributions.

Despite the absence of statistically significant departures from normality, many of the plots showed a slight change of slope near the middle of the distribution. This phenomenon indicated that the distribution of sums of T scores did not extend as far above the mean as it did below the mean and, in turn, implied that intersubtest scatter was greater at high ability levels than at low ability levels. This finding is consistent with those from other ability batteries (Kaufman, 1979; Matarazzo, Daniel, Prifitera, & Herman, 1988). Greater scatter implies lower correlations among subtests and fewer cases obtaining very high scores on all of the subtests. Because of this observed bend in the plots of sums of T scores against normalized standard scores, the project team read the final norms from the curves, rather than calculating them from a linear equation. This slight asymmetry in the distributions of sums of T scores means that the standard-score range of each composite extends farther above the mean than below it before reaching the limits imposed by the minimum and maximum sums of subtest T scores.

Grade Norms for Achievement Tests

Grade-based percentile norms for the three achievement tests were constructed from the mid-interval percentiles corresponding to obtained ability scores for each grade group (representing the second half of the school year). Percentiles were then smoothed both across grades and within each grade. Interpolation yielded percentiles for the first half of the year.

Age and Grade Equivalents

The project team calculated these scores by plotting the median ability score for a subtest against age or grade and then drawing a smooth curve through the points. An *age equivalent* represents the age (in years and months) at which a particular ability score is the median score. A *grade equivalent* represents the grade and month of school at which a particular ability score is the median score. Age and grade equivalents are reported only for those ages and grades for which a particular subtest is appropriate.

Extended GCA Norms

Traditionally, a shortcoming of cognitive ability tests has been the lack of accurate norms for extremely low performance levels (more than 3 or 4 standard deviations below the mean). Standardization samples often exclude severely retarded children who score at such low levels. Even if these children were included, the test materials normally administered to children of their age would probably be inappropriate for them.

To address this problem, the DAS provides extended GCA norms for levels of performance that are below the lower limit (3 ⅔ standard deviations below the mean, or a standard score of about 45) of the standard GCA norms. These extended norms are based on the observed relationship between GCA standard scores for the child's chronological age and GCA standard scores at a younger age (referred to as the *reference age*). For each level of the Cognitive Battery, the reference age is the youngest age group in the usual age range for that level (2:6–2:8, 3:6–3:8, and 6:0–6:2).

The rationale for the extended GCA norms is as follows. Each GCA standard score at the child's chronological age corresponds to a certain level of ''raw'' performance on the subtests. That same level of raw performance would yield a different—and higher—GCA score at the younger reference age. Plotting the GCA score at the **chronological age** against the GCA score at the **reference age** that corresponds to the same level of raw performance reveals the relationship between GCA scores at the two ages. Extending this relationship downward yields the GCA score at the reference age that is equivalent (in raw performance level) to GCA standard scores below 45 at the chronological age, that is, scores that cannot be obtained from the usual norms. Finally, by scoring the child's performance with the subtest norms for the reference age and obtaining the GCA for the reference age, we can find the equivalent GCA at the child's chronological age.

Figure 7.2 illustrates the relationship between GCA scores at ages 9:0–9:5 and ages 6:0–6:2 (the reference age range for the School-Age Level of the Cognitive Battery). The graph indicates that a GCA score of 50 at ages 9:0–9:5 reflects the same level of raw performance as a GCA score of 78 at ages 6:0–6:2. In other words, if a child aged 9:0–9:5 with a GCA score of 50 were scored on norms for ages 6:0–6:2, the GCA score would be 78. An extrapolation of the relationship (as shown by the dotted line) shows that a GCA of 65 obtained from the reference-age norms (ages 6:0–6:2) corresponds to a GCA score of 40 at ages 9:0–9:5.

Because no single raw-score scale underlies the GCA, "raw" performance was measured in the following way. At each level of the Cognitive Battery, each GCA score corresponds to a particular sum of T scores. For a given GCA score at the chronological age, it is assumed for the sake of convenience that the child scored at the same T-score level on each of the core subtests, that is, at the level of the mean T score. The ability score on each core subtest corresponding to that mean T score is then found in the norm table for the chronological age. Next, these ability scores are referred to the norm table for the reference age and converted to T scores for that younger age. The sum of those T scores yields the GCA score for the reference age.

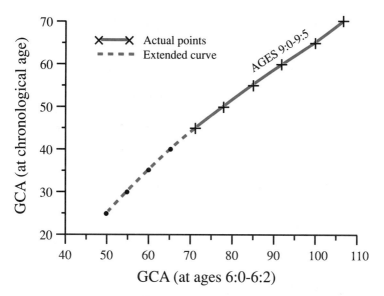

Figure 7.2. GCA Scores at Ages 6:0–6:2 and 9:0–9:5 That Correspond to the Same Level of Performance

Often, administering a lower level of the Cognitive Battery is desirable for testing children who are very low in ability. Such a lower level will often have more suitable materials and items of more appropriate difficulty. The extended GCA norms accommodate this out-of-level use of the Cognitive Battery by covering several years of age above the usual age range of each level. Thus, the extended GCA norms for the lower Preschool Level extend to age 6:11, and those for the upper Preschool Level extend to age 13:11. The norms stop at these points because the reference-age GCA scores are near their upper limits.

These across-level extended GCA norms are possible because the normative age ranges of each level overlapped in standardization. Thus, children in the reference age group for the upper Preschool Level (ages 3:6–3:8) also took all of the core subtests of the lower Preschool Level (ages 2:6–3:5), and children at the reference age for the School-Age Level (ages 6:0–6:2) also took the core subtests of the upper Preschool Level. This overlap allows a GCA score for a reference age group of an upper level of the Cognitive Battery to be equated to a GCA score for the reference age group of a lower level. As illustrated in Figure 7.2, a GCA score of 40 for a child aged 9:0–9:5 on the School-Age Level corresponds to a GCA score of 65 for the reference age (6:0–6:2) of that level; that GCA score, if translated to the upper Preschool Level of the Cognitive Battery, is equivalent to a GCA score of 116 for that level's reference age (3:6–3:8). Overall, then, if a child aged 9:0–9:5 takes the upper Preschool Level and obtains a GCA of 116 when scored on norms for ages 3:6–3:8, we estimate that this is equivalent to a GCA of 40 for ages 9:0–9:5.

The extended GCA norms address a substantial need in the assessment of very low-functioning children. The norms' accuracy depends in part on the reasonableness of the graphic extrapolations of the empirical relationships between GCA scores at different ages. As shown in Figure 7.2, these relationships are approximately linear. By simultaneously plotting the relationships for all ages and making them parallel, the project staff removed age-to-age fluctuations caused by minor variations in the data of the norm tables. For ages with extended GCA norms for more than one level of the Cognitive Battery, internal consistency was achieved by ensuring that the values obtained from the two levels were in agreement. In a similar way, the upper levels of the extended norms (above 45) were checked against empirical norms for the child's age.

Another important factor influencing the accuracy of the across-level extended GCA norms is the equivalence of meaning of the GCA scores obtained from the Preschool and School-Age Levels of the Cognitive Battery. Across-level equating assumes that these two GCA scores measure the same construct. Empirical evidence, presented in Chapter 9, strongly supports this assumption.

The extended GCA norms necessarily depend to some degree on extrapolation and therefore have some margin of error. Nevertheless they enable us to administer items and subtests that are appropriate in content and difficulty to the abilities of the individual child being assessed. This tailoring of content to the child's ability is fundamental to accurate measurement.

When to Use the Extended GCA Norms

When a child of low ability is given a level of the Cognitive Battery lower than the level usually administered for his or her age, and the core subtests of that level are not fully normed at the child's chronological age, then the extended GCA norms provide the only means of obtaining a composite score. Thus, the performance of an 8-year-old who is given the upper Preschool Level can be scored only on the extended GCA norms. In contrast, the performance of a 6-year-old taking that level could be scored on the actual subtest norms for his or her age because the upper Preschool Level is fully normed at age 6 years; we would then obtain cluster and GCA scores from the usual composite norm tables for the upper Preschool Level.

The extended GCA norms may also be useful for a child who has taken a level that is fully normed for his or her age but whose performance is so low that the subtest norms for that age fail to discriminate. The norm tables provide a T score of 20 for any performance that is 3 standard deviations or more below the average performance at that age. Thus, these tables do not differentiate between children who score just at 3 standard deviations below the mean and those who score lower. If a child obtains several core-subtest ability scores that are well below the highest ability score that earns a T score of 20, then the subtest norms are failing to measure the actual level of the child's performance. The subtest norm table for the (younger) reference age will provide the needed discrimination at the level of the child's ability, and the extended GCA norms based on these reference-age T scores will better reflect the child's overall performance.

Chapter 8

Reliability, Accuracy, and Specificity

This chapter focuses on various ways of evaluating how accurately the scores obtained from the DAS measure general and specific abilities—that is, reliability. Reliability refers to several factors that influence the interpretation of test scores, including:

- the *homogeneity*, or internal consistency, of the test's content;
- the *accuracy of individual items*, that is, the extent to which item-response scores are a function of ability rather than of error;
- the *appropriateness of item difficulty* for the group of people taking the test;
- the *temporal stability* of the person's normative score; and
- *interrater reliability*, or the consistency with which test performance is scored by different scorers.

This chapter explores all of these dimensions with reference to the DAS subtests and composites.

Reliability and Accuracy

Before empirical results can be discussed, the important issue of the relationship between reliability and accuracy must be addressed. The two terms are often used almost interchangeably, and they are closely related. However, underlying the development of the DAS is the view that accuracy rather than reliability should be our primary consideration when we select tests for individual examinees and when we interpret test scores. Furthermore, modern test theory provides a means of shifting the focus from reliability to accuracy.

In classical test theory, any test score is an approximation of the examinee's hypothetical *true score*, that is, the score the individual would receive if the measuring instrument were perfectly accurate. The difference between the person's true score, which can never be known, and the score the person actually obtains on a single administration is *measurement error*. The smaller the average amount of measurement error on a test, the more *accurately* the observed score will estimate the true score. The index of measurement error is the *standard error of measurement* (SE_M), which is the standard deviation of measurement errors.

The standard error of a test score varies according to the ability level of the examinee. On an instrument such as the DAS that uses item response theory

(IRT) to estimate each person's score on an ability scale, we can evaluate the amount of error in that ability estimate. As shown in the raw-score-to-ability-score tables (Figure 7.1, pp. 149–163), the standard errors are smallest for raw scores near the middle of the raw-score range and are substantially larger for raw scores near either end of that range. The accuracy of an examinee's score is a function of the number of administered items that are near the examinee's level of ability. Very difficult items, which the examinee will likely answer incorrectly, and very easy items, which the examinee will likely answer correctly, give little information about the person's ability. Items on which the probability of the person's answering correctly is between, say, 20% and 80% provide the most information about the person's ability.[a]

The implication for test selection and administration is clear. In order to estimate accurately the individual examinee's ability, we should select items that are near the examinee's level of ability. Of course we do not know the examinee's ability before testing begins. We do, however, often have some basis for an expectation about the examinee's ability and can therefore choose test items that are likely to be appropriate. Even if we have no prior information, we can obtain evidence about the examinee's ability during the course of administration and use this information to "tailor" the administration so that appropriate items are given.

The DAS provides three methods of tailoring content to the examinee. First, although each subtest's Starting and Decision Points were placed so that the items will be appropriate for almost all examinees in the designated age range, we are free (and encouraged) to use the Starting and Decision Points for a younger age if the examinee is expected to be very low in ability. Second, using the Decision Point rules, we can determine, according to the examinee's performance on the items already given, whether or not to administer additional harder or easier items. Third, many subtests can be administered out of level if we decide that their content and difficulty are appropriate for the individual child. With these procedures we can select items and subtests that will give the most accurate estimate of ability for a particular examinee; that is, we can minimize the amount of measurement error for the individual.

How is reliability related to accuracy? In general terms, reliability is the proportion of test-score variance that is true variance rather than error variance. (Error variance is the square of the standard error.) For a given group of examinees taking a given set of items, reliability is estimated by squaring the standard error of each person's estimated ability score (SE_A), finding the mean of these squared

---

[a]The standard error of estimate of an ability score is computed as

$$SE_A = \sqrt{\dfrac{1}{\displaystyle\sum_{i=1}^{m} P_i Q_i}} \; ,$$

where m is the number of items, P_i is the probability of passing item i, and Q_i is $(1 - P_i)$. The product $P_i Q_i$ is largest when $P_i = .5$ and smallest when P_i is near .0 or 1.0. The more items there are with P_i near .5, the smaller the standard error of the ability estimate will be.

standard errors (or error variances), and inserting that mean error variance into the basic formula for reliability:

$$Reliability = 1 - \frac{SE_A^2}{s_x^2} \ , \tag{8.1}$$

where s_x^2 is the variance of observed ability scores (Samejima, 1977). This reliability value reflects the average accuracy with which the test measures the abilities of the group members.

For examinees in a particular range of ability, the reliability of a test is found by inserting only those specific standard errors that apply at that level into the basic reliability equation (Equation 8.1). The resulting value is still referenced to a group (such as an age group) because the standard deviation of ability scores (s_x) is a group statistic. This modified reliability coefficient reflects the accuracy of the test for examinees at the selected ability level because it uses the average of their actual standard errors rather than the average standard errors for the entire reference group.

The traditional reliability coefficient that describes how a test works for an entire group (such as all children of a particular age) may be an inappropriate guide to selecting tests for individual examinees who are near either the low or the high end of the ability distribution for their age. Because the standard error at these extremes may differ from that of the average range of ability, the reliability coefficient for the age group may tell us little about the accuracy of the test for low- and high-ability examinees. A test whose age-group reliability is high may have insufficient items that are easy enough to measure accurately the performance of a very low-ability person of that age group. Equally important is the corollary that a test with low reliability for the group may be very accurate for the low-ability examinee. The inaccuracy of a test for people of average and high ability is of no consequence to the assessment of the low-ability individual.

We are well aware that some tests have *floor* or *ceiling* effects at certain ages; that is, the test cannot differentiate among examinees who score at the low or the high end of the scale. Figure 8.1(A) illustrates the distribution of raw scores from a test with a ceiling; it lacks a sufficient number of difficult items to measure the performance of high-ability examinees. The great benefit of the Rasch-based approach to reliability estimation is that it provides the means of showing us that even a test with such a strong ceiling effect can yield highly reliable (that is, accurate) scores for examinees whose abilities are near the low end of the scale. For the person at score level X, the test whose raw-score distribution is illustrated in Figure 8.1(A) is just as accurate as the one whose raw-score distribution is shown in Figure 8.1(B) and which has many difficult items, even though the overall reliability coefficients are quite different.

Later sections of this chapter will describe practical methods for selecting tests that are appropriate for the individual examinee, including out-of-level testing, and will report reliability coefficients for some subtests at specific levels of ability.

a) Ceiling Effect (Reliability = .76)

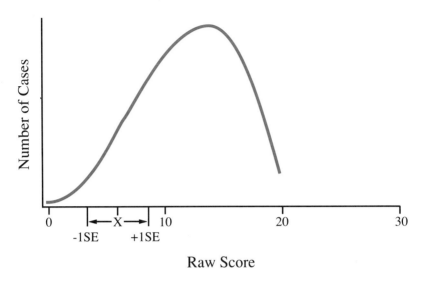

b) No Ceiling Effect (Reliability = .84)

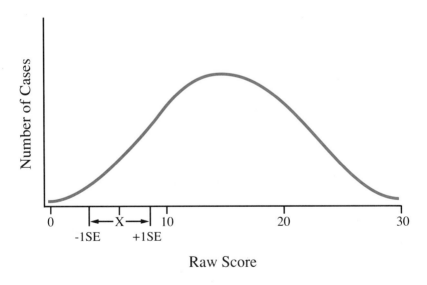

Figure 8.1. Raw-Score Distributions for a Test With and Without a Ceiling Effect

Internal Reliabilities of Subtests and Composites

Subtests

During standardization, the items in each DAS subtest were administered in pre-determined sets, with rules governing the administration of additional easy or difficult items (see Chapter 7). Generally, examinees did not establish traditional basals or ceilings. Therefore, internal-consistency reliabilities could not be calculated in the usual way, which assumes that examinees would have passed all of the easier, unadministered items and failed all of the harder, unadministered items. Moreover, because the item-selection procedures of the final edition more efficiently target items to the individual child, it would have been inappropriate to divide the items into parallel halves, estimate the ability from each half, calculate the split-half correlation, and adjust it by the Spearman–Brown formula. An alternative method of estimating reliability was developed. This method takes into account the effects on reliability of the item-selection procedures incorporated in the final edition. That is, it is based purely on the items expected to be taken by an individual and makes no assumptions about the person's performance on unadministered items. This method played a key role in the design of the final Starting and Decision Points for each subtest.

The standard error of a person's estimated ability score is a function of the number of administered items that were appropriate in difficulty for the examinee; the more items given on which the examinee has a moderate probability of responding correctly, the smaller the standard error. If we knew which items each examinee would take, we could calculate each examinee's standard error and then find the mean error variance for all of the examinees in a group (such as all of the children of a particular age). This mean error variance, in combination with the variance of ability scores in the group, would yield the reliability for that group.

To estimate a subtest's reliability for each age group, the DAS team first assumed that all children of a given age start at the same point. (In reality, we would start at an earlier point than the usual Starting Point for the child's age if we suspected that the child was very low in ability. Such modifications will increase the accuracy obtained in practice and make the given reliability estimate conservative.) However, even though the children in an age group all start at the same point, they do not all take the same set of items. Those who perform very well on the initial set of items continue with an additional set of more difficult items to increase the accuracy of their scores; others who have difficulty with the initial set of items drop back to an earlier Starting Point to take easier items.

The DAS Decision Point rules that govern item selection allowed the team to calculate the probability that an examinee at a particular level of ability would take any one of the possible sets of items. For a given ability level, the Rasch model provided the probability of the child's passing each item on the subtest. Therefore, it was possible to calculate the probability of the child's passing three or more items and failing three or more items in the initially assigned item set and thereby stopping at the Decision Point; the probability of the child's failing fewer than three items and continuing to the next higher Decision Point (where some examinees would stop and the rest would continue); and the probability of the child's passing fewer than three items in the initial set and taking a set of easier items. The project team calculated each of these probabilities by summing the probabilities of all possible patterns of item passes and failures that would lead to a particular decision at the Decision Point. Each possible set of administered items yields a different standard error of the ability score.

The project team used the distribution of ability scores at each age group obtained during standardization as an estimate of the population distribution of ability scores for children within that age range. The *expected error variance* was calculated separately for each ability score represented in that group. The expected error variance is the weighted mean of the ability-score error variances associated with each of the possible item sets, with the probability of the child's taking each item set as the weight. Thus, the expected error variance is the mean error variance for cases at that ability score. Finally, the mean of the expected error variances for all of the cases in the age group, along with the variance of ability scores, was inserted in Equation 8.1 to obtain the reliability for the group.

To summarize, to estimate reliability for an age group, the DAS team

1. Used the observed distribution of ability scores for an age range in the norm sample as an estimate of the distribution of abilities at that age in the population.

2. Assumed that all examinees in the group started at the same Starting Point.

3. For each case, used the Rasch model to calculate the probability that an examinee at that ability level would take each possible set of items, according to the specified Starting and Decision Points, Decision Point rules, and Alternative Stopping Point rule.

4. For each case, calculated the standard error of estimate for each possible set of items.

5. Calculated the expected error variance for the case by taking the weighted average of the squared standard errors.

6. Inserted the mean expected error variance along with the variance of ability scores for all cases in the sample into Equation 8.1 to compute the reliability.

For two subtests (Recall of Objects—Immediate and Speed of Information Processing), it was possible to use the traditional reliability procedure because standardization examinees took all of the final items, and these subtests do not use Decision Point rules. Both of these subtests have polychotomous items, which are not as well suited as dichotomous items to the IRT-based reliability estimation procedure. Therefore, the reliability values in Tables 8.1 and 8.2 for Recall of Objects—Immediate and Speed of Information Processing are coefficient alpha.

Tables 8.1 and 8.2 report reliability coefficients for each subtest for each age in the preschool and school-age levels of the DAS, respectively. The tables also show the average reliability of each subtest at the ages where it is on level. Reliabilities for out-of-level ages (discussed later in this chapter) appear in parentheses. The reliability coefficients in Tables 8.1 and 8.2 are the best possible estimates of the reliability based on the final configuration of test items with their Starting and Decision Point rules.

Constructing Item-Selection Rules for Each Subtest

The DAS subtest reliabilities are sensitive to both the set of items in the subtest and the specific item-selection procedure (the locations of the Starting and Decision Points and the Decision Point and Alternative Stopping Point rules). To determine the item-selection procedure for each subtest, the DAS team systematically varied the procedures and observed the effects on the overall reliability for each age group. Various combinations of Starting and Stopping Points, Decision Point rules, and Alternative Stopping Point rules were evaluated to find an efficient balance of reliability and test length. Through this experimentation, the DAS team constructed the item-selection procedure so that the reliability of the subtest administered according to those rules nearly equals the reliability that would be obtained if all items were administered.

These simulations indicated the percentage of children in each age group expected to pass fewer than three items in the initial set of items and therefore expected to drop back to an earlier Starting Point. Because starting with difficult items can decrease a child's motivation, and because dropping back to an earlier Starting Point is inefficient, the Starting Point for each age group was placed so that no more than a very small percentage of children would need to drop back.

The Alternative Stopping Point rules were also evaluated with Rasch-based simulations. The DAS generally uses Decision Points rather than ceiling rules to determine when testing should stop. Occasionally, however, a child will fail many items in succession before reaching the Decision Point. Using the Rasch model, the project team calculated the probability of an examinee's answering additional items correctly after failing a specified number of successive items. These analyses were used to determine the Alternative Stopping Point rule for each subtest.

Table 8.1. Internal Reliabilities of Subtests and Composites for the Preschool Level of the Cognitive Battery

Subtest or Composite	Age									Mean[a]
	2:6–2:11	3:0–3:5	3:6–3:11	4:0–4:5	4:6–4:11	5:0–5:11	6:0–6:11	7:0–7:11	8:0–8:11	
Verbal Comprehension	.86	.83	.85	.85	.82	.83	(.74)	—	—	.84
Naming Vocabulary	.77	.74	.73	.79	.76	.84	.78	.77	(.64)	.78
Block Building	.68	.74	.80	.84	.76	—	—	—	—	.77
Picture Similarities	.84	.78	.76	.70	.73	.72	(.60)	(.33)	—	.76
Pattern Construction	—	(.80)	.84	.89	.82	.90	.90	.89	.90	.88
Pattern Construction (Alt.)	—	(.37)	.66	.78	.76	.82	.85	.81	.82	.79
Copying	—	—	.82	.86	.88	.88	.85	.82	—	.86
Early Number Concepts	(.53)	(.80)	.88	.87	.85	.87	.81	(.57)	—	.86
Matching Letter-Like Forms	—	—	—	(.78)	.84	.87	(.68)	(.49)	—	.85
Recall of Digits	(.86)	.90	.87	.89	.85	.88	.88	.88	.86	.87
Recall of Objects—Imm.[b]	—	—	—	.76	.66	.67	.77	.69	.71	.71
Recognition of Pictures	(.68)	.78	.78	.80	.74	.74	.66	.71	(.54)	.73
Verbal Ability	.89	.86	.88	.89	.86	.90	(.85)	—	—	.88
Nonverbal Ability	—	—	.88	.90	.88	.90	(.88)	(.83)	—	.89
GCA (Lower Level)	.91	.89	.91	.91	.89	—	—	—	—	.90[c]
GCA (Upper Level)	—	—	.94	.94	.94	.95	(.93)	—	—	.94
Special Nonverbal (Lower Level)	.82	.81	.84	.83	.80	—	—	—	—	.81[c]

Note. N = 175 for each age range from 2:6–4:11; N = 200 for each age range from 5:0–8:11. Values in parentheses are for ages at which the subtest or composite is out of level.
[a]Mean of on-level values, calculated by Fisher's *z* transformation.
[b]Coefficient alpha. All other reliabilities are IRT-based (see text).
[c]Mean of values for ages 2:6–3:5.

Table 8.2. Internal Reliabilities of Subtests, Achievement Tests, and Composites for the School-Age Level

Subtest or Composite	Age													Mean[a]
	5	6	7	8	9	10	11	12	13	14	15	16	17	
Word Definitions	(.75)	.81	.83	.84	.84	.84	.83	.84	.85	.81	.81	.83	.82	.83
Similarities	(.84)	.82	.77	.75	.77	.81	.78	.82	.82	.77	.78	.77	.73	.79
Matrices	.72	.79	.86	.87	.86	.86	.80	.85	.84	.82	.80	.81	.78	.82
Seq. & Quant. Reasoning	(.78)	.83	.88	.86	.84	.86	.82	.87	.86	.85	.85	.84	.83	.85
Recall of Designs	.80	.83	.80	.79	.81	.79	.84	.85	.86	.86	.87	.89	.88	.84
Pattern Construction	.90	.90	.89	.90	.87	.91	.92	.92	.93	.92	.93	.92	.91	.91
Pattern Construction (Alt.)	.82	.85	.81	.83	.84	.84	.83	.82	(.79)	(.69)	(.69)	(.62)	(.54)	.83
Recall of Digits	.88	.88	.88	.86	.86	.87	.87	.85	.87	.88	.86	.87	.85	.87
Recall of Objects—Imm.[b]	.67	.77	.69	.71	.76	.76	.80	.77	.76	.79	.83	.75	.81	.76
Recognition of Pictures	.74	.66	.71	(.54)	(.55)	(.55)	(.49)	(.40)	(.35)	(.13)	(.17)	(.07)	(.00)	.70
Speed of Info. Processing[b]	(.86)	.89	.89	.89	.92	.89	.91	.92	.90	.92	.93	.92	.94	.91
Basic Number Skills	—	.88	.90	.85	.88	.88	.88	.89	.90	.86	.86	.86	.82	.87
Spelling	—	.90	.94	.91	.92	.91	.92	.91	.92	.92	.92	.91	.91	.92
Word Reading	(.68)	.94	.94	.94	.95	.93	.93	.90	.93	.90	.90	.89	.88	.92
Verbal Ability	(.87)	.88	.88	.87	.88	.89	.88	.90	.90	.87	.88	.88	.86	.88
Nonverbal Reas. Ability	(.83)	.88	.92	.91	.91	.91	.88	.91	.91	.89	.89	.89	.88	.90
Spatial Ability	.90	.91	.89	.89	.90	.90	.92	.93	.94	.94	.94	.94	.93	.92
GCA	(.94)	.95	.95	.95	.95	.95	.95	.96	.96	.95	.95	.96	.95	.95
Special Nonverbal	(.91)	.94	.94	.94	.94	.94	.94	.95	.95	.94	.94	.95	.94	.94

Note. N = 200 for each age. Values in parentheses are for ages at which the subtest or composite is out of level.
[a]Mean of on-level values, calculated by Fisher's z transformation.
[b]Coefficient alpha. All other reliabilities are IRT-based (see text).

Composite Scores

Tables 8.1 and 8.2 also report the reliabilities of the cluster, GCA, and Special Nonverbal Composite scores for each age group. For calculating these values, the project team used the formula for the reliability of a composite score composed of fixed components (Nunnally, 1978). This formula uses the internal reliabilities of the subtests and the variance of the sum of subtest scores.

The reliability of the GCA is high at all ages, averaging .90 for the lower Preschool Level, .94 for the upper Preschool Level, and .95 for the School-Age Level. The cluster scores also have consistently high reliabilities, averaging between .88 and .92. For the School-Age Level, the Special Nonverbal Composite is nearly as reliable as the GCA, averaging .94. At the lower Preschool Level (ages 2:6–3:5), however, the two-subtest Special Nonverbal Composite has only moderate reliability and should be used only when the GCA is inappropriate because of its verbal content.

Standard Errors of Subtest and Composite Scores

The reliability coefficients in Table 8.1 and 8.2 relate to the average standard error of measurement. Although the standard error of a particular ability score is useful for many purposes, the traditionally estimated standard errors in standard-score units are necessary for establishing confidence intervals for composite scores and for evaluating a variety of differences between scores. Tables 8.3 and 8.4 give the standard errors of measurement for the subtests and composites in T-score and standard-score units. These values are derived from the internal reliability coefficients reported in Tables 8.1 and 8.2.

Reliability at Different Ability Levels: Out-of-Level Testing

Information about the reliability of subtests at different ability levels aids us in selecting tests that are appropriate in difficulty, and therefore accurate, for examinees who are low or high in ability relative to others of their age. Tables 8.1 and 8.2 include reliabilities (in parentheses) for ages at which a subtest is out of level, that is, appropriate at these ages only for examinees who are expected to be either low or high in ability. Table 8.5 separately reports the reliability of each subtest at these out-of-level ages for four segments of the T-score distribution: 40 and below (the lowest scoring 16% at that age), 41–50 (the next higher 34%), 51–59 (the next 34%), and 60 and above (the highest scoring 16%). The values illustrate that large differences in reliability may exist between different ability levels within a single age group. More important, the values show how subtests with low overall reliabilities for an age group may nevertheless be useful for assessing low-ability or high-ability children of that age. We can use this table, in addition to the shading in the subtest norm tables, as a guide for selecting subtests for individual examinees.

Table 8.3. Standard Errors of Measurement of Subtests and Composites for the Preschool Level of the Cognitive Battery

Subtest or Composite	Age									Mean[a]
	2:6–2:11	3:0–3:5	3:6–3:11	4:0–4:5	4:6–4:11	5:0–5:11	6:0–6:11	7:0–7:11	8:0–8:11	
Verbal Comprehension	3.75	3.99	4.02	3.70	4.00	4.23	(4.78)	—	—	3.95
Naming Vocabulary	4.68	5.16	4.89	4.52	4.69	4.33	4.46	4.81	(5.82)	4.69
Block Building	5.86	4.78	4.23	4.19	4.73	—	—	—	—	4.76
Picture Similarities	4.29	4.45	4.77	5.10	5.41	5.49	(6.25)	(7.87)	—	4.92
Pattern Construction	—	(4.36)	3.73	3.50	4.36	2.86	3.12	3.10	3.09	3.40
Pattern Construction (Alt.)	—	(7.84)	5.77	4.99	4.28	4.20	3.94	4.07	4.31	4.51
Copying	—	—	4.41	3.48	3.26	3.35	3.71	4.52	—	3.79
Early Number Concepts	(6.00)	(4.26)	3.56	3.56	3.64	3.45	4.25	(6.10)	—	3.69
Matching Letter-Like Forms	—	—	—	(4.60)	3.91	3.55	(5.61)	(7.22)	—	3.73
Recall of Digits	(3.48)	3.42	3.46	3.52	3.61	3.50	3.54	3.66	3.64	3.54
Recall of Objects—Imm.	—	—	—	5.29	5.53	5.29	5.05	5.35	5.44	5.33
Recognition of Pictures	(5.18)	4.80	4.51	4.61	5.16	4.98	5.43	6.07	(6.09)	5.20
Verbal Ability	5.04	5.56	5.35	4.92	5.21	5.14	(5.51)	—	—	5.15
Nonverbal Ability	—	—	5.08	4.77	5.13	4.70	(5.29)	(6.41)	—	4.92
GCA (Lower Level)	4.65	4.62	4.52	4.39	4.73	—	—	—	—	4.63
GCA (Upper Level)	—	—	3.65	3.40	3.61	3.41	(3.81)	—	—	3.51
Special Nonverbal (Lower Level)	6.76	6.07	5.97	6.17	6.71	—	—	—	—	6.42

Note. Values are in *T*-score units (cognitive subtests) or standard-score units (composites). Values are based on the reliabilities in Table 8.1 and the actual standard deviations of *T* scores or standard scores at each age. Values in parentheses are for ages at which the subtest or composite is out of level.
[a]Mean of on-level values.

Table 8.4. Standard Errors of Measurement of Subtests, Achievement Tests, and Composites for the School-Age Level

Subtest or Composite	Age													Mean[a]
	5	6	7	8	9	10	11	12	13	14	15	16	17	
Word Definitions	(4.94)	4.22	3.90	3.64	3.81	3.92	4.08	4.02	4.06	4.32	4.36	4.41	4.37	4.09
Similarities	(3.78)	4.05	4.65	4.81	4.77	4.60	4.44	4.42	4.41	4.57	4.72	4.95	5.40	4.65
Matrices	4.91	4.53	3.95	3.70	3.84	4.00	4.14	4.11	4.20	4.50	4.49	4.61	4.69	4.28
Seq. & Quant. Reasoning	(4.03)	3.93	3.55	3.66	3.86	3.77	3.89	3.81	3.80	3.99	4.02	3.98	4.21	3.87
Recall of Designs	4.19	4.10	4.60	4.42	4.39	4.44	4.27	3.83	3.75	3.58	3.56	3.47	3.48	4.01
Pattern Construction	2.86	3.12	3.10	3.09	3.15	2.94	2.88	2.85	2.72	2.77	2.66	2.98	2.98	2.93
Pattern Construction (Alt.)	4.20	3.94	4.07	4.31	3.77	3.68	4.26	4.39	(4.72)	(4.84)	(5.12)	(5.55)	(6.03)	4.08
Recall of Digits	3.50	3.54	3.66	3.64	3.82	3.71	3.60	3.73	3.71	3.69	3.60	3.64	3.72	3.66
Recall of Objects—Imm.	5.29	5.05	5.35	5.44	4.92	5.11	4.63	4.79	5.14	4.57	4.71	4.80	4.40	4.94
Recognition of Pictures	4.98	5.43	6.07	(6.09)	(6.71)	(6.91)	(7.30)	(7.53)	(7.89)	(8.20)	(8.56)	(8.64)	(8.59)	5.49
Speed of Info. Processing	(3.58)	3.20	3.19	3.25	3.23	3.07	3.05	2.98	3.07	2.86	2.62	2.79	2.44	2.98
Basic Number Skills	—	4.72	4.58	5.05	5.07	5.06	4.91	4.98	5.07	5.55	5.66	5.77	6.05	5.20
Spelling	—	4.43	3.45	4.07	4.34	4.35	4.34	4.31	4.19	4.35	4.38	4.61	4.42	4.27
Word Reading	(6.52)	3.21	3.51	3.57	3.33	3.86	4.14	4.30	4.16	4.52	4.69	4.95	5.13	4.11
Verbal Ability	(5.19)	4.86	5.02	4.98	5.05	4.99	5.01	4.92	4.98	5.24	5.28	5.47	5.76	5.13
Nonverbal Reas. Ability	(5.27)	5.12	4.21	4.12	4.45	4.39	5.16	4.55	4.87	4.93	4.99	5.33	5.16	4.77
Spatial Ability	4.27	4.37	4.71	4.54	4.57	4.52	4.36	4.05	3.90	3.83	3.72	3.87	3.88	4.19
GCA	(3.40)	3.28	3.26	3.18	3.24	3.22	3.23	3.14	3.10	3.30	3.26	3.32	3.47	3.25
Special Nonverbal	(3.90)	3.65	3.77	3.69	3.69	3.75	3.30	3.52	3.31	3.64	3.56	3.40	3.74	3.58

Note. Values are in T-score units (cognitive subtests) or standard-score units (achievement tests) or standard-score units (achievement tests and composites). Values are based on the reliabilities given in Table 8.2 and the actual standard deviations of T scores or standard scores at each age. Values in parentheses are for ages at which the subtest or composite is out of level.
[a]Mean of on-level values.

Table 8.5. Out-of-Level Subtests: Reliability at Different Levels of Ability

Subtest	Age	T Score			
		≤40	41–50	51–59	≥60
Early Number Concepts	2:6–2:11	.24	.30	.74	.82
	3:0–3:5	.54	.83	.88	.89
	6:6–6:11	.90	.88	.83	.56
	7:0–7:11	.85	.76	.39	.16
Matching Letter-Like Forms	4:0–4:5	.57	.82	.89	.84
	6:0–6:11	.89	.87	.74	.08
	7:0–7:11	.87	.77	.46	.00
Naming Vocabulary	8:0–8:11	.79	.73	.61	.36
Pattern Construction	3:0–3:5	.47	.84	.90	.93
Pattern Construction (Alternative)	3:0–3:5	.06	.24	.54	.75
	13:0–13:11	.89	.87	.82	.52
	14:0–14:11	.85	.82	.72	.35
	15:0–15:11	.86	.83	.72	.41
	16:0–16:11	.84	.81	.45	—[a]
	17:0–17:11	.80	.70	.21	—[a]
Picture Similarities	6:0–6:11	.77	.70	.58	.15
	7:0–7:11	.66	.54	.35	.00
Recall of Digits	2:6–2:11	.69	.90	.91	.91
Recognition of Pictures	2:6–2:11	.38	.72	.78	.83
	8:0–8:11	.65	.65	.57	.18
	9:0–9:11	.73	.71	.61	.00
	10:0–10:11	.76	.71	.62	.01
	11:0–11:11	.74	.69	.56	.03
	12:0–12:11	.72	.65	.36	.00
	13:0–13:11	.73	.61	.27	.00
	14:0–14:11	.67	.53	.13	.00
	15:0–15:11	.71	.56	.20	.00
	16:0–16:11	.67	.53	.13	.00
	17:0–17:11	.61	.46	.00	.00
Seq. & Quant. Reasoning	5:0–5:11	.52	.79	.85	.85
Similarities	5:0–5:11	.63	.88	.89	.89
Verbal Comprehension	6:0–6:11	.90	.84	.70	.30
Word Definitions	5:0–5:11	.42	.73	.87	.90
Word Reading[b]	5:0–5:11	—	.60	.86	.95

Note. See text for explanation of how reliability is calculated for an ability level. Speed of Information Processing (for age 5) is omitted because its reliability is calculated by coefficient alpha rather than by the IRT-based method.
[a]For ages 16–17, the Pattern Construction (Alternative) norms do not extend above a *T* score of 59.
[b]The ranges for Word Reading standard scores are 86–100, 101–114, and ≥115. For age 5, the Word Reading norms do not extend below a standard score of 86.

All of the reliability values in Table 8.5 are underestimates because each of the ability distributions is truncated by a floor or ceiling at the end of the scale opposite from the region where the test is recommended for use. This restriction of range lowers the reliability coefficient: the greater the floor or ceiling effect, the greater the underestimation.

Test–Retest Reliability

Information on the temporal stability of test scores tells us how much the child's normative score might possibly change on retesting. Change could reflect the examinee's growth or fluctuation in the ability being measured or the examinee's recollection of the earlier administration.

About 100 examinees at each of three age ranges—3:6–4:5, 5:0–6:11, and 12:0–13:11— were randomly selected from the DAS standardization sample for retesting after an interval of 2–7 weeks ($M = 30$ days). The cases are reasonably representative of the U.S. population with respect to sex, race, region, and parent education. To reduce practice effects, examiners did not inform examinees at the time of first testing that they would be tested again. Most retesting was done by the same examiner who had administered the test the first time. For purposes of analysis, the examinees in the 5:0–6:11 age range, who took both the Preschool and School-Age Levels of the Cognitive Battery, were divided into two over-lapping groups: Those aged 5:0–6:3 were given scores on the Preschool Level subtests and composites, and those aged 5:9–6:11 were given scores on the School-Age Level subtests and composites. Tables 8.6 and 8.7 present the means, standard deviations, and retest correlations for subtest and composite scores.

The GCA and cluster scores are highly stable, as are many of the subtests. The subtests that have high internal reliability also tend to have high retest reliability. Measures of verbal ability are somewhat more stable and show smaller practice effects than nonverbal measures, perhaps because the latter often include novel tasks that are more affected by exposure. The practice effect for the Recall of Objects—Immediate subtest is unusually large (averaging about 7 points) and should be kept in mind when we retest children within a few months. At the level of the composites, the average score for the Verbal cluster increases about 2 points at the Preschool Level and 4 points at the School-Age Level. The nonverbal clusters increase somewhat more—about 4 points (Preschool) and 6 points (School-Age). The practice effect for the GCA is about 3 points for younger children and 6 points for school-aged children.

The test–retest study provides further evidence of the reliability of the subtests and composites. We must keep practice effects in mind when interpreting the scores of a child retested within a few months of initial testing.

Table 8.6. Test–Retest Reliabilities of Preschool Subtests and Composites

| Variable | Ages 3:6–4:5 (N = 100) | | | | | Ages 5:0–6:3 (N = 90) | | | | |
	r	Mean 1	Mean 2	SD 1	SD 2	r	Mean 1	Mean 2	SD 1	SD 2
Verbal Comprehension	.81	48.8	50.8	9.3	10.6	.77	47.3	47.9	8.1	8.9
Naming Vocabulary	.80	49.2	49.8	9.1	9.3	.89	48.0	48.8	9.5	9.6
Picture Similarities	.56	48.9	50.7	8.6	11.2	.63	48.4	52.6	9.1	9.3
Pattern Construction	.62	49.1	51.4	9.8	9.7	.73	49.5	52.4	9.4	9.7
Pattern Construction (Alt.)	.65	49.2	52.2	10.2	11.3	.73	49.5	52.7	9.5	9.8
Copying	.71	50.5	51.1	10.8	9.7	.68[a]	50.1	49.1	10.2	10.7
Early Number Concepts	.68	50.2	50.6	10.6	9.5	.83	47.6	48.9	8.7	9.2
Block Building	.67	50.9	51.0	10.1	11.1	—	—	—	—	—
Matching Letter-Like Forms	.62[b]	49.4	51.6	9.8	11.5	.68	48.9	51.4	10.0	10.4
Recall of Digits	.81	50.4	52.7	10.6	10.4	.80	48.9	48.5	8.9	8.8
Recall of Objects—Imm.	.61[b]	50.8	53.4	9.1	9.9	.54[a]	48.5	54.0	9.1	10.5
Recall of Objects—Del.	.38[b]	53.7	52.5	9.4	10.6	.58[a]	49.4	51.7	10.5	12.2
Recognition of Pictures	.58	51.6	52.6	9.1	9.4	.54	51.5	52.7	9.9	9.9
Word Reading	—	—	—	—	—	.93[c]	96.9	97.4	9.4	10.3
Verbal Ability	.84	98.2	100.3	13.9	14.7	.89	95.8	97.0	13.3	13.5
Nonverbal Ability	.79[d]	98.4	101.7	14.1	16.0	.86[a]	98.2	102.7	15.2	15.9
GCA	.90[e]	98.9	101.9	13.9	15.1	.94[a]	96.6	100.0	12.8	14.2

Note. The retest interval was 2–6 weeks. All correlations are corrected for restriction of range on the initial score.
[a] N = 88.
[b] N = 44.
[c] N = 84.
[d] N = 99.
[e] N = 97.

Table 8.7. Test-Retest Reliabilities of School-Age Subtests, Composites, and Achievement Tests

Variable	Ages 5:9-6:11 (N = 81)					Ages 12:0-13:11 (N = 122)				
		Mean		SD			Mean		SD	
	r	1	2	1	2	r	1	2	1	2
Word Definitions	.80	49.8	51.0	9.8	9.0	.87	49.2	51.5	10.1	10.6
Similarities	.75	49.7	51.5	9.1	8.0	.77	49.1	52.9	10.1	10.7
Matrices	.65	50.5	53.9	8.6	9.0	.76	49.0	52.7	10.1	10.1
Seq. & Quant. Reasoning	.78	49.0	52.5	8.6	8.8	.71	48.5	52.6	9.4	9.7
Recall of Designs	.65	51.2	51.7	8.6	10.3	.80	51.0	54.9	8.9	10.2
Pattern Construction	.76	50.2	55.1	9.1	8.6	.90	50.8	55.7	9.2	10.4
Pattern Construction (Alt.)	.66	50.9	54.5	8.8	7.9	.80	50.6	54.6	9.7	9.5
Recall of Digits	.83	50.0	51.3	9.1	9.5	.72[a]	50.2	52.1	9.6	10.0
Recall of Objects—Imm.	.53	49.8	56.0	11.1	11.8	.72	49.5	58.5	9.5	10.2
Recall of Objects—Del.	.56[b]	49.6	53.9	11.0	13.1	.71[c]	50.7	56.2	9.3	9.1
Recognition of Pictures	.54	52.3	52.8	10.1	9.3	.47	51.3	53.1	8.4	9.0
Speed of Info. Processing	.78	50.0	53.2	9.6	9.9	.80[a]	52.6	54.5	10.1	10.2
Basic Number Skills	.79[d]	102.1	102.1	12.0	12.6	.85[e]	100.6	102.2	15.5	16.8
Spelling	.89[f]	98.9	100.3	13.9	12.5	.94[g]	99.3	100.7	14.7	14.8
Word Reading	.97[h]	99.5	99.5	12.2	13.1	.94[e]	99.0	101.3	14.2	14.2
Verbal Ability	.87	99.0	101.5	13.5	12.5	.89	98.0	103.1	14.8	16.5
Nonverbal Reas. Ability	.80	99.2	105.0	12.8	13.2	.83	97.5	104.1	14.4	15.4
Spatial Ability	.79	100.6	105.3	13.0	13.5	.90	101.0	108.6	13.5	16.1
GCA	.89	99.6	104.7	12.6	12.4	.93	98.6	106.4	14.3	16.4
Special Nonverbal	.85	99.8	105.6	12.9	13.0	.92	99.1	107.0	13.9	15.9

Note. The retest interval was 2-6 weeks. All correlations are corrected for restriction of range on the initial score.

[a] N = 120.   [e] N = 121.
[b] N = 74.   [f] N = 62.
[c] N = 115.   [g] N = 118.
[d] N = 67.   [h] N = 79.

Interrater Reliability of Four Subtests with Open-Ended Responses

Although most DAS subtests are scored objectively, four require a significant amount of judgment. Two of these subtests, Copying and Recall of Designs, require us to evaluate various features of a child's drawings; the other two, Similarities and Word Definitions, require us to determine whether or not the child's verbal responses meet the criteria for correctness. The interrater reliability of each of these four subtests was analyzed statistically.

The purpose of an interrater reliability study is to determine to what extent scorers can be considered interchangeable. Unlike previous analyses (including those done for the BAS) that examined only the agreement among raters in their rank-ordering of cases, the DAS analyses follow the recommendation of Shrout and Fleiss (1979) of using a form of intraclass correlation that additionally accounts for differences in the leniency of scorers (that is, the levels of their scores). The formula for intraclass correlation used in these analyses is

$$\frac{MS_p - MS_{ps}}{MS_p + (k-1)\,MS_{ps} + \dfrac{k(MS_s - MS_{ps})}{n}} \qquad (8.2)$$

where MS_p is the mean square for persons (examinees), MS_s is the mean square for scorers, MS_{ps} is the mean square of the person-by-scorer interaction, k is the number of scorers, and n is the number of cases. This method is somewhat more conservative than the usual form of intraclass correlation and also more directly estimates the degree of scorer interchangeability.

For three of the subtests (Copying, Similarities, and Word Definitions), four sets (corresponding to different age ranges) of approximately 50 cases each were randomly drawn from the standardization sample. Three sets of 100 cases each were similarly selected for the Recall of Designs subtest. Scorers were school psychologists and graduate and undergraduate psychology students who were trained on the scoring procedures and who demonstrated competence in the scoring of practice cases. The scorers were divided into two groups of four scorers each, and each group scored all of the cases in a set. Thus, every case was scored by four raters.

Raw scores on the drawing subtests were analyzed because during standardization all children of a given age took the same set of items. For the verbal subtests, for which Decision Points were used to tailor items to individual children, Rasch ability scores were analyzed.

The project team calculated the interrater reliability of each subtest separately for each set of cases and computed the weighted average, using Fisher's z transformation. Table 8.8 reports the resulting interrater reliability coefficients. Average reliabilities are 0.9 or above for all four subtests.

Table 8.8. Interrater Reliabilities of Four Subtests

Subtest	N	Age	Reliability
Word Definitions	50	6	.93
	49	9	.92
	51	13	.96
	50	16	.96
Mean[a]			**.95**
Similarities	50	6	.98
	50	9	.97
	50	13	.97
	50	16	.91
Mean[a]			**.96**
Copying	50	3:6–4:5	.96
	50	3:6–4:5	.95
	49	6–7	.85
	50	6–7	.74
Mean[a]			**.90**
Recall of Designs	100	6	.91
	100	11	.95
	100	16	.97
Mean[a]			**.95**

Note. See text for explanation of method of calculation.
[a]Weighted mean, calculated by Fisher's z transformation.

Confidence Intervals

Confidence intervals contribute to the proper interpretation of test scores by indicating the extent to which the observed test score may be influenced by measurement error. Typically, a confidence interval gives a range within which the person's true score is likely to fall, with a specified probability.

A confidence interval may be constructed for a subtest score with the use of the standard error of the ability score presented in the raw-score-to-ability-score tables on the Record Forms (also reprinted in Figure 7.1, pp. 149–163). Because this standard error is sensitive to the particular set of items administered to the child, it is more accurate than a standard error derived from the overall reliability of the subtest for all children of the same age. An interval extending from one standard error below to one standard error above the observed score has a 68% likelihood of including the examinee's true ability score.[b] An interval twice as wide (two standard

---

[b]We could construct more accurate confidence intervals by centering the interval on the estimated true ability score and by using the standard error of estimate of the true ability score to determine the interval's width. However, this procedure is cumbersome, and no simple method was found that would retain the advantage provided by using the examinee's own standard error of measurement. The more accurate procedure was used, however, for the DAS composite scores.

errors above and below the observed score) has a 95% chance of including the true score. Using the subtest norm table for the child's age, we could convert the upper and lower limits of this confidence interval to T-scores and percentiles. For example, for a child aged 8:2 who obtains a raw score of 5 on Items 4–25 of the Word Definitions subtest, the corresponding ability score of 54 has a standard error of 6 ability-score points. Thus, a 68% confidence interval would include ability scores ranging from 48 (54 − 6) to 60 (54 + 6), which is equivalent to a range of T scores from 38 to 45, or a percentile range from 12 to 31. The more conservative 95% confidence interval includes ability scores ranging from 42 (54 − 12) to 66 (54 + 12) and T scores ranging from 34 to 49.

For our convenience, the DAS norm tables include the standard score confidence intervals for the composites and achievement tests, so we can obtain confidence intervals without calculation. For composite scores we cannot easily compute a standard error reflecting the appropriateness of the test content to the child's ability level. For each composite, then, we must use the average standard error from Tables 8.3 and 8.4 (pp. 181–182).

The standard-score confidence interval for each composite and each achievement test is centered on the estimated true standard score, and its width is determined by the standard error of estimate of the true standard score. These confidence intervals therefore give accurate estimates of the range within which the examinee's true standard score is likely to fall. The true standard score is the score that indicates where the examinee's true ability stands in relation to the distribution of true abilities in the normative population.[c]

---

[c]The procedure for estimating true standard scores differs from that used to estimate true raw scores. The difference arises because the standard deviation of true standard scores is, by definition, the same as that of observed standard scores (in the case of the DAS composites and achievement tests, 15). By contrast, the standard deviation of true raw scores is only $r_{xx}^{1/2}$ as great as that of observed raw scores (where r_{xx} is the test's reliability). As a result, the formula for predicting true standard scores from observed standard scores is

$$M + \sqrt{r_{xx}}\ \left(X - M\right)$$

where M is the mean standard score and X is the observed standard score. The estimation formula for true raw scores differs by using the reliability, rather than the square root of the reliability, as the coefficient. Again because true and observed standard scores have the same standard deviation, the standard error of estimate of the true standard score is the same as the standard error of measurement, whereas the standard error of estimate of the true raw score is smaller than the standard error of measurement of raw scores.

Specificity

An important characteristic of a test battery designed for interpretable profile analysis is the *specificity* of its scores. Specificity is the proportion of score variance that is reliable and unique to that subtest. The greater the proportion of reliable specific variance in a subtest, the more confidently we can interpret its score as a measure of a distinct ability.

The specificity of a battery can be examined at several levels. In principle, any score at a level of generality lower than the GCA score can have specificity, whether it is a subtest score or a cluster score. To the extent that a cluster score measures an ability that is independent of the other variables in the battery, it has specificity. Because the two or three subtests within a cluster share both general-factor variance and specific-ability variance, the abilities they measure overlap substantially, and the subtest scores individually will not have as much specificity as the cluster score that they create.

Tables 8.9 and 8.10 report specificity for all cognitive subtests and cluster scores. Following Silverstein's (1976) recommendation, shared variance is measured by the squared multiple correlation of the variable with all other subtests. This method counts as specific variance only variance that is not shared with any other cognitive subtest.

At both the Preschool and School-Age Levels, about 50% of the variance of the cognitive subtests is reliable specific variance. Not surprisingly, the diagnostic subtests have relatively high specificity. However, even the core subtests have substantial specificity that is always larger than the subtest's error variance. These results support the use of the DAS for analysis of cognitive strengths and weaknesses.

Comparison of IRT-Based and Traditional Methods of Estimating Reliability

The Rasch-based method of estimating subtest reliability has several advantages. First, it makes no assumptions about how examinees would have performed on items not administered to them. Second, the method gives the test developer a powerful tool for modeling test performance in order to design flexible item-selection procedures that combine accuracy with efficiency. Third, and perhaps most important, the model provides information about the accuracy of a test for examinees at various levels of ability. How do the results of this method compare with those of the most frequently used methods of estimating internal-consistency reliability—the split-half technique and coefficient alpha?

This chapter began by discussing five variables reflected in reliability coefficients: homogeneity of content, item accuracy, appropriateness of difficulty, temporal stability, and interrater reliability. The split-half method and coefficient alpha are highly sensitive to homogeneity of content; for this reason they are often referred

Table 8.9. Specificities of Subtests and Composites for the Preschool Level of the Cognitive Battery

Subtest or Composite	Age						Mean	Error Variance[a]
	2:6–2:11	3:0–3:5	3:6–3:11	4:0–4:5	4:6–4:11	5:0–5:11		
Verbal Comprehension	.41	.40	.22	.35	.34	.30	.34	.16
Naming Vocabulary	.38	.32	.26	.35	.39	.36	.34	.22
Block Building	.48	.51	.37	.44	.43	—	.44	.23
Picture Similarities	.63	.57	.51	.44	.48	.43	.51	.24
Pattern Construction	—	—	.53	.51	.50	.55	.52	.12
Copying	—	—	.51	.48	.56	.50	.51	.14
Early Number Concepts	—	—	.32	.34	.30	.29	.31	.14
Matching Letter-Like Forms	—	—	—	—	.47	.47	.47	.15
Recall of Digits	—	.68	.66	.64	.71	.57	.65	.13
Recall of Objects—Imm.	—	—	—	.68	.62	.54	.61	.29
Recognition of Pictures	—	.48	.48	.51	.47	.60	.51	.27
Verbal Ability	—	—	.38	.50	.43	.50	.45	.12
Nonverbal Ability	—	—	.34	.35	.33	.36	.35	.11

Note. Specificity is calculated by subtracting from the internal reliability of the subtest or composite the squared multiple correlation of the subtest or composite with all other subtests in the cognitive battery. Only on-level subtests were used for the calculations.

[a] Average proportion of test-score variance that is error variance, based on the average reliability shown in Table 8.1.

Table 8.10. Specificities of Subtests and Composites for the School-Age Level of the Cognitive Battery

Subtest or Composite	Age												Mean	Error Var.[a]
	6	7	8	9	10	11	12	13	14	15	16	17		
Word Definitions	45	26	41	37	40	31	37	39	33	31	25	39	.35	.17
Similarities	46	20	30	31	37	32	35	33	26	22	22	29	.30	.21
Matrices	34	41	46	32	37	46	36	36	43	41	44	37	.39	.18
Seq. & Quant. Reasoning	32	40	36	36	39	36	43	32	32	40	22	35	.35	.15
Recall of Designs	40	47	53	49	51	42	50	44	44	49	41	47	.46	.16
Pattern Construction	47	49	56	40	48	44	37	37	45	50	35	46	.44	.09
Recall of Digits	74	72	76	71	73	81	72	82	73	72	68	75	.74	.13
Recall of Objects—Imm.	62	55	60	66	64	66	62	66	69	71	63	68	.64	.24
Speed of Info. Processing	70	84	82	77	86	83	81	80	84	86	81	92	.82	.09
Verbal Ability	51	49	54	50	53	53	41	41	42	46	36	51	.47	.12
Nonverbal Reas. Ability	36	48	46	36	43	36	40	29	41	40	32	45	.39	.10
Spatial Ability	43	49	58	46	52	50	52	42	54	49	43	54	.49	.08

Note. Specificity is calculated by subtracting from the internal reliability of the subtest or composite the squared multiple correlation of the subtest or composite with all other subtests in the cognitive battery. Only on-level subtests were used for the calculations.

[a] Average proportion of test-score variance that is error variance, based on the average reliability shown in Table 8.2.

to as measures of *internal consistency*. (In the remainder of this section, split-half reliability and coefficient alpha will be referred to jointly as internal-consistency methods.) The IRT-based method is also sensitive to homogeneity of content, for two reasons. First, when IRT methods are used to develop a test, the homogeneity of the items is evaluated through goodness-of-fit tests (such as those described in Chapter 7); hence, a reasonable level of homogeneity is assured. Second, the more homogeneous the items are, the stronger the average relationship between each item and the total raw score will be. This strengthened relationship increases the variance of calibrated person abilities and thereby increases the IRT-based reliability index.

Item accuracy, or the amount of error in item scores, affects both internal-consistency and IRT-based reliability indexes in the same way as item homogeneity affects these indexes. When item scores are highly accurate, inter-item and split-half correlations increase. Also, the relationship between item-response scores and the total raw score is strengthened; this result produces greater dispersion of person abilities and a higher IRT-based reliability value.

Both the internal-consistency and IRT-based reliability methods are also sensitive to the appropriateness of item difficulty for the group for which reliability is being calculated. The effect on the IRT-based method is direct: the more items for which the probability of passing is near 0.5, the lower the standard error. Internal-consistency methods are also affected by item difficulty; this effect is clear when we consider the parallel halves of a test. In order for the halves to correlate highly, each half must exhibit reliable score variance, which can occur only if each half includes items appropriate in difficulty for the group.

Neither internal-consistency nor IRT-based methods are sensitive to interrater consistency or temporal stability (except for instability of ability during the period of test administration, which has the same effect as error in the item scores).

In summary, the IRT-based approach to estimating reliability appears to reflect the same test characteristics—homogeneity, item accuracy, and appropriateness of difficulty—as do the traditional internal-consistency methods.

The comparability of the two methods can be further evaluated by applying both methods to data. Because the split-half technique and coefficient alpha require data sets in which all examinees have taken all items, such data sets are used for the comparison. Two types of comparisons are reported below. One type used standardization data for the DAS Verbal Comprehension subtest for two age groups (3:6–3:11 and 4:0–4:5). Almost all examinees in these age ranges took all of the 23 items that use the toys and the inset tray. (Some of the children also took easier or harder items, increasing the accuracy of their scores; therefore, the reliabilities reported below are underestimates of the actual reliabilities of the subtest at these ages.) For the very few children who did not take all items because they failed five or more in succession and were stopped, items at the end of the set that were not administered were scored as failures.

The other comparisons used hypothetical, synthetic data sets. These sets allow computed reliability coefficients to be compared not only with one another but also with the "true" reliability. The project team constructed these data sets by (1) randomly generating a normal distribution of Rasch person abilities and a rectangular distribution of Rasch item difficulties, both centered at zero; (2) computing, from the Rasch model, the probability of each person's passing each item; and finally, (3) assigning to each item a score of 0 or 1 based on a comparison of the person's probability of passing, with a randomly sampled number between 0 and 1. The team then applied the MSTEPS program to the data to obtain estimated item difficulties and person abilities. The "true" reliability is calculated by the square of the correlation between the initially generated true abilities and the calibrated abilities from the Rasch scaling. The DAS team calculated internal consistency coefficients in the usual way (the split-half reliability is the odd–even correlation adjusted by the Spearman–Brown formula).

The results of these comparisons are presented in Table 8.11. For both the actual and synthetic data sets, the IRT-based reliability coefficients agree very closely with the split-half reliabilities and coefficient alpha. Furthermore, in the synthetic data sets, both the internal-consistency and IRT-based reliabilities closely estimate the "true" reliabilities. These findings support interpreting the IRT-based reliability coefficient in the same way as the traditional internal-consistency coefficients are interpreted.

One possible source of difference between the IRT-based and traditional methods is the way in which polychotomous items were scaled with the use of dummy items for the different point levels (described in Chapter 7). The IRT-based reliability-estimation method assumes that each dummy item is an independent contributor of information. Because the dummy items within an actual item are not independent, they may not contribute as much information about ability as the model assumes they do.

The two DAS subtests most likely to be affected are Speed of Information Processing and the standard version of Pattern Construction, each of which uses a multipoint scale of up to 3 to 6 points for each item. As mentioned earlier, coefficient alpha was used to measure the reliability of the Speed of Information Processing and Recall of Objects subtests because those subtests do not use Decision Point rules. Pattern Construction could not be analyzed in this way because it uses adaptive testing procedures. To determine whether or not polychotomous scoring affects IRT-based reliability estimates, the DAS team, using both IRT-based and traditional methods, analyzed sets of Pattern Construction items that had been given to almost all children at various ages. Results suggest that the IRT-based reliability values in Tables 8.1 and 8.2 for the Standard version of Pattern Construction are probably slightly higher (by around .04) than the split-half reliabilities would be if they could be computed. This difference, however, has very little practical effect on profile analysis. For example, if we assume that the average reliability at the school-age level is .87 rather than the .91 reported in Table 8.2, the score differences involving Pattern Construction or the Spatial Ability cluster

Table 8.11. Comparison of IRT-Based Reliability Estimates, Traditional Estimates, and "True" Reliabilities

Real Data (Verbal Comprehension)[a]

Age	N	Reliability		
		Alpha	Odd–Even	IRT–Based
3:6–3:11	174	.83	.86	.85
4:0–4:5	171	.80	.84	.80

Simulated Data

Ability[b]		Range of Item Difficulties[b]	N	"True"[c]	Reliability		
Mean	SD				Alpha	Odd–Even	IRT–Based
0	1	−1.5 to 1.5	2000	.80	.82	.82	.81
0	1	−2.0 to 2.0	2000	.81	.80	.80	.81
0	1	−2.5 to 2.5	2000	.80	.80	.80	.81
0	2	−3 to 3	2000	.91	.91	.92	.90
0	2	−4 to 4	2000	.90	.90	.91	.91
0	2	−5 to 5	2000	.89	.87	.89	.89

[a]The Verbal Comprehension data are for Items 7–29 only.
[b] "True" ability and difficulty values used to generate data. The simulated test contains 25 items.
[c]The "true" reliability is the squared correlation between the true ability scores (used for data generation) and the ability estimates generated by the Rasch scaling.

required for statistical significance at the .05 level would be increased by only 1/2 to 1 point. The differences on the other subtests with polychotomous items (Copying, Recall of Designs, and Similarities) would be even smaller because the items on those subtests have point scales of only up to 2 to 3 points.

Conclusion

This chapter has been concerned with showing that DAS scores are not only reliable in the traditional sense of the term, but are also accurate, even for some applications where the accuracy would not be obvious from the reliability coefficient. Thus, in the case of a test with a ceiling effect (where higher ability persons obtain near-maximum scores), the reliability coefficient is reduced, but measurement can be accurate for lower ability individuals. Because accuracy of measurement depends on administering items that are appropriate for the child's ability level, we will sometimes turn to out-of-level testing to obtain the most accurate results.

Chapter 9

Validity

Validating a test battery is an ongoing and cumulative process. This chapter presents and discusses the findings of a number of DAS validity studies as a groundwork for interpretation of and research with the DAS. The chapter discusses both the *internal* validity of the DAS—that is, the empirical support for its structure of scores—and the battery's *external* validity, the data from external sources that illuminate what the battery measures and how well it predicts.

The intercorrelations of the DAS subtests and composites for each of 17 age groups and 3 broad age ranges are presented first. Next, the internal structure of the DAS is examined through confirmatory and exploratory factor analyses. Finally, the external validity of the DAS is addressed through studies of its correlations with other indicators of cognitive abilities and achievement and through examination of the performance of special populations.

Internal Validity

As discussed in Chapter 2, the DAS arises from a perspective that abilities are hierarchically structured, with a higher-order factor measuring psychometric *g*, group factors representing narrower ability areas, and finally, specific abilities, some of which are largely independent of *g*. The original DAS developers included measures of a wide range of specific abilities that have been well documented, and anticipated that some of these would form a core battery that might include verbal and nonverbal dimensions, while others would be relatively independent. However, the DAS developers did not impose a detailed, preconceived organization of ability factors on the battery. Instead, the structure of the composite scores arose from a series of analyses of the data from the norm sample, which are described below.

Intercorrelations of Subtests and Composites

The intercorrelations of the core, diagnostic, and achievement subtests and the composite scores of the DAS for each 6-month or 1-year age group of the norm sample are presented in Appendix C. Tables 9.1–9.3 present these correlation coefficients for three broad age ranges: 2:6–3:5, 3:6–5:11, and 6:0–17:11. Correlations of the core subtests with the GCA and, at ages 6:0–17:11, with the Special Nonverbal Composite are shown in two ways: the raw correlation and the correlation of the subtest score with the sum of scores on the other subtests in the composite. (This latter correlation, referred to as the correlation "corrected for contamination," avoids the inflation that results from correlating a whole with one of its parts.) Appendix C also presents the correlations between the Preschool and School-Age Level scores of the Cognitive Battery for children aged 5:0–7:11.

197

Table 9.1. Intercorrelation of Subtests and Composites
by Age Range: Ages 2:6–3:5

Variable	VCom	NVoc	BB	PSim	ENC	RDig	RPic	GCA	SNV
Naming Vocabulary	.61	—							
Block Building	.39	.32	—						
Picture Similarities	.40	.39	.28	—					
Early Number Concepts	.53	.50	.38	.39	—				
Recall of Digits	.39	.34	.28	.33	.42	—			
Recognition of Pictures	.39	.38	.39	.23	.36	.25	—		
GCA	.81	.79	.67	.70	.61	.44	.47	—	
Special Nonverbal	.49	.45	.79	.80	.49	.38	.39	.85	—
Corrected Correlations[a]									
GCA	.63	.59	.41	.45	—	—	—	—	.53
Mean	50.4	50.1	50.0	50.5	50.3	50.2	49.7	100.3	99.7
SD	9.8	10.0	9.9	10.1	9.1	10.0	9.8	14.7	14.8

Note. N = 350.
[a]Correlation of the subtest with the sum of scores on the other subtests making up the composite.

Confirmatory Methods of Factor Analysis

To determine the actual structure of the abilities measured by the DAS, the project team employed the technique of confirmatory factor analysis. Like the more familiar exploratory techniques of principal-component and principal-factor analysis, confirmatory factor analysis attempts to represent the subtests as measures of a relatively small number of underlying factors. A subtest that is largely a measure of a particular factor or dimension of ability is said to have a high loading on (or correlation with) that factor. A model specifying which subtests load on which factors is said to fit the data well if it predicts the observed correlations among the subtests.

A fundamental difference between confirmatory and exploratory techniques is the approach to creating the model. In an exploratory analysis, the computer program generates a model from the correlations; the model shows the investigator how the variables align themselves, or "hang together." In a confirmatory analysis, on the other hand, the investigator specifies the model and obtains information about how well the model fits the data (that is, explains the correlations among the variables).

Confirmatory factor analysis can be used in an exploratory mode. The investigator specifies a number of theoretically plausible models ranging from very simple to complex. By comparing the degree of fit of each model, the investigator can identify the one that both fits well and is relatively simple. A usual strategy is to proceed from the simplest model to increasingly complex models and to observe the improvement of fit at each step. When a more complex model fails to improve the fit substantially, the simpler model is preferred because it is more parsimonious.

Table 9.2. Intercorrelation of Subtests and Composites by Age Range: Ages 3:6–5:11

Variable	VCom	NVoc	PSim	PC	PC(A)	Copy	ENC	BB	MLLF	RDig	RObI	RObD	RPic	Verb	NV	GCA
Naming Vocabulary	.64	—														
Picture Similarities	.40	.33	—													
Pattern Const.	.40	.29	.33	—												
Pattern Const. (Alt.)	.42	.30	.35	.87	—											
Copying	.35	.30	.31	.39	.40	—										
Early Number Concepts	.61	.51	.44	.48	.50	.49	—									
Block Building	.35	.31	.34	.48	.49	.51	.47	—								
Matching Letter-Like Forms	.32	.31	.31	.45	.44	.43	.44	.43	—							
Recall of Digits	.38	.37	.24	.21	.24	.27	.41	.34	.19	—						
Recall of Objects—Imm.	.18	.16	.17	.11	.13	.14	.19	.13	.11	.25	—					
Recall of Objects—Del.	.12	.10	.07	.14	.17	.16	.19	.18	.15	.15	.47	—				
Recognition of Pictures	.36	.31	.31	.35	.36	.28	.43	.35	.31	.22	.24	.23	—			
Verbal Ability	.90	.91	.40	.38	.40	.36	.62	.37	.34	.41	.19	.12	.37	—		
Nonverbal Ability	.51	.41	.73	.76	.72	.75	.62	.60	.52	.31	.19	.16	.41	.51	—	
GCA	.79	.71	.65	.67	.66	.65	.82	.58	.51	.44	.22	.18	.47	.83	.88	—
Corrected Correlations[a] GCA	.68	.57	.48	.51	.53	.49	.71							.59	.60	—
Mean	49.7	49.9	50.0	50.3	50.4	49.9	49.7	50.0	49.5	49.8	50.0	50.2	50.2	99.5	99.6	99.8
SD	9.9	10.0	10.0	9.9	9.8	9.8	9.7	9.8	9.7	9.9	9.8	9.5	9.9	15.2	14.9	14.7
N	725	725	725	725	725	725	725	525	550	725	550	531	725	725	725	725

[a]Correlation of the subtest with the sum of scores on the other subtests making up the composite.

Table 9.3. Intercorrelation of Subtests and Composites by Age Range: Ages 6:0-17:11

Variable	WDef	Sim	Mat	SQR	RDes	PC	PC(A)	RDig	RObI	RObD	RPic	SIP	Verb	NVR	Spat	GCA	SNV	BNS	Spel	WR
Similarities	.64	—																		
Matrices	.43	.44	—																	
S & Q Reas.	.52	.51	.58	—																
Rec. Designs	.38	.38	.44	.44	—															
Patt. Const.	.41	.44	.53	.54	.57	—														
Patt. Const. (Alt.)	.38	.42	.51	.51	.52	.89	—													
Rec. Digits	.28	.27	.24	.29	.19	.21	.19	—												
Rec. Ob.—Imm.	.24	.25	.22	.22	.25	.21	.17	.18	—											
Rec. Ob.—Del.	.13	.15	.14	.14	.22	.15	.12	.10	.68	—										
Recog. Pictures	.25	.25	.31	.28	.35	.28	.26	.16	.24	.23	—									
SIP	.19	.17	.18	.22	.16	.22	.16	.12	.20	.13	.14	—								
Verbal	.90	.91	.48	.57	.42	.47	.44	.30	.27	.16	.28	.20	—							
Nonverbal Reas.	.53	.53	.89	.89	.49	.60	.57	.30	.25	.15	.33	.22	.59	—						
Spatial	.45	.46	.55	.55	.88	.88	.80	.22	.26	.21	.35	.21	.50	.61	—					
GCA	.74	.75	.76	.79	.71	.77	.71	.33	.31	.20	.38	.25	.83	.87	.83	—				
SNV	.54	.55	.80	.80	.76	.82	.76	.29	.28	.20	.38	.24	.61	.90	.90	.95	—			
Corrected Correlations[a]																				
GCA	.62	.63	.63	.68	.57	.65	.61						.61	.69	.63	—				
SNV			.63	.63	.57	.67	.63										—			
Basic Number	.45	.41	.48	.57	.36	.44	.40	.28	.20	.14	.25	.29	.48	.59	.45	.60	.58	—		
Spelling	.49	.40	.39	.49	.28	.32	.30	.36	.22	.13	.23	.31	.49	.49	.34	.52	.46	.56	—	
Word Reading	.57	.50	.42	.50	.33	.38	.36	.38	.22	.14	.24	.26	.59	.52	.40	.60	.51	.53	.81	—
Mean	50.0	50.0	50.1	50.1	50.3	50.1	50.0	50.1	49.9	50.1	49.7	50.3	99.5	99.8	99.8	99.7	99.8	100.6	100.3	99.9
SD	9.9	10.0	10.2	10.0	10.0	10.0	9.6	10.0	10.2	9.9	9.6	9.9	15.0	15.1	14.9	15.0	14.9	14.6	14.9	14.7

Note. N = 2400 for all variables except Recall of Objects—Delayed, for which N = 2249.
[a]Correlation of the subtest with the sum of scores on the other subtests making up the composite.

The project team used this strategy to analyze the DAS norm-sample data. For each of several broad age levels, they evaluated the fit of a single-factor model, a two-factor (verbal–nonverbal) model, and, if theoretically appropriate, more complex models, and computed the improvement of fit from one model to the next. The age levels were determined by the ages at which the content of the Cognitive Battery stayed the same. The data for the broad School-Age Level were analyzed both within narrow age bands and across the whole group. The achievement tests were not included in these analyses because the focus was on creating a structure for the scores of the Cognitive Battery.

For each age level, the analysis initially included all of the cognitive subtests. As the analyses proceeded, subtests that did not load highly on any factors were classified as *diagnostic* and excluded from further analyses. Subtests were also excluded from the *core* battery on the grounds that they did not appear to measure conceptual and reasoning ability (for example, Matching Letter-Like Forms) or if they were not normed and on level for the full age range. The core subtests, then, had relatively high loadings on the general factor in the one-factor model and also were on level for the full age range. The discussion of the analyses for each age range includes the details of core- and diagnostic-subtest selection.

The purpose of the analyses reported here was to determine the differences in degrees of fit among the models rather than to find a model that fit the data perfectly. The fit of each model was evaluated according to several statistical indexes. Because no single index has been found to be completely satisfactory, several indexes are provided. The simplest index is *chi-square* (χ^2), which is smaller when the model fits the data well. The probability associated with chi-square and its degrees of freedom (*df*) is a test of the hypothesis that the model fully explains the data. When the probability value *p* based on chi-square is small (such as $< .01$), we can be confident that the model does not fit the data perfectly. With large samples, the hypothesis of perfect fit can almost always be rejected (that is, the *p* value will be small). Because of this fact, other indexes have been developed that also reflect the degree of fit. Two of these, the *goodness-of-fit index* (GFI) and the *adjusted goodness-of-fit index* (AGFI), take values up to 1, with larger values indicating better fit. The *root mean squared residual* (RMSR) reflects the average discrepancy between the intercorrelations predicted by the model and those actually observed. The closer the RMSR is to 0, the better the model fits the data. All of these indexes are generated by the maximum-likelihood estimation procedure of the LISREL VI program used for these analyses (Jöreskog & Sörbom, 1986) and the indexes are described in detail in that program's manual.

Chi-square is also quite useful for comparisons between models. When a model is made more complex by the addition of factors or by an increase in the number of loadings, the degrees of freedom—and usually the value of chi-square—decrease. The decrease of chi-square relative to the change in degrees of freedom is a direct test of the statistical significance of the difference in fit between the two models. If the more complex model produces a significantly smaller value of chi-square, then it significantly improves the fit to the data.

Ages 2:6–3:5

Six cognitive subtests were evaluated for ages 2:6–3:5. Although Recall of Digits and Recognition of Pictures are out of level at ages 2:6–2:11, they are appropriate for all but a small proportion of children at that age and were therefore included in the analyses.

The project team evaluated two models: a one-factor model, and a two-factor model in which three subtests formed a verbal factor and three subtests a nonverbal factor. As shown in Table 9.4, the one-factor model fit the data extremely well, and the two-factor model did not fit the data significantly better. The subtest loadings (shown in Table 9.5) indicate that all six subtests are reasonably good measures of the general factor, although the subtests measuring verbal comprehension and verbal expression are most strongly related. Verbal Comprehension, Naming Vocabulary, Block Building, and Picture Similarities were selected as the core subtests for this age range. The two memory subtests, Recall of Digits and Recognition of Pictures, were not included in the core because they demonstrated some floor effects for ages 2:6–2:11.

Table 9.4. Confirmatory Factor Analyses: Ages 2:6–3:5 (Six Subtests)

Model	Indexes of Fit[a]						Improvement in Fit		
	χ^2	df	p	GFI	AGFI	RMSR	χ^2	df	p
One Factor	21.75	9	.010	.980	.965	.037			
Two Factors	18.64	8	.017	.983	.972	.035	3.11	1	.100

Verbal (Verbal Comprehension, Naming Vocabulary, Recall of Digits)

Nonverbal (Block Building, Picture Similarities, Recognition of Pictures)

Note. N = 350.
[a]GFI = goodness of fit index; AGFI = adjusted goodness of fit index; RMSR = root mean squared residual. See the text for an explanation of these indexes.

Table 9.5. Confirmatory Factor Analysis—Subtest Correlations with the General Factor: Ages 2:6–3:5

Subtest	Factor Loading
Verbal Comprehension	0.80
Naming Vocabulary	0.74
Block Building	0.51
Picture Similarities	0.52
Recall of Digits	0.50
Recognition of Pictures	0.52

Ages 4:0–5:11

The next age range for analysis (4:0–5:11) started at age 4:0 rather than at age 3:6 so that the Recall of Objects and Matching Letter-Like Forms subtests could be included. Ten cognitive subtests were analyzed. (Block Building could not be included because it was administered to children only up to age 4:11.) The project team first evaluated three models: a one-factor model, a two-factor (verbal-nonverbal) model, and a three-factor (verbal–nonverbal–memory) model. Table 9.6 presents the results of these analyses.

The two-factor model fit the data significantly better than did the general-factor model. The three-factor model, however, fit the data worse than did the two-factor model; this result indicates that the memory subtests do not share much common variance. The two-factor solution was therefore chosen to represent the structure of the DAS for this age range.

Table 9.6. Confirmatory Factor Analyses: Ages 4:0–5:11 (Ten Subtests)

Model	Indexes of Fit						Improvement in Fit		
	χ^2	df	p	GFI	AGFI	RMSR	χ^2	df	p
One Factor	181.73	35	<.001	.932	.812	.052			
Two Factors[a]	135.69	34	<.001	.951	.873	.045	46.04	1	<.001
Three Factors	140.36	32	<.001	.948	.876	.046			

    Verbal (Verbal Comprehension, Naming Vocabulary, Early Number Concepts)

    Nonverbal (Picture Similarities, Pattern Construction, Copying, Matching Letter-Like Forms)

    Memory (Recall of Digits, Recall of Objects, Recognition of Pictures)

Note. N = 550.
[a]See Table 9.7 for the composition of the factors.

To select subtests for the core battery, the project team examined the loadings on the general factor (shown in Table 9.7) and retained six of the seven subtests with the highest *g* loadings. The Matching Letter-Like Forms subtest was excluded from the core because it appeared to be a measure more of perceptual ability than of conceptual or reasoning ability and because it is on level only for a relatively narrow age range (4:6–5:11).

The project team reanalyzed the six retained core subtests to determine whether or not the two-factor model still fit well. Because 3 1/2-year-olds had taken all six core subtests, the age range for this analysis was widened to 3:6–5:11. As shown in Table 9.8, the two-factor model again fit significantly better than did the one-factor model. However, the analysis indicated that the model's requirement that the Early Number Concepts subtest load only on the verbal factor caused much of the remaining misfit of the model to the data. Loading this subtest on the non-verbal factor instead substantially improved the overall fit, although much of the remaining misfit was still attributable to the subtest. Loading the Early Number

Table 9.7. Confirmatory Factor Analyses—Subtest Loadings for the One-Factor and Two-Factor Models: Ages 4:0–5:11

		Factor Loadings	
			Two Factors
Subtest	One Factor	Verbal	Nonverbal
Verbal Comprehension	.72	.76	
Naming Vocabulary	.64	.69	
Early Number Concepts	.82	.81	
Recall of Digits	.47	.49	
Recall of Objects	.27	.27	
Picture Similarities	.54		.55
Pattern Construction	.59		.66
Copying	.59		.63
Matching Letter-Like Forms	.55		.62
Recognition of Pictures	.49		.52

Note. N = 550.

Table 9.8. Confirmatory Factor Analyses: Ages 3:6–5:11 (Six Core Subtests)

	Indexes of Fit						Improvement in Fit		
Model	χ^2	*df*	*p*	GFI	AGFI	RMSR	χ^2	*df*	*p*
One Factor	103.85	9	<.001	.948	.910	.048			
Two Factors	86.77	8	<.001	.958	.932	.043	17.08	1	<.001
Verbal (Verbal Comprehension, Naming Vocabulary, Early Number Concepts [ENC])									
Nonverbal (Picture Similarities, Pattern Construction, Copying)									
Two Factors (ENC on Nonverbal only)	18.28	8	.019	.992	.987	.023	85.57[a]	1	<.001
Two Factors (ENC on both)	11.53	7	.117	.995	.992	.018	6.75[b]	1	<.01

Note. N = 725.
[a]Compared with the one-factor model.
[b]Compared with the two-factor model with ENC on the Nonverbal Factor only.

Concepts subtest on both factors further improved the fit and yielded the loadings shown in Table 9.9.

From a practical point of view, allowing a subtest to contribute to two factors would seriously detract from the distinctiveness and interpretability of those composites. However, its high *g* loading and conceptual content mandated the inclusion of the Early Number Concepts subtest in the GCA, and its strong verbal content made it inappropriate as part of the nonverbal factor. Early Number Concepts was therefore retained as a core subtest contributing only to the GCA but not contributing to either the Verbal Ability or the Nonverbal Ability cluster score.

Table 9.9. Confirmatory Factor Analyses—Subtest Loadings for the Two-Factor Model (ENC on Both): Ages 3:6–5:11

	Factor Loadings	
Subtest	Verbal	Nonverbal
Verbal Comprehension	.88	
Naming Vocabulary	.73	
Early Number Concepts	.22	.64
Picture Similarities		.56
Pattern Construction		.61
Copying		.60

Note. N = 725.

Ages 6:0–17:11

The ten cognitive subtests analyzed for ages 6:0–17:11 included Recognition of Pictures, which is out of level for ages 8:0–17:11 but which is normed through age 17:11. The project team evaluated one-factor, two-factor (verbal–nonverbal), and three-factor (verbal–nonverbal–memory) models. Results are presented in Table 9.10.

Table 9.10. Confirmatory Factor Analyses: Ages 6:0–17:11 (Ten Subtests)

	Indexes of Fit						Improvement in Fit		
Model	χ^2	df	p	GFI	AGFI	RMSR	χ^2	df	p
One Factor	705.53	35	<.001	.942	.840	.045			
Two Factors[a] Verbal Nonverbal	376.76	34	<.001	.969	.918	.039	328.77	1	<.001
Three Factors[a] Verbal Nonverbal Memory	329.43	32	<.001	.972	.933	.034	376.10[b]	3	<.001

Note. N = 2400.
[a]See Table 9.11 for the composition of the factors.
[b]Compared with the one-factor model.

All three models fit the data reasonably well. The two-factor model fit the data significantly better than did the one-factor model. The three-factor model fit even better, although the improvement relative to the two-factor model could not be evaluated for statistical significance because the two-factor model was not "nested" in the three-factor model. Table 9.11 shows the subtest loadings of all three models. Despite the good fit of the three-factor model, its memory factor was not supported by the loadings: Only the Recall of Designs subtest loaded highly. Futhermore, the analysis indicated that allowing Recall of Designs to load as well on the nonverbal factor would substantially improve the fit. These findings suggested that a memory factor separate from the verbal and nonverbal factors was not justified.

205

Table 9.11. Confirmatory Factor Analyses—Subtest Loadings for the One-, Two-, and Three-Factor Models: Ages 6:0–17:11

		Factor Loadings				
		Two Factors		Three Factors		
Subtest	One Factor	Verbal	Non-verbal	Verbal	Non-verbal	Memory
Word Definitions	.68	.79		.79		
Similarities	.69	.79		.80		
Matrices	.71		.73		.73	
Seq. & Quant. Reasoning	.76		.76		.77	
Pattern Construction	.70		.73		.73	
Speed of Info. Processing	.28		.28		.29	
Recognition of Pictures	.42		.42			.47
Recall of Designs	.63		.65			.70
Recall of Digits	.36	.37				.37
Recall of Objects	.35	.34				.38

Note. N = 2400.

Six subtests clearly loaded more highly on the general factor than did the others, and these were selected to compose the core. The project team analyzed these highly *g* loaded subtests for their fit to one-factor and two-factor models. Again, as shown in Table 9.12, the two-factor model had significantly better fit. Analysis of the residual correlations also indicated, however, that the Pattern Construction and Recall of Designs subtests correlated with each other much more highly than the model would predict, and that both the Sequential and Quantitative Reasoning and the Matrices subtests correlated lower with the Pattern Construction and Recall of Designs subtests than the model predicted. These indications suggested the creation of two separate factors out of the original nonverbal factor: one consisting of the Matrices and Sequential and Quantitative Reasoning subtests, the nonverbal reasoning factor; and the other including the Pattern Construction and Recall of Designs subtests, the spatial factor. Table 9.12 shows that, according to all of the fit indexes, this three-factor (verbal–nonverbal reasoning–spatial) model fit significantly better than did the two-factor model.

To determine whether the three-factor structure or the two-factor model fit better for the youngest as well as the oldest age groups in the school-aged sample, the project team separately analyzed the core subtests for three age ranges: 6:0–9:11, 10:0–13:11, and 14:0–17:11. Results appear in Table 9.13.

For all three subsamples, the one-factor model fit the data relatively poorly, whereas the two-factor (verbal–nonverbal) model fit significantly better. The three-factor model, however, fit the data significantly better than did the two-factor model for every age range. Loadings as well as fit indexes were highly consistent at all three age ranges. Thus, for the entire school-aged sample, a three-factor model comprising Verbal Ability, Nonverbal Reasoning Ability, and Spatial Ability dimensions provides the best explanation of the correlations among the core subtests.

Table 9.12. Confirmatory Factor Analyses: Ages 6:0–17:11 (Six Core Subtests)

Model	χ²	df	p	GFI	AGFI	RMSR	χ²	df	p
			Indexes of Fit				Improvement in Fit		
One Factor	515.47	9	<.001	.930	.877	.055			
Two Factors	160.39	8	<.001	.977	.963	.030	355.08	1	<.001
Verbal									
Nonverbal									
Three Factors	28.07	6	<.001	.996	.995	.013	132.32[a]	2	<.001
Verbal									
Nonverbal Reasoning									
Spatial									

Subtest	Verbal	Nonverbal Reasoning	Spatial
		Factor Loadings	
Word Definitions	.79		
Similarities	.81		
Matrices		.74	
Seq. & Quant. Reasoning		.80	
Recall of Designs			.69
Pattern Construction			.82

Note. N = 2400.
[a]Compared with the two-factor model.

Summary of Confirmatory Factor Analyses

The confirmatory factor analyses suggest that the structure of abilities becomes more differentiated with the examinee's increasing age. It has been a robust, but often overlooked, finding that as the child's age and ability increase, abilities become more differentiated (Anastasi, 1970). This development is true for the DAS, for which one factor provides the best fit for the core subtests for the youngest children, two factors emerge as the child's cognitive development increases, and three factors represent the abilities of the school-aged child. In addition to these factors among the relatively highly *g* loaded subtests, the diagnostic subtests represent further dimensions of ability, which become more independent of the core subtests with the examinee's increasing age.

The lack of statistical support for a factor underlying the various memory subtests is consistent with results of experimental investigations of memory in children. For example, Hitch, Halliday, Schaafstal, and Schraagen (1988) have emphasized that there is a distinction between modality-specific auditory-verbal and visual subsystems of temporary information storage. These separate memory systems offer a more satisfactory account of how individuals retain information than does a single, undifferentiated memory system.

Table 9.13. Confirmatory Factor Analyses—One-, Two-, and Three-Factor Models for School-Aged Subsamples (Six Core Subtests)

Age and Model	Indexes of Fit						Improvement in Fit		
	χ^2	*df*	*p*	GFI	AGFI	RMSR	χ^2	*df*	*p*
Ages 6:0–9:11									
One Factor	190.49	9	<.001	.925	.869	.061			
Two Factors	50.65	8	<.001	.979	.966	.030	139.84	1	<.001
Verbal									
Nonverbal									
Three Factors	19.71	6	<.003	.992	.989	.019	30.94[a]	2	<.001
Verbal									
Nonverbal Reasoning									
Spatial									
Ages 10:0–13:11									
One Factor	172.66	9	<.001	.929	.875	.055			
Two Factors	65.59	8	<.001	.972	.955	.034	107.07	1	<.001
Verbal									
Nonverbal									
Three Factors	16.79	6	<.01	.993	.990	.016	48.80[a]	2	<.001
Verbal									
Nonverbal Reasoning									
Spatial									
Ages 14:0–17:11									
One Factor	190.18	9	<.001	.924	.867	.054			
Two Factors	77.94	8	<.001	.967	.947	.034	112.24	1	<.001
Verbal									
Nonverbal									
Three Factors	19.79	6	<.003	.992	.989	.016	58.15[a]	2	<.001
Verbal									
Nonverbal Reasoning									
Spatial									

Note. N = 800 for each age range.
[a]Compared with the two-factor model.

Exploratory Methods of Factor Analysis

The technique of exploratory factor analysis was used with the DAS data as a secondary procedure to the confirmatory factor analyses. As stated in the previous section, in an exploratory analysis the computer program generates a model from the correlations between subtests. The factor loadings are an index of how the various subtests align themselves.

Paradoxically, just as confirmatory factor analytic techniques were used in an exploratory way to investigate a number of models, the exploratory factor analyses reported here were intended to be confirmatory. In other words, the exploratory analyses would indicate whether the models identified in the previous analyses offered the most plausible accounts of the interrelationships between the subtests or whether there were alternative patterns that would lead to different models.

One of the problems of exploratory factor analysis is the lack of a commonly accepted criterion to determine the number of factors that underlie a set of data. Consequently, a number of solutions are presented for each major age group represented in the confirmatory analyses, namely, 2:6–3:5, 4:0–5:11, and 6:0–17:11.

To examine the common factors underlying the subtest intercorrelations, with error variance excluded, the project team used the technique of principal-factor analysis. (Initial communality estimates were squared multiple correlations.) Because cognitive abilities tend to covary, a type of factor solution in which the factors, when rotated, would be correlated was deemed the most realistic. Thus, the factors were obliquely rotated to the Promax criterion. The tables for each solution consist of factor-pattern coefficients for the rotated factors.

Factor loadings for a single (general) factor for the three age groups have been reported with the confirmatory analyses. The exploratory analyses reported here present two-, three-, or four-factor solutions for each age group. Subtests that have been designed to have high levels of reliable specificity create a difficulty for exploratory factor analysis: At some point during the extraction of factors, a strong but unique factor that is determined largely by one subtest will emerge. One way to prevent this occurrence is to delete the subtest concerned from the set of tests to be analyzed. Experience showed, however, that this solution would mean that all of the diagnostic subtests would be deleted because all have high levels of reliable specificity. In the solutions presented below, all of the diagnostic subtests are retained. Factor extraction was discontinued at the point when no further common factors determined by two or more high-loading subtests emerged.

Ages 2:6–3:5

Six cognitive subtests were evaluated for ages 2:6–3:5. Only one solution, for two factors, was obtained for this age group (in addition to the one-factor solution discussed earlier). The results appear in Table 9.14. Factor 1 is a verbal factor that is strongly defined by high loadings for the Naming Vocabulary and Verbal

Table 9.14. Exploratory Principal-Factor Analysis—
Promax Factor Pattern: Ages 2:6–3:5

	Factor	
Subtest	1	2
Verbal Comprehension	.74	.09
Naming Vocabulary	.76	.00
Block Building	.02	.70
Picture Similarities	.48	.07
Recall of Digits	.41	.13
Recognition of Pictures	.22	.41

Correlation Between Factors 1 and 2: .60

Note. N = 350.

Comprehension subtests. Factor 2 is largely determined by a high loading for the Block Building subtest and a moderate one for the Recognition of Pictures subtest. These loadings might suggest a weak nonverbal factor, but the near-zero loading of the Picture Similarities subtest on the factor makes the interpretation and labeling of the factor uncertain. With only one subtest having a high loading on the factor, evidence for a two-factor structure is weak, and the data best support the one-factor model for this age level. These results support the conclusion from the confirmatory analyses of these data that a one-factor model provides the best fit for this age.

Ages 4:0–5:11

This age range started at 4:0 so that the Recall of Objects and Matching Letter-Like Forms subtests could be included in the battery. Ten cognitive subtests were analyzed with two-, three-, and four-factor solutions, shown in Table 9.15. The two-factor solution was interpretable as a nonverbal–verbal dichotomy. Factor 1 (nonverbal) is strongly defined by the high loadings of the Pattern Construction, Matching Letter-Like Forms, and Copying subtests, with an additional, moderate loading for the Early Number Concepts subtest (the loadings for Early Number Concepts seemed balanced about equally between the two factors). The moderate loadings of the Picture Similarities and Recognition of Pictures subtests also supported the interpretation of this factor as nonverbal. Factor 2 (verbal) is principally defined by the Verbal Comprehension and Naming Vocabulary subtests, with moderate loadings for the Recall of Digits and Early Number Concepts subtests. As discussed earlier in relation to the confirmatory analyses, Early Number Concepts appeared to have both verbal and nonverbal components and was therefore not included in either DAS cluster. The results of the exploratory factor analysis support that decision.

Table 9.15. Exploratory Principal-Factor Analyses—
Promax Factor Patterns: Ages 4:0–5:11

| | Solution 1 | | Solution 2 | | | Solution 3 | | | |
| | Factor | | Factor | | | Factor | | | |
Subtest	1	2	1	2	3	1	2	3	4
Picture Similarities	.34	.25	.35	.21	.07	.31	.20	.10	.02
Pattern Construction	.70	−.02	.72	−.02	−.06	.67	.05	.02	−.12
Early Number Concepts	.47	.42	.49	.38	.03	.48	.29	.05	.16
Copying	.58	.08	.59	.06	.00	.67	−.05	−.08	.18
Verbal Comprehension	.06	.76	.06	.79	−.04	.02	.87	−.04	−.02
Naming Vocabulary	−.04	.77	−.04	.80	−.03	.00	.71	−.02	.09
Matching LL Forms	.67	−.03	.68	−.04	−.04	.67	−.02	−.02	−.01
Recall of Digits	.03	.48	.02	.39	.22	−.01	.16	.17	.49
Recall of Objects	.07	.23	.00	.01	.65	−.07	−.06	.47	.26
Recognition of Pictures	.40	.15	.41	.05	.19	.27	.04	.44	−.07

Correlations Between Factors:

Solution 1	Solution 2	Solution 3
1 and 2: .62	1 and 2: .64	1 and 2: .63
	1 and 3: .32	1 and 3: .48
	2 and 3: .35	1 and 4: .29
		2 and 3: .45
		2 and 4: .42
		3 and 4: .12

Note. N = 550.

The three-factor solution is also shown in Table 9.15. The first two factors were virtually identical to those of the two-factor solution, and Factor 3 appeared to be a unique factor defined solely by the Recall of Objects subtest. Thus, this solution did not add substantively to the information derived from the two-factor solution.

Finally, in the four-factor solution, the first two factors remained relatively strongly defined as nonverbal and verbal abilities, respectively. Their loadings were very similar to those of Factors 1 and 2 in the two previous solutions. Factors 3 and 4 were both relatively weak, with no loadings exceeding .50. Factor 3 was defined by moderate loadings for the Recall of Objects and Recognition of Pictures subtests, while Factor 4 appeared to be a unique factor defined by a moderate loading for the Recall of Digits subtest. Both Factors 3 and 4 were weakly defined by diagnostic subtests which themselves had relatively low *g* loadings (see Table 9.7). Consequently, little justification appeared for interpreting Factors 3 and 4 as significant contributors to the ability structure of this sample of 4- and 5-year-olds.

In summary, Factors 1 and 2 remained robust for all solutions, strongly supporting the confirmatory factor analyses in determining that a two-factor model best fits the data for this age group.

Ages 6:0–17:11

The ten cognitive subtests for this age range (6:0–17:11) were also analyzed with two-, three-, and four-factor exploratory solutions. The results are shown in Table 9.16.

Table 9.16. Exploratory Principal-Factor Analyses—
Promax Factor Patterns: Ages 6:0–17:11

Subtest	Solution 1 Factor		Solution 2 Factor			Solution 3 Factor			
	1	2	1	2	3	1	2	3	4
Word Definitions	.02	.79	.00	.80	.02	.79	.02	.01	.01
Similarities	.07	.73	.07	.72	.02	.72	.06	.04	.00
Matrices	.55	.21	.57	.19	.00	.04	.62	.12	.04
Seq. & Quant. Reasoning	.46	.36	.48	.35	−.02	.17	.67	.00	.02
Recall of Designs	.69	.01	.64	−.03	.14	.02	−.02	.83	.02
Pattern Construction	.72	.06	.79	.01	−.03	.03	.40	.42	−.03
Recall of Digits	.13	.28	.06	.26	.14	.18	.18	−.06	.17
Recall of Objects	.24	.15	.01	.07	.58	.04	−.02	.05	.58
Recognition of Pictures	.41	.06	.30	.01	.27	.01	.11	.23	.24
Speed of Info. Processing	.21	.11	.12	.07	.21	.01	.17	−.02	.24

Correlations Between Factors:

1 and 2: .62	1 and 2: .65	1 and 2: .65
	1 and 3: .41	1 and 3: .52
	2 and 3: .38	1 and 4: .41
		2 and 3: .63
		2 and 4: .35
		3 and 4: .41

Note. $N = 2400$.

The two-factor solution yielded a nonverbal factor (Factor 1) defined by high loadings for the Pattern Construction and Recall of Designs subtests and by moderate loadings for the Matrices, Sequential and Quantitative Reasoning, and Recognition of Pictures subtests. Factor 2, the verbal factor, was defined by high loadings for the Word Definitions and Similarities subtests.

The three-factor solution produced a result very similar to that produced by the three-factor solution for 4- and 5-year-olds. Once again the loadings on Factors 1 and 2 were virtually identical to the factor pattern of the two-factor solution. And once again, Factor 3 was a unique factor defined by the Recall of Objects subtest.

To examine whether or not the cluster of subtests loading highly on Factor 1 would subdivide, the project team obtained a four-factor solution. The four core subtests that loaded on the previous Factor 1 (the nonverbal factor) split into two pairs, defining Factors 2 and 3, respectively. Thus, Factor 2 had high loadings for the Sequential and Quantitative Reasoning and Matrices subtests and was therefore interpretable as a nonverbal reasoning factor. Factor 3, defined largely by the

Recall of Designs subtest, and with a moderate loading for Pattern Construction, was a spatial ability factor. Factor 1 became the verbal factor, defined by the same subtests (Word Definitions and Similarities) as Factor 2 in the two- and three-factor solutions. The first three factors strongly support the confirmatory factor analysis for this age group.

Factor 4 was again largely defined by the Recall of Objects subtest. The small, but positive, association between this subtest and the Speed of Information Processing subtest emerged consistently throughout the school-age range and appeared in a number of similar analyses for narrower age ranges, which are not reported here.

Summary of Exploratory Factor Analyses

The analyses described above support the results and factor interpretations of the confirmatory factor analyses. They provide additional evidence of the differentiation of abilities as children become older. Even when three or four factors are extracted, the analyses do not suggest groupings of subtests other than those that were evaluated in the confirmatory phase.

Equivalence of the Preschool and School-Age GCA

Continuity in the meaning of the GCA score at different ages is crucial for longitudinal interpretation of the DAS. Because both the Preschool and School-Age Levels of the Cognitive Battery were administered during standardization to all children aged 5:0–6:11, a comparison of the GCA scores produced by the two levels is possible. This comparison is not ideal because the Preschool Level is somewhat too easy for the higher ability 6-year-olds and because parts of the School-Age Level are difficult for the lower ability 5-year-olds. These floor and ceiling effects diminish reliability and attenuate the correlations. The method of confirmatory factor analysis, however, makes possible a reliable test of the hypothesis that the two GCA scores reflect the same dimension of ability.

The intercorrelation matrix of all eleven core subtests making up the separate levels of the battery was computed for all 400 children (see Table 9.17). Two GCA scores were calculated for each child, one from the Preschool and the other from the School-Age core subtests. The correlation between the two GCA scores is .86, indicating that these composite scores have a high degree of convergence. Two simple factor models were constructed and compared, as shown in Figure 9.1. The first model had a single factor underlying all eleven subtests, whereas the second model had two distinct, but correlated, factors, one for the Preschool core subtests and the other for the School-Age core subtests. If the GCA scores from the two levels differed at all, then the two-factor model would fit the data better than would the one-factor model. Results are presented in Table 9.18.

Table 9.17. Intercorrelation of Preschool and School-Age Core Subtests: Ages 5:0–6:11

Subtest	NVoc	VCom	Copy	PSim	ENC	PC	Sim	WDef	Mat	SQR	RDes
Verbal Comprehension	.62	—									
Copying	.34	.35	—								
Picture Similarities	.32	.38	.37	—							
Early Number Concepts	.50	.55	.47	.39	—						
Pattern Construction	.30	.37	.48	.36	.46	—					
Similarities	.58	.58	.42	.36	.52	.32	—				
Word Definitions	.59	.53	.42	.34	.52	.33	.56	—			
Matrices	.31	.42	.45	.35	.46	.45	.40	.33	—		
Seq. & Quant. Reas.	.39	.48	.47	.40	.62	.45	.50	.45	.55	—	
Recall of Designs	.32	.35	.64	.34	.43	.49	.39	.42	.44	.53	—
Mean	50.0	49.1	50.5	49.6	49.4	49.8	50.3	50.4	50.1	50.3	50.1
SD	10.2	9.8	9.7	10.1	9.7	9.7	9.5	9.8	9.6	9.1	9.6

Note. N = 400.

Table 9.18. Confirmatory Factor Analyses Testing the Equivalence of the Preschool and School-Age GCA Scores

Model	Indexes of Fit						Improvement in Fit		
	χ^2	df	p	GFI	AGFI	RMSR	χ^2	df	p
One Factor	289.87	44	< .001	.856	.569	.066			
Two Factors Preschool and School-Age GCAs	289.29	42	< .001	.857	.608	.066	0.58	2	NS

Note. N = 400 children aged 5:0–6:11 from the norm sample.

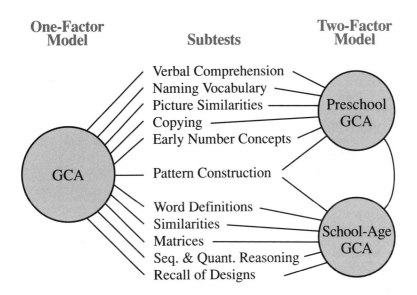

Figure 9.1. Models Used for the Comparison of the GCAs from the Preschool and School-Age Levels

Clearly the fit did not improve when separate factors were introduced to represent the GCAs of the Preschool and School-Age Levels. The small and nonsignificant change in chi-square indicated that a single factor well represents the underlying structure of the core subtests across age. This conclusion was reinforced by the correlation of approximately 1.00 between the underlying factors in the two-factor model. We can therefore infer that the GCA holds equal interpretive significance at the Preschool and School-Age Levels.

Equivalence of the Two Versions of the Pattern Construction Subtest

The Alternative (unspeeded) version of the Pattern Construction subtest is intended to measure the same ability as the standard version. At the same time, it is intended to be fairer for those children for whom a motor impairment or other extraneous factor might make speed of response an invalid index of their ability. In substituting the Alternative for the Standard version, we assume that the Alternative version measures the same construct and fits into the underlying factor model equally well.

The two versions have similar correlations with other variables, as shown in Tables 9.2 and 9.3 (pp. 199 and 200). The equivalence of the two versions was tested statistically with confirmatory factor analysis. Two variations of the intercorrelation matrix of the core subtests analyzed were identical except that one included the Standard version and the other the Alternative version of the Pattern Construction subtest. The same factor model was applied to each intercorrelation matrix. One analysis was performed with the restriction that all factor loadings and factor intercorrelations were identical for the two matrices. The second analysis differed only in permitting the loadings for Pattern Construction to be different for each matrix. If the Standard and Alternative versions of Pattern Construction had the same relationship to the other variables, the overall fit would be the same for both analyses. If the two versions of the subtest differed, the fit would be better when their loadings were permitted to differ.

Results for three age groups appear in Table 9.19. The school-aged sample was split into two subsamples, 6:0–11:11 and 12:0–17:11, because the Alternative version of Pattern Construction has a ceiling effect for older adolescents.

Allowing the Pattern Construction loadings to differ did not improve the fit for either of the first two age groups. For the oldest group, the fit improved significantly, with the Pattern Construction loadings on the spatial factor at .85 (Standard) and .78 (Alternative). The ceiling effect of the Alternative version for children aged 13 and over caused a reduction in the correlations that probably accounted for this difference; for this age range, the Alternative version should be used only with children of low or average spatial ability. Overall, these results support the use of the Alternative version of the Pattern Construction subtest in place of the Standard version for both subtest and composite scoring.

Table 9.19. Confirmatory Factor Analyses Comparing the Two Versions of the Pattern Construction Subtest

Age Range	Condition	Indexes of Fit (Total for Both Matrices)					Improvement of Fit		
		χ^2	df	p	GFI	RMSR	χ^2	df	p
3:6–5:11	Equal Loadings	25.77	22	.262	.994	.019			
	Variable Loadings	25.48	21	.227	.994	.019	0.29	1	NS
6:0–11:11	Equal Loadings	30.75	21	.078	.996	.015			
	Variable Loadings	30.65	20	.060	.996	.014	0.10	1	NS
12:0–17:11	Equal Loadings	51.27	21	<.001	.992	.023			
	Variable Loadings	46.89	20	<.001	.993	.016	4.38	1	<.05

Note. N = 725 for Ages 3:6–5:11; N = 1200 each for Ages 6:0–11:11 and 12:0–17:11. See text for explanation of method.

Correlations with Other Cognitive Measures

The studies described in this section address several fundamental issues, including the similarities and differences between the DAS and other instruments, the relationship between the DAS and academic achievement, and performance on the DAS by special populations. Most of the studies provide evidence regarding the convergent and discriminant validity of the DAS subtests and composites. Convergent validity is shown by relatively high correlations with other measures of the same ability, and discriminant validity is demonstrated by lower correlations with measures of different constructs.

Correlations with Other Ability Batteries

In the first group of studies, the project team, in cooperation with several independent researchers, investigated the correlations of DAS composite and subtest scores with scores from other cognitive-ability batteries. Most of these studies were concerned with the general population of children and were carried out in conjunction with the standardization of the DAS. This arrangement enabled the samples for studies of the WPPSI-R, WISC-R, and SB-IV to be reasonably representative of the U.S. population according to sex, race, SES, and region. These data were collected by numerous examiners in various parts of the United States. The samples of a few of the studies, conducted by independent researchers, were local samples, as noted below.

In most of the studies, the sequence of administration of the batteries was counterbalanced so that differences in mean scores from the two different batteries could be measured, independent of practice effects. For these studies, the estimated practice effects were removed from second-administration scores by adjustments to the mean composite scores. The practice effect was estimated by computing, for each of the two subsamples (those taking the DAS first and those taking the DAS second), the average increase in mean scores on like composites from first to second testing and then by finding the unweighted mean of these two average increases. The estimated practice effect for each composite was then subtracted from the scores obtained on the second administrations.

When comparing scores from different batteries, we should keep in mind that because the overall level of performance of children has tended to increase over the decades, recently normed tests will produce lower normative scores than do tests standardized in the past (Flynn, 1984). Differences between tests in their levels of scores often are due to this phenomenon.

In studies incorporating counterbalanced administrations, correlations of the DAS with the other battery were computed separately for each of the two sub-groups and were corrected for restriction of range of the DAS score. The weighted average of the two corrected correlations was then found with Fisher's z transformation.

The following section first presents correlational studies of the Preschool Level of the Cognitive Battery and continues with studies of the School-Age Level of the battery. The information about the demographic characteristics of each sample can be compared with the distributions for the U.S. population presented in Chapter 6.

Preschool Level of the DAS Cognitive Battery

Wechsler Preschool and Primary Scale of Intelligence— Revised (WPPSI–R)

The DAS and the WPPSI–R (Wechsler, 1989) were administered in counterbalanced order to 62 children aged 4:6–5:11, with a mean age of 5:3 (SD = 5 months). The interval between test administrations averaged 14 days, ranging from 7 to 41 days. The sample had the following composition:

Sex: Females (50%) and Males (50%)

Race/Ethnicity: Black (8%), Hispanic (2%), White (88%), and Other (2%)

Parent Education (for the 60 cases for whom data were available)**:** 4 or more years of college (38%), 1–3 years of college or technical school (23%), high school graduation or equivalent (28%), and less than high school graduation (10%)

Geography: North Central (47%), South (42%), and West (11%)

Table 9.20 reports the correlations and mean scores.

Table 9.20. Correlations of the DAS with the Wechsler Preschool and Primary Scale of Intelligence— Revised (WPPSI–R): 4- and 5-Year-Olds

DAS	WPPSI–R			DAS	
	Verbal IQ	Perform-ance IQ	Full Scale IQ	Mean	SD
Composites					
Verbal Ability	.74	.62	.77	97.6	14.8
Nonverbal Ability	.51	.75	.72	99.0	12.5
GCA	.76	.83	.89	98.3	12.8
Core Subtests					
Verbal Comprehension	.72	.67	.80		
Naming Vocabulary	.70	.53	.69		
Picture Similarities	.49	.34	.45		
Pattern Construction	.50	.66	.65		
Copying	.22	.66	.51		
Early Number Concepts	.52	.60	.64		
Diagnostic Subtests					
Matching Letter-Like Forms	.57	.51	.61		
Recall of Digits	.22	.31	.31		
Recall of Objects	.34	.24	.34		
Recognition of Pictures	.31	.35	.37		
WPPSI–R					
Mean	101.2	99.9	101.0		
SD	13.6	14.7	14.7		

Note. $N = 62$. All correlations are corrected for restriction of range of DAS scores. To compute the mean scores, estimated practice effects were subtracted from second administration scores.

The high correlations between composite scores indicate that the two batteries have much in common. The Verbal Ability and Nonverbal Ability cluster scores of the DAS show a differential pattern of correlations with the WPPSI–R's Verbal and Performance IQs. Each DAS core-subtest score correlates above .4 (median = .645) with the WPPSI–R Full Scale IQ. The higher correlation of the Picture Similarities score with Verbal IQ than with Performance IQ probably reflects the influence of verbal mediation on this nonverbally administered subtest. Mean scores on the two instruments are very similar, as would be expected for tests normed at about the same time.

Scores on three of the four DAS diagnostic subtests correlate below .4 with the WPPSI–R Full Scale IQ, as is expected for subtests that do not have high g loadings. However, the Matching Letter-Like Forms score correlates substantially with each of the WPPSI–R composites. This perceptual-matching task appears to have a relatively strong relationship to g, a finding consistent with the DAS factor analytic results.

To assist in the interpretation of the DAS subtest scores, Table 9.21 reports selected correlations with those WPPSI–R subtests that are most similar in content.

Table 9.21. Selected Correlations Between DAS and WPPSI–R Subtests

DAS Subtest	WPPSI–R Subtest	r
Verbal Comprehension	Comprehension	.47
Verbal Comprehension	Vocabulary	.54
Naming Vocabulary	Vocabulary	.72
Pattern Construction	Block Design	.45
Copying	Geometric Design	.72
Early Number Concepts	Arithmetic	.46

Note. $N = 62$.

Stanford–Binet Intelligence Scale, Fourth Edition (SB–IV)

The DAS and the SB–IV (Thorndike, Hagen, & Sattler, 1986) were administered in counterbalanced order to 58 children aged 4:0–5:11, with a mean age of 5:0 (SD = 7.5 months). The interval between test administrations averaged 9 days, ranging from 1 to 43 days. The sample had the following composition:

Sex: Females (54%) and Males (46%)

Race/Ethnicity: Black (7%) and White (93%)

Parent Education (n = 44): 4 or more years of college (25%), 1–3 years of college or technical school (39%), high school graduation or equivalent (30%), and less than high school graduation (7%)

Geography: North Central (74%) and South (26%)

Table 9.22 reports the correlations and mean scores.

The correlations between verbal composites of each battery and between the DAS GCA score and the SB–IV Composite score are fairly high. The DAS Nonverbal Ability cluster score correlates higher with the SB–IV Abstract-Visual Reasoning score than with any of the other SB–IV composites, except the overall score. Mean scores on the two instruments are very similar.

The correlations of DAS core-subtest scores with the SB–IV Composite score show a pattern very similar to the pattern of correlations with the WPPSI–R Full Scale IQ. The Picture Similarities subtest again correlates higher with the verbal composite than with the other components. Several verbal and nonverbal core subtests correlate quite highly with the SB–IV Short-Term Memory area score. The two verbal-memory subtests of the DAS correlate higher with the SB–IV Memory scale than with any other SB–IV component, although the Recognition of Pictures subtest has a low correlation with that SB–IV area score.

Table 9.22. Correlations of the DAS with the Stanford–Binet Intelligence Scale, Fourth Edition (SB–IV): 4- and 5-Year-Olds

DAS	SB–IV					DAS	
	Verbal Reas.	Abstract-Visual Reas.	Quantitative Reas.	Short-Term Memory	Composite	Mean	SD
Composites							
Verbal Ability	.72	.54	.44	.66	.74	104.5	15.1
Nonverbal Ability	.55	.64	.51	.46	.69	101.9	15.6
GCA	.67	.64	.48	.62	.77	104.5	16.4
Core Subtests							
Verbal Comprehension	.66	.53	.48	.59	.71		
Naming Vocabulary	.70	.49	.35	.63	.68		
Picture Similarities	.46	.36	.31	.39	.47		
Pattern Construction	.51	.68	.55	.58	.74		
Copying	.39	.56	.40	.21	.47		
Early Number Concepts	.61	.58	.44	.56	.68		
Diagnostic Subtests							
Matching Letter-Like Forms	.36	.39	.32	.42	.48		
Recall of Digits	.23	.28	.21	.31	.34		
Recall of Objects	.07	.08	.15	.25	.17		
Recognition of Pictures	.36	.37	.28	.17	.37		
SB–IV							
Mean	109.0	107.1	104.6	101.3	106.9		
SD	11.9	16.6	11.7	15.8	13.3		

Note. $N = 58$. All correlations are corrected for restriction of range of DAS scores. To compute the mean scores, estimated practice effects were subtracted from second administration scores.

Correlations between the scores of selected pairs of DAS and SB–IV subtests for the same 58 children are shown in Table 9.23. Generally, the verbal subtest scores appear more similar across instruments than do the nonverbal subtest scores.

Table 9.23. Selected Correlations Between DAS and SB–IV Subtests: Preschool

DAS Subtest	SB–IV	r
Verbal Comprehension	Vocabulary	.65
Verbal Comprehension	Comprehension	.55
Naming Vocabulary	Vocabulary	.60
Pattern Construction	Pattern Analysis	.53
Copying	Copying	.42
Early Number Concepts	Quantitative	.43

Note. $N = 58$.

McCarthy Scales of Children's Abilities (MSCA)

The DAS and the MSCA (McCarthy, 1972) were administered in counterbalanced order to 49 British preschool children aged 3:4–3:7 in a study carried out by Janet Muscutt. The MSCA Motor scale was omitted because the focus of the study was on cognitive abilities. The sample was stratified by parent education, race, sex, and community size (urban vs. rural) in order to be representative of the British population. The sample had the following composition:

Sex: Females (49%) and Males (51%)

Race/Ethnicity: Minority (14%) and White (86%)

The data were analyzed in two ways: First, the lower Preschool Level subtest and composite scores for all of the children were analyzed; second, the upper Preschool Level subtest and composite scores for 40 children aged 3:6–3:7 were analyzed. Results are given in Table 9.24.

For the older subgroup, the DAS Verbal Ability cluster score correlates very highly with most of the MSCA composite scores. The Nonverbal Ability cluster score correlates less highly but shows the expected pattern of correlations with the MSCA composite scores. The DAS GCA score correlates highly with the General Cognitive Index (GCI) score of the MSCA. The difference of about 7 points between GCA and GCI mean scores is consistent with what would be expected from the 18-year interval between standardizations (Flynn, 1984).

Scores on the DAS core subtests also show the anticipated patterns of correlations with MSCA composite scores, correlating highest with the Verbal, Perceptual-Performance, or (in the case of Early Number Concepts) Quantitative scales. For the full sample, the Block Building score correlates moderately highly only with the MSCA Perceptual-Performance score, and the Picture Similarities score again shows its propensity to correlate with both verbal and nonverbal measures. Like the Memory scale of the SB–IV, the MSCA Memory scale correlates highest with the DAS verbal subtests, a pattern suggesting that this MSCA score is most strongly related to verbal memory. The Recognition of Pictures score correlates higher with the Perceptual-Performance composite than with the MSCA Verbal composite, whereas Recall of Digits correlations show the opposite pattern.

WPPSI–R, Woodcock–Johnson Psycho-Educational Battery Preschool Skills Cluster (WJ–PSSC), and Kaufman Assessment Battery for Children (K–ABC)

The DAS was administered after administration of the WPPSI-R, WJ-PSSC (Woodcock & Johnson, 1977), and K–ABC (Kaufman & Kaufman, 1983) to 23 Louisiana preschool children aged 3:6–5:11, with a mean age of 4:6 (*SD* = 9 months). The sample was collected under the direction of Dr. Paulette Thomas. The preschool Skills Cluster of the Woodcock–Johnson Psycho-Educational Battery measures the child's abilities to recognize and write simple letters and words, to count, and to perform simple arithmetic. The interval between WPPSI-R and DAS administrations averaged 74 days, ranging from 56 to 106

Table 9.24. Correlations of the DAS with the McCarthy Scales of Children's Abilities (MSCA): British 3-Year-Olds

	MSCA					DAS	
DAS	Verbal	Perceptual-Performance	Quanti-tative	GCI	Memory	Mean	SD
Ages 3:4–3:7 (N = 49)							
Composites							
GCA (4 subtests)	.68	.70	.42	.76	.56	94.7	10.7
Special Nonverbal	.21	.54	−.08	.34	.24	94.0	11.0
Core Subtests							
Block Building	.19	.47	.02	.30	.23		
Picture Similarities	.37	.31	.02	.33	.24		
Verbal Comprehension	.79	.51	.54	.76	.58		
Naming Vocabulary	.61	.40	.48	.60	.33		
Diagnostic Subtests							
Recall of Digits	.31	−.01	.33	.25	.29		
Recognition of Pictures	.49	.58	.18	.53	.24		
MSCA							
Mean	52.4	51.8	47.0	101.9	50.3		
SD	7.4	8.6	6.6	11.9	7.7		
Ages 3:6–3:7 (N = 40)							
Composites							
Verbal Ability	.79	.64	.72	.84	.66	98.7	12.9
Nonverbal Ability	.37	.66	.39	.55	.50	93.1	12.8
GCA (6 subtests)	.70	.78	.70	.82	.69	94.8	11.9
Core Subtests							
Verbal Comprehension	.75	.64	.59	.80	.65		
Naming Vocabulary	.64	.48	.64	.68	.48		
Picture Similarities	.37	.42	.19	.43	.41		
Pattern Construction	.36	.47	.27	.46	.36		
Copying	−.11	.33	.18	.08	.13		
Early Number Concepts	.50	.52	.65	.60	.44		
MSCA							
Mean	52.6	51.7	47.6	102.5	50.8		
SD	7.4	8.5	6.7	12.1	7.5		

Note. All correlations are corrected for restriction of range of DAS scores. To compute the mean scores, estimated practice effects were subtracted from second administration scores.

days; that between K–ABC and DAS administrations also averaged 74 days, ranging from 62 to 111 days; and that between WJ–PSSC and DAS administrations averaged 65 days, ranging from 44 to 100 days. The sample had the following composition:

Sex: Females (52%) and Males (48%)

Race/Ethnicity: Black (30%) and White (70%)

Results are presented in Table 9.25.

Table 9.25. Correlations of the DAS with the Wechsler
Preschool and Primary Scale of Intelligence—
Revised (WPPSI–R), Woodcock–Johnson
Psycho-Educational Battery Preschool Skills
Cluster (WJ–PSSC), and Kaufman Assessment
Battery for Children (K–ABC): 3- to 5-Year-Olds

DAS	WPPSI–R			WJ–PSSC	K–ABC			DAS	
	VIQ	PIQ	FSIQ		Seq. Proc.	Simul. Proc.	Mental Proc. Comp.	Mean	SD
Composites									
Verbal Ability	.75	.57	.70	.56	.62	.50	.63	94.1	12.7
Nonverbal Ability	.63	.80	.76	.67	.75	.45	.67	99.0	11.2
GCA	.77	.77	.81	.67	.74	.49	.68	96.5	11.8
Core Subtests									
Verbal Comprehension	.73	.45	.63	.56	.57	.36	.52		
Naming Vocabulary	.64	.56	.64	.41	.52	.50	.60		
Picture Similarities	.38	.45	.45	.34	.53	.35	.50		
Pattern Construction	.29	.48	.41	.21	.31	.34	.38		
Copying	.39	.58	.51	.58	.45	.04	.22		
Early Number Concepts	.58	.58	.63	.44	.47	.24	.39		
Diagnostic Subtests									
Recall of Digits	.20	.21	.22	.19	.48	.18	.38		
Recognition of Pictures	.39	.29	.36	−.04	−.08	.30	.14		
WPPSI–R, WJ–PSSC, & K–ABC									
Mean	97.7	99.0	97.9	102.0	106.8	96.9	101.4		
SD	12.2	14.4	13.8	13.9	14.7	13.2	13.7		

Note. N = 23. The DAS was administered about two months after the other instruments. All correlations are corrected for restriction of range of DAS scores.

Correlations with the WPPSI–R are consistent with those in the study reported earlier (which does not share any cases with this study). The three DAS composites correlate highly with their WPPSI–R counterparts; the verbal core subtests correlate higher with the Verbal IQ, and the nonverbal core subtests correlate higher with the Performance IQ. Early Number Concepts correlates equally with the Verbal and Performance IQs. Mean composite scores indicate that the sample closely approximates the normal population.

Although the DAS composites and most of the core subtests correlate moderately with the WJ–PSSC, the DAS diagnostic subtests are virtually uncorrelated with this preschool academic-achievement measure.

The DAS composites and core subtests generally correlate higher with the K–ABC Sequential Processing score than with the Simultaneous Processing score, and their correlations with the Mental Processing Composite are, in this study, somewhat lower than with the overall scores from other cognitive batteries. However, the small size of this sample makes any generalizations tentative. The DAS diagnostic subtest Recognition of Pictures appears more "simultaneous" than "sequential," whereas the opposite is true for the Recall of Digits subtest.

School-Age Level of the DAS Cognitive Battery

Wechsler Intelligence Scale for Children—Revised (WISC–R)

The DAS and the WISC-R (Wechsler, 1974) were administered in counterbalanced sequence to two samples, one consisting of 66 children aged 8:0–10:2, and the other consisting of 60 adolescents aged 14:0–15:11. Results from the two studies are reported separately. For additional information about the construct validity of both the DAS and the WISC-R, scores on the WISC-R "Third Factor" were calculated from WISC-R scaled scores with the following formula (from Sattler, 1988, p. 816):

WISC-R Third Factor = 2.20 (Arithmetic + Digit Span + Coding) + 34.0

This formula converts the sum of subtest scaled scores to a standard score with a mean of 100 and standard deviation of 15.

Ages 8:0–10:2

The mean age of the children in the first sample was 9:2 (SD = 6 months). The interval between test administrations averaged 16 days, ranging from 1 to 63 days. The sample had the following composition:

Sex: Females (50%) and Males (50%)

Race/Ethnicity: Black (3%), Hispanic (8%), White (84%), and Other (5%)

Parent Education (n = 57): 4 or more years of college (26%), 1–3 years of college or technical school (35%), high school graduation or equivalent (32%), and less than high school graduation (7%)

Geography: North Central (21%), Northeast (26%), South (45%), and West (8%)

Correlations and mean scores are presented in Table 9.26.

All of the DAS composites correlate highly with the WISC-R Full Scale IQ. The DAS Verbal Ability cluster correlates very highly with the WISC-R Verbal IQ. The DAS Nonverbal Reasoning Ability cluster correlates higher with both the WISC-R Verbal IQ and Third Factor than with the Performance IQ, a pattern suggesting that Nonverbal Reasoning Ability may be a measure more of reasoning than of perceptual-organizational ability. The DAS Spatial Ability cluster correlates strongly with the WISC-R Performance IQ. The mean GCA score on the DAS is lower than the WISC-R Full Scale IQ, a difference consistent with the interval between the standardizations of the instruments.

Table 9.26. Correlations of the DAS with the Wechsler Intelligence Scale for Children—Revised (WISC–R): 8- to 10-Year-Olds

DAS	WISC–R				DAS	
	Verbal IQ	Perform-ance IQ	Full Scale IQ	Third Factor[a]	Mean	SD
Composites						
Verbal Ability	.84	.42	.72	.56	106.2	15.0
Nonverbal Reas. Ability	.77	.57	.75	.70	106.0	13.6
Spatial Ability	.55	.69	.68	.50	105.2	14.5
GCA	.85	.66	.84	.70	107.2	14.4
Special Nonverbal	.74	.71	.80	.67	106.4	14.0
Core Subtests						
Word Definitions	.87	.46	.77	.57		
Similarities	.72	.36	.62	.46		
Matrices	.69	.53	.68	.54		
Seq. & Quant. Reasoning	.68	.51	.68	.58		
Recall of Designs	.48	.52	.56	.41		
Pattern Construction	.61	.74	.75	.53		
Diagnostic Subtests						
Recall of Digits	.63	.49	.62	.58		
Recall of Objects	.38	.22	.34	.23		
Recognition of Pictures	.30	.30	.33	.30		
Speed of Info. Processing	.35	.40	.42	.56		
Achievement Tests						
Basic Number Skills	.62	.53	.68	.69		
Spelling	.57	.34	.50	.47		
Word Reading	.68	.50	.66	.50		
WISC–R						
Mean	114.8	112.5	115.3	106.1		
SD	15.5	13.6	14.8	13.9		

Note. $N = 66$. All correlations are corrected for restriction of range of DAS scores. To compute the mean scores, estimated practice effects were subtracted from second administration scores.
[a]The WISC–R "Third Factor" is calculated by the formula provided by Sattler (1988, p. 816). $N = 63$.

The DAS Special Nonverbal Composite correlates highly with all WISC–R composites, particularly the Full Scale IQ. This pattern further supports the use of the Special Nonverbal Composite when the DAS verbal subtests cannot be administered.

Both of the DAS verbal core subtests correlate highly with the WISC–R Verbal IQ. The DAS nonverbal reasoning core subtests also correlate more highly with the WISC–R Verbal IQ than with the Performance IQ. The DAS nonverbal reasoning subtests appear to be strong measures of general reasoning ability within a nonverbal format. The Pattern Construction and Recall of Designs subtests correlate higher with the Performance IQ than with the Verbal IQ.

With two exceptions, the DAS diagnostic subtests have fairly low correlations with the WISC-R composite scores. The Recall of Digits subtest correlates moderately highly with the WISC-R Verbal IQ, Full Scale IQ, and Third Factor score; and the Speed of Information Processing subtest also correlates fairly highly with the WISC-R Third Factor. Recall of Digits and Speed of Information Processing each have a related subtest in the WISC-R Third Factor—Digit Span and Coding, respectively.

The WISC-R Verbal and Full Scale IQs correlate quite highly with the DAS Basic Number Skills and Word Reading achievement tests, and the WISC-R Third Factor is strongly related to Basic Number Skills. The Performance IQ has moderate but lower correlations with all three DAS achievement tests.

Correlations between scores of selected pairs of subtests are shown in Table 9.27. There is a large amount of overlap between some of the subtest pairs.

Table 9.27. Selected Correlations Between DAS and WISC-R Subtests: Ages 8:0–10:2

DAS Subtest	WISC-R Subtest	N	r
Word Definitions	Vocabulary	66	.82
Similarities	Similarities	66	.68
Sequential and Quantitative Reasoning	Arithmetic	66	.55
Pattern Construction	Block Design	66	.80
Recall of Digits	Digit Span	63	.72
Speed of Information Processing	Coding	66	.50
Speed of Information Processing	Mazes	52	.19
Basic Number Skills	Arithmetic	66	.66

Note. A few examinees did not take the optional WISC-R Digit Span and Mazes subtests.

Ages 14:0–15:11

The mean age of the 60 adolescents in the second sample was 15:0 (*SD* = 7 months). The interval between test administrations averaged 21 days, ranging from 5 to 32 days. The sample had the following composition:

Sex: Females (52%) and Males (48%)

Race/Ethnicity: Black (12%), Hispanic (8%), White (75%), and Other (5%)

Parent Education (*n* = 51): 4 or more years of college (22%), 1–3 years of college or technical school (24%), high school graduation or equivalent (43%), and less than high school graduation (12%)

Geography: North Central (5%), Northeast (8%), South (77%), and West (10%)

Correlations and mean scores are presented in Table 9.28.

Table 9.28. Correlations of the DAS with the Wechsler
Intelligence Scale for Children—Revised
(WISC–R): 14- and 15-Year-Olds

| | WISC–R | | | | DAS | |
DAS	Verbal IQ	Perform-ance IQ	Full Scale IQ	Third Factor[a]	Mean	SD
Composites						
Verbal Ability	.84	.47	.82	.48	101.0	15.4
Nonverbal Reas. Ability	.68	.69	.79	.69	98.5	14.1
Spatial Ability	.27	.77	.59	.30	101.3	13.1
GCA	.79	.80	.91	.69	100.5	13.5
Special Nonverbal	.68	.84	.82	.69	100.0	12.8
Core Subtests						
Word Definitions	.79	.44	.75	.48		
Similarities	.83	.47	.80	.48		
Matrices	.44	.55	.56	.56		
Seq. & Quant. Reasoning	.73	.68	.81	.69		
Recall of Designs	.20	.53	.40	.22		
Pattern Construction	.20	.70	.49	.23		
Diagnostic Subtests						
Recall of Digits	.36	.34	.41	.60		
Recall of Objects	.34	.34	.42	.11		
Speed of Info. Processing	−.09	.24	.07	.37		
Achievement Tests						
Basic Number Skills	.66	.40	.68	.63		
Spelling	.57	.34	.55	.47		
Word Reading	.74	.38	.72	.63		
WISC–R						
Mean	103.4	108.3	106.2	104.8		
SD	13.9	12.5	12.6	13.0		

Note. N = 60. All correlations are corrected for restriction of range of DAS scores. To compute the mean scores, estimated practice effects were subtracted from second administration scores.
[a]The WISC-R "Third Factor" is calculated by the formula provided by Sattler (1988, p. 816). N = 52.

The verbal composites of both tests again correlate very highly. The Nonverbal Reasoning Ability cluster correlates fairly evenly with all WISC–R indexes (including the Third Factor). The Spatial Ability cluster again aligns with the Performance IQ, and the Special Nonverbal Composite again correlates highly with the WISC–R Performance and Full Scale IQs. The DAS GCA score correlates very highly with the WISC–R Full Scale IQ.

The correlations of DAS core-subtest scores with the WISC–R composite scores show a pattern similar to that shown by the scores of the younger sample. The DAS verbal core subtests correlate more highly with the WISC–R Verbal IQ than with any other measures. The DAS nonverbal reasoning subtests correlate about equally with the WISC–R Verbal and Performance IQs and with the Third Factor. The DAS spatial subtests correlate much more strongly with the WISC–R Performance IQ than with the Verbal IQ or the Third Factor.

The DAS diagnostic subtests correlate at a fairly low level with all WISC–R indexes, with the same two exceptions as before: Recall of Digits again correlates substantially with the Third Factor, and Speed of Information Processing's highest correlation is with the WISC–R Third Factor.

The results from both WISC–R samples are consistent in indicating that the WISC–R Third Factor is strongly related to nonverbal reasoning ability as measured by both the Matrices and the Sequential and Quantitative Reasoning subtests of the DAS. The results also suggest that the Third Factor has components of sequential information processing related to speed and short-term auditory memory.

The pattern of WISC–R composite-score correlations with DAS achievement tests is very similar to that found in the younger sample. Both Basic Number Skills and Word Reading correlate highly with the Verbal and Full Scale IQs and the Third Factor.

Correlations between the scores of selected pairs of subtests are shown in Table 9.29.

Table 9.29. Selected Correlations Between DAS and WISC–R Subtests: Ages 14:0–15:11

DAS Subtest	WISC–R Subtest	N	r
Word Definitions	Vocabulary	60	.82
Similarities	Similarities	60	.75
Sequential and Quantitative Reasoning	Arithmetic	60	.81
Pattern Construction	Block Design	60	.86
Recall of Digits	Digit Span	52	.74
Speed of Information Processing	Coding	59	.54
Speed of Information Processing	Mazes	59	− .01
Basic Number Skills	Arithmetic	60	.67

Note. A few examinees did not take the WISC–R Digit Span, Coding, or Mazes subtests.

These correlations are similar to those found for 8- to 10-year-olds. A number of the correlations are quite high, near the reliabilities of the subtests. Speed of Information Processing again has a moderate correlation with Coding and a low correlation with Mazes. Sequential and Quantitative Reasoning correlates higher with Arithmetic at this age level, perhaps because its content shifts from figures to numbers for the older ages.

Stanford–Binet Intelligence Scale, Fourth Edition (SB–IV)

The DAS and SB–IV were administered in counterbalanced order to 55 children aged 9:0 - 10:11, with a mean age of 9:11 (*SD* = 6 months). The interval between test administrations averaged 11 days, ranging from 1 to 62 days. The sample had the following composition:

Sex: Females (45%) and Males (55%)

Race/Ethnicity: Black (11%), Hispanic (4%), and White (85%)

Parent Education (*n* = 47): 4 or more years of college (19%), 1-3 years of college or technical school (36%), high school graduation or equivalent (43%), and less than high school graduation (2%)

Geography: North Central (44%), Northeast (13%), and South (44%)

Correlations and mean scores are presented in Table 9.30.

Table 9.30. Correlations of the DAS with the Stanford–Binet Intelligence Scale, Fourth Edition (SB-IV): 9- and 10-Year-Olds

DAS	SB–IV					DAS	
	Verbal Reas.	Abstract-Visual Reas.	Quanti-tative Reas.	Short-Term Memory	Com-posite	Mean	SD
Composites							
Verbal Ability	.79	.44	.63	.50	.73	103.8	14.7
Nonverbal Reas. Ability	.58	.76	.75	.55	.82	104.8	15.0
Spatial Ability	.37	.67	.46	.42	.60	102.8	13.6
GCA	.73	.77	.76	.61	.88	106.3	13.4
Special Nonverbal	.54	.81	.69	.56	.80	103.4	14.1
Core Subtests							
Word Definitions	.80	.45	.61	.48	.72		
Similarities	.68	.40	.58	.44	.65		
Matrices	.49	.70	.61	.47	.70		
Seq. & Quant. Reasoning	.58	.64	.72	.50	.76		
Recall of Designs	.22	.42	.25	.33	.38		
Pattern Construction	.45	.65	.50	.33	.61		
Diagnostic Subtests							
Recall of Digits	.20	.17	.23	.48	.34		
Recall of Objects	.18	.23	.25	.13	.25		
Recognition of Pictures	.36	.33	.37	.36	.44		
Speed of Info. Processing	.22	.28	.27	.18	.30		
Achievement Tests							
Basic Number Skills	.55	.56	.69	.28	.66		
Spelling	.34	.44	.50	.39	.49		
Word Reading	.58	.48	.63	.45	.66		
SB–IV							
Mean	109.6	107.9	106.9	105.1	109.8		
SD	12.5	14.8	13.6	13.3	12.8		

Note. N = 55. All correlations are corrected for restriction of range of DAS scores. To compute the mean scores, estimated practice effects were subtracted from second administration scores.

The verbal composites of the two instruments correlate very highly. The Non-verbal Reasoning Ability cluster of the DAS shows a very strong relationship with both the Abstract–Visual Reasoning and the Quantitative Reasoning area scores of the SB–IV. The DAS Spatial Ability cluster also correlates strongly with the Abstract–Visual Reasoning area score, but much less strongly with the Quantitative Reasoning area score. The Special Nonverbal Composite shows very strong relationships with the Abstract–Visual Reasoning area score and the overall Composite and a somewhat smaller, but still substantial, relationship with the Quantitative Reasoning area score. The DAS GCA and SB–IV Composite scores correlate very highly, with a mean difference between them of only about 3 points.

The DAS verbal core subtests are strongly related to the SB–IV Verbal area score. The DAS core subtests Matrices, Pattern Construction, and Recall of Designs correlate highest with the SB–IV Abstract–Visual Reasoning area score, whereas the Sequential and Quantitative Reasoning subtest correlates highest with the Quantitative Reasoning area score. Aside from a moderate correlation of the DAS Recall of Digits subtest with the SB–IV Short-Term Memory score, the DAS diagnostic subtests are distinct from the SB–IV composites. The DAS Basic Number Skills and Word Reading achievement tests correlate fairly highly with the Quantitative Reasoning area score and the Composite and slightly lower with the Verbal Reasoning and Abstract–Visual Reasoning area scores.

Correlations between scores of selected pairs of subtests are shown in Table 9.31. Most of the comparable subtests correlate fairly highly, although the memory subtests exhibit somewhat less consistency than do the others.

Table 9.31. Selected Correlations Between DAS and SB–IV Subtests: School-Age

DAS Subtest	SB–IV	N	r
Word Definitions	Vocabulary	55	.75
Matrices	Matrices	53	.71
Sequential and Quantitative Reasoning	Quantitative	55	.50
Sequential and Quantitative Reasoning	Number Series	54	.72
Pattern Construction	Pattern Analysis	55	.62
Recall of Digits	Memory for Digits	55	.55
Recall of Objects	Memory for Objects	55	.12

Note. A few examinees did not take the SB–IV Number Series and Matrices subtests.

231

Stanford–Binet Intelligence Scale, Fourth Edition: Gifted Referrals

This sample of 29 children, aged 7:1–11:4, with a mean age of 8:7 (SD = 14 months), was administered the DAS and the SB-IV in counterbalanced order. Subjects were referred by parents for assessment of possible giftedness. The study was conducted in central Wisconsin under the direction of Dr. Elizabeth Doll. The interval between test administrations averaged 16 days, ranging from 5 to 41 days. The sample had the following composition:

Sex: Females (52%) and Males (48%)

Race/Ethnicity: Hispanic (3%), White (90%), and Other (7%)

Correlations and mean scores are shown in Table 9.32.

Table 9.32. Correlations of the DAS with the Stanford–Binet Intelligence Scale, Fourth Edition (SB–IV): 7- to 11-Year-Old Gifted Referrals

	SB–IV					DAS	
DAS	Verbal Reas.	Abstract-Visual Reas.	Quanti-tative Reas.	Short-Term Memory	Com-posite	Mean	SD
Composites							
Verbal Ability	.74	.53	.43	.47	.68	123.3	12.0
Nonverbal Reas. Ability	.29	.76	.66	.51	.73	115.9	13.3
Spatial Ability	.49	.77	.45	.45	.73	109.9	14.0
GCA	.60	.83	.67	.58	.85	119.7	13.2
Special Nonverbal	.43	.84	.64	.52	.80	113.0	14.0
Core Subtests							
Word Definitions	.59	.48	.53	.52	.67		
Similarities	.57	.34	.16	.19	.39		
Matrices	.26	.76	.59	.39	.67		
Seq. & Quant. Reasoning	.28	.60	.58	.52	.65		
Recall of Designs	.37	.50	.15	.25	.42		
Pattern Construction	.40	.79	.69	.55	.80		
Diagnostic Subtests							
Recall of Digits	−.19	.22	.33	.40	.29		
Recall of Objects	−.11	.35	.12	.24	.24		
Speed of Info. Processing	.36	.50	.43	.21	.51		
Achievement Tests							
Basic Number Skills	.28	.52	.64	.37	.57		
Spelling	.24	.36	.43	.35	.46		
Word Reading	.50	.51	.52	.43	.61		
SB–IV							
Mean	128.2	121.1	118.9	117.6	125.5		
SD	13.6	12.7	12.8	14.6	13.6		

Note. N = 29. All correlations are corrected for restriction of range of DAS scores. To compute the mean scores, estimated practice effects were subtracted from second administration scores.

The overall pattern of correlations between the DAS and the SB–IV is quite similar to that for the sample of 9- and 10-year-old children discussed previously. The most notable exceptions are the increased correlations of about .5 between the DAS Speed of Information Processing subtest and the SB–IV Abstract-Visual Reasoning and Composite scores. The correlation between the DAS GCA and SB–IV Composite scores is very high, with a mean difference between them of about 6 points.

Kaufman Assessment Battery for Children (K–ABC)

The DAS and K–ABC were administered to 27 children aged 5:0–7:11, with a mean age of 6:0 (SD = 12 months). Eighteen of the cases were collected in Illinois under the direction of Dr. Mark Swerdlik, while the remaining 9 cases came from the Louisiana study conducted by Dr. Paulette Thomas (see pp. 222–225). These latter cases were included again because in the previous study the children's scores were based on the Preschool Level of the DAS Cognitive Battery, whereas for this study the children's scores were based on the School-Age Level. For the Illinois sample, tests were administered in counterbalanced order, and all children in the Louisiana sample took the DAS about two to three months after taking the K–ABC. The sample had the following composition:

Sex: Females (63%) and Males (37%)

Race/Ethnicity: Black (7%) and White (93%)

Correlations and mean scores are shown in Table 9.33.

The correlations of the DAS scores with the K–ABC processing scales are considerably higher than those in the study of younger children. The DAS Spatial Ability cluster shares considerable variance with all of the K–ABC processing composites. In contrast, the DAS Verbal Ability cluster has little in common with the K–ABC processing composites. The Nonverbal Reasoning Ability cluster is strongly related to the Simultaneous Processing score but only weakly related to Sequential Processing. Overall, the correlation between the GCA and the Mental Processing Composite is fairly high. The K–ABC Achievement composite has a low correlation with the Spatial Ability cluster but correlates highly with the other DAS composites. The mean difference between the DAS GCA score and the K–ABC Mental Processing Composite score is about 9 points.

Table 9.33. Correlations of the DAS with the Kaufman
Assessment Battery for Children (K–ABC):
5- to 7-Year-Olds

| DAS | K–ABC | | | | DAS | |
	Sequen-tial Proc.	Simul-taneous Proc.	Mental Proc. Composite	Achieve-ment[a]	Mean	SD
Composites						
Verbal Ability	.18	.35	.32	.64	106.2	10.5
Nonverbal Reas. Ability	.24	.68	.56	.72	101.6	13.1
Spatial Ability	.62	.74	.81	.39	100.6	14.1
GCA	.46	.78	.75	.78	102.8	11.1
Special Nonverbal	.49	.82	.80	.64	100.3	12.0
Core Subtests						
Word Definitions	.13	.25	.20	.72		
Similarities	.19	.33	.32	.31		
Matrices	.45	.54	.58	.37		
Seq. & Quant. Reasoning	.01	.59	.39	.64		
Recall of Designs	.56	.56	.68	.43		
Pattern Construction	.50	.79	.79	.27		
Diagnostic Subtests						
Naming Vocabulary	.29	.20	.29	.27		
Recall of Digits	.57	−.14	.21	.01		
Recall of Objects	.32	.02	.17	.34		
Recognition of Pictures	.25	.10	.17	.24		
Speed of Info. Processing	.04	−.10	−.05	.36		
Achievement Tests						
Basic Number Skills[a]	.58	.38	.66	.64		
Spelling[a]	.49	.38	.51	.60		
Word Reading	.34	.38	.38	.83		
K–ABC						
Mean	110.6	110.5	111.9	110.5		
SD	13.8	12.1	12.5	7.4		

Note. N = 27 except as noted. All correlations are corrected for restriction of range of DAS scores. To compute
the mean scores, estimated practice effects were subtracted from second administration scores.
[a]N = 18.

Correlations with Tests of Specific Cognitive Abilities

Peabody Picture Vocabulary Test—Revised (PPVT–R), Test for Auditory Comprehension of Language—Revised (TACL–R), and Columbia Mental Maturity Scale (CMMS)

Three DAS subtests (Verbal Comprehension, Naming Vocabulary, and Picture Similarities), PPVT-R (Dunn & Dunn, 1981), TACL-R (Carrow-Woolfolk, 1985), and CMMS (Burgemeister, Blum, & Lorge, 1972) were administered on the same day to 39 children aged 3:6–5:6, with a mean age of 4:8 (*SD* = 7 months). The majority of cases for this study was collected from a New York State preschool by Rocco Persico. The sample had the following composition:

Sex: Females (46%) and Males (54%)

Race/Ethnicity: Black (10%), Hispanic (13%), and White (77%)

Results are shown in Table 9.34.

Table 9.34. Correlations of Three DAS Subtests with the Peabody Picture Vocabulary Test—Revised (PPVT-R), Test for Auditory Comprehension of Language—Revised (TACL-R), and Columbia Mental Maturity Scale (CMMS): 3- to 5-Year Olds

| | | TACL–R | | | | | DAS | |
DAS	PPVT–R	Word Classes	Grammatical Morphemes	Elaborated Sentences	Total	CMMS	Mean	SD
Composite								
Verbal Ability	.84	.64	.68	.59	.75	.61	98.6	12.8
Core Subtests								
Verbal Comprehension	.78	.66	.65	.59	.75	.60	48.9	9.3
Naming Vocabulary	.76	.51	.62	.50	.65	.54	50.1	10.2
Picture Similarities	.52	.63	.44	.45	.51	.70	53.0	11.0
PPVT–R, TACL–R, & CMMS								
Mean	100.8	107.9	108.2	109.1	109.1	107.7		
SD	15.6	13.0	12.0	14.6	13.1	11.1		

Note. N = 39. All tests were administered on the same day. All correlations are corrected for restriction of range on the DAS scores.

Not surprisingly, the DAS verbal measures correlate highly with the PPVT–R (a receptive-vocabulary test) and the TACL–R (a complex language-comprehension test), while correlating lower with the CMMS (a nonverbal reasoning test). The Verbal Comprehension subtest apparently is a strong measure of both receptive-vocabulary and language-comprehension skills. The Naming Vocabulary subtest focuses more on receptive-vocabulary skills as measured by the PPVT–R. The Picture Similarities subtest correlates highly with the CMMS, a pattern supporting its interpretation as a measure of nonverbal reasoning. It correlates at a lower level with both the receptive and expressive verbal measures.

Peabody Picture Vocabulary Test—Revised (PPVT–R)

This study was directed by Dr. Nancy McKellar. The DAS and PPVT–R were administered in counterbalanced order to 32 first-grade children and 32 third-grade children in regular education classes of a large urban school district in Kansas. The sample included 53% males and ranged in age from 6:0 to 10:9. The first-grade sample had a mean age of 7:4 (SD = 7 months), and the third grade sample had a mean age of 9:4 (SD = 5 months). Half of the children in each grade received Form L of the PPVT–R, and the other half, Form M. Each child took all of the DAS subtests normed for their age; thus, almost all of the first-graders took Naming Vocabulary, Early Number Concepts, and Picture Similarities, in addition to the School-Age Level subtests, but few of the third-graders took these Preschool Level subtests. Correlations and mean scores are shown in Table 9.35.

As we would expect, the PPVT–R correlates substantially higher with the DAS Naming Vocabulary subtest than with any other DAS score. The school-age GCA and Verbal Ability cluster (which do not include Naming Vocabulary) show fairly substantial relationships with the PPVT–R. Finally, the PPVT–R correlates moderately with the DAS Word Reading achievement test.

DAS Matrices and Speed of Information Processing Subtests with WISC–R Performance IQ, Selected Neuropsychological Measures, and *Stanford Achievement Test* (SAT) Scores for Hearing-Impaired Children

Thirty hearing-impaired adolescents aged 12:6–14:9, with a mean age of 13:9 (SD = 6 months), from the Florida State School for the Deaf and Blind in St. Augustine, Florida, were tested with the Matrices and Speed of Information Processing subtests from the DAS, the WISC–R Performance scale, and the Category and Trail-Making tests from the *Halstead–Reitan Neuropsychological Test Battery for Children* (Reitan, 1969). All tests were administered on the same day in the following sequence: WISC–R, Category test, Trail-Making test, Matrices, and Speed of Information Processing. Recent scores on the Stanford Achievement Test—Special Edition for the Hearing Impaired (Madden, Gardner, Rudman, Karlsen, & Merwin, 1982) were also available. Cases were collected under the supervision of Mark Kelly and Dr. Raymond S. Dean. The examinees were randomly sampled from students aged 12–14 at the school. All were severely or profoundly

Table 9.35. Correlations of the DAS with the Peabody Picture Vocabulary Test—Revised (PPVT-R): 1st- and 3rd-Graders

	PPVT–R			DAS	
DAS	1st Grade	3rd Grade	Total	Mean	SD
Composites					
Verbal Ability	.54	.55	.57	107.5	17.4
Nonverbal Reas. Ability	.48	.23	.38	108.9	13.8
Spatial Ability	−.02	.35	.16	100.2	13.5
GCA	.53	.59	.56	105.7	12.2
Special Nonverbal	.32	.34	.32	105.6	12.6
Diagnostic Subtests					
Naming Vocabulary	.74[a]	—	.70[b]	53.9	6.6
Picture Similarities	.26	—	—	52.4	9.8
Early Number Concepts	.51[a]	—	—	59.8	6.7
Achievement Tests					
Basic Number Skills	.42	.16	.31	101.8	13.6
Spelling	.41	.41	.42	104.8	11.2
Word Reading	.47	.48	.48	104.2	12.9
PPVT–R					
Mean	106.2	106.6	106.4		
SD	13.5	11.7	12.6		

Note. $N = 32$ for each grade, except as noted. All correlations are corrected for restriction of range of the DAS score.
[a]$N = 30$.
[b]$N = 40$.

Table 9.36. Correlations of Two DAS Subtests with Selected Cognitive and Neuropsychological Tests: Hearing-Impaired 12- to 14-Year-Olds

	WISC-R	Halstead–Reitan Neuropsychological Battery (H-R NB)				Stanford Achievement Test (SAT-HI)[a]		DAS	
		Category Test	Trail-Making						
DAS	Perform-ance IQ	Total Errors	Correct Resp. Time	A	B	Verbal	Math	Mean	SD
Matrices	.43	.27	−.13	−.07	.26	.60	.42	50.6	8.5
Speed of Info. Processing	−.08	.05	−.48	−.59	−.43	.53	.37	42.8	6.8
WISC–R PIQ, SAT-HI									
Mean	107.3					51.0	52.0		
SD	8.6					15.1	11.4		

Note. $N = 30$, except as noted. All tests (except the SAT) were administered on the same day in the following sequence: WISC-R, H-R NB, Matrices, and Speed of Information Processing. All correlations are corrected for restriction of range of the DAS subtest.
[a]$N = 25$. Scores are normal curve equivalents.

hearing impaired, but none had additional handicapping conditions. All children were male and right-handed. Examiners administered the tests using "simultaneous" communication. Correlations and mean scores are shown in Table 9.36.The DAS Matrices subtest displays a moderately strong relationship with the WISC–R Performance IQ and with SAT Verbal and Mathematics scores. Speed of Information Processing is moderately related to speed of correctly responding on the Category test and the Trail-Making tests and to SAT scores. The sample obtained relatively low Speed of Information Processing scores compared with their WISC–R Performance IQs and DAS Matrices scores. Hearing-impaired children typically perform poorly on the WISC–R Coding subtest (Sattler, 1988, p. 640), which correlates moderately with Speed of Information Processing.

DAS Speed of Information Processing Subtest with Measures of Speed and Reasoning

This study, conducted and published independently by Buckhalt and Jensen (1989), involved the Speed of Information Processing subtest from the *British Ability Scales* (BAS). Because this BAS subtest was the forerunner of the DAS subtest, the Buckhalt and Jensen study is very relevant to the construct validity of the corresponding DAS subtest.

The BAS and DAS subtests have the same content. They differ principally in the method of scoring. In the BAS, each item response was scored either 1 or 0 points according to completion time, whereas in the DAS version, responses are scored on a 0–6 point scale according to completion time. The DAS scoring method incorporates more information from the completion time for each item into the ability estimates. The nature of the items themselves, however, is the same for both versions.

Buckhalt and Jensen administered four BAS subtests to 78 sixth-grade students, with a mean age of 12:4 (*SD* = 10 months), from a rural county elementary school. The subtests were Speed of Information Processing, Matrices, Similarities, and Recall of Digits. In addition, the following measures were given:

- *Raven Standard Progressive Matrices* (Raven, 1958);
- *Otis–Lennon School Ability Test* (OLSAT; Otis & Lennon, 1982); and
- reaction time measures, separated into *reaction time* (RT) and *movement time* (MT), from the Jensen and Munro (1979) apparatus. The Hick and "odd-man-out" paradigms were used.

Buckhalt and Jensen reported correlations of each psychometric test score with various reaction-time measures. A hierarchical factor analysis was performed on the intercorrelated variables. As well as an overall factor of general speed, the following first-order factors were identified:

- psychometric ability,
- consistency of performance in RT and MT tasks,
- speed of movement (MT), and
- speed of apprehension (RT).

238

The authors reported that the correlations of the BAS measures with RT suggested both convergent and divergent validity for the Speed of Information Processing subtest. Speed of Information Processing scores had a substantial loading on Factor 4 (RT), which also had moderate loadings for a range of experimental RT measures. Speed of Information Processing had near-zero loadings on the other three first-order factors. In particular, the subtest was not related to movement time (MT). All of the other psychometric tests loaded significantly on Factor 1 but negligibly on Factor 4. Buckhalt and Jensen interpreted these findings as indicating that Speed of Information Processing is a credible indicator of speed in the child's performance of very simple cognitive operations. They reported that the results showed that the expressed goal of having high levels of subtest specificity (a goal shared by the DAS) had been achieved for the Speed of Information Processing subtest.

The authors also found some differences between nonnumerical and numerical items (Items 1–6 and 7–18, respectively, in the DAS). Although the correlation between the scores on the two types of items was .75, the authors suggested that the numerical items may in part reflect numerical knowledge. The items in Speed of Information Processing are deliberately designed to be simple and, thus, to minimize the contribution of individual differences in knowledge. Buckhalt and Jensen further suggested that as an aid to clearer interpretation of high and low scores, provision for scoring the nonnumerical and numerical items separately should be made in future revisions of Speed of Information Processing. Because the ability ranges covered by the nonnumerical and the easiest numerical items greatly overlap, the DAS makes such score interpretations possible. Buckhalt and Jensen's comments underscore the need for us to establish the students' familiarity with numerals before administering the Speed of Information Processing numerical items.

Summary of Correlation Studies with Other Cognitive Measures

The DAS GCA score correlates consistently highly with the overall composite scores of other cognitive batteries. Although some of the DAS core subtests are similar in content to subtests in other batteries, there is a fundamental difference — the GCA includes only subtests that are strong measures of g, whereas the overall composites of most other batteries comprise more diverse subtests whose g loadings vary more widely. Nevertheless, those composites primarily reflect the common factor, which in most cases is close to g. Thus, although the major goal of the DAS is to enhance the assessment and interpretability of intra-individual differences, the GCA score of the DAS is a focused measure of the general ability dimension that underlies most other cognitive batteries. As such, the GCA is capable of serving the same purpose as these other overall composites with which it has been shown to correlate highly.

Over a range of studies, the DAS cluster and subtest scores have shown both convergent and discriminant validity. All of the studies reported here demonstrate convergent and discriminant validity of the Verbal Ability cluster. The Verbal Ability score correlates considerably higher with the Verbal Composites than with the nonverbal composites of other batteries. Similarly, the DAS Nonverbal Ability, Nonverbal Reasoning Ability, and Spatial Ability cluster scores always have lower correlations than the DAS Verbal Ability cluster score with verbal composites in other batteries.

The Nonverbal Ability cluster at the Preschool Level also shows convergent and discriminant validity. It correlates highly with nonverbal reasoning and conceptual ability composites from other batteries, and correlates somewhat lower with measures of other dimensions such as verbal ability and memory.

The Nonverbal Reasoning Ability cluster correlates fairly highly with a variety of other measures, including measures of verbal reasoning, quantitative reasoning, and spatial–perceptual ability. It tends to correlate higher than the other DAS cluster scores with the overall composite scores of other cognitive batteries, and it also has the lowest level of specificity of any of the school-age DAS clusters. One interpretation of these findings is that the Nonverbal Reasoning Ability cluster is a particularly good measure of the complex reasoning skills that are central to psychometric g. Furthermore, both of its subtests—Matrices and Sequential and Quantitative Reasoning—present problems visually but lend themselves to verbal mediation.

The Nonverbal Reasoning Ability cluster also correlates highly with the WISC–R Third Factor. Because the construct measured by the Third Factor has not been fully explicated, the significance of the high correlations is unclear; the relatively focused measures in the DAS may shed some light on its interpretation. Only one of the two DAS subtests in the Nonverbal Reasoning Ability cluster has numerical content, a characteristic of all of the Third Factor subtests.

The Spatial Ability cluster correlates highly with measures of perceptual organization and visual–spatial reasoning and at a much lower level with measures of verbal ability.

The School-Age Special Nonverbal Composite, composed of the Nonverbal Reasoning Ability and Spatial Ability clusters, correlates quite highly with overall composite scores and with broad nonverbal composites from other cognitive batteries. Apparently this scale's combination of general nonverbal reasoning and visual–spatial measures is a strong substitute for the broader GCA score when verbal information is unobtainable or likely to be invalid.

Because the core subtests contribute to the clusters, they show patterns of convergent and divergent validity very similar to those of the clusters themselves. In contrast, the diagnostic subtests are fairly independent of the composite scores from other batteries. Therefore, these subtests are capable of providing unique information beyond that provided by composite scores from the DAS or other instruments. Speed of Information Processing and Recall of Objects correlate very little with other measures, and the very high reliability of the former gives it a high level of specificity. Recall of Digits and Recognition of Pictures correlate only moderately with composite scores from the DAS and other batteries.

The Matching Letter-Like Forms subtest appears to be related to a range of abilities rather than simply to perceptual matching. The subtest is apparently related to the development of letter–discrimination skills in young children, a development that typically occurs within a relatively narrow age range.

Correlations with Measures of Academic Achievement

Correlations Within the DAS Between Ability and Achievement

Correlations between the DAS school-age cognitive-composite scores and the DAS achievement-test scores for all children aged 6:0–17:11 in the norm sample are presented in Table 9.37. The achievement tests were administered in varied sequences but always after the core cognitive battery, usually on the same day but sometimes with a short interval (up to one week) between administrations.

Table 9.37. Correlations of the DAS Cognitive Composites with the DAS Achievement Tests: 6- to 17-Year-Olds from the Norm Sample

Composites	Basic Number Skills	Spelling	Word Reading
Verbal Ability	.48	.49	.59
Nonverbal Reasoning Ability	.59	.49	.52
Spatial Ability	.45	.34	.40
GCA	.60	.52	.60
Special Nonverbal	.58	.46	.51

Note. $N = 2400$. All scores are age-based standard scores.

Regression equations predicting achievement-test scores from GCA and Special Nonverbal Composite scores were derived from this sample. The prediction equations based on GCA scores are the following:

$$\text{BNS}_{\text{pred}} = 42.5 + .583(\text{GCA})$$
$$\text{SPEL}_{\text{pred}} = 48.9 + .515(\text{GCA})$$
$$\text{WR}_{\text{pred}} = 43.0 + .570(\text{GCA})$$

The prediction equations based on Special Nonverbal Composite scores are as follows:

$$\text{BNS}_{\text{pred}} = 44.0 + .568(\text{SNV})$$
$$\text{SPEL}_{\text{pred}} = 54.7 + .458(\text{SNV})$$
$$\text{WR}_{\text{pred}} = 49.6 + .503(\text{SNV})$$

Tables 14 and 15 in the **Manual** provide predicted achievement-test scores for each possible GCA or Special Nonverbal Composite score.

In general, the GCA correlates about as highly as the highest correlating cluster score with each of the DAS achievement tests. The GCA appears to be a versatile predictor of achievement. Likewise, the Special Nonverbal Composite is a good predictor of scores on Basic Number Skills, although it does not correlate as highly as does the GCA with Word Reading or Spelling.

Of the three cluster scores, the best predictor of Word Reading and Spelling is Verbal Ability. The Nonverbal Reasoning Ability cluster has the strongest relationship with Basic Number Skills. The Spatial Ability cluster is not strongly related to any of the achievement measures but has a moderate (.5) correlation with Basic Number Skills.

To detect any trends in these correlations across age, the project team partitioned the norm sample into three subsamples representing three age ranges, 6:0–9:11, 10:0–13:11, and 14:0–17:11. Results for these samples are presented in Table 9.38.

Table 9.38. Correlations of the DAS Cognitive Composites with the DAS Achievement Tests: Three Age Ranges of the Norm Sample

| Composites | Ages 6:0–9:11 | | | Ages 10:0–13:11 | | | Ages 14:0–17:11 | | |
	Basic Number Skills	Spelling	Word Reading	Basic Number Skills	Spelling	Word Reading	Basic Number Skills	Spelling	Word Reading
Verbal Ability	.46	.45	.54	.47	.50	.59	.50	.53	.65
NV Reas. Ability	.55	.50	.52	.58	.49	.52	.63	.48	.51
Spatial Ability	.40	.33	.36	.45	.35	.40	.50	.33	.44
GCA	.56	.51	.57	.59	.52	.59	.64	.53	.63
Special Nonverbal	.53	.46	.50	.57	.46	.51	.63	.45	.53

Note. $N = 800$ for each age range. All scores are age-based standard scores.

The correlation of cognitive ability with achievement generally tends to increase with the child's age. Among the cluster scores, this trend is particularly true for the most important pairings: Verbal Ability with Word Reading and Spelling, and Nonverbal Reasoning Ability and Spatial Ability with Basic Number Skills. The same pattern of correlations is observed at each age level. The GCA's correlation with the separate achievement tests is as high (or higher) as any other DAS cognitive composite's correlation with those tests. The Special Nonverbal Composite displays a fairly strong relationship with all of the achievement areas and may be a useful predictor of achievement when verbal information is unobtainable.

For each age level, the Nonverbal Reasoning Ability cluster correlates with Basic Number Skills more highly than does either of the other two cluster scores. For the youngest level, the Nonverbal Reasoning Ability and Verbal Ability composites correlate about equally with Word Reading, but for increasingly older groups, the Verbal Ability correlation increases markedly, while that for Nonverbal Reasoning Ability remains the same.

To investigate the correlations of the DAS preschool-level composites with achievement as measured by the DAS, the project team computed correlations for all 6-year-olds in the norm sample. Correlations were corrected for restriction of range of the cognitive measures because some of the cognitive subtests for age 6 have ceiling effects. For 6-year-olds of average or low ability, for whom these composites would be appropriate, the corrected correlations better estimate the relationship between ability and achievement. Correlations and mean scores are shown in Table 9.39.

Table 9.39. Correlations of the DAS Preschool and School-Age Cognitive Composites with DAS Achievement Tests: 6-Year-Olds from the Norm Sample

| Cognitive Composites | Achievement Test | | | Cognitive Composite | |
	Basic Number Skills	Spelling	Word Reading	Mean	SD
Preschool					
Verbal Ability	.45	.42	.46	99.0	14.2
Nonverbal Ability	.41	.45	.43	98.9	15.4
GCA	.60	.59	.61	99.3	14.2
Early Number Concepts	.74	.66	.71	49.9	9.8
School-Age					
Verbal Ability	.45	.42	.51	99.9	14.0
Nonverbal Reas. Ability	.51	.54	.57	100.0	14.8
Spatial Ability	.39	.42	.42	99.6	14.9
GCA	.54	.54	.59	99.9	14.5
Special Nonverbal	.49	.52	.54	99.8	14.9
Achievement Tests					
Mean	101.1	98.6	100.0		
SD	13.8	14.4	13.1		

Note. $N = 200$. Correlations with the Preschool Level composites and subtests are corrected for restriction of range on the cognitive variable.

For these 6-year-olds, the preschool GCA correlates substantially higher than does either of the preschool clusters with the achievement tests. This pattern results from the exclusion of the Early Number Concepts subtest from both the Verbal and Nonverbal Ability clusters and its inclusion in the GCA composite. The separate correlations of Early Number Concepts with achievement (shown in the table) are even higher than those of the GCA with achievement.

For comparison, correlations of the DAS school-age cognitive composites with the achievement tests are also shown in Table 9.39. No adjustment for restriction of range is needed for these correlations because all of the subtests are on level. The correlations for the school-age GCA are slightly lower than those for the preschool GCA, undoubtedly because of the influence of Early Number Concepts. However, correlations with achievement are higher for the school-age Verbal Ability and Nonverbal Reasoning Ability clusters than for the preschool clusters.

Correlations with Other Individually Administered Achievement Tests

Basic Achievement Skills Individual Screener (BASIS)

Almost all children aged 7:0–7:11 and 11:0–11:11 in the DAS standardization sample were administered BASIS (The Psychological Corporation, 1983) within 2 weeks after administration of the DAS. Correlations and mean scores are shown in Table 9.40.

Table 9.40. Correlations of the DAS Cognitive Composites and Achievement Tests with the Basic Achievement Skills Individual Screener (BASIS)

| | BASIS | | | | | | DAS | | | |
| | Age 7 | | | Age 11 | | | Age 7 | | Age 11 | |
DAS	Mathe-matics	Spell-ing	Read-ing	Mathe-matics	Spell-ing	Read-ing	Mean	SD	Mean	SD
Composites										
Verbal Ability	.49	.41	.56	.34	.46	.60	98.0	14.4	100.9	14.0
NV Reas. Ability	.54	.52	.62	.66	.36	.49	100.4	14.4	102.1	12.7
Spatial Ability	.38	.35	.45	.38	.27	.33	98.9	13.6	102.0	15.1
GCA	.58	.52	.66	.57	.46	.59	99.0	13.8	102.0	13.6
Special Nonverbal	.53	.50	.61	.59	.36	.46	99.6	13.7	102.2	13.6
Achievement Tests										
Basic Number Skills	.75			.79			101.5	13.4	102.3	13.8
Spelling		.88			.87		100.8	12.8	101.8	14.3
Word Reading			.79			.64	100.2	13.5	101.5	14.9
BASIS										
Mean	103.6	102.7	99.2	106.6	102.6	102.3				
SD	16.4	12.6	13.4	16.0	15.0	15.4				

Note. N = 198 for Age 7; N = 157 for Age 11. All correlations are corrected for restriction of range on the DAS. All scores are age-based standard scores.

In general, the GCA score predicts achievement as well as or better than any of the other DAS cognitive composites, with one exception. For ages 11:0–11:11, the DAS Nonverbal Reasoning Ability cluster correlates higher than the GCA with BASIS Mathematics scores. The pattern of correlations is very similar to that of the DAS cognitive composites with the DAS achievement tests for the same age levels.

The correlation between each BASIS score and its corresponding DAS achievement test is generally high. The only correlation below .75 is the one between DAS Word Reading and BASIS Reading for ages 11:0–11:11. The BASIS Reading task differs greatly from the DAS Word Reading task: It involves the cloze procedure in which the child supplies words missing from text, basing the decision on context. Mean achievement scores on the two instruments are similar.

Kaufman Test of Educational Achievement (K–TEA)

In a study conducted by Dr. Elizabeth Doll at a Midwestern university clinic, the DAS and the K–TEA (Kaufman & Kaufman, 1985) were administered in counter-balanced order to 29 children aged 7:1–11:4, with a mean age of 8:7 (*SD* = 14 months). Parents had referred their children for assessment for giftedness. The interval between test administrations averaged 16 days, ranging from 5 to 41 days. The sample had the following composition:

Sex: Females (48%) and Males (52%)

Race/Ethnicity: Hispanic (3%), White (90%), and Other (7%)

Correlations and mean scores are presented in Table 9.41.

Table 9.41. Correlations of the DAS with the Kaufman Test of Educational Achievement (K–TEA): 7- to 11-Year-Old Gifted Referrals

| | K–TEA | | | | | | | | DAS | |
| | Reading | | | | Mathematics | | | | | |
DAS	Decoding	Compre-hension	Com-posite	Spelling	Appli-cations	Compu-tation	Com-posite	Total Battery	Mean	SD
Composites										
Verbal Ability	.48	.58	.56	.38	.51	.49	.55	.51	123.3	12.0
NV Reas. Ability	.34	.47	.43	.44	.55	.53	.59	.47	115.9	13.3
Spatial Ability	.30	.32	.32	.25	.49	.27	.41	.34	109.9	14.0
GCA	.49	.59	.57	.53	.65	.55	.69	.56	119.7	13.2
Special Nonverbal	.37	.46	.48	.40	.58	.46	.56	.46	113.0	14.0
Achievement Tests										
Basic No. Skills	.58	.55	.58	.53	.68	.87	.84	.71	118.8	14.4
Spelling	.75	.71	.76	.85	.48	.52	.52	.78	111.9	16.8
Word Reading	.79	.80	.85	.84	.64	.65	.68	.81	116.9	17.5
K–TEA										
Mean	123.9	127.1	127.3	116.4	127.6	115.6	122.8	125.6		
SD	19.0	20.2	20.0	22.7	16.5	17.0	16.1	19.1		

Note. N = 29. All correlations are corrected for restriction of range on the DAS. All scores are age-based standard scores. To compute the mean scores, estimated practice effects were subtracted from second administration scores.

The DAS achievement tests yield scores that are about the same or somewhat lower than those on the K–TEA. The DAS Basic Number Skills subtest correlates highest with Mathematics Computation and lower with Mathematics Applications. The Spelling tests from both measures are highly correlated. The DAS Word Reading test correlates equally highly with the K–TEA's Reading Comprehension and Reading Decoding scales and has a very high correlation with the Reading Composite. Overall, these results support the DAS achievement tests as measures of achievement.

Woodcock Reading Mastery Tests—Revised (WRMT–R)

The DAS Word Definitions and Word Reading subtests and the WRMT-R (Woodcock, 1987) were administered to 100 children aged 8:5-11:6, with a mean age of 9:8 (*SD* = 9 months), who were in the third, fourth, or fifth grade of an urban Midwestern university laboratory school. The study was directed by Dr. Betty Gridley and David McIntosh. The sample included 53% males. Each child took the WRMT-R, DAS Word Reading, and DAS Word Definitions subtests in that sequence on the same day. Correlations and mean scores are shown in Table 9.42.

Table 9.42. Correlations of Two DAS Subtests with the Woodcock Reading Mastery Tests—Revised (WRMT–R): 8- to 11-Year-Olds

DAS	WRMT–R							DAS	
	Word Identi-fication	Word Attack	Word Compre-hension	Passage Compre-hension	Basic Skills Cluster	Reading Cluster	Total Reading	Mean	*SD*
Word Definitions	.53	.45	.65	.53	.49	.62	.55	55.0	8.9
Word Reading	.84	.78	.73	.71	.84	.78	.83	105.5	13.6
WRMT–R									
Mean	104.1	102.7	110.5	100.4	104.6	104.5	106.2		
SD	14.0	15.3	15.3	16.1	15.2	15.4	16.0		

Note. N = 100. All tests were administered on the same day in the following sequence: WRMT-R, Word Reading, and Word Definitions. All correlations are corrected for restriction of range on the DAS.

The DAS Word Definitions subtest correlates moderately with the numerous aspects of reading ability measured by the WRMT-R. Its highest correlation is with Word Comprehension. Word Reading, one of the DAS achievement tests, correlates quite highly with all of the WRMT-R indexes. Not surprisingly, Word Reading's correlations with Word Identification and Word Attack are higher than those with the comprehension measures, but the overall high level of correlation supports the Word Reading test as a measure of important aspects of reading achievement. Mean scores are comparable for the DAS Word Reading test and the WRMT-R Total Reading score.

Correlations with Group-Administered, Standardized Tests of School Achievement

Group achievement-test data were gathered from participating schools for many of the children in the DAS standardization sample. The school provided the child's most recent scores on a nationally standardized group achievement test. Because a variety of achievement-test series and forms had been used, for which norms would not be equivalent, the project team analyzed the data separately for five groups and averaged the results using Fisher's *z* transformation. The groups were determined by the number of children who had taken each test series. If ten or more children at a grade level had taken equivalent forms of the same series, that group's scores were analyzed separately. The five resulting groups were:

- *California Achievement Test*
- *California Test of Basic Skills*
- *Iowa Test of Basic Skills*
- *Stanford Achievement Test*
- Other

All group achievement-test scores are grade-based normal curve equivalents (NCEs). After averaging the within-group correlations, the project team adjusted the mean correlation for restriction of range of the DAS composite score.

Because the various achievement-test series did not provide identical categories of scores or use identical labels, a small number of criterion variables that reflected the most frequently reported scores were formed. To maximize the number of cases available for analysis, the team used some subscores in place of overall scores, if the latter were not reported. The following rules governed construction of the Total Reading, Total Mathematics, and Total Achievement scores.

- **Total Reading.** The overall Reading score was used, if available. Otherwise the Reading Comprehension score was used or, if that score was unavailable, the Vocabulary score was used.
- **Total Mathematics.** The overall Mathematics score was used, if available. Otherwise the Mathematics Problem Solving score was used or, if that score was also unavailable, the Mathematics Computation score was used.
- **Total Achievement.** The mean of the NCE scores for Total Reading and Total Mathematics was used.

Only those children who had scores for both Total Reading and Total Mathematics were included in the analyses. Correlations performed on the scores of the entire sample of children in the 1st through 12th grades are presented in Table 9.43.

The GCA correlates higher than does any of the cluster scores with Total Achievement, although the DAS Verbal Ability cluster correlates higher than does the GCA with Total Reading, Reading Comprehension, and Spelling, and the Nonverbal Reasoning Ability cluster correlates almost as high as does the GCA with Total Mathematics and with Mathematics Computation. The Special Nonverbal Composite is also a good predictor of Total Achievement and the two mathematics achievement scores.

The Basic Number Skills test has its highest correlation with Total Mathematics, and the DAS Spelling test correlates strongly with the group measure of spelling. The DAS Word Reading test correlates highly with Total Reading and Spelling and slightly lower with Reading Comprehension.

Tables 9.44–9.46 present the same correlations with achievement-test scores for three grade levels: 1–3, 4–7, and 8–12. As Table 9.44 indicates, the GCA correlates

Table 9.43. Correlations of DAS Cognitive Composites and Achievement Tests with Group Achievement Tests: Grades 1–12 in the Standardization Sample

DAS	Total Achievement[b]	Reading Comprehension	Reading Total	Mathematics Computation	Mathematics Total	Spelling	DAS Mean	DAS SD
Composites								
Verbal Ability	.66	.64	.66	.41	.54	.54	99.4	13.9
Nonverbal Reas. Ability	.63	.50	.51	.51	.64	.42	99.7	14.9
Spatial Ability	.48	.35	.41	.34	.46	.16	99.5	14.2
GCA	.72	.60	.63	.53	.66	.44	99.5	14.1
Special Nonverbal	.64	.49	.52	.51	.63	.34	99.5	14.3
Achievement Tests								
Basic Number Skills	.60	.43	.47	.53	.62	.36	100.4	13.7
Spelling	.60	.56	.60	.44	.47	.77	101.2	14.8
Word Reading	.63	.62	.67	.37	.48	.69	100.6	14.6
Group Achievement Tests (NCEs)								
Mean	58.7	57.5	57.7	58.6	59.6	54.7		
SD	17.3	18.7	18.9	19.7	19.2	19.0		
N	729	633	729	573	729	282	729	729

Note. All correlations are corrected for restriction of range of DAS scores.
[a]See text for identification of achievement test series.
[b]Mean of the NCEs for Total Reading and Total Mathematics.

higher than other cognitive composites with Total Achievement for grades 1–3. The GCA and the Verbal Ability cluster both correlate fairly highly with Total Reading, and the Verbal Ability score is a somewhat better predictor than the GCA of Reading Comprehension. The GCA, the Nonverbal Reasoning Ability cluster, and the Special Nonverbal Composite all correlate fairly strongly with Total Mathematics.

The Basic Number Skills test correlates moderately with Total Mathematics, and the DAS Spelling test correlates quite highly with its group achievement counterpart. The DAS Word Reading test correlates highly with Total Reading and Reading Comprehension.

As presented in Table 9.45, the pattern of correlations for grades 4–7 is the same as that for the earlier grades. However, as similarly found in the correlations of DAS cognitive scores with DAS achievement scores, the level of correlation between ability and achievement is somewhat higher for these older students. Total Reading correlates highest with the Verbal Ability cluster and next highest with the GCA. Total Mathematics correlates about equally with the Nonverbal Reasoning Ability cluster, GCA, and Special Nonverbal Composite. The correlation of the Basic Number Skills test with Total Mathematics is slightly higher than the correlation at the younger grades, and that between the Word Reading test and Total Reading is slightly lower than the corresponding correlation for the earlier grades.

Table 9.44. Correlations of DAS Cognitive Composites and Achievement Tests with Group Achievement Tests: Grades 1–3 in the Standardization Sample

| | Group Achievement Tests[a] | | | | | | DAS | |
| | Total | Reading | | Mathematics | | | | |
DAS	Achieve-ment[b]	Compre-hension	Total	Compu-tation	Total	Spelling	Mean	SD
Composites								
Verbal Ability	.64	.60	.61	.38	.52	.51	99.2	14.6
Nonverbal Reas. Ability	.60	.45	.49	.49	.62	.40	101.5	15.5
Spatial Ability	.46	.31	.37	.36	.47	.15	98.1	13.8
GCA	.69	.55	.59	.50	.64	.41	99.6	14.7
Special Nonverbal	.61	.44	.48	.48	.61	.32	99.7	14.5
Achievement Tests								
Basic Number Skills	.59	.48	.49	.52	.59	.35	101.2	13.8
Spelling	.58	.60	.60	.41	.45	.78	102.3	14.6
Word Reading	.63	.68	.72	.39	.47	.68	102.1	14.1
Group Achievement Tests (NCEs)								
Mean	61.9	60.3	60.9	62.1	62.9	55.3		
SD	18.0	19.1	20.4	19.4	19.5	22.4		
N	187	163	187	149	187	77	187	187

Note. All correlations are corrected for restriction of range of DAS scores.
[a]See text for identification of achievement test series.
[b]Mean of the NCEs for Total Reading and Total Mathematics.

The correlation coefficients for grades 8–12 are presented in Table 9.46. The pattern and level of correlations are generally the same as those for the earlier grades, with the exception of higher correlations of the Spatial Ability cluster with most of the achievement indexes. The Verbal Ability cluster and the GCA correlate fairly highly with Total Reading, and the Nonverbal Reasoning Ability cluster, GCA, and Special Nonverbal Composite each correlate highly with Total Mathematics. The correlation of the DAS Basic Number Skills test with Total Mathematics is highest for these grades, and the DAS Word Reading subtest maintains its high correlation with Total Reading.

In summary, for all grade levels, the GCA score was found to correlate highly with reading and mathematics achievement. The Verbal Ability cluster correlates highly with reading achievement, and the Nonverbal Reasoning Ability cluster and the Special Nonverbal Composite correlate highly with mathematics achievement. The DAS achievement tests correlate distinctively and fairly highly with their group achievement counterparts. Taken together, these results provide strong, initial support for the validity of the GCA and cluster scores as predictors of school achievement as assessed by a variety of group-administered and individually administered achievement tests.

Table 9.45. Correlations of DAS Cognitive Composites and Achievement Tests with Group Achievement Tests: Grades 4–7 in the Standardization Sample

DAS	Total Achievement[b]	Reading Compre-hension	Reading Total	Mathematics Compu-tation	Mathematics Total	Spelling	DAS Mean	DAS SD
Composites								
Verbal Ability	.68	.63	.69	.41	.56	.55	100.0	13.8
Nonverbal Reas. Ability	.69	.51	.55	.53	.69	.41	99.3	14.8
Spatial Ability	.46	.33	.40	.34	.46	.18	100.8	14.0
GCA	.73	.59	.66	.51	.68	.45	100.1	13.9
Special Nonverbal	.64	.48	.54	.50	.66	.36	100.1	14.1
Achievement Tests								
Basic Number Skills	.61	.39	.46	.50	.63	.36	100.0	14.7
Spelling	.61	.52	.60	.41	.41	.80	101.2	15.2
Word Reading	.63	.62	.66	.34	.46	.68	100.8	14.8
Group Achievement Tests (NCEs)								
Mean	59.0	57.5	58.0	57.5	60.0	55.1		
SD	16.7	17.8	17.2	20.1	19.3	18.9		
N	295	256	295	270	295	114	295	295

Note. All correlations are corrected for restriction of range of DAS scores.
[a]See text for identification of achievement test series.
[b]Mean of the NCEs for Total Reading and Total Mathematics.

Correlations with Teacher-Assigned School Grades

Many of the schools participating in the standardization of the DAS also provided the students' grades from the most recent marking period. The grades, which reflected a variety of scoring scales, were converted to a single numerical system (50–100) so that the data could be combined. The tendency of grades to be less reliable than scores on standardized group achievement tests reduces the level of correlation. To obtain the most reliable possible index of grades, the project team calculated a grade point average (GPA) as the mean of grades in English, mathematics, and (for grades K–7) reading. Only those students who had grades in all of the subject areas contributing to the GPA were included in the analysis.

Table 9.47 presents the correlations of the DAS cognitive composites and achievement tests with school grades for the entire sample. The results are highly predictable and are generally parallel to the patterns of correlations of DAS GCA and cluster scores with scores on group and individual achievement tests. Overall, the GCA has the strongest relationship with school grades. The Verbal and Nonverbal Reasoning Ability clusters correlate about as highly as does the GPA

251

Table 9.46. Correlations of DAS Cognitive Composites and Achievement Tests with Group Achievement Tests: Grades 8–12 in the Standardization Sample

DAS	Total Achievement[b]	Reading Compre-hension	Reading Total	Mathematics Compu-tation	Mathematics Total	Spelling	DAS Mean	DAS SD
		Group Achievement Tests[a]					DAS	
Composites								
Verbal Ability	.69	.63	.69	.42	.58	.51	98.6	13.6
Nonverbal Reas. Ability	.66	.50	.53	.52	.68	.41	98.7	14.5
Spatial Ability	.54	.40	.45	.37	.56	.14	99.0	14.8
GCA	.76	.62	.68	.55	.70	.40	98.6	13.9
Special Nonverbal	.68	.50	.54	.53	.69	.32	98.7	14.4
Achievement Tests								
Basic Number Skills	.61	.42	.48	.57	.69	.32	100.2	12.5
Spelling	.59	.56	.61	.49	.46	.74	100.4	14.5
Word Reading	.62	.62	.67	.40	.47	.66	99.0	14.5
Group Achievement Tests (NCEs)								
Mean	55.8	55.1	55.0	57.3	56.7	53.7		
SD	16.9	19.3	19.4	19.1	18.6	15.7		
N	247	214	247	154	247	91	247	247

Note. All correlations are corrected for restriction of range of DAS scores.
[a]See text for identification of achievement test series.
[b]Mean of the NCEs for Total Reading and Total Mathematics.

with reading, English, and spelling; the Nonverbal Reasoning Ability cluster has the same correlation as does the GCA with mathematics. The DAS achievement tests correlate highest with their respective subject-grade counterparts.

Table 9.48 presents the correlation coefficients for grades K–3. The pattern of correlations at this grade level is similar to the pattern for all grades combined. Again, the GCA score is the best overall predictor of grades, although for specific subjects, other clusters approximate or exceed the GCA in the magnitude of their correlations.

Table 9.49 gives the correlation coefficients for grades 4–7. The pattern and the levels of correlations are similar to the pattern for all ages combined, although the Verbal Ability and Nonverbal Reasoning Ability clusters correlate higher than does the GCA with grades in particular subject areas.

Table 9.50 presents the correlations for students in grades 8–12. The pattern of correlations is nearly identical to that for the earlier grades.

Table 9.47. Correlations of DAS Cognitive Composites and Achievement Tests with School Grades: Grades K–12 in the Standardization Sample

DAS	GPA[a]	Mathematics	Spelling	Reading	English	DAS Mean	SD
Composites							
Verbal Ability	.40	.34	.30	.37	.37	99.2	14.1
Nonverbal Reas. Ability	.42	.40	.21	.36	.38	99.7	14.9
Spatial Ability	.25	.23	.11	.21	.23	99.5	14.2
GCA	.45	.40	.25	.38	.40	99.4	14.2
Special Nonverbal	.39	.36	.19	.32	.35	99.5	14.3
Achievement Tests							
Basic Number Skills		.43				100.2	13.8
Spelling			.60			101.1	14.6
Word Reading				.48		100.2	14.6
N	626	626	338	410	626	626	626

Note. All correlations are corrected for restriction of range of DAS scores.
[a]GPA = mean of grades in mathematics and English.

Table 9.48. Correlations of DAS Cognitive Composites and Achievement Tests with School Grades: Grades K–3 in the Standardization Sample

DAS	GPA[a]	Mathematics	Spelling	Reading	English	DAS Mean	SD
Composites							
Verbal Ability	.41	.40	.34	.32	.37	99.5	14.4
Nonverbal Reas. Ability	.41	.36	.23	.36	.36	101.7	15.3
Spatial Ability	.29	.26	.08	.24	.28	98.9	13.4
GCA	.45	.41	.26	.37	.41	100.1	14.3
Special Nonverbal	.40	.35	.18	.34	.36	100.3	14.1
Achievement Tests							
Basic Number Skills		.35				101.6	13.8
Spelling			.59			101.9	14.3
Word Reading				.49		101.8	14.3
N	175	175	163	175	175	175	175

Note. All correlations are corrected for restriction of range of DAS scores.
[a]GPA = mean of grades in reading, mathematics, and English.

Table 9.49. Correlations of DAS Cognitive Composites and Achievement Tests with School Grades: Grades 4–7 in the Standardization Sample

DAS	GPA[a]	Mathematics	Spelling	Reading	English	DAS Mean	DAS SD
Composites							
Verbal Ability	.42	.31	.27	.41	.36	99.7	14.2
Nonverbal Reas. Ability	.47	.44	.21	.35	.39	99.4	15.2
Spatial Ability	.24	.22	.12	.18	.20	100.9	14.4
GCA	.45	.39	.24	.38	.38	100.1	14.5
Special Nonverbal	.40	.38	.19	.31	.34	100.2	14.6
Achievement Tests							
Basic Number Skills		.44				100.1	15.0
Spelling			.61			101.5	15.1
Word Reading				.47		100.5	15.0
N	229	229	174	229	229	229	229

Note. All correlations are corrected for restriction of range of DAS scores.
[a]GPA = mean of grades in reading, mathematics, and English.

Table 9.50. Correlations of DAS Cognitive Composites and Achievement Tests with School Grades: Grades 8–12 in the Standardization Sample

DAS	GPA[a]	Mathematics	English	DAS Mean	DAS SD
Composites					
Verbal Ability	.36	.22	.39	98.7	13.4
Nonverbal Reas. Ability	.40	.34	.34	98.9	14.3
Spatial Ability	.24	.25	.15	99.1	14.2
GCA	.44	.36	.39	98.7	13.5
Special Nonverbal	.38	.35	.29	98.9	13.8
Achievement Tests					
Basic Number Skills		.46		100.4	12.2
Spelling			.34	100.5	13.8
Word Reading			.28	98.8	14.2
N	222	222	222	222	222

Note. All correlations are corrected for restriction of range of DAS scores.
[a]GPA = mean of grades in mathematics and English.

Summary of Correlation Studies with Measures of Academic Achievement

Studies of a variety of achievement measures, including the DAS achievement tests, other individually administered or group-administered achievement tests, and teacher-assigned grades, present a consistent pattern of convergent and divergent validity for the DAS school-age composite scores. The GCA score is the best overall predictor of achievement. Among the cluster scores, Verbal Ability has the highest correlations with measures of reading and spelling, and Nonverbal Reasoning Ability is the best predictor of mathematics achievement. The Special Nonverbal Composite correlates about as highly as the GCA with mathematics achievement, but at a somewhat lower level with reading.

High correlations between the DAS achievement tests and their group-administered or individually administered counterparts support the validity of these achievement measures. Despite the focus of the DAS Word Reading test on one aspect of reading, namely decoding, many of the studies showed it to correlate highly with more global indexes of reading ability. The Spelling test shows a very high degree of convergence with similar measures, and the Basic Number Skills test correlates fairly highly with measures of mathematics computation and applications.

DAS Score Profiles of Special Populations

Individually administered cognitive-ability tests such as the DAS often are used with children who are exceptional in some way. As examiners, we are naturally interested in how such children perform on any new instrument. Our interest in the DAS is likely to be especially strong because of its inclusion of separately interpretable diagnostic and core subtests. The following section provides data on the test performance of gifted, retarded, and learning-disabled children.

Gifted Students

The DAS scores of 62 students who had previously been classified as gifted were selected from the standardization sample. State and district classification guidelines vary widely, and this sample reflects this variability. The children were aged 6:0–17:8, with a mean age of 11:11 (SD = 39 months). The sample had the following composition:

Sex: Females (57%) and Males (43%)

Race/Ethnicity: Black (3%), Hispanic (8%), White (82%), and Other (6%)

Parent Education: 4 or more years of college (42%), 1–3 years of college or technical school (29%), high school graduation or equivalent (23%), and less than high school graduation (6%)

Geography: North Central (21%), Northeast (23%), South (26%), and West (31%).

Table 9.51 reports mean scores for this sample.

Mean scores on the DAS composites are about one standard deviation above the general-population averages, and GCA scores range from 100 to 141. The core-subtest and achievement-test average scores are slightly less than one standard deviation above the mean. The diagnostic-subtest average scores, however, are much closer to the mean for the norm sample. Recall of Objects—Immediate and Speed of Information Processing show the lowest average scores and the greatest variability of all of the subtests for this sample. Because the diagnostic subtests are relatively uncorrelated with *g*, we would not expect to find particularly high scores on them in a sample selected for a high level of general intellectual ability.

Table 9.51. DAS Scores of Students Classified as Gifted

DAS	Mean	*SD*
Composites		
Verbal Ability	115.3	9.7
Nonverbal Reas. Ability	115.5	11.5
Spatial Ability	114.2	12.0
GCA	118.1	10.3
Special Nonverbal	116.9	11.4
Core Subtests		
Word Definitions	59.9	6.9
Similarities	59.0	7.4
Matrices	59.2	9.3
Seq. & Quant. Reasoning	59.6	7.2
Recall of Designs	58.6	7.8
Pattern Construction	58.6	8.1
Diagnostic Subtests		
Recall of Digits	56.0	7.5
Recall of Objects	54.1	10.8
Speed of Info. Processing	54.6	10.1
Recognition of Pictures	55.9	8.4
Achievement Tests		
Basic Number Skills	114.6	12.8
Spelling	113.8	14.2
Word Reading	113.9	12.1

Note. N = 62.

Educable Mentally Retarded Students

A sample of 25 students previously and independently classified as educable mentally retarded (EMR) were tested with the DAS. Twelve of these students were part of the standardization sample, and the other 13 cases were gathered from various locations. The children were aged 6:10–16:8, with a mean age of 11:6 (SD = 33 months). The sample had the following composition:

Sex: Females (52%) and Males (48%)

Race/Ethnicity (n = 20): Black (25%), Hispanic (20%), and White (55%)

Parent Education (n = 18): 4 or more years of college (6%), 1–3 years of college or technical school (17%), high school graduation or equivalent (39%), and less than high school graduation (39%)

Geography: North Central (32%), South (64%), and West (4%).

The mean DAS scores are shown in Table 9.52.

Average scores on all composites are below 70, that is, more than two standard deviations below the general population mean, and GCA scores range from 45 to 78. The Spatial Ability cluster has the highest average score and greatest standard deviation.

Table 9.52. DAS Scores of Students Classified as Educable Mentally Retarded

DAS	Mean	SD
Composites		
Verbal Ability	63.8	9.7
Nonverbal Reas. Ability	63.4	7.9
Spatial Ability	65.8	11.0
GCA	59.4	9.0
Special Nonverbal	61.8	8.7
Core Subtests		
Word Definitions	28.8	6.3
Similarities	27.1	7.0
Matrices	27.9	7.1
Seq. & Quant. Reasoning	27.2	6.0
Recall of Designs	29.4	8.3
Pattern Construction	29.8	7.0
Diagnostic Subtests		
Recall of Digits	32.4	11.9
Recall of Objects	30.1	9.1
Recognition of Pictures	33.2	9.9
Speed of Info. Processing	33.2	10.5
Achievement Tests		
Basic Number Skills	61.8	8.5
Spelling	67.9	12.9
Word Reading	67.7	13.2

Note. N = 25.

For this sample, all core-subtest average scores are below 30, but the diagnostic subtests have somewhat higher average scores and much greater standard deviations. This score pattern suggests that the diagnostic subtests, which have low g loadings, are potential indicators of strengths and weaknesses in children who might otherwise show a flat profile. Scores on the achievement subtests, while on average higher than the cognitive composite scores, are still more than two standard deviations below the mean of the norm sample.

Learning-Disabled Students

Independently Classified Learning-Disabled Students

DAS scores were obtained for 110 children who had been independently classified as learning disabled (LD) by their school districts. About a third (41) of these cases were gathered from the DAS standardization sample, and the remaining 69 cases were specially collected. Criteria for classifying children as LD vary among states and districts, although in order to conform to the Federal definition of LD, the local criteria must require some demonstration of an ability–achievement discrepancy.

The children were aged 7:2–15:8, with a mean age of 11:5 (SD = 25 months). As is often found in LD samples, males outnumbered females; this sample included 88 males (80%) and 22 females (20%). The sample had the following composition:

Race/Ethnicity: Black (12%), Hispanic (9%), White (78%), and Other (1%)

Parent Education (n = 103): 4 or more years of college (8%), 1–3 years of college or technical school (29%), high school graduation or equivalent (41%), and less than high school graduation (22%)

Geography: North Central (17%), Northeast (8%), South (42%), and West (33%)

The means and standard deviations of DAS scores for this sample are presented in Table 9.53.

The LD students' scores average about a half standard deviation below the population means on the core cognitive subtests, while averaging from 1 to 1 2/3 standard deviations below the means on the achievement subtests. Because learning disabilities are most often defined by poor reading skills, it is not surprising that the Word Reading and Spelling scores are substantially lower than the Basic Number Skills scores. Perhaps the most interesting finding is that the greatest variability is found, as it is in the other special populations, in the diagnostic subtests. The standard deviations of the core-subtest scores are all less than 10, whereas those of the diagnostic-subtest scores are all greater than 10. Furthermore, in contrast to the gifted and EMR samples whose diagnostic-subtest scores were closer than their core-subtest scores to the mean of 50, the LD students tend to score lower on the diagnostic subtests than on the core subtests. This pattern suggests that the diagnostic subtests, especially Recall of Objects, Recognition of

Pictures, and Speed of Information Processing, may possibly measure cognitive processes that are implicated in learning disability.

Table 9.53. DAS Scores of Students Classified as Learning Disabled

DAS	Mean	*SD*
Composites		
Verbal Ability	91.7	12.0
Nonverbal Reasoning Ability	89.4	12.2
Spatial Ability	92.4	14.2
GCA	89.6	12.0
Special Nonverbal	89.9	12.5
Core Subtests		
Word Definitions	45.4	8.5
Similarities	45.2	8.2
Matrices	44.9	8.7
Seq. & Quant. Reasoning	43.0	8.3
Recall of Designs	45.0	9.8
Pattern Construction	46.6	9.7
Diagnostic Subtests		
Recall of Digits	45.3	10.9
Recall of Objects	39.5	10.7
Speed of Info. Processing	42.5	10.7
Recognition of Pictures	42.6	11.2
Achievement Tests		
Basic Number Skills	86.2	13.9
Spelling	78.2	13.0
Word Reading	76.5	12.8

Note. N = 110.

Reading-Disabled Students as Defined by DAS Scores

We should not assume that all, or even most, learning-disabled children will show the profile of scores depicted in Table 9.53. Numerous studies have shown a variety of profile patterns among LD children (Kavale & Forness, 1984). The large standard deviations of the diagnostic subtests suggest that DAS profiles will vary considerably.

To explore this possibility, the DAS project team applied cluster analysis to the scores of a somewhat different sample of 136 children from the standardization sample who demonstrated a reading disability according to the following criteria:

- GCA scores above 85,
- Word Reading scores below 85, and
- Word Reading scores at least 15 points below the score predicted from the GCA.

The last criterion is consistent with the regression approach to the comparison of GCA and Word Reading scores. A 15-point discrepancy between observed and predicted achievement is significant at the .01 level and is found in about 10% of children (see Appendix B).

Of the 136 reading-disabled children, 57 were also included in the original sample of 110 school-classified LD students. Although for many of the other 79 children information on LD classification was not available, some of these children undoubtedly were so classified. The sample had the following composition:

Sex: Females (26%) and Males (74%)

Race/Ethnicity: Black (10%), Hispanic (13%), White (74%), and Other (3%)

Parent Education (n = 132): 4 or more years of college (11%), 1–3 years of college or technical school (25%), high school graduation or equivalent (42%), and less than high school graduation (21%)

Geography: North Central (16%), Northeast (14%), South (40%), and West (30%)

The means and standard deviations for this sample are shown in Table 9.54.

Table 9.54. Means and Standard Deviations for Four Clusters of Reading-Disabled Students on DAS Subtests and Composites

DAS	Cluster 1 Mean	SD	Cluster 2 Mean	SD	Cluster 3 Mean	SD	Cluster 4 Mean	SD	Total Mean	SD
Composites										
Verbal Ability	95.7	11.2	103.2	8.6	90.2	10.1	93.2	8.6	95.5	10.5
NV Reas. Ability	95.9	8.0	96.3	12.2	100.1	11.1	95.9	8.8	97.0	10.2
Spatial Ability	102.7	10.4	94.5	9.6	107.9	9.6	98.6	8.6	100.5	10.5
GCA	97.7	7.6	97.5	9.2	99.2	8.7	95.1	5.9	97.2	7.9
Special Nonverbal	99.2	7.3	94.8	9.6	104.3	8.8	97.0	7.6	98.5	9.0
Core Subtests										
Word Definitions	46.3	9.4	51.4	6.3	44.4	7.4	46.4	5.9	47.2	7.5
Similarities	49.3	7.6	53.2	8.1	44.5	7.1	46.1	6.7	48.1	8.0
Matrices	47.8	6.9	48.0	8.2	53.2	8.1	49.5	7.8	49.6	8.0
Seq. & Quant. Reas.	47.8	5.6	48.2	8.2	47.5	7.6	46.3	5.0	47.3	6.6
Recall of Designs	49.8	7.0	47.3	7.1	54.8	6.5	51.2	6.3	50.8	7.1
Pattern Construction	54.1	6.9	46.8	8.2	55.2	6.5	47.7	7.2	50.4	8.1
Diagnostic Subtests										
Recall of Digits	35.8	7.3	52.0	9.7	44.7	7.7	46.4	8.1	47.7	11.1
Recall of Objects	57.8	8.2	41.3	11.8	40.3	7.9	51.8	6.9	45.4	10.2
Recog. of Pictures	44.9	8.6	43.7	8.4	55.7	9.1	47.6	6.6	45.4	9.7
Speed of Info. Proc.	43.1	6.8	37.2	7.9	44.5	9.0	53.6	8.0	48.0	9.2
Achievement Subtests										
Basic Number Skills	93.3	11.8	89.4	12.5	91.0	12.4	93.0	14.0	91.7	12.8
Spelling	80.5	8.7	77.1	10.5	78.5	10.5	82.1	8.0	79.7	9.5
Word Reading	75.3	5.6	73.4	8.0	73.8	8.3	76.8	5.6	75.0	7.0
Age in Months	149	31	136	28	140	27	146	31	143	29
N		26		34		31		45		136

Note. The clusters were derived from a cluster analysis, as described in the text.

A comparison of the means and standard deviations in Tables 9.53 and 9.54 shows that the average GCA for the reading-disabled sample is higher, and that the standard deviations for the GCA and for the Word Reading scores are lower than those for the general LD sample. The use of these DAS scores as selection criteria causes these differences in standard deviation. Again, the diagnostic subtests have larger standard deviations than do the core subtests.

The purpose of a cluster analysis is to group children with similar score profiles into clusters. We should interpret groupings with caution, however, until they can be validated through external information such as teacher descriptions of apparent problems or independent test scores. Nevertheless, the clusters do illustrate the variability of profiles among reading-disabled students.

The clustering procedure was applied to the children's cognitive-subtest scores. In order to focus on profile shape, the project team converted each child's subtest scores to within-child deviation scores by subtracting the child's own mean score on all of the cognitive subtests. The team used the FASTCLUS procedure (SAS Institute, 1985) to form non-overlapping clusters (that is, each child belongs to one and only one cluster). Four solutions were considered, with 2 to 5 clusters being identified. The four-cluster solution was the most appealing on clinical grounds, and it is this solution which is presented here.

The means and standard deviations of each cluster group's scores on the ten DAS cognitive subtests, the cognitive composites, and the achievement tests are shown in Table 9.54.

Cluster 1 has a high Spatial Ability mean score relative to the Verbal Ability and Nonverbal Reasoning Ability scores. By far, the lowest score is on Recall of Digits for this group, which also has a slightly depressed score on Speed of Information Processing.

Cluster 2 provides a marked contrast. These children tend to have higher scores on verbal than on nonverbal subtests and have an above-average mean score on Recall of Digits. They have a low mean score on Speed of Information Processing and somewhat depressed scores on Recall of Objects and Recognition of Pictures.

Cluster 3 shows a particular contrast between the Verbal and Spatial Ability cluster scores, with the Spatial cluster score nearly 18 points higher. On the diagnostic subtests the group's lowest score is on Recall of Objects, and the Recall of Digits and Speed of Information Processing scores are near the same level as that of the verbal subtests. This cluster of students has high mean scores on visual-spatial tasks, particularly on the short-term visual-memory subtests of Recall of Designs and Recognition of Pictures.

Cluster 4 shows a relatively flat cognitive profile. While having somewhat lower verbal than nonverbal scores, this group of students has no extremely low or extremely high mean scores.

This study, based on a diverse sample of children with severe discrepancies between GCA and Word Reading scores, and conducted with a single disjoint-clustering procedure, has yielded results which are suggestive rather than definitive. The results nevertheless provide good evidence of different configurations of test scores among children labeled as LD or reading-disabled. These labels encompass heterogeneous groups of individuals whose only common test characteristics are poor achievement and a severe discrepancy between measures of ability and achievement. The results suggest that the DAS and particularly its diagnostic subtests may be able to make useful distinctions between subgroups of these children based upon characteristic patterns of cognitive strengths and weaknesses.

Concluding Comments

The results of the various studies reported in this chapter on the internal and external validity of the DAS have shown substantial evidence for the hierarchical structure of the battery and for the relationship of the DAS composites, cognitive subtests, and achievement tests with other cognitive and achievement measures. In particular, the convergent and discriminant validity of the DAS core subtests and achievement tests is supported by the consistent interrelationships and patterns of correlations of the DAS measures with external measures. There is similar evidence, too, for the validity of the diagnostic subtests, although this evidence is perhaps not as strong. A notable contribution to the validation of the diagnostic subtests is the study of the Speed of Information Processing subtest by Buckhalt and Jensen (1989), reported in this chapter. In general, results suggest that the diagnostic subtests show relatively low correlations with the core subtests and with other g-loaded measures, and that they thereby help to fulfill a goal of the DAS of including a range of subtests with high levels of reliable specificity.

The evidence from samples of gifted, retarded, and learning-disabled students indicates that the scores of these special populations on the diagnostic subtests are more variable than their scores on the core subtests. Of course, such samples are often selected partly on the basis of measures, such as cognitive tests, with high g loadings. It is not surprising, therefore, that in such samples the DAS subtests with high g loadings show smaller score variances than subtests with low g loadings. Nevertheless, the results of the cluster analysis of the LD sample suggest that the diagnostic subtests may play a major role in identifying meaningful subgroupings of LD children. Further specific investigation into the validity of the diagnostic subtests would therefore appear to be a particularly fruitful research area.

Chapter 10

Fairness

The *fairness* of a test is the degree to which it is an equally valid measure of ability for individuals with different demographic characteristics or backgrounds. A test score should reflect the same level of ability regardless of the examinee's sex, race, ethnicity, region of the country, and so on. If a test or item does not meet this criterion of fairness, it may be considered biased.

Two aspects of the development of the DAS contribute to its fairness. First, great care was taken to ensure that the standardization sample was representative of U.S. children. This aspect of the development is fully described in Chapter 7.

Second, the development of the DAS as a joint British and American instrument helped to preclude content that might be unfair to individuals with different cultural backgrounds. The project team carefully selected content intended to be equally meaningful not only in the United States and Great Britain but also in other English-speaking countries. To this end, Canadians and Australians reviewed the test content before the final materials were produced. Thus, the DAS does not include subtests that depend on knowledge of terms, symbols, or information that is likely to be familiar to residents of only one country.

In addition, the DAS project team took three specific steps to make the test fair: having the test content reviewed by a bias panel, exploring item bias using standardization data (including a substantial oversample of Black and Hispanic children), and comparing the test's predictions of outside criteria for separate subgroups.

Bias Review Panel

As mentioned in Chapter 3, a panel representing the perspectives of women, Blacks, Hispanics, and Native Americans reviewed all test materials before the standardization edition was produced. The panel members were asked to consider items and subtests for possible bias against children of either sex or of any particular racial, ethnic, cultural, or other subgroup of the U.S. population. The panel members were also asked to suggest changes that might correct any such faults. The panel's recommendations led to the deletion or modification of items on several subtests, particularly the verbal subtests.

The following panel members are thanked for their contributions. Responsibility for the fairness of the final content of the DAS, however, rests entirely with the author and publisher.

Ernesto M. Bernal, Ph.D.
Sylvia T. Johnson, Ph.D.
Damian A. McShane, Ph.D.
Julia M. Ramos-McKay, Ph.D.
Cecil R. Reynolds, Ph.D.
Jonathan H. Sandoval, Ph.D.

Statistical Analyses of Item Bias

The DAS team selected the following subtests for empirical analyses of item bias based on standardization data:

Basic Number Skills
Early Number Concepts
Matrices
Naming Vocabulary
Picture Similarities
Recognition of Pictures
Sequential and Quantitative Reasoning
Similarities
Spelling
Verbal Comprehension
Word Definitions
Word Reading

These subtests were selected for several reasons. First, item bias due to sex or race/ethnicity would more likely be found in verbal and achievement subtests or in nonverbal subtests, such as Picture Similarities or Recognition of Pictures, that use representational drawings, than in subtests with nonverbal, abstract content. Second, the Matrices and Sequential and Quantitative Reasoning subtests were analyzed as "control" subtests, because item bias was not anticipated on these nonverbal, abstract subtests. The Recall of Objects subtest, although verbal, was not analyzed because the nature of the task made dropping any objects from scoring after the subtest had been standardized inappropriate.

An item is biased against a group if it is more difficult for that group (relative to the other items in the subtest) than it is for other groups. Something about that item may be causing members of the first group particular difficulty answering the item correctly. Biased items can be detected by scaling the subtest separately for each group and determining whether or not the items have the same sequence of difficulties and similar distances between item difficulties for all groups. This comparative scaling can be readily achieved with the Rasch model (see Appendix D).

With the Rasch model, item-difficulty estimates for a test are sample free. Consequently, even if two samples have different mean abilities, the calibrated difficulties of a given set of items should be the same in both samples. Through studies of item bias, we can discover any items in a subtest that have different difficulty values for different samples.

Collection of Additional Samples of Black and Hispanic Children

Item-bias evaluation depends on stable estimates of item difficulty, and stable estimates necessitate sufficiently large samples of each group. The standard error of each item-difficulty estimate depends largely on the number of examinees taking the item. For analyses of sex or regional bias, the norm sample included many children of each group who took each item. However, for analyses of racial/ethnic bias, the norm sample did not include a sufficient number of Black (15%) and Hispanic (11%) children to give accurate within-group estimates of difficulty for all of the items. Therefore, about 600 additional Black and Hispanic children were tested during standardization to enable more accurate analyses of item bias, as well as to help ensure that item-scoring rules would be sensitive to minority children's responses.

Table 10.1 shows the average number of Black and Hispanic children *per item* whose test data contributed to item-bias analyses for the 12 subtests analyzed.

Table 10.1. Average Number of Black and Hispanic Children Taking Each Item for Item Bias Analysis

Subtest	Black		Hispanic	
	\multicolumn{4}{c}{Mean (Range) of Number of Cases per Item}
Basic Number Skills	150	(72–274)	137	(83–248)
Early Number Concepts	155	(82–231)	131	(59–181)
Matrices	219	(72–343)	192	(91–296)
Naming Vocabulary	273	(127–436)	209	(112–345)
Picture Similarities	256	(156–363)	194	(105–270)
Recognition of Pictures	345	(137–515)	259	(44–366)
Seq. & Quant. Reasoning	197	(141–253)	175	(141–224)
Similarities	287	(172–287)	253	(177–387)
Spelling	160	(74–314)	145	(72–315)
Verbal Comprehension	198	(85–297)	148	(79–219)
Word Definitions	197	(55–294)	186	(62–272)
Word Reading	221	(79–375)	216	(74–360)

All of the subtests listed in Table 10.1 were also evaluated for sex bias. In addition, regional bias was investigated for the Naming Vocabulary, Similarities, and Word Definitions subtests.

Procedure for Item Bias Analysis

Bias analysis of each subtest began with the reduced set of items that remained after poorly fitting items for the entire sample had been deleted from the subtest. Using the MSTEPS program, the project team scaled the item-difficulty values separately for each group. First, the within-group fit of each item was examined. The analyses would identify an item that fit poorly for one group despite its fitting well for the entire sample. Such an item apparently would be functioning differently for that group and would need to be deleted. The analyses identified very few such item-fit differences.

Next, the project team considered the magnitude and the statistical significance of between-group differences in item difficulty. These evaluations were the grounds for most item deletions.

For most of these statistically identified items, there was a plausible reason for the item's possible unfairness to a particular group. A particularly clear example is the Naming Vocabulary item "Cactus," which was found to be biased against children living in the Northeast and North Central regions. The interpretability of the bias-analysis results lent credibility to the statistical method used to identify biased items.

Fairness of Prediction

A third, important index of a test's fairness is its fairness of prediction. Does the test predict relevant external criteria in the same way for each of the different groups with whom the test is used? If it does, then in a fundamental sense, the test can be said to be fair.

Using various measures of school achievement as the criteria, the project team investigated the fairness of the DAS GCA score for Black, Hispanic, and White children in this way. The question of interest was whether or not children with the same GCA score would obtain the same average achievement score regardless of the group to which they belonged. Using multiple regression to address this question, the project team compared Black with White children and Hispanic with White children. For each comparison, achievement was predicted from the GCA score, the race/ethnic group, and the interaction of GCA and race/ethnicity.

The logic of the multiple regression analysis is as follows. First, for the sample consisting of the two groups being compared, the project team calculated the squared multiple correlation of GCA and race/ethnicity with the criterion (achievement). (The square of a multiple correlation indicates the proportion of variance in the criterion which is accounted for by the predictors.) Second, the interaction of GCA and race/ethnicity was added as a predictor. If the proportion of criterion variance explained by the predictors increased significantly, then the slope of the regression line—that is, the strength of the relationship between GCA and achievement—differed for the two groups. This type of bias is illustrated in Figure 10.1(A).

If the interaction did not add significantly to the prediction of achievement, then the prediction with GCA and race/ethnicity as predictors was compared with the prediction from GCA alone. A statistically significant effect for race/ethnicity, in comparison with GCA alone, would mean that children in one group obtained higher achievement scores than children in the other group having the same GCA scores, that is, that the GCA predicts a higher level of achievement for one group than for the other (see Figure 10.1(B)). If neither the interaction of GCA with race/ethnicity nor race/ethnicity alone added significantly to the prediction of achievement, then the prediction of achievement from GCA is the same for both groups, as illustrated in Figure 10.1(C).

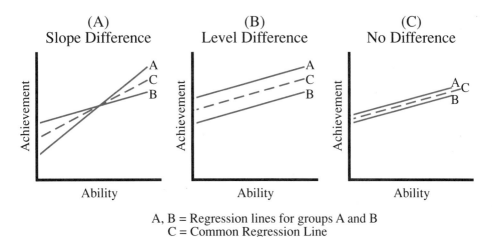

| (A) | (B) | (C) |
| Slope Difference | Level Difference | No Difference |

A, B = Regression lines for groups A and B
C = Common Regression Line

Figure 10.1. Relationship Between Ability and Achievement for Different Groups

The DAS team ran these analyses for all cases, aged 5 through 17, from the standardization sample and the bias oversample for whom school achievement data had been obtained. Three achievement variables were used separately in the analyses: the mean of the NCEs for total reading and total mathematics from one of a range of standardized group achievement tests (see Chapter 9, p. 248, for details on this criterion); Reading and Mathematics standard scores from the individually administered *Basic Achievement Skills Individual Screener* (BASIS); and grade point average (the average of teacher-assigned grades in reading and mathematics during the most recent grading period).

Results of the analyses incorporating the three criteria are presented in Table 10.2. None of the analyses showed statistically significant differences in regression slope—that is, in the strength of the relationship between achievement and GCA—for either Blacks or Hispanics compared with Whites. The analyses revealed statistically significant differences between the levels of the regression lines for Hispanic and White children when group achievement-test scores were the criteria. In each case, Hispanics obtained lower group achievement-test scores than did Whites for the same GCA scores. This result means that a common regression line would overpredict Hispanic achievement; the opposite result would be expected if the GCA were biased against Hispanics. Thus, none of the analyses suggests that the GCA is an unfair measure of the ability of Black and Hispanic children, when the context of evaluation is the prediction of school achievement.

Conclusion

The DAS team used both subjective and empirical methods to identify and either delete or modify items that were possibly unfair according to sex, race, ethnicity, or region. The remaining item content predicted school achievement in the same way for Black and White children, and the differences between the predictions for Hispanic and White children were not of the type that would suggest unfair measurement of the ability of Hispanic children.

These procedures and results support the DAS as a fair measure of ability. However, we should not infer that there will be no differences in performance on the subtests or composites among demographic subgroups. Because ability tests measure developed abilities, such differences can reflect environment and experience. We may, however, have confidence that the subtest content was carefully scrutinized to eliminate items that work differently for children of one group than for children of another group.

Table 10.2. Prediction of Academic Achievement From GCA and Race/Ethnicity

Achievement Criterion	N Black	N His-panic	N White	Squared Multiple Correlations Predictors (Black vs. White) GCA	GCA, Race	GCA, Race, Inter.[a]	Predictors (Hispanic vs. White) GCA	GCA, Race	GCA, Race, Inter.[a]	Regression Slope Black	His-panic	White
Group Achievement Test NCE												
Reading	125	133	467	.365	.367	.368	.373	.385[b]	.385	.75	.80	.84
Mathematics	125	133	467	.392	.392	.392	.386	.407[c]	.407	.78	.86	.84
Total	125	133	467	.467	.468	.469	.468	.487[d]	.488	.77	.83	.84
BASIS Standard Score												
Reading	54	58	226	.321	.322	.323	.335	.335	.336	.67	.69	.61
Mathematics	55	61	227	.296	.302	.302	.247	.248	.248	.64	.60	.60
Spelling	55	61	227	.181	.189	.191	.181	.183	.183	.59	.50	.44
Grade Point Average	110	127	436	.163	.166	.167	.154	.155	.159	.21	.17	.27

Note. Except as noted, none of the changes in the squared multiple correlation resulting from the addition of race/ethnicity and GCA, or the interaction of race/ethnicity and GCA, as predictors is statistically significant at $p < .05$.

[a]Interaction of GCA and race.

[b]Significantly ($p < .01$) larger than the squared multiple correlation for GCA alone. For children with a given GCA score, the average Reading NCE score is 5.0 points lower for Hispanic than for White children.

[c]Significantly ($p < .001$) larger than the squared multiple correlation for GCA alone. For children with a given GCA score, the average Mathematics NCE score is 6.9 points lower for Hispanic than for White children.

[d]Significantly ($p < .001$) larger than the squared multiple correlation for GCA alone. For children with a given GCA score, the average Total NCE score is 6.0 points lower for Hispanic than for White children.

Appendix A

Acknowledgments

The publisher and author greatly appreciate the cooperation and participation of the following individuals, schools, and other institutions in the various developmental phases of the *Differential Ability Scales*. Their help during tryout, standardization, and validation has ensured the quality and completion of this test.

Field Supervisors and Examiners

Alabama

Auburn University, Auburn

Joseph A. Buckhalt, Ph.D.
Field Supervisor

Diane Byrd
Frances Childs
Gabriel Denes
James Logan
Susanne MacGuire
Stephen Stratton

University of Alabama, Huntsville

James W. Fleming, Ph.D.
Field Supervisor

Phyllis Coffield
Jennifer Herndon

Arizona

Douglas

William G. Masten, Ph.D.
Field Supervisor

Constance Gamble

California

California Lutheran University, Thousand Oaks

C. Douglas Saddler, Ph.D.
Field Supervisor

Madeleine Edelman

California School of Professional Psychology, San Diego

Thomas F. McGee, Ph.D.
Field Supervisor

Beatriz Netter

California State University, Fullerton

Ernest H. Dondis, Ph.D.
Field Supervisor

Karen Kiszelewski
Shelley Kuecks
Cynthia Larson
Lynne McGowan
Heidi Scott

California State University, Northridge

Joseph Morris, Ph.D.
Field Supervisor

Deanne Nolte
Rhonda Solomon

California State University, San Bernardino

Steve R. Wagner, Ph.D.
Field Supervisor

Barbara Hamilton

Chapman College, Fort Ord

J. David Bigelow, Ph.D.
Field Supervisor

Dee Linde
Maureen Ploen

Claremont Graduate School, Claremont

Kathy Pezdek, Ph.D.
Field Supervisor

Laura Kaufmann
Anita Rosenfield
Lauren Whetstone

**Pepperdine University,
Los Angeles**

Paul H. Henkin, Ph.D.
Field Supervisor

> Elizabeth Balcom
> Jo Kontzer
> Terri Lintz
> Samuel Zepeda

San Jose State University, San Jose

John S. Kelly, Ph.D.
Field Supervisor

> Jo Ann Bathurst
> Richard Bromberg
> Anna Lorenzi
> Lori Loson
> Fred Luskin
> Barbara Morton
> Cliff Siegel

University of California, Davis

Jonathan H. Sandoval, Ph.D.
Field Supervisor

> Elizabeth Boyer
> Mary Campbell
> Catherine Christo
> Carolyn Fitzgerald
> Andrew Kercher

Colorado

University of Colorado, Boulder

Stephen E. Hodge, Ph.D.
Field Supervisor

> Janice Culler
> Patricia Hayes
> Linda Sims

**University of Northern Colorado,
Greeley**

Ellis P. Copeland, Ph.D.
Field Supervisor

Elizabeth J. Rave, Ed.D.
Field Supervisor

> Jerry Beffert
> Joanne Pierce
> Sherry Schenk
> Nancy Snowden
> Colleen Swendson

Connecticut

**Southern Connecticut State
University, New Haven**

Jack I. Novick, Ph.D.
Field Supervisor

> Martha Kardok
> Michael Rattley
> Robert Swan, Jr.

Florida

**Florida A & M University,
Tallahassee**

James L. Byrd,
Field Supervisor

> Chandra Nims

**University of Central Florida,
Orlando**

David J. Mealor, Ph.D.
Field Supervisor

> James Fierro

Florida (Continued)

University of Florida, Gainesville

Jeffery P. Braden, Ph.D.
Field Supervisor

Robert Blanchette
William Brown
Tracey Bryant
Amy Endsley
Linda Fraze
Laurie McNulte
Justine Neville

University of South Florida, Tampa

James W. Barnard, Ph.D.
Field Supervisor

Linda Bythway
Mary Lisa Cummins
Sharon Headley
Joyce Poklemba
Silvia Romano

Bradenton

Thomas P. O'Donnell, Ed.D.
Field Supervisor

Gail Swanson
Susan Tate
Patricia Wilson-Lavigne

Jarrett Pence
Field Supervisor

Maitland

Claire H. Chepenik
Field Supervisor

James Fierro

Sarasota

Steven R. Shoemaker, Ph.D.
Field Supervisor

South Miami

Erwin Lesser, Ph.D.
Field Supervisor

Steven Shapiro
Patricia Wick

Tallahassee

Elizabeth F. Carter
Field Supervisor

Fae Hartsfield
Kathleen Leighton

Georgia

Georgia State University, Atlanta

R. Wayne Jones, Ph.D.
Field Supervisor

Ethel Craig
Lynda Fraizer

Georgia State University, Atlanta

Robin Morris, Ph.D.
Field Supervisor

Wendy Hanevold
Elizabeth Karlstrom
Suzann Lawry
John Lutz

Illinois

Illinois State University, Normal

Mark E. Swerdlik, Ph.D.
Field Supervisor

Greg Greenwood
Wanda Hughes
Jual Johnson
Julie Odette
Lisa Raufheisen

University of Illinois at Chicago

Billie S. Strauss, Ph.D.
Field Supervisor

Nancy Dassoff
Ron Pavone

Chicago

Stanley S. Selinger, Ph.D.
Field Supervisor

> John Paglini
> Albert Tuskenis

Streator

Robert E. Friedle, Ed.D.
Field Supervisor

> Kent Terry
> Rex Williamson

Indiana

Ball State University, Muncie

Betty E. Gridley, Ed.D.
Field Supervisor

> Christine Barry
> Diana Brummer
> Mark Kelly
> Vicki Mayer
> David McIntosh
> Rachel Nijakowski
> Kathleen Williams

Indiana University, Bloomington

Graydon E. Estabrook, Ph.D.
Field Supervisor

> Janet Broeren
> Lisa Anne Kelly
> Michael Vance

Indianapolis

Dennis F. Bowman, Jr.
Field Supervisor

> Anthony Kochert

Kansas

Wichita State University, Wichita

Nancy A. McKellar, Ph.D.
Field Supervisor

> Alisyn Andreas
> Diane Farnsworth
> Carolyn James

Liberal

James Cromer
Field Supervisor

Louisiana

University of New Orleans, New Orleans

Paulette J. Thomas, Ph.D.
Field Supervisor

> Brenda Burrell
> Susan Neel
> Laura Porter
> Joanne Rinardo
> Andrew Sandler

Massachusetts

American International University, Springfield

Gregory T. Schmutte, Ph.D.
Field Supervisor

> Brian Topor

Northeastern University, Boston

Peter Entwistle, Ph.D.
Field Supervisor

> James Thompson

Salem State College, Salem

Leonard P. Zani, Ed.D.
Field Supervisor

> Alba De Simone

Michigan

Central Michigan University, Mt. Pleasant

Susan Jacob, Ph.D.
Field Supervisor

Mary Abraham
Ruth Fodness
Larry Gandee

University of Michigan, Ann Arbor

Calvin O. Dyer, Ph.D.
Field Supervisor

Linda Lange

Detroit

Marion A. Smith
Field Supervisor

Ronald August

Minnesota

University of Minnesota, Minneapolis

James E. Ysseldyke, Ph.D.
Field Supervisor

Kirk Diment
David Schrot

Mississippi

Mississippi State University, Starkville

Alpha S. Humble
Field Supervisor

Cherri Parks

University of Southern Mississippi, Hattiesburg

Lee K. Hildman
Field Supervisor

Glenda Bailey
Catherine Capelli
Ralph Ott
Philip Spoto

Missouri

University of Missouri, Columbia

LeAdelle Phelps, Ph.D.
Field Supervisor

Christine Bell
Deborah Duncan
Clara Elliott
Shirley Hendricks
Jill Johnson
Tamara Mathews

Nebraska

University of Nebraska, Lincoln

Wayne C. Piersel, Ph.D.
Field Supervisor

Sarah Allen
Rebecca Braymen
Debra Sabers

New Jersey

Montclair State College, Upper Montclair

Joan M. Silverstein, Ph.D.
Field Supervisor

Patricia Carroll

New York

Alfred University, Alfred

Carla M. Narrett, Ph.D.
Field Supervisor

Susan Binley
Jennifer Daniels
Laurie Fiorella
Wanda Heath
Karen Hetey
Margaret Leutbecher
Rocco Persico
Lynne Russo
Cora Saxton
Catherine Warda

Cornell University, Ithaca

Marsha E. Williams
Field Supervisor

Julie Eisele
Melody Miller

New York City Board of Education, Brooklyn

Mary-Georgia A. Pollock
Field Supervisor

St. Joseph's College, Brooklyn

Sister Rosamond O'Keefe
Field Supervisor

Richard Azueta
Sophie Silverstein
Robert Weiss

State University of New York, Binghamton

Ian M. Evans, Ph.D.
Field Supervisor

Brooke Cannon

Syracuse University, Syracuse

S. Yancey Padget
Field Supervisor

Christine Müller-Schwarze

Yeshiva University, Bronx

Judith Kaufman, Ph.D.
Field Supervisor

Mark Biblow
Yvette Vogel

North Carolina

Greenville

Betty P. Robertson, Ph.D.
Field Supervisor

Ohio

Case Western Reserve University, Cleveland

Douglas K. Detterman, Ph.D.
Field Supervisor

Amy Lauderback
Marcia Lewis

Kent State University, Kent

Caven McLoughlin, Ph.D.
Field Supervisor

Barbara Bakos
Diane Bush
Jann Dolan
Valerie Gruber
Michelle Henry
Kathy Jurca
Paul Mooradian
Margo Siebert

Ohio State University, Columbus

Jack A. Naglieri, Ph.D.
Field Supervisor

Wanda Lillis
Julie Vondrell

University of Toledo, Toledo

Robert N. Wendt, Ph.D.
Field Supervisor

Mariane Osentoski

Ohio *(Continued)*

Cincinnati

Joseph T. Olasov, Ph.D.
Field Supervisor

Pennsylvania

Bryn Mawr College, Bryn Mawr

Leslie A. Rescorla, Ph.D.
Field Supervisor

    Marijke Goossens

Erie School District, Erie

Cyndy Quadri
Field Supervisor

    Katherine Bailey
    Tim Baronner
    Karen Cocco

Kutztown University, Kutztown

Constance P. Dent, Ph.D.
Field Supervisor

    Sue Freeman
    Sheila Fulton
    Ann Gundry

Lehigh University, Bethlehem

Edward S. Shapiro, Ph.D.
Field Supervisor

    Eileen Brennan
    Alison Brown
    Marilyn Herwig
    Cheryl Houser

University of Pennsylvania, Philadelphia

Judith Z. Nathanson, Ph.D.
Field Supervisor

    Judith Alperin
    Susan Bell
    Joseph Keenan
    Susan McGroarty

South Dakota

Sioux Falls

Janet Shelver, Ed.D.
Field Supervisor

Tennessee

Memphis Public Schools, Memphis

A. Lee Steward
Field Supervisor

Memphis State University

Bruce A. Bracken, Ph.D.
Field Supervisor

    Anne Graves

University of Tennessee, Knoxville

R. Steve McCallum, Ph.D.
Field Supervisor

    Edward Bloser
    Jann Cupp
    Richard Jones
    Susan Koller
    Isabella Thomas-Heinsohn
    George Traver

Texas

Houston Independent School District, Houston

Robert A. Guercio
Field Supervisor

    Susan Kollister

Texas A & M University, College Station

Cecil R. Reynolds, Ph.D.
Field Supervisor

    Joanna Gol
    Bonnie Raskin

Trinity University, San Antonio

Albert E. Riester, Ph.D.
Field Supervisor

> Gloria Collins
> Kimla Cotropia
> Nancy de Wied
> Janet LaVallee
> Julie Miller
> Ronald Morrell
> Christina Petofi-Casal

University of Texas, Austin

Thomas D. Oakland, Ph.D.
Field Supervisor

> Therese Adam
> Dina Hijazi
> Sherman Hu

Houston

Robert Huzinec
Field Supervisor

> Kathryn C. Bradford
> Rita Braunberger

Virginia E. Kibler, Ph.D.
Field Supervisor

San Antonio

Vera R. Wiser
Field Supervisor

> Mary Barbee
> Joseph DiRaddo
> Kenneth Frontman
> Mark Sexton
> Nancy Smith

Utah

University of Utah, Salt Lake City

Elaine Clark, Ph.D.
Field Supervisor

> Douglas Goldsmith
> Vernon Jesse
> Karen Malm

Utah State University, Logan

Glen Casto, Ph.D.
Field Supervisor

> Helen Mitchell

Washington

University of Washington, Seattle

Stanton P. Thalberg, Ph.D.
Field Supervisor

> Margaret McCool
> Sherrie Morrison
> Kari Seeger

Wisconsin

University of Wisconsin, Madison

Elizabeth J. Doll, Ph.D.
Field Supervisor

> Beth Ann Crain
> Deborah Levin
> Mary Rhoades
> Sharon Sanderson
> Stacy Weimer
> Denise Youngerman

University of Wisconsin, Milwaukee

Lindsay S. Gross
Field Supervisor

> Daryl Hanneman
> Jeffrey Molter
> Jim Neubert
> Karen Van Handel

Schools, Preschools, and Day-Care Centers

Alabama

Schools

Athens City School District
Decatur City School District
Huntsville City School District
Lee County School District
Lee–Scott Academy, Auburn
Macon County School District
Madison County Schools
Russell County School District

Preschools and Day-Care Centers

Auburn Day Care Center
Lanett First Baptist Day Care
The Learning Connection, Auburn
Love and Care Daycare Center, Inc.,
  Montgomery
Springwood Child Development
  Center, Lanett
University (of Alabama) Preschool,
  Huntsville

Arizona

Schools

Marana School District 6, Tucson
Sunnyside Unified School District 12,
  Tucson
Tucson Unified School District

California

Schools

Adelanto Elementary School District
Alhambra School District, Alhambra
Anaheim City School District
Berryessa Union School District,
  San Jose

Cajon Valley Union Elementary
  District, El Cajon
Campbell Christian School
Claremont Unified School District
Galt Joint Union High School
  District
Gilroy Christian School
Grace Lutheran Church Day School,
  Corona
Grant Joint Union High School
  District, Sacramento
Healdsburg Union Elementary
  Schools
Los Angeles Unified School District
Lynwood Unified School District
Milpitas Christian School, San Jose
Monterey Peninsula Unified School
  District
Newark Unified School District
Oak Grove Elementary School
  District, San Jose
Pasadena Unified School District
San Jose Unified School District
South Whittier Elementary School
  District
Ventura Unified School District
West Valley SDA Elementary School,
  Campbell
Winters Joint Unified School District
Yuba City Unified School District

Preschools and Day-Care Centers

Bear Necessities, Seaside
Ben Ali Children's Center,
  Sacramento
Children's Center of Santa Ana
Conley School, Chino
Creative Center for Children,
  Los Angeles
Davis Parent Nursery School
Fairplex Child Development Center,
  Pomona

Forrest Day School, Montclair
Garden Grove Country Dayschool &
  Preschool
Grace Christian Academy, Yuba City
Kid's Country School, Van Nuys
Lampson Grove Day School, Garden
  Grove
Little Promises Preschool, Ontario
Mother Goose Nursery, Yuba City
Park Vista School, Inc., Sacramento
Plaza Child Observation &
  Development Center, Los Angeles
San Fernando Valley Child Guidance
  Clinic, Northridge
Washington Children's Center, West
  Sacramento

Colorado

Schools

Ault Highland School District RE9,
  Ault
Denver School District 1
Park School District R3, Estes Park
Poudre School District R1, Fort
  Collins

Preschools and Day-Care Centers

Burlington Community Preschool,
  Longment
Campus Child Care Center, Greeley
Parent Child Center, LaSalle
Sunshine Lane Christian Academy,
  Greeley

Connecticut

Schools

East Haven School District

Preschools and Day-Care Centers

Chip & Dale Nursery, New Haven

Florida

Schools

Alachua County School District
Charlotte County School District
Columbia County School District
Florida School for the Deaf and
  Blind, St. Augustine
Hillsborough County School District
Jefferson County School District
Levy County School District
Manatee County School District
McClellan Park School, Sarasota
Osceola County School District
Our Redeemer Lutheran School,
  Temple Terrace
Tampa Baptist Academy
Tampa Junior Academy
Trinity Christian School, Apopka
Union County School District
Volusia County School District

Preschools and Day-Care Centers

A+ Preschool & Daycare, Bradenton
Advent Day School, Tallahassee
All Angel's Episcopal School, Miami
  Springs
Bizzy Bee Child Care, Sarasota
Child Care Center, Inc., Miami
Christ United Methodist Preschool,
  Bradenton
Colonial Park United Methodist
  Child Development Center, Lake
  Mary
Concordia Lutheran Preschool,
  Sarasota
Countryside Montessori School,
  Sarasota
Educational Imagery, Tallahassee
Heritage Christian School,
  Gainesville
Kinder Care, Bradenton
Lake Magdalene Methodist
  Preschool, Tampa

Florida (*Continued*)

My School Childcare Center,
    Gainesville
Oak Grove Child Care Development
    Center, Miami
Oakridge Child Development Center,
    Tallahassee
Palmer King Day Care Center,
    Gainesville
Playschool of Gainesville
Project Child Care, Bradenton
Robin's Nest, Tampa
Sarasota County Preschool
    Compensatory Program, Sarasota
Sarasota Day Nursery, Inc., Sarasota
South Miami Lutheran School, Miami
Wayside Baptist Church, Miami
Wee Care Preschool, Bradenton

Other

Boy's Club, Sarasota
YMCA, Sarasota

Georgia

Schools

Atlanta Adventist Academy
Barrow County School District
Brooks County School District
Brookstone School, Columbus
Clayton County School District
Colonial Hills Christian School, East
    Point
Fulton County School District
Old National Christian Academy,
    College Park
Paulding County School District
Thomasville City School District
Wesleyan Day School, Atlanta

Preschools and Day-Care Centers

Barrow County Child Development
    Center, Winder
Bridge to Learning, Athens
Buckhead Baptist Day School,
    Atlanta
Canterbury School, Atlanta

International Preparatory Institute,
    Atlanta
Sheltering Arms, Baker, Atlanta
Sheltering Arms, Brown Street,
    Douglasville
Sheltering Arms, Estoria, Atlanta
Sheltering Arms, Jere Via Center,
    Douglasville
Sheltering Arms, Memorial, Atlanta
Sheltering Arms, West Circle,
    Conyers

Illinois

Schools

Christian Day School of St. Luke,
    Chicago
Heyworth School District 4
Leo High School, Chicago
Marseilles Unit School District 155
North Chicago School District 64
Our Lady of the Snows School,
    Chicago
Peace Lutheran School, Chicago
Seneca Community Consolidated
    District 170
Streator School District 45
Streator Township High School
    District 40

Preschools and Day-Care Centers

Candlestick Day Care, Chicago
Cherub Preschool, Peoria
A Child's World/A Child's World
    Nursery, Peoria
Danvers Community School, Danvers
Evanston Day Nursery
Hilltop Private Nursery School,
    Normal
Pals' Preschool, Peoria
Putnam County Day Care
St. Andrew's Day Care, Peoria
Sunshine Learning Center, Peoria
Trinity Lutheran Preschool and Day
    Care Center, Des Plaines

Other

YWCA of Peoria

Indiana

Schools

Hammond City School District
Monroe County Community School
  Corporation

Preschools and Day-Care Centers

Burris Laboratory School, Muncie
Happy Day Care Center, Bloomington
Kinder-Care Learning Center,
  Bloomington
Penny Lane Day Care Center,
  Bloomington

Kansas

Schools

Derby Unified School District 260
Sedgwick Unified School District 439

Preschools and Day-Care Centers

Gideon Day Care Center, Wichita
Kids Connection, Liberal
Little Pals Day Care Center, Wichita
Northwest Wichita Early Childhood
  Center
Rainbow Room, Liberal
West Wichita Children's Center

Louisiana

Schools

Archdiocese of New Orleans (New
  Orleans Area Catholic Schools)

Preschools and Day-Care Centers

Storyland Nursery, Inc., Kenner

Massachusetts

Schools

Hampden School District
Lawrence School District
Randolph School District
Revere School District

Preschools and Day-Care Centers

Foster Memorial Nursery School,
  Springfield

Michigan

Schools

Chippewa Hills School District,
  Remus
St. Louis Public School District

Preschools and Day-Care Centers

Appleblossom Learning Center,
  Lansing
Gingerbread House Nursery School,
  Claire
Isabella Child Development Center,
  Mt. Pleasant
Kinder-Kare, Midland
Zion Lutheran Nursery, Mt. Pleasant

Minnesota

Schools

Magnolia School District
St. Paul Independent School
  District 625

Preschools and Day-Care Centers

Community Child Care Center,
  Minneapolis
Jack & Jill Learning Center, Luverne
Little Lambs Preschool, Luverne

Mississippi

Schools

Forrest County School District
Lowndes County School District
Oktibbeha County School District
Perry County School District
Starkville School District

Preschools and Day-Care Centers

Gateway Learning Center,
  Hattiesburg

Missouri

Schools

Boone County School District R4
Center School District 58, Kansas
  City
Howard County School District R2
Springfield School District R12
Sturgeon School District R5
Walnut Grove School District R5
Waynesville School District R6
Willard School District

Preschools and Day-Care Centers

Audrey Webb Child Study Center,
  Columbia
Developmental Learning Center,
  Columbia
Kids Farm, Columbia
Progressive Day Care Center,
  Columbia

Nebraska

Schools

Lincoln Christian Academy
Malcolm Public Schools
Norris School District 160, Firth
St. Mary Elementary School, Lincoln

Preschools and Day-Care Centers

Central Day Care and Preschool,
  Lincoln
Family Service Child Care, Lincoln

New Jersey

Schools

Belleville School District
Pascack Valley Regional High
  School, Hillsdale

New York

Schools

Arkport Central School District
Bethlehem Baptist Academy,
  Brooklyn
Bronx Community School District 9
Brooklyn Community School
  District 14
Brooklyn Community School
  District 19
Brooklyn Community School
  District 22
Dryden Central School District
Groton Central School District
Hebrew Academy of Nassau County,
  Uniondale
Hornell City School District
Letchworth Central School District,
  Gainesville
Newfield Central School District
New York City Community School
  District 6
St. Angela Hall Academy, Brooklyn
St. Joseph High School, Brooklyn
Watkins Glen Central School District
Wellsville Central School District

Preschools and Day-Care Centers

Blodgett-Hughes School, Syracuse
Blodgett-St. Anthony School,
  Syracuse

New York (*Continued*)

Blodgett–Sumner School, Syracuse
Grace Children's Academy, Syracuse
Happy Day Playschool, Ithaca
Happy House Nursery, Elmira
Ithaca Area Church & Community
  Day Care
Just Kids, Middle Island
Kid Korral Day Care Center,
  Binghamton
Lollipops Nursery School, Delmar
Love-N-Learn Day Care, Elmira
Place of Learning, Corning

Ohio

Schools

Akron City School District, Akron
Apostolate for the Mentally Retarded,
  Cleveland
Cleveland City School District
Clintonville Academy, Columbus
Crestwood Local School District,
  Mantua
Gahanna–Jefferson School District,
  Gahanna
Maumee City Schools
Southeast Local School District,
  Ravenna
Southwestern City School District,
  Grove City
Tree of Life Christian School,
  Columbus

Preschools and Day-Care Centers

Color Our Rainbow, Akron
Creative Play Center, Worthington
Gerber Children's Center, Akron
Gerber Children's Center, Brookpark
Gerber Children's Center, North
  Olmstead
Little People's Day Care, Columbus

Pennsylvania

Schools

Allentown City School District
Bristol Township School District
East Penn School District, Emmaus
Erie City School District
Kutztown Area School District
Philadelphia School District
Southeast Delco School District,
  Folcroft

Preschools and Day-Care Centers

Bellefonte Child Development Center
Delco Child Day Care Association,
  Darby
Delco Child Day Care Association,
  Drexel Hill
First Impressions Child Development
  Center, State College
The Learning Station, State College
Mount St. Benedict East Coast
  Migrant Head Start, Harbor Creek
Research Learning Center, Kutztown

Tennessee

Schools

Alcoa City School District
Blount County School District
Briarcrest Baptist Schools System,
  Memphis
Knoxville City Schools
Lamplighter Montessori School,
  Memphis
Lenoir City School District
Shelby County School District
Southern Baptist Educational Center
Whitehaven Methodist

Tennessee *(Continued)*

Preschools and Day-Care Centers

Arnstein Jewish Community Center,
    Knoxville
Bethel Temple Day Care, Memphis
Broadway Baptist Child Development
    Center, Knoxville
Buntyn Preschool, Memphis
Children's Center of Knoxville
Golden Leaf Baptist Day Care Center,
    Memphis
Greenwood Learning Center,
    Memphis

Texas

Schools

Archdiocese of San Antonio Schools
Bastrop Independent School District
Brentwood Christian School, Austin
Cypress Fairbanks School District,
    Houston
Dallas Independent School District
Dripping Springs Independent School
    District
Elgin Independent School District
Harlandale Independent School
    District, San Antonio
Houston Independent School District
Judson Independent School District,
    Converse
Melrose Baptist School, Houston
New Age School, San Antonio
North Forest Independent School
    District, Houston
Northside Independent School
    District, San Antonio
Northwest Academy, Houston
Pflugerville Independent School
    District
Royal Independent School District,
    Brookshire
St. Luke's Episcopal School, San
    Antonio
San Antonio Independent School
    District
Second Baptist School, Houston

Southwest Independent School
    District, San Antonio

Preschools and Day-Care Centers

A Child's World, Austin
Creative Rapid Learning Center,
    Austin
Discovery School, San Antonio
Early Learning Center, San Antonio
First Class, San Antonio
Keystone School, San Antonio
Landauer Child Care Center, Dallas
Manor Baptist Child Development
    Center, San Antonio
Martin Luther King Child Care,
    Dallas
San Antonio Country Day School
South San Baptist Day Care Center,
    San Antonio

Utah

Schools

Cache County School District
Granite School District, Salt Lake
    City
Jordan School District, Sandy
Ogden City School DistrictPreschools
    and Day-Care Centers
Mary's Nursery School, Salt Lake
    City

Washington

Schools

Bellevue Montessori School
Kent School District 415
King's Elementary, Seattle

Preschools and Day-Care Centers

Child Development Center, Seattle
Children's World Montessori, Seattle
Nazarene Creative Day Care,
    Bremerton

Wisconsin

Schools

Atonement Lutheran School,
Milwaukee
Bruce Guadalupe Community School,
Milwaukee
Glendale–River Hills Joint District 1,
Milwaukee
Greenfield School District
Holy Cross Lutheran School, Madison
New Glarus School District
Nicolet High School District 1,
Glendale
Northwest Lutheran Grade School,
Milwaukee
Oakwood Discovery Stage, Inc.,
Franklin
Our Father's Evangelical Lutheran
School, Greenfield
Pecatonica Area School District,
Blanchardville
Racine Unified School District
St. Francis School District 6
St. Jacobi Lutheran School,
Greenfield
St. Peter–Immanuel Lutheran School,
Milwaukee
Sauk Prairie School District
South Milwaukee School District
Sun Prairie School District

Preschools and Day-Care Centers

Bernie's Place, Inc., Madison
Bluemond Preschools, Waunatosa
Campus for Kids, Madison
Christian Day Care, Madison
Creative Child Care, Madison
Silver Spring Day Care Center &
Neighborhood Center, Milwaukee
South Day Care of St. Joseph, Inc.,
Milwaukee

Wyoming

Schools

Laramie County School
District 1, Cheyenne

Appendix B

Statistical Significance and Frequency of Score Differences

The following tables show the differences between various scores required for statistical significance, based on the standard errors of measurement reported in Tables 8.3 and 8.4. They also report the sizes of differences shown by various percentages of children in the norm sample.

Table B.1. Between-Cluster and Within-Cluster Score Differences Required for Statistical Significance: Ages 3:6–5:11

Table B.2. Between-Cluster and Within-Cluster Score Differences Shown by Various Percentages of the Norm Sample: Ages 3:6–5:11

Table B.3. Between-Cluster and Within-Cluster Score Differences Shown by Various Percentages of the Norm Sample: Ages 6:0–17:11

Table B.4. Between-Cluster and Within-Cluster Score Differences Required for Statistical Significance: Ages 6:0–17:11

Table B.5. Differences Between Cognitive-Subtest T Scores and the Mean T Score on the Core Subtests Required for Statistical Significance

Table B.6. Differences Between Cognitive-Subtest T Scores and the Mean T Score on the Core Subtests Shown by Various Percentages of the Norm Sample: Ages 2:6–3:5

Table B.7. Differences Between Cognitive-Subtest T Scores and the Mean T Score on the Core Subtests Shown by Various Percentages of the Norm Sample: Ages 3:6–5:11

Table B.8. Differences Between Cognitive-Subtest T Scores and the Mean T Score on the Core Subtests Shown by Various Percentages of the Norm Sample: Ages 6:0–17:11

Table B.9. Differences Between Subtest T Scores Required for Statistical Significance

Table B.10. Differences Between Achievement-Test Standard Scores and GCA or SNC Scores Required for Statistical Significance

Table B.11. Achievement-Test Standard Scores Predicted from GCA or Special Nonverbal Composite Scores

Table B.12. Differences Between Observed and Predicted Achievement-Test Standard Scores Required for Statistical Significance

Table B.13. Differences Between Observed and Predicted Achievement-Test Standard Scores Shown by Various Percentages of the Norm Sample

Table B.1. Between-Cluster and Within-Cluster Score Differences Required for Statistical Significance: Ages 3:6-5:11

Comparison	p	Mean	Age 3:6-3:11	4:0-4:5	4:6-4:11	5:0-5:11
Cluster vs. GCA[a]						
Verbal Ability	.15	7.4	7.6	7.1	7.6	7.3
	.05	9.3	9.6	8.9	9.5	9.1
	.01	11.7	12.0	11.2	12.0	11.5
Nonverbal Ability	.15	6.1	6.3	5.9	6.2	5.9
	.05	7.6	7.9	7.4	7.8	7.4
	.01	9.6	9.9	9.3	9.8	9.3
Cluster vs. Cluster						
Verbal vs. Nonverbal	.15	10.3	10.6	9.9	10.5	10.0
	.05	14.0	14.5	13.4	14.3	13.6
	.01	18.4	19.0	17.7	18.9	18.0
Within Cluster						
Verbal Comprehension	.15	8.8	9.1	8.4	8.9	8.7
vs. Naming Vocabulary	.05	12.0	12.4	11.5	12.1	11.9
	.01	15.7	16.3	15.1	15.9	15.6
Picture Similarities	.15	12.4	11.9	12.1	13.6	12.1
vs. Pattern Construction[a]	.05	15.2	14.5	14.8	16.6	14.8
	.01	18.6	17.7	18.1	20.4	18.1
Picture Similarities	.15	13.9	14.7	14.0	13.5	13.6
vs. Pattern Construction	.05	17.0	17.9	17.0	16.5	16.5
(Alternative)[a]	.01	20.8	21.9	20.9	20.2	20.3
Picture Similarities	.15	12.5	12.7	12.1	12.4	12.6
vs. Copying[a]	.05	15.2	15.5	14.8	15.1	15.4
	.01	18.6	19.0	18.1	18.5	18.9
Pattern Construction	.15	10.1	11.3	9.7	10.7	8.6
vs. Copying[a]	.05	12.3	13.8	11.8	13.0	10.5
	.01	15.1	16.9	14.5	16.0	12.9
Pattern Construction	.15	11.8	14.2	11.9	10.5	10.5
(Alternative) vs.	.05	14.4	17.3	14.5	12.9	12.8
Copying[a]	.01	17.6	21.3	17.8	15.8	15.8

Note. Cluster vs. GCA differences have been calculated in a way that takes into account the part-whole relationship.

[a] Values have been adjusted for multiple, simultaneous comparisons.

Table B.2. Between-Cluster and Within-Cluster Score Differences Shown by Various Percentages of the Norm Sample: Ages 3:6–5:11

Comparison	Percentage					
	25	15	10	5	2	1
Cluster vs. GCA						
Verbal Ability	10	13	15	19	22	25
Nonverbal Ability	9	11	13	15	18	20
Cluster vs. Cluster						
Verbal vs. Nonverbal	17	21	25	30	36	40
Within-Cluster						
Verb. Comp. vs. N. Voc.	9	11	13	16	19	21
Pict. Sim. vs. Pattern Construction	13	16	19	23	26	29
Pict. Sim. vs. Pattern Construction (Alt.)	13	16	18	22	26	28
Pict. Sim. vs. Copying	13	16	18	23	27	29
Pattern Construction vs. Copying	11	15	17	21	28	30
Pattern Construction (Alt.) vs. Copying	12	15	17	20	25	29

Table B.3. Between-Cluster and Within-Cluster Score Differences Shown by Various Percentages of the Norm Sample: Ages 6:0–17:11

Comparison	Percentage					
	25	15	10	5	2	1
Cluster vs. GCA						
Verbal Ability	11	13	15	18	20	23
Nonverbal Reas. Ability	9	11	13	16	19	22
Spatial Ability	10	13	15	17	21	23
Cluster vs. Cluster						
Verbal vs. Nonverbal Reas.	15	19	22	26	32	36
Verbal vs. Spatial	17	21	24	28	34	37
Nonverbal Reas. vs. Spatial	14	19	21	25	30	34
Within-Cluster						
Word Def. vs. Similarities	9	11	13	16	19	22
Matrices vs. Sequential & Quantitative Reasoning	10	13	15	18	20	23
Rec. of Designs vs. Pattern Construction	10	13	15	18	23	25
Rec. of Designs vs. Pattern Construction (Alt.)	10	13	15	19	23	26

Table B.4. Between-Cluster and Within-Cluster Score Differences Required for Statistical Significance: Ages 6:0–17:11

Comparison	p	Mean	6	7	8	9	10	11	12	13	14	15	16	17
Cluster vs. GCA [a]														
Verbal Ability	.15	7.8	7.7	7.7	7.6	7.7	7.7	7.7	7.5	7.6	7.9	7.9	8.1	8.5
	.05	9.5	9.4	9.4	9.3	9.4	9.4	9.4	9.1	9.2	9.6	9.6	9.9	10.3
	.01	11.7	11.5	11.6	11.4	11.6	11.5	11.5	11.2	11.3	11.8	11.8	12.1	12.7
Nonverbal Reas. Ability	.15	7.7	7.9	7.5	7.4	7.6	7.6	7.7	7.5	7.5	7.9	7.9	8.0	8.3
	.05	9.4	9.6	9.2	9.0	9.3	9.2	9.4	9.1	9.1	9.6	9.6	9.8	10.2
	.01	11.6	11.8	11.2	11.0	11.4	11.3	11.5	11.1	11.2	11.8	11.8	12.0	12.5
Spatial Ability	.15	7.4	7.6	7.7	7.5	7.6	7.6	7.5	7.2	7.1	7.3	7.2	7.4	7.7
	.05	9.1	9.2	9.4	9.1	9.3	9.2	9.1	8.8	8.6	8.9	8.8	9.1	9.3
	.01	11.1	11.3	11.5	11.2	11.4	11.3	11.2	10.7	10.6	10.9	10.8	11.1	11.5
Cluster vs. Cluster [a]														
Verbal vs. Nonverbal Reasoning	.15	13.8	13.8	13.1	13.0	13.4	13.3	13.6	13.3	13.5	14.3	14.4	14.7	15.4
	.05	16.8	16.8	16.0	15.8	16.3	16.2	16.6	16.3	16.5	17.4	17.5	17.9	18.8
	.01	20.7	20.6	19.7	19.4	20.0	19.9	20.3	19.9	20.2	21.4	21.5	22.0	23.0
Verbal vs. Spatial	.15	13.0	12.8	13.5	13.2	13.3	13.2	13.0	12.5	12.4	12.7	12.7	13.1	13.6
	.05	15.9	15.6	16.5	16.1	16.3	16.1	15.9	15.2	15.1	15.5	15.4	16.0	16.6
	.01	19.4	19.1	20.2	19.7	20.0	19.7	19.5	18.7	18.5	19.0	18.9	19.6	20.4
Nonverbal Reasoning vs. Spatial	.15	12.6	13.1	12.7	12.4	12.7	12.7	12.7	12.1	12.1	12.5	12.4	12.6	12.9
	.05	15.3	16.0	15.5	15.1	15.5	15.4	15.5	14.8	14.7	15.2	15.1	15.3	15.7
	.01	18.8	19.6	18.5	18.5	19.0	18.9	19.0	18.2	18.0	18.6	18.5	18.8	19.3

Note. Cluster vs. GCA differences have been calculated in a way that takes into account the part-whole relationship.
[a] Values have been adjusted for multiple, simultaneous comparisons.

Table B.4. Between-Cluster and Within-Cluster Score Differences Required for Statistical Significance: Ages 6:0–17:11 *(Continued)*

Comparison	p	Mean	6	7	8	9	10	11	12	13	14	15	16	17
Within Cluster														
Word Def. vs.	.15	8.9	8.4	8.7	8.7	8.8	8.7	8.7	8.6	8.6	9.1	9.2	9.5	10.0
Similarities	.05	12.1	11.5	11.9	11.8	12.0	11.8	11.8	11.7	11.7	12.3	12.6	13.0	13.6
	.01	16.0	15.1	15.7	15.6	15.8	15.6	15.6	15.4	15.5	16.2	16.6	17.1	17.9
Matrices vs.	.15	8.3	8.6	7.6	7.5	7.8	7.9	8.2	8.1	8.2	8.7	8.7	8.8	9.1
Seq. & Quant. Reas.	.05	11.2	11.7	10.4	10.2	10.7	10.8	11.1	11.0	11.1	11.8	11.8	11.9	12.4
	.01	14.8	15.5	13.7	13.4	14.0	14.2	14.6	14.5	14.6	15.5	15.5	15.7	16.3
Recall of Designs vs.	.15	7.1	7.4	8.0	7.8	7.8	7.7	7.4	6.9	6.7	6.5	6.4	6.6	6.6
Pattern Construction	.05	9.7	10.1	10.9	10.6	10.6	10.4	10.1	9.4	9.1	8.9	8.7	9.0	9.0
	.01	12.8	13.3	14.3	13.9	13.9	13.7	13.3	12.3	11.9	11.7	11.5	11.8	11.8
Recall of Designs vs.	.15	8.8	8.2	8.9	8.9	8.3	8.3	8.7	8.4	8.7	8.7	9.0	9.4	10.0
Pattern Construction	.05	12.0	11.1	12.0	12.1	11.3	11.3	11.8	11.4	11.8	11.8	12.2	12.8	13.6
(Alternative)	.01	15.7	14.7	15.9	15.9	14.9	14.9	15.6	15.0	15.5	15.5	16.1	16.9	18.0

293

Table B.5. Differences Between Cognitive-Subtest *T* Scores and the Mean *T* Score on the Core Subtests Required for Statistical Significance

Subtest	Lower Preschool Level			Upper Preschool Level			School-Age Level		
	.15	.05	.01	.15	.05	.01	.15	.05	.01
GCA: Mean *T* Score									
Block Building	10	12	14	12	13	16	—	—	—
Verbal Comprehension	8	10	11	9	10	12	—	—	—
Picture Similarities	9	10	12	11	13	15	—	—	—
Naming Vocabulary	9	11	13	10	12	14	—	—	—
Pattern Construction	—	—	—	8	10	11	—	—	—
Pattern Const. (Alt.)	—	—	—	11	12	14	—	—	—
Early Number Concepts	—	—	—	8	9	11	—	—	—
Copying	—	—	—	8	9	11	—	—	—
Recall of Designs	—	—	—	—	—	—	9	10	12
Word Definitions	—	—	—	—	—	—	9	10	12
Pattern Construction	—	—	—	—	—	—	7	8	9
Pattern Const. (Alt.)	—	—	—	—	—	—	9	10	12
Matrices	—	—	—	—	—	—	9	11	12
Similarities	—	—	—	—	—	—	10	11	13
Seq. & Quant. Reas.	—	—	—	—	—	—	9	10	12
Matching LL Forms	—	—	—	10	12	14	—	—	—
Recall of Digits	9	11	13	10	11	13	10	11	13
Recall of Objects—Imm.	—	—	—	14	16	19	12	14	17
Recognition of Pictures	12	15	17	13	14	17	—	—	—
Speed of Info. Processing	—	—	—	—	—	—	8	9	11
Special Nonverbal Composite: Mean *T* Score									
Block Building	8	9	11	12	14	17	—	—	—
Verbal Comprehension	12	14	16	12	13	15	—	—	—
Picture Similarities	8	9	11	10	11	13	—	—	—
Naming Vocabulary	13	16	19	13	15	17	—	—	—
Pattern Construction	—	—	—	8	9	11	—	—	—
Pattern Const. (Alt.)	—	—	—	10	11	13	—	—	—
Early Number Concepts	—	—	—	11	12	14	—	—	—
Copying	—	—	—	8	9	11	—	—	—
Recall of Designs	—	—	—	—	—	—	8	10	11
Word Definitions	—	—	—	—	—	—	11	13	15
Pattern Construction	—	—	—	—	—	—	7	8	9
Pattern Const. (Alt.)	—	—	—	—	—	—	8	10	11
Matrices	—	—	—	—	—	—	9	10	12
Similarities	—	—	—	—	—	—	12	14	16
Seq. & Quant. Reas.	—	—	—	—	—	—	8	9	11
Matching LL Forms	—	—	—	12	13	16	—	—	—
Recall of Digits	11	13	15	11	12	14	10	12	13
Recall of Objects—Imm.	—	—	—	15	17	19	13	15	17
Recognition of Pictures	14	16	19	13	15	18	—	—	—
Speed of Info. Processing	—	—	—	—	—	—	9	10	12

Note. Differences involving core subtests have been calculated in a way that takes into account the part-whole relationship betweeen core-subtest scores and the mean *T* score. Values have been adjusted for multiple, simultaneous comparisons.

Table B.6. Differences Between Cognitive-Subtest T Scores and the Mean T Score on the Core Subtests Shown By Various Percentages of the Norm Sample: Ages 2:6–3:5

Subtest	Percentage					
	25	15	10	5	2	1
GCA: Mean T Score						
Block Building	9	11	13	15	18	20
Verbal Comprehension	7	9	10	12	14	15
Picture Similarities	9	11	12	14	18	20
Naming Vocabulary	8	9	11	13	15	17
Pattern Construction[a]	10	12	14	16	18	23
Pattern Const. (Alt.)[a]	10	13	15	17	19	24
Early Number Concepts	9	11	13	15	19	21
Recall of Digits	11	14	16	19	22	24
Recognition of Pictures	10	13	16	19	23	26
Special Nonverbal Composite: Mean T Score						
Block Building	6	8	10	12	14	15
Verbal Comprehension	10	13	14	17	19	22
Picture Similarities	6	8	9	11	14	15
Naming Vocabulary	10	13	16	19	22	24
Pattern Construction[a]	9	12	14	17	18	19
Pattern Const. (Alt.)[a]	9	12	14	17	20	23
Early Number Concepts	9	12	14	17	21	24
Recall of Digits	11	14	16	19	24	26
Recognition of Pictures	10	14	16	20	23	25

Note. $N = 350$ except as noted.
[a]$N = 175$.

Table B.7. Differences Between Cognitive-Subtest T Scores and the Mean T Score on the Core Subtests Shown By Various Percentages of the Norm Sample: Ages 3:6–5:11

Subtest	Percentage					
	25	15	10	5	2	1
GCA: Mean T Score						
Verbal Comprehension	6	8	10	12	14	16
Picture Similarities	8	10	12	15	17	19
Naming Vocabulary	8	10	11	13	16	18
Pattern Construction	8	10	11	14	17	20
Pattern Const. (Alt.)	8	10	11	14	17	19
Early Number Concepts	6	8	9	11	13	15
Copying	7	10	11	14	18	21
Block Building[a]	9	11	13	15	18	22
Matching LL Forms[b]	9	12	14	17	19	22
Recall of Digits	10	13	14	17	21	25
Recall of Objects—Imm.[b]	12	15	17	20	24	27
Recognition of Pictures	10	13	15	17	19	22
Nonverbal Cluster:						
Mean T Score						
Verbal Comprehension	9	12	15	17	19	21
Picture Similarities	7	9	11	13	15	17
Naming Vocabulary	10	14	16	20	23	24
Pattern Construction	7	9	10	13	15	17
Pattern Const. (Alt.)	7	9	10	12	14	15
Early Number Concepts	8	10	12	15	18	20
Copying	7	9	10	12	15	18
Block Building[a]	9	11	12	15	19	20
Matching LL Forms[b]	10	12	14	16	19	21
Recall of Digits	11	14	16	19	23	28
Recall of Objects—Imm.[b]	12	16	18	22	26	28
Recognition of Pictures	10	13	16	18	21	25

Note. $N = 725$ except as noted.
[a]$N = 525$.
[b]$N = 550$.

Table B.8. Differences Between Cognitive-Subtest T Scores and the Mean T Score on the Core Subtests Shown By Various Percentages of the Norm Sample: Ages 6:0–17:11

Subtest	Percentage					
	25	15	10	5	2	1
GCA: Mean T Score						
Recall of Designs	7	10	11	13	16	19
Word Definitions	7	9	11	12	15	17
Pattern Construction	7	9	10	12	14	16
Pattern Const. (Alt.)	7	9	10	12	15	17
Matrices	7	9	10	13	15	17
Similarities	7	9	10	13	15	17
Seq. & Quant. Reas.	7	8	10	12	14	15
Recall of Digits	11	14	17	20	24	27
Recall of Objects—Imm.	12	15	17	20	25	28
Recognition of Pictures	11	13	15	19	22	25
Speed of Info. Processing	12	15	17	21	25	27
Special Nonverbal Composite: Mean T Score						
Recall of Designs	7	9	10	12	15	16
Word Definitions	10	12	14	17	19	22
Pattern Construction	6	8	9	11	13	15
Pattern Const. (Alt.)	6	8	9	11	13	15
Matrices	6	8	10	12	15	17
Similarities	9	12	14	17	20	22
Seq. & Quant. Reas.	6	8	9	11	13	15
Recall of Digits	12	15	18	21	25	28
Recall of Objects—Imm.	12	15	17	21	26	28
Recognition of Pictures	11	14	16	19	23	25
Speed of Info. Processing	12	15	18	22	26	28

Note. N = 2400.

Table B.9. Differences Between Subtest T Scores Required for Statistical Significance

Subtest	Block Building	Verbal Comprehension	Picture Similarities	Naming Vocabulary	Pattern Construction	Early Number Concepts	Copying	Matching Letter-Like Forms	Recall of Digits	Recall of Objects—Immediate	Recognition of Pictures
Block Building		12.1	13.4	13.1	11.6	11.8	11.6	11.8	11.6	13.9	13.5
Verbal Comprehension	8.9		12.4	12.0	10.4	10.6	10.4	10.6	10.3	12.9	12.4
Picture Similarities	9.8	9.1		13.3	11.8	12.0	11.9	12.1	11.8	14.1	13.7
Naming Vocabulary	9.6	8.8	9.8		11.5	11.7	11.5	11.7	11.5	13.8	13.3
Pattern Construction	8.5	7.6	8.7	8.4		10.0	9.8	10.0	9.7	12.4	11.9
Early Number Concepts	8.7	7.8	8.9	8.6	7.3		10.0	10.3	10.0	12.6	12.1
Copying	8.5	7.6	8.7	8.4	7.2	7.4		10.1	9.8	12.5	11.9
Matching Letter-Like Forms	8.7	7.8	8.9	8.6	7.4	7.6	7.4		10.0	12.7	12.2
Recall of Digits	8.5	7.6	8.7	8.4	7.1	7.3	7.2	7.4		12.4	11.9
Recall of Objects—Immediate	10.2	9.5	10.4	10.2	9.1	9.3	9.2	9.3	9.1		14.2
Recognition of Pictures	9.9	9.1	10.0	9.8	8.7	8.9	8.8	8.9	8.7	10.4	

Note. Differences at the .05 level of significance are shown above the diagonal, and those at the .15 level are shown below the diagonal. Values are not adjusted for multiple, simultaneous comparisons.

Table B.9. Differences Between Subtest *T* Scores Required for Statistical Significance (*Continued*)

Subtest	Recall of Designs	Word Definitions	Pattern Construction	Matrices	Similarities	Sequent. & Quant. Reasoning	Recall of Digits	Recall of Objects Immed.	Speed of Inform. Process.
Recall of Designs		11.2	9.7	11.4	12.0	10.9	10.6	12.4	9.7
Word Definitions	8.2		9.9	11.5	12.1	11.0	10.8	12.5	9.8
Pattern Construction	7.1	7.3		10.1	10.8	9.5	9.2	11.2	8.1
Matrices	8.4	8.5	7.4		12.3	11.2	11.0	12.7	10.1
Similarities	8.8	8.9	7.9	9.1		11.9	11.6	13.3	10.8
Sequential & Quantitative Reasoning	8.0	8.1	7.0	8.3	8.7		10.5	12.3	9.5
Recall of Digits	7.8	7.9	6.8	8.1	8.5	7.7		12.0	9.2
Recall of Objects— Immediate	9.1	9.2	8.2	9.3	9.7	9.0	8.8		11.2
Speed of Information Processing	7.1	7.2	6.0	7.4	7.9	7.0	6.7	8.2	

Note. Differences at the .05 level of significance are shown above the diagonal, and those at the .15 level are shown below the diagonal. Values are not adjusted for multiple, simultaneous comparisons.

Table B.10. Differences Between Achievement-Test Standard Scores and GCA or SNC Scores Required for Statistical Significance

Achievement Test	p	Mean	Age												
			6	7	8	9	10	11	12	13	14	15	16	17
Compared with the GCA															
Basic Number Skills	.15	8.8	8.3	8.1	8.6	8.7	8.6	8.5	8.5	8.6	9.3	9.4	9.6	10.0
	.05	12.0	11.3	11.0	11.7	11.8	11.8	11.5	11.5	11.6	12.7	12.8	13.1	13.7
	.01	15.8	14.8	14.5	15.4	15.5	15.5	15.2	15.2	15.3	16.7	16.8	17.2	18.0
Spelling	.15	7.7	7.9	6.8	7.4	7.8	7.8	7.8	7.7	7.5	7.9	7.9	8.2	8.1
	.05	10.5	10.8	9.3	10.1	10.6	10.6	10.6	10.4	10.2	10.7	10.7	11.1	11.0
	.01	13.9	14.2	12.2	13.3	14.0	14.0	14.0	13.8	13.4	14.1	14.1	14.7	14.5
Word Reading[a]	.15	7.6	6.6	6.9	6.9	6.7	7.2	7.6	7.7	7.5	8.1	8.2	8.6	8.9
	.05	10.3	9.0	9.4	9.4	9.1	9.8	10.3	10.4	10.2	11.0	11.2	11.7	12.1
	.01	13.6	11.8	12.3	12.3	12.0	12.9	13.5	13.7	13.4	14.4	14.7	15.4	16.0
Compared with the Special Nonverbal Composite															
Basic Number Skills	.15	9.1	8.6	8.4	8.8	8.9	8.9	8.7	8.7	8.8	9.5	9.6	9.8	10.2
	.05	12.3	11.7	11.4	12.0	12.2	12.1	11.9	11.8	11.9	12.9	13.0	13.3	13.8
	.01	16.2	15.4	15.0	15.8	16.0	16.0	15.6	15.6	15.7	17.0	17.1	17.5	18.2
Spelling	.15	8.0	8.3	7.2	7.7	8.1	8.1	8.1	7.9	7.8	8.1	8.1	8.4	8.2
	.05	10.9	11.3	9.7	10.5	11.0	11.0	11.0	10.8	10.6	11.0	11.0	11.4	11.2
	.01	14.3	14.9	12.8	13.8	14.5	14.5	14.5	14.2	13.9	14.5	14.4	15.0	14.8
Word Reading[a]	.15	7.8	7.0	7.2	7.2	7.0	7.6	7.9	7.9	7.7	8.3	8.4	8.8	9.0
	.05	10.7	9.6	9.8	9.8	9.6	10.3	10.7	10.8	10.5	11.2	11.4	11.9	12.3
	.01	14.0	12.6	12.9	12.9	12.6	13.5	14.1	14.2	13.8	14.8	15.1	15.7	16.2

[a]Values are larger at ages 14-17 because at those ages the Word Reading test is less accurate for high-achieving examinees. For examinees aged 14-17 who score in the low or average range on Word Reading, the difference values for ages 6-13 are more appropriate.

Table B.11 Achievement-Test Standard Scores Predicted from GCA or Special Nonverbal Composite Scores

GCA	Basic Number Skills	Spelling	Word Reading	GCA	Basic Number Skills	Spelling	Word Reading
45	69	72	69	106	104	104	103
46	69	73	69	107	105	104	104
47	70	73	70	108	105	105	105
48	71	74	70	109	106	105	105
49	71	74	71	110	107	106	106
50	72	75	72	111	107	106	106
51	72	75	72	112	108	107	107
52	73	76	73	113	108	107	107
53	73	76	73	114	109	108	108
54	74	77	74	115	110	108	109
55	75	77	74	116	110	109	109
56	75	78	75	117	111	109	110
57	76	78	76	118	111	110	110
58	76	79	76	119	112	110	111
59	77	79	77	120	112	111	111
60	78	80	77	121	113	111	112
61	78	80	78	122	114	112	113
62	79	81	78	123	114	112	113
63	79	81	79	124	115	113	114
64	80	82	79	125	115	113	114
65	80	82	80	126	116	114	115
66	81	83	81	127	117	114	115
67	82	83	81	128	117	115	116
68	82	84	82	129	118	115	117
69	83	84	82	130	118	116	117
70	83	85	83	131	119	116	118
71	84	85	83	132	119	117	118
72	85	86	84	133	120	117	119
73	85	87	85	134	121	118	119
74	86	87	85	135	121	118	120
75	86	88	86	136	122	119	121
76	87	88	86	137	122	119	121
77	87	89	87	138	123	120	122
78	88	89	87	139	124	121	122
79	89	90	88	140	124	121	123
80	89	90	89	141	125	122	123
81	90	91	89	142	125	122	124
82	90	91	90	143	126	123	125
83	91	92	90	144	126	123	125
84	92	92	91	145	127	124	126
85	92	93	91	146	128	124	126
86	93	93	92	147	128	125	127
87	93	94	93	148	129	125	127
88	94	94	93	149	129	126	128
89	94	95	94	150	130	126	129
90	95	95	94	151	131	127	129
91	96	96	95	152	131	127	130
92	96	96	95	153	132	128	130
93	97	97	96	154	132	128	131
94	97	97	97	155	133	129	131
95	98	98	97	156	133	129	132
96	98	98	98	157	134	130	133
97	99	99	98	158	135	130	133
98	99	99	99	159	135	131	134
99	100	100	99	160	136	131	134
100	100	100	100	161	136	132	135
101	101	101	101	162	137	132	135
102	102	101	101	163	138	133	136
103	102	102	102	164	138	133	136
104	103	102	102				
105	104	103	103				

Table B.11 Achievement-Test Standard Scores Predicted from GCA or Special Nonverbal Composite Scores

(Continued)

Special Nonverbal Composite	Basic Number Skills	Spelling	Word Reading	Special Nonverbal Composite	Basic Number Skills	Spelling	Word Reading
45	70	75	73	106	104	103	103
46	70	76	73	107	105	104	103
47	71	76	74	108	105	104	104
48	71	77	74	109	106	105	104
49	72	77	75	110	106	105	105
50	72	78	75	111	107	106	105
51	73	78	76	112	108	106	106
52	74	78	76	113	108	106	106
53	74	79	77	114	109	107	107
54	75	79	77	115	109	107	107
55	75	80	78	116	110	108	108
56	76	80	78	117	110	108	108
57	76	81	79	118	111	109	109
58	77	81	79	119	112	109	109
59	78	82	80	120	112	110	110
60	78	82	80	121	113	110	110
61	79	83	81	122	113	111	111
62	79	83	81	123	114	111	111
63	80	84	82	124	114	111	112
64	80	84	82	125	115	112	112
65	81	84	83	126	116	112	113
66	81	85	83	127	116	113	113
67	82	85	84	128	117	113	114
68	83	86	84	129	117	114	114
69	83	86	85	130	118	114	115
70	84	87	85	131	118	115	115
71	84	87	86	132	119	115	116
72	85	88	86	133	120	116	116
73	85	88	87	134	120	116	117
74	86	89	87	135	121	117	117
75	87	89	88	136	121	117	118
76	87	89	88	137	122	117	118
77	88	90	89	138	122	118	119
78	88	90	89	139	123	118	119
79	89	91	90	140	124	119	120
80	89	91	90	141	124	119	120
81	90	92	91	142	125	120	121
82	91	92	91	143	125	120	121
83	91	93	92	144	126	121	122
84	92	93	92	145	126	121	122
85	92	94	93	146	127	122	123
86	93	94	93	147	127	122	123
87	93	95	94	148	128	122	124
88	94	95	94	149	129	123	124
89	95	95	95	150	129	123	125
90	95	96	95	151	130	124	125
91	96	96	96	152	130	124	126
92	96	97	96	153	131	125	126
93	97	97	97	154	131	125	127
94	97	98	97	155	132	126	127
95	98	98	98	156	133	126	128
96	99	99	98	157	133	127	128
97	99	99	99	158	134	127	129
98	100	100	99	159	134	127	129
99	100	100	99	160	135	128	130
100	101	100	100	161	135	128	130
101	101	101	100	162	136	129	131
102	102	101	101				
103	102	102	101				
104	103	102	102				
105	104	103	102				

Table B.12. Differences Between Observed and Predicted Achievement-Test Standard Scores Required for Statistical Significance

Achievement Test	p	Mean	Age 6	7	8	9	10	11	12	13	14	15	16	17
Predicted From GCA														
Basic Number Skills	.15	8.0	7.3	7.1	7.7	7.8	7.8	7.6	7.6	7.7	8.5	8.6	8.8	9.2
	.05	10.9	10.0	9.7	10.5	10.6	10.6	10.3	10.4	10.5	11.5	11.7	11.9	12.5
	.01	14.3	13.1	12.8	13.9	14.0	13.9	13.6	13.7	13.9	15.2	15.4	15.7	16.5
Spelling	.15	6.6	6.8	5.5	6.3	6.7	6.7	6.7	6.6	6.5	6.7	6.8	7.1	6.9
	.05	9.0	9.3	7.5	8.6	9.1	9.1	9.1	9.0	8.8	9.1	9.2	9.6	9.4
	.01	11.8	12.2	9.9	11.3	12.0	12.0	12.0	11.9	11.6	12.0	12.1	12.7	12.3
Word Reading[a]	.15	6.5	5.4	5.7	5.8	5.5	6.1	6.5	6.7	6.5	7.0	7.3	7.6	7.9
	.05	8.9	7.3	7.8	7.8	7.5	8.4	8.9	9.1	8.9	9.6	9.9	10.4	10.8
	.01	11.7	9.6	10.2	10.3	9.8	11.0	11.7	12.0	11.7	12.6	13.0	13.7	14.2
Predicted from the Special Nonverbal Composite														
Basic Number Skills	.15	8.0	7.4	7.2	7.8	7.9	7.8	7.6	7.7	7.8	8.5	8.6	8.8	9.2
	.05	10.9	10.1	9.8	10.6	10.7	10.7	10.4	10.5	10.6	11.6	11.8	12.0	12.5
	.01	14.4	13.3	12.9	14.0	14.1	14.1	13.7	13.8	14.0	15.2	15.5	15.8	16.5
Spelling	.15	6.6	6.8	5.5	6.3	6.7	6.7	6.7	6.6	6.4	6.7	6.7	7.0	6.8
	.05	9.0	9.3	7.5	8.6	9.1	9.1	9.1	9.0	8.8	9.1	9.1	9.6	9.3
	.01	11.8	12.2	9.9	11.3	12.0	12.0	12.0	11.8	11.5	12.0	12.0	12.6	12.2
Word Reading[a]	.15	6.4	5.3	5.7	5.7	5.4	6.1	6.5	6.6	6.5	7.0	7.2	7.6	7.8
	.05	8.8	7.2	7.7	7.8	7.4	8.3	8.8	9.0	8.8	9.5	9.8	10.3	10.6
	.01	11.5	9.5	10.1	10.2	9.7	10.9	11.6	11.9	11.6	12.5	12.9	13.5	14.0

[a] Values are larger at ages 14-17 because at those ages the Word Reading test is less accurate for high-achieving examinees. For examinees aged 14-17 who score in the low or average range on Word Reading, the difference values for ages 6-13 are more appropriate.

Table B.13. Differences Between Observed and Predicted Achievement-Test Standard Scores Shown by Various Percentages of the Norm Sample[a]

Achievement Test	Percentage								
	25	20	15	10	5	4	3	2	1
Predicted from the GCA									
Basic Number Skills	8	10	13	15	20	21	22	24	27
Spelling	9	11	14	17	22	23	24	26	29
Word Reading	8	11	13	15	20	21	22	24	28
Predicted from the Special Nonverbal Composite									
Basic Number Skills	9	11	13	16	20	21	23	26	28
Spelling	9	12	14	18	23	24	25	27	30
Word Reading	9	11	13	16	21	22	24	26	29

[a]Percentage of children whose observed achievement test score was *below* their predicted score by the specified amount or more.

Appendix C

Intercorrelation of Subtests, Composites, and Achievement Tests by Age

Table C.1. Intercorrelation of Preschool Subtests and Composites by Age: 2:6–2:11

Variable	VCom	NVoc	BB	PSim	ENC	RDig	RPic	GCA	SNV
Naming Vocabulary	.62	—							
Block Building	.43	.34	—						
Picture Similarities	.43	.39	.31	—					
Early Number Concepts	.48	.51	.37	.39	—				
Recall of Digits	.38	.35	.27	.31	.40	—			
Recognition of Pictures	.38	.33	.33	.16	.28	.19	—		
GCA	.82	.77	.69	.72	.58	.43	.40	—	
Special Nonverbal	.53	.45	.80	.82	.47	.36	.30	.87	—
Corrected Correlations[a]									
GCA	.65	.58	.45	.47	—	—	—	—	.55
Mean	50.0	49.6	50.0	50.6	50.6	49.5	49.2	99.9	99.9
SD	10.0	9.8	10.3	10.7	8.7	9.3	9.2	15.2	15.8

Note. N = 175.

[a] Correlation of the subtest with the sum of scores on the other subtests making up the composite.

Table C.2. Intercorrelation of Preschool Subtests and Composites by Age: 3:0–3:5

Variable	VCom	NVoc	BB	PSim	PC	PC(A)	ENC	RDig	RPic	GCA	SNV
Naming Vocabulary	.61										
Block Building	.35	.30	—								
Picture Similarities	.37	.40	.23	—							
Pattern Construction	.41	.44	.47	.39	—						
Pattern Construction (Alt.)	.37	.41	.47	.40	.97	—					
Early Number Concepts	.59	.50	.40	.40	.43	.43	—				
Recall of Digits	.41	.32	.29	.35	.32	.29	.44	—			
Recognition of Pictures	.39	.42	.46	.30	.36	.37	.43	.30	—		
GCA	.80	.80	.63	.68	.59	.57	.64	.46	.53	—	
Special Nonverbal	.45	.45	.79	.78	.55	.55	.51	.41	.48	.83	—
Corrected Correlations[a]											
GCA	.60	.60	.37	.43	—	—	—	—	—	—	.50
Mean	50.9	50.5	50.0	50.4	50.1	49.1	50.1	51.0	50.2	100.7	99.6
SD	9.6	10.1	9.4	9.5	9.8	9.8	9.5	10.6	10.3	14.2	13.9

Note. N = 175.
[a]Correlation of the subtest with the sum of scores on the other subtests making up the composite.

Table C.3. Intercorrelation of Preschool Subtests and Composites by Age: 3:6–3:11

Variable	VCom	NVoc	PSim	PC	PC(A)	Copy	ENC	BB	RDig	RPic	Verb	NV	GCA
Naming Vocabulary	.68	—											
Picture Similarities	.42	.38	—										
Pattern Construction	.45	.30	.33	—									
Pattern Construction (Alt.)	.50	.35	.38	.93	—								
Copying	.33	.28	.31	.30	.32	—							
Early Number Concepts	.68	.53	.45	.46	.49	.43	—						
Block Building	.35	.30	.36	.49	.50	.54	.50	—					
Recall of Digits	.42	.38	.30	.29	.31	.28	.44	.33	—				
Recognition of Pictures	.50	.41	.40	.32	.35	.31	.49	.35	.31	—			
Verbal Ability	.92	.91	.43	.41	.47	.33	.66	.36	.44	.50	—		
Nonverbal Ability	.54	.43	.74	.72	.73	.75	.61	.63	.39	.47	.53	—	
GCA	.82	.73	.67	.65	.69	.62	.83	.59	.49	.56	.85	.87	—
Corrected Correlations[a]													
GCA	.72	.60	.51	.49	.55	.44	.72	—	—	—	.63	.61	—
Mean	49.6	50.4	50.4	49.9	50.1	50.3	50.1	49.9	50.0	50.7	99.8	99.8	100.2
SD	10.2	9.5	9.7	9.4	9.8	10.4	10.1	9.5	9.6	9.6	15.3	14.7	15.0

Note. N = 175.

[a] Correlation of the subtest with the sum of scores on the other subtests making up the composite.

Table C.4. Intercorrelation of Preschool Subtests and Composites by Age: 4:0–4:5

Variable	VCom	NVoc	PSim	PC	PC(A)	Copy	ENC	BB	MLLF	RDig	RObI	RObD	RPic	Verb	NV	GCA
Naming Vocabulary	.63	—														
Picture Similarities	.41	.21	—													
Pattern Construction	.36	.22	.36	—												
Pattern Construction (Alt.)	.40	.24	.35	.91	—											
Copying	.35	.30	.35	.44	.42	—										
Early Number Concepts	.57	.50	.39	.53	.53	.55	—									
Block Building	.39	.33	.34	.50	.55	.53	.50	—								
Matching Letter-Like Forms	.27	.19	.22	.39	.42	.34	.34	.44	—							
Recall of Digits	.38	.39	.27	.22	.21	.34	.38	.38	.31	—						
Recall of Objects—Imm.	.18	.19	.21	.10	.14	.22	.20	.20	.11	.27	—					
Recall of Objects—Del.	.11	.15	.10	.17	.22	.23	.15	.33	.13	.18	.41	—				
Recognition of Pictures	.38	.30	.39	.43	.44	.31	.46	.37	.29	.21	.22	.23	—			
Verbal Ability	.90	.90	.34	.32	.35	.36	.59	.40	.26	.43	.20	.15	.38	—		
Nonverbal Ability	.49	.31	.73	.80	.74	.77	.64	.60	.42	.36	.22	.22	.49	.44	—	
GCA	.78	.66	.63	.69	.67	.69	.83	.61	.41	.46	.25	.22	.53	.80	.87	—
Corrected Correlations[a]																
GCA	.65	.50	.46	.52	.53	.54	.73	—	—	—	—	—	—	.53	.57	—
Mean	48.9	48.7	48.4	50.8	51.0	50.1	50.1	49.7	49.4	48.9	49.6	50.5	49.5	97.9	99.0	98.9
SD	9.7	9.9	9.3	10.6	10.7	9.4	9.9	10.4	9.9	10.4	10.7	9.5	10.3	14.9	15.2	14.5

Note. N = 175 for all variables except Recall of Objects—Delayed, for which *N* = 166.
[a]Correlation of the subtest with the sum of scores on the other subtests making up the composite.

Table C.5. Intercorrelation of Preschool Subtests and Composites by Age: 4:6–4:11

Variable	VCom	NVoc	PSim	PC	PC(A)	Copy	ENC	BB	MLLF	RDig	RObI	RObD	RPic	Verb	NV	GCA
Naming Vocabulary	.58	—														
Picture Similarities	.39	.41	—													
Pattern Construction	.43	.33	.29	—												
Pattern Construction (Alt.)	.44	.27	.34	.81	—											
Copying	.44	.33	.19	.39	.42	—										
Early Number Concepts	.60	.51	.46	.47	.52	.44	—									
Block Building	.31	.31	.31	.44	.42	.46	.41	—								
Matching Letter-Like Forms	.37	.35	.27	.44	.43	.42	.54	.43	—							
Recall of Digits	.31	.27	.27	.17	.18	.25	.32	.30	.15	—						
Recall of Objects—Imm.	.09	.07	.03	.03	.02	.08	.13	.03	.09	.12	—					
Recall of Objects—Del.	.04	−.01	−.01	.08	.11	.08	.16	.03	.14	.09	.53	—				
Recognition of Pictures	.27	.28	.24	.32	.30	.26	.46	.32	.38	.24	.28	.19	—			
Verbal Ability	.88	.89	.45	.43	.40	.43	.62	.35	.40	.33	.09	.01	.31	—		
Nonverbal Ability	.58	.49	.69	.78	.72	.70	.62	.56	.52	.31	.06	.07	.38	.60	—	
GCA	.79	.73	.64	.68	.65	.64	.80	.53	.55	.37	.09	.07	.42	.86	.90	—
Corrected Correlations[a]																
GCA	.68	.59	.46	.51	.53	.48	.70	—	—	—	—	—	—	.66	.67	—
Mean	50.7	50.7	50.9	50.8	50.1	48.5	49.8	50.3	49.5	50.7	50.8	49.8	50.0	101.0	99.5	100.4
SD	9.4	9.5	10.4	10.4	8.7	9.4	9.4	9.7	9.7	9.3	9.4	9.6	10.1	14.2	14.6	14.4

Note. N = 175 for all variables except Recall of Objects—Delayed, for which N = 169.
[a] Correlation of the subtest with the sum of scores on the other subtests making up the composite.

Table C.6. Intercorrelation of Preschool Subtests and Composites by Age: 5:0–5:11

Variable	VCom	NVoc	PSim	PC	PC(A)	Copy	ENC	MLLF	RDig	RObI	RObD	RPic	Verb	NV	GCA
Naming Vocabulary	.67	—													
Picture Similarities	.37	.32	—												
Pattern Construction	.38	.34	.36	—											
Pattern Construction (Alt.)	.38	.34	.36	.83	—										
Copying	.34	.31	.41	.44	.47	—									
Early Number Concepts	.60	.52	.47	.47	.47	.55	—								
Matching Letter-Like Forms	.32	.37	.42	.52	.48	.51	.45	—							
Recall of Digits	.38	.40	.12	.17	.26	.22	.49	.12	—						
Recall of Objects—Imm.	.26	.20	.25	.22	.22	.14	.25	.13	.31	—					
Recall of Objects—Del.	.21	.15	.13	.17	.17	.17	.24	.17	.19	.49	—				
Recognition of Pictures	.30	.25	.22	.32	.34	.24	.33	.28	.16	.22	.26	—			
Verbal Ability	.91	.92	.37	.39	.39	.35	.60	.37	.42	.25	.19	.30	—		
Nonverbal Ability	.46	.41	.78	.76	.70	.79	.63	.62	.22	.26	.20	.33	.47	—	
GCA	.78	.74	.67	.66	.64	.69	.82	.58	.41	.30	.24	.37	.82	.87	—
Corrected Correlations[a]															
GCA	.65	.58	.51	.53	.54	.54	.72	—	—	—	—	—	.56	.58	—
Mean	49.4	49.9	50.2	50.0	50.4	50.5	48.9	49.7	49.4	49.6	50.3	50.5	99.3	100.0	99.6
SD	10.2	10.9	10.3	9.3	10.0	9.8	9.6	9.7	10.1	9.2	9.4	9.7	16.3	15.2	15.1

Note. N = 200 for all variables except Recall of Objects—Delayed, for which N = 196.
[a]Correlation of the subtest with the sum of scores on the other subtests making up the composite.

Table C.7. Intercorrelation of Preschool Subtests and Composites by Age: 6:0–6:11

Variable	VCom	NVoc	PSim	PC	PC(A)	Copy	ENC	MLLF	RDig	RObI	RObD	RPic	Verb	NV	GCA
Naming Vocabulary	.57	—													
Picture Similarities	.38	.33	—												
Pattern Construction	.35	.26	.37	—											
Pattern Construction (Alt.)	.36	.32	.36	.89	—										
Copying	.37	.37	.32	.51	.49	—									
Early Number Concepts	.51	.49	.31	.45	.49	.40	—								
Matching Letter-Like Forms	.38	.28	.40	.44	.48	.41	.38	—							
Recall of Digits	.38	.21	.11	.26	.30	.25	.42	.32	—						
Recall of Objects—Imm.	.24	.32	.17	.28	.29	.22	.33	.19	.17	—					
Recall of Objects—Del.	.21	.31	.15	.26	.24	.23	.28	.16	.11	.72	—				
Recognition of Pictures	.23	.14	.33	.36	.31	.27	.29	.30	.21	.29	.27	—			
Verbal Ability	.88	.89	.40	.35	.38	.42	.56	.37	.33	.32	.29	.21	—		
Nonverbal Ability	.48	.41	.73	.81	.75	.78	.50	.54	.26	.29	.28	.41	.50	—	
GCA	.75	.70	.64	.70	.69	.70	.74	.53	.38	.37	.35	.38	.82	.88	—
Corrected Correlations[a]															
GCA	.61	.56	.47	.54	.56	.55	.60	—	—	—	—	—	.58	.56	—
Mean	48.8	50.2	49.0	49.6	49.8	50.5	49.9	50.6	50.3	50.0	49.9	49.9	98.9	98.9	99.3
SD	9.4	9.6	9.9	10.1	10.2	9.6	9.8	9.9	10.2	10.6	10.1	9.4	14.2	15.4	14.2

Note. N = 200 for all variables except Recall of Objects–Delayed, for which N = 182.
[a]Correlation of the subtest with the sum of scores on the other subtests making up the composite.

Table C.8. Intercorrelation of Preschool Subtests and Composites by Age: 7:0–7:11

Variable	NVoc	PSim	PC	PC(A)	Copy	ENC	MLLF	RDig	RObI	RObD	RPic	NV
Picture Similarities	.31	—										
Pattern Construction	.47	.41	—									
Pattern Construction (Alt.)	.43	.41	.89	—								
Copying	.26	.34	.52	.56	—							
Early Number Concepts	.37	.40	.49	.52	.41	—						
Matching Letter-Like Forms	.34	.34	.47	.46	.44	.36	—					
Recall of Digits	.31	.14	.25	.32	.24	.34	.20	—				
Recall of Objects—Imm.	.30	.05	.19	.16	.17	.32	.14	.25	—			
Recall of Objects—Del.	.14	.02	.11	.07	.18	.15	.08	.15	.61	—		
Recognition of Pictures	.22	.27	.28	.27	.26	.21	.22	.14	.22	.26	—	
Nonverbal Ability	.43	.73	.81	.78	.81	.55	.52	.26	.17	.14	.34	—
Mean	50.0	49.5	49.5	49.6	49.8	50.0	50.0	51.1	50.1	49.7	48.6	98.7
SD	10.0	9.6	9.2	9.3	10.7	9.3	10.1	10.4	9.6	9.8	11.3	15.5

Note. $N = 200$ for all variables except Recall of Objects—Delayed, for which $N = 187$.

Table C.9. Intercorrelation of School-Age Subtests, Composites, and Achievement Tests by Age: 5:0–5:11

Variable	WDef	Sim	Mat	SQR	RDes	PC	PC(A)	RDig	RObI	RObD	RPic	SIP	Verb	NVR	Spat	GCA	SNV	WR
Similarities	.61	—																
Matrices	.34	.37	—															
Seq. & Quant. Reas.	.48	.53	.48	—														
Recall of Designs	.42	.43	.39	.48	—													
Pattern Const.	.30	.34	.39	.34	.43	—												
Pattern Const. (Alt.)	.35	.39	.43	.39	.45	.83	—											
Recall of Digits	.47	.49	.21	.34	.24	.17	.26	—										
Recall of Ob.—Imm.	.25	.34	.04	.18	.17	.22	.22	.31	—									
Recall of Ob.—Del.	.21	.26	.09	.15	.12	.17	.17	.19	.49	—								
Recognition of Pictures	.23	.30	.29	.27	.23	.32	.34	.16	.22	.26	—							
Speed of Info. Processing	.27	.29	.31	.31	.29	.43	.34	.16	.22	.12	.25	—						
Verbal	.90	.90	.39	.56	.47	.35	.41	.53	.32	.26	.29	.31	—					
Nonverbal Reasoning	.47	.52	.87	.85	.50	.43	.48	.32	.12	.14	.32	.36	.55	—				
Spatial	.42	.45	.46	.49	.85	.84	.76	.24	.23	.17	.33	.43	.48	.55	—			
GCA	.74	.77	.69	.76	.72	.64	.65	.45	.28	.23	.38	.44	.83	.84	.81	—		
Special Nonverbal	.51	.56	.75	.76	.77	.72	.69	.32	.21	.18	.37	.45	.59	.88	.88	.94	—	
Corrected Correlations[a]																		
GCA	.59	.63	.53	.64	.58	.48	.54	—	—	—	—	—	.59	.64	.59	—	—	
Special Nonverbal	—	—	.53	.56	.55	.48	.53	—	—	—	—	—	—	—	—	—	—	
Word Reading	.33	.42	.27	.46	.25	.15	.18	.39	.08	.07	.10	.28	.42	.42	.23	.44	.38	—
Mean	50.4	50.5	50.1	50.1	49.7	50.0	50.4	49.4	49.6	50.3	50.5	49.8	100.2	99.8	99.2	99.7	99.4	100.0
SD	9.8	9.6	9.3	8.6	9.4	9.3	10.0	10.1	9.2	9.4	9.7	9.6	14.5	13.1	13.2	13.4	12.8	11.5

Note. $N = 200$ for all variables except Recall of Objects—Delayed, for which $N = 196$.
[a]Correlation of the subtest with the sum of scores on the other subtests making up the composite.

Table C.10. Intercorrelation of School-Age Subtests, Composites, and Achievement Tests by Age: 6:0–6:11

Variable	WDef	Sim	Mat	SQR	RDes	PC	PC(A)	RDig	RObI	RObD	RPic	SIP	Verb	NVR	Spat	GCA	SNV	BNS	Spel	WR
Similarities	.52	—																		
Matrices	.32	.44	—																	
S & Q Reas.	.42	.47	.61	—																
Rec. Designs	.43	.36	.49	.56	—															
Patt. Const.	.36	.31	.51	.55	.56	—														
Patt. Const. (Alt.)	.37	.32	.49	.58	.53	.89	—													
Rec. Digits	.30	.31	.26	.29	.20	.26	.30	—												
Rec. Ob.—Imm.	.31	.28	.31	.35	.27	.28	.29	.17	—											
Rec. Ob.—Del.	.27	.21	.31	.29	.27	.26	.24	.11	.72	—										
Recog. Pictures	.23	.25	.41	.33	.39	.36	.31	.21	.29	.27	—									
SIP	.30	.25	.30	.28	.23	.37	.28	.01	.28	.15	.24	—								
Verbal	.87	.87	.44	.51	.45	.38	.40	.35	.33	.28	.27	.31	—							
Nonverbal Reas.	.41	.51	.90	.89	.59	.59	.59	.31	.36	.33	.41	.33	.53	—						
Spatial	.45	.38	.57	.63	.88	.88	.81	.26	.31	.30	.42	.34	.48	.67	—					
GCA	.69	.69	.76	.81	.77	.74	.72	.36	.40	.36	.44	.39	.79	.87	.86	—				
SNV	.47	.48	.80	.84	.80	.81	.77	.31	.37	.35	.45	.36	.55	.91	.91	.94	—			
Corrected Correlations[a]																				
GCA	.53	.55	.63	.71	.64	.61	.61	—	—	—	—	—	.55	.70	.66	—	—			
SNV	.47	—	.64	.70	.64	.64	.64	—	—	—	—	—	—	—	—	—	—			
Basic Number	.38	.41	.40	.51	.34	.36	.38	.43	.29	.19	.30	.32	.45	.51	.39	.54	.49	—		
Spelling	.34	.40	.46	.50	.37	.37	.39	.42	.27	.19	.34	.33	.42	.54	.42	.54	.52	.71	—	
Word Reading	.43	.45	.46	.55	.41	.34	.39	.48	.27	.17	.32	.30	.51	.57	.42	.59	.54	.75	.88	—
Mean	50.5	50.1	50.2	50.4	50.4	49.6	49.8	50.3	50.0	49.9	49.9	49.8	99.9	100.0	99.6	99.9	99.8	101.1	98.6	100.0
SD	9.8	9.5	9.8	9.6	9.8	10.1	10.2	10.2	10.6	10.1	9.4	9.7	14.0	14.8	14.9	14.5	14.9	13.8	14.4	13.1

Note. N = 200 for all variables except Recall of Objects—Delayed, for which N = 182.
[a]Correlation of the subtest with the sum of scores on the other subtests making up the composite.

315

Table C.11. Intercorrelation of School-Age Subtests, Composites, and Achievement Tests by Age: 7:0–7:11

Variable	WDef	Sim	Mat	SQR	RDes	PC	PC(A)	RDig	RObI	RObD	RPic	SIP	Verb	NVR	Spat	GCA	SNV	BNS	Spel	WR
Similarities	.72	—																		
Matrices	.44	.45	—																	
S & Q Reas.	.49	.46	.63	—																
Rec. Designs	.43	.29	.41	.43	—															
Patt. Const.	.42	.41	.50	.51	.50	—														
Patt. Const. (Alt.)	.43	.43	.50	.50	.49	.89	—													
Rec. Digits	.33	.41	.28	.25	.13	.25	.32	—												
Rec. Ob.–Imm.	.29	.37	.25	.25	.22	.19	.16	.25	—											
Rec. Ob.–Del.	.08	.15	.13	.19	.18	.11	.07	.15	.61	—										
Recog. Pictures	.27	.27	.39	.29	.33	.28	.27	.14	.22	.26	—									
SIP	.16	.13	.12	.19	.22	.25	.25	.07	.15	.06	.11	—								
Verbal	.92	.93	.48	.51	.38	.44	.46	.40	.36	.13	.29	.16	—							
Nonverbal Reas.	.51	.51	.90	.90	.47	.56	.56	.29	.27	.17	.38	.17	.55	—						
Spatial	.49	.40	.53	.54	.88	.85	.78	.22	.24	.17	.35	.27	.48	.59	—					
GCA	.77	.74	.77	.79	.69	.73	.71	.36	.35	.19	.41	.24	.81	.86	.82	—				
SNV	.56	.51	.81	.82	.74	.78	.74	.29	.29	.19	.41	.24	.58	.90	.88	.94	—			
Corrected Correlations[a]																				
GCA	.66	.61	.64	.68	.53	.62	.62						.58	.66	.61	—				
SNV	—	—	.64	.66	.53	.62	.61						—	—	—	—	—			
Basic Number	.55	.51	.51	.56	.35	.42	.41	.31	.29	.16	.20	.31	.57	.59	.44	.64	.58	—		
Spelling	.39	.47	.38	.50	.31	.32	.33	.33	.27	.31	.20	.28	.46	.49	.36	.52	.48	.65	—	
Word Reading	.45	.54	.43	.52	.29	.37	.38	.29	.31	.28	.17	.26	.53	.52	.38	.58	.51	.67	.90	—
Mean	48.9	50.1	49.8	51.0	50.3	49.5	49.6	51.1	50.1	49.7	48.6	50.7	98.6	100.3	99.3	99.4	99.8	100.7	101.0	100.3
SD	9.5	9.8	10.4	10.1	10.2	9.2	9.3	10.4	9.6	9.8	11.3	9.6	14.8	15.5	14.3	14.7	14.7	14.8	14.2	14.3

Note. N = 200 for all variables except Recall of Objects—Delayed, for which N = 187.

[a]Correlation of the subtest with the sum of scores on the other subtests making up the composite.

Table C.12. Intercorrelation of School-Age Subtests, Composites, and Achievement Tests by Age: 8:0–8:11

Variable	WDef	Sim	Mat	SQR	RDes	PC	PC(A)	RDig	RObI	RObD	RPic	SIP	Verb	NVR	Spat	GCA	SNV	BNS	Spel	WR
Similarities	.62	—																		
Matrices	.37	.37	—																	
S & Q Reas.	.45	.53	.60	—																
Rec. Designs	.34	.28	.39	.36	—															
Patt. Const.	.33	.31	.47	.47	.47	—														
Patt. Const. (Alt.)	.30	.28	.46	.47	.51	.88	—													
Rec. Digits	.19	.23	.27	.31	.13	.11	.07	—												
Rec. Ob.–Imm.	.29	.20	.15	.19	.12	.17	.09	.11	—											
Rec. Ob.–Del.	.28	.20	.10	.06	.13	.09	.02	.08	.62	—										
Recog. Pictures	.29	.28	.31	.30	.20	.30	.20	.22	.21	.29	—									
SIP	.18	.12	.10	.14	.02	.09	.06	-.03	.29	.19	.22	—								
Verbal	.89	.91	.41	.55	.34	.36	.32	.24	.27	.26	.32	.16	—							
Nonverbal Reas.	.46	.50	.90	.89	.42	.53	.52	.32	.19	.09	.34	.14	.53	—						
Spatial	.39	.35	.50	.48	.86	.86	.81	.14	.16	.13	.28	.07	.41	.55	—					
GCA	.71	.72	.75	.78	.66	.71	.67	.28	.26	.20	.38	.15	.79	.86	.80	—				
SNV	.48	.48	.81	.78	.71	.78	.75	.26	.20	.13	.35	.11	.54	.89	.87	.94	—			
Corrected Correlations[a]																				
GCA	.57	.60	.60	.67	.49	.56	.55	—	—	—	—	—	.54	.64	.55	—				
SNV	—	.62	.62	.60	.49	.59	.60	—	—	—	—	—	—	—	—		—			
Basic Number	.41	.38	.45	.55	.32	.24	.30	.26	.18	.20	.21	.25	.44	.55	.32	.54	.50	—		
Spelling	.42	.40	.32	.42	.19	.15	.17	.22	.19	.20	.23	.24	.45	.41	.20	.43	.35	.58	—	
Word Reading	.45	.49	.39	.43	.22	.23	.22	.25	.15	.20	.25	.21	.52	.46	.26	.51	.41	.56	.85	—
Mean	50.4	49.7	50.4	50.1	50.5	50.3	51.0	50.0	50.3	50.9	50.3	49.9	99.5	100.1	100.3	100.0	100.1	101.2	101.5	100.3
SD	9.1	9.6	10.1	9.6	9.6	9.7	10.3	9.6	10.1	9.8	9.0	9.8	14.0	14.8	13.9	13.8	14.0	12.9	13.9	14.6

Note. $N = 200$ for all variables except Recall of Objects–Delayed, for which $N = 187$.

[a] Correlation of the subtest with the sum of scores on the other subtests making up the composite.

Table C.13. Intercorrelation of School-Age Subtests, Composites, and Achievement Tests by Age: 9:0–9:11

Variable	WDef	Sim	Mat	SQR	RDes	PC	PC(A)	RDig	RObI	RObD	RPic	SIP	Verb	NVR	Spat	GCA	SNV	BNS	Spel	WR
Similarities	.64	—																		
Matrices	.45	.50	—																	
S & Q Reas.	.53	.46	.62	—																
Rec. Designs	.36	.40	.49	.37	—															
Patt. Const.	.36	.44	.61	.51	.54	—														
Patt. Const. (Alt.)	.35	.44	.65	.50	.49	.89	—													
Rec. Digits	.29	.29	.38	.36	.19	.26	.23	—												
Rec. Ob.—Imm.	.25	.22	.21	.16	.17	.21	.16	.17	—											
Rec. Ob.—Del.	.03	.06	.12	-.01	.15	.13	.10	.06	.65	—										
Recog. Pictures	.05	.14	.27	.11	.33	.29	.31	.04	.09	.16	—									
SIP	.23	.21	.21	.28	.21	.33	.22	.14	.28	.17	.06	—								
Verbal	.90	.91	.52	.54	.42	.44	.43	.32	.26	.05	.10	.24	—							
Nonverbal Reas.	.55	.53	.91	.89	.48	.62	.64	.41	.21	.06	.21	.28	.59	—						
Spatial	.41	.48	.62	.49	.90	.86	.77	.25	.21	.15	.35	.30	.49	.62	—					
GCA	.74	.76	.81	.77	.70	.76	.73	.39	.27	.10	.26	.32	.83	.88	.83	—				
SNV	.53	.56	.85	.78	.76	.82	.78	.37	.23	.12	.31	.32	.60	.91	.89	.95	—			
Corrected Correlations[a]																				
GCA	.61	.64	.70	.65	.55	.64	.63	—	—	—	—	—	.60	.70	.62	—	—			
SNV	—	—	.71	.60	.55	.68	.67	—	—	—	—	—	—	—	—	—	—			
Basic Number	.41	.26	.46	.51	.38	.41	.35	.32	.23	.11	.10	.36	.37	.53	.45	.53	.55	—		
Spelling	.52	.36	.47	.52	.27	.33	.29	.38	.28	.06	.13	.36	.48	.55	.34	.55	.50	.60	—	
Word Reading	.59	.51	.51	.48	.29	.39	.34	.44	.28	.08	.15	.36	.61	.55	.39	.61	.53	.57	.85	—
Mean	49.7	50.7	51.1	50.3	50.0	50.4	50.6	49.5	50.4	51.0	50.9	50.5	99.8	100.8	99.9	100.3	100.3	100.1	101.2	99.9
SD	9.7	10.0	10.1	9.5	10.2	8.8	9.4	10.1	10.1	10.2	10.0	11.1	14.8	14.9	14.2	14.7	14.4	14.8	15.3	15.0

Note. $N = 200$ for all variables except Recall of Objects—Delayed, for which $N = 184$.
[a]Correlation of the subtest with the sum of scores on the other subtests making up the composite.

Table C.14. Intercorrelation of School-Age Subtests, Composites, and Achievement Tests by Age: 10:0–10:11

Variable	WDef	Sim	Mat	SQR	RDes	PC	PC(A)	RDig	RObI	RObD	RPic	SIP	Verb	NVR	Spat	GCA	SNV	BNS	Spel	WR
Similarities	.62	—																		
Matrices	.47	.38	—																	
S & Q Reas.	.48	.51	.57	—																
Rec. Designs	.27	.33	.39	.37	—															
Patt. Const.	.41	.38	.60	.45	.49	—														
Patt. Const. (Alt.)	.39	.41	.57	.47	.45	.88	—													
Rec. Digits	.24	.25	.15	.38	.24	.19	.27	—												
Rec. Ob.—Imm.	.28	.29	.29	.29	.28	.26	.19	.17	—											
Rec. Ob.—Del.	.09	.10	.13	.16	.23	.08	.04	.11	.60	—										
Recog. Pictures	.31	.32	.33	.32	.32	.22	.28	.23	.27	.20	—									
SIP	.15	.19	.17	.16	.20	.17	.15	.06	.17	-.04	.11	—								
Verbal	.89	.91	.47	.55	.33	.44	.44	.28	.31	.11	.35	.19	—							
Nonverbal Reas.	.54	.50	.89	.88	.42	.59	.58	.29	.33	.16	.36	.18	.57	—						
Spatial	.39	.41	.57	.47	.86	.87	.77	.24	.31	.18	.31	.22	.45	.58	—					
GCA	.73	.73	.78	.77	.64	.76	.72	.33	.38	.18	.41	.23	.81	.87	.81	—				
SNV	.52	.51	.83	.77	.71	.81	.75	.30	.36	.19	.38	.23	.57	.90	.88	.94	—			
Corrected Correlations[a]																				
GCA	.61	.59	.66	.64	.48	.63	.61	—	—	—	—	—	.57	.68	.58	—	—			
SNV	—	—	.57	.66	.50	.65	.62	—	—	—	—	—	—	—	—	—	—			
Basic Number	.37	.36	.40	.45	.38	.41	.38	.24	.33	.19	.28	.30	.40	.48	.46	.54	.52	—		
Spelling	.48	.37	.32	.43	.26	.29	.31	.45	.28	.12	.30	.29	.47	.42	.32	.49	.41	.55	—	
Word Reading	.49	.49	.31	.50	.27	.31	.37	.47	.29	.14	.33	.29	.55	.45	.34	.54	.44	.48	.80	—
Mean	49.3	50.2	49.9	49.8	50.6	50.2	49.4	50.4	49.2	49.8	49.6	49.7	99.0	99.4	100.2	99.5	99.8	100.8	99.7	99.8
SD	9.8	10.5	10.7	10.2	9.8	10.0	9.3	10.4	10.5	9.9	10.3	9.2	15.1	15.6	14.5	14.9	14.8	14.7	14.7	14.6

Note. N = 200 for all variables except Recall of Objects—Delayed, for which *N* = 189.
[a]Correlation of the subtest with the sum of scores on the other subtests making up the composite.

Table C.15. Intercorrelation of School-Age Subtests, Composites, and Achievement Tests by Age: 11:0–11:11

Variable	WDef	Sim	Mat	SQR	RDes	PC	PC(A)	RDig	RObI	RObD	RPic	SIP	Verb	NVR	Spat	GCA	SNV	BNS	Spel	WR
Similarities	.67	—																		
Matrices	.45	.37	—																	
S & Q Reas.	.50	.43	.50	—																
Rec. Designs	.38	.38	.43	.51	—															
Patt. Const.	.37	.37	.49	.57	.60	—														
Patt. Const. (Alt.)	.37	.38	.47	.56	.58	.92	—													
Rec. Digits	.22	.10	.19	.23	.15	.14	.13	—												
Rec. Ob.—Imm.	.34	.33	.26	.19	.25	.13	.13	.17	—											
Rec. Ob.—Del.	.18	.24	.19	.17	.24	.07	.06	.06	.66	—										
Recog. Pictures	.36	.30	.40	.31	.42	.31	.30	.12	.21	.30	—									
SIP	.17	.13	.17	.29	.13	.25	.21	.14	.12	.10	.14	—								
Verbal	.92	.91	.45	.50	.41	.41	.41	.17	.37	.23	.36	.16	—							
Nonverbal Reas.	.54	.46	.87	.86	.55	.61	.60	.23	.26	.21	.41	.27	.55	—						
Spatial	.42	.41	.51	.60	.90	.89	.83	.16	.21	.18	.41	.22	.45	.65	—					
GCA	.75	.71	.72	.78	.75	.77	.74	.22	.33	.24	.47	.25	.80	.86	.84	—				
SNV	.52	.48	.75	.80	.81	.84	.80	.21	.26	.21	.45	.26	.55	.89	.92	.94	—			
Corrected Correlations[a]																				
GCA	.62	.58	.59	.67	.61	.64	.63	—	—	—	—	—	.55	.70	.62	—				
SNV	—	—	.56	.64	.63	.69	.67	—	—	—	—	—	—	—	—	—	—			
Basic Number	.43	.35	.43	.56	.29	.44	.42	.19	.12	.06	.28	.38	.43	.57	.41	.55	.53	—		
Spelling	.53	.38	.34	.48	.28	.33	.31	.30	.19	.04	.24	.31	.50	.47	.34	.51	.44	.59	—	
Word Reading	.60	.44	.41	.47	.37	.38	.36	.32	.20	.02	.20	.28	.57	.50	.41	.59	.50	.51	.81	—
Mean	51.4	49.9	51.3	50.7	50.5	49.9	50.3	50.1	50.7	49.1	49.9	50.5	100.6	101.3	99.9	100.8	100.6	102.8	102.2	101.5
SD	9.8	9.6	9.3	9.3	10.6	10.2	10.4	9.8	10.3	9.9	10.2	10.0	14.7	13.6	15.7	14.6	14.7	14.3	15.1	15.2

Note. $N = 200$ for all variables except Recall of Objects—Delayed, for which $N = 189$.

[a]Correlation of the subtest with the sum of scores on the other subtests making up the composite.

Table C.16. Intercorrelation of School-Age Subtests, Composites, and Achievement Tests by Age: 12:0–12:11

Variable	WDef	Sim	Mat	SQR	RDes	PC	PC(A)	RDig	RObI	RObD	RPic	SIP	Verb	NVR	Spat	GCA	SNV	BNS	Spel	WR
Similarities	.61	—																		
Matrices	.50	.52	—																	
S & Q Reas.	.51	.51	.60	—																
Rec. Designs	.31	.33	.42	.33	—															
Patt. Const.	.44	.54	.61	.52	.59	—														
Patt. Const. (Alt.)	.39	.53	.59	.48	.56	.91	—													
Rec. Digits	.37	.31	.23	.31	.11	.16	.18	—												
Rec. Ob.–Imm.	.31	.29	.24	.25	.31	.32	.30	.11	—											
Rec. Ob.–Del.	.18	.14	.12	.19	.18	.21	.23	.10	.72	—										
Recog. Pictures	.34	.21	.38	.28	.27	.24	.24	.26	.30	.22	—									
SIP	.33	.27	.22	.25	.08	.22	.17	.15	.25	.22	.11	—								
Verbal	.89	.90	.57	.57	.35	.55	.51	.37	.33	.17	.30	.32	—							
Nonverbal Reas.	.57	.57	.90	.89	.42	.63	.59	.30	.27	.17	.37	.26	.63	—						
Spatial	.42	.49	.57	.48	.89	.89	.82	.15	.35	.22	.28	.17	.51	.59	—					
GCA	.74	.77	.80	.77	.65	.81	.76	.32	.37	.22	.37	.29	.84	.88	.82	—				
SNV	.55	.59	.83	.78	.73	.85	.79	.25	.35	.22	.36	.24	.64	.90	.89	.95	—			
Corrected Correlations[a]																				
GCA	.62	.66	.70	.65	.50	.72	.67	—	—	—	—	—	.64	.70	.61	—	—			
SNV	—	—	.67	.59	.53	.72	.68	—	—	—	—	—	—	—	—	—	—			
Basic Number	.47	.43	.46	.55	.21	.42	.36	.19	.29	.25	.30	.30	.50	.56	.35	.55	.51	—		
Spelling	.46	.34	.37	.46	.14	.29	.26	.28	.20	.21	.23	.27	.44	.46	.24	.45	.40	.50	—	
Word Reading	.58	.41	.41	.56	.17	.36	.35	.36	.16	.16	.24	.24	.55	.54	.30	.55	.48	.43	.78	—
Mean	49.9	50.1	49.2	49.4	49.9	49.5	50.1	49.8	48.9	49.8	49.6	50.3	99.4	98.5	99.0	98.9	98.6	99.3	100.7	99.0
SD	10.1	10.5	10.6	10.4	10.0	10.3	10.4	9.5	9.9	10.4	9.7	10.4	15.3	15.7	15.3	15.5	15.2	14.7	14.8	13.7

Note. N = 200 for all variables except Recall of Objects—Delayed, for which N = 188.

[a]Correlation of the subtest with the sum of scores on the other subtests making up the composite.

Table C.17. Intercorrelation of School-Age Subtests, Composites, and Achievement Tests by Age: 13:0–13:11

Variable	WDef	Sim	Mat	SQR	RDes	PC	PC(A)	RDig	RObI	RObD	RPic	SIP	Verb	NVR	Spat	GCA	SNV	BNS	Spel	WR
Similarities	.62	—																		
Matrices	.46	.51	—																	
S & Q Reas.	.58	.61	.59	—																
Rec. Designs	.44	.39	.52	.51	—															
Patt. Const.	.51	.54	.64	.61	.61	—														
Patt. Const. (Alt.)	.49	.54	.59	.59	.59	.91	—													
Rec. Digits	.20	.22	.17	.20	.20	.21	.19	—												
Rec. Ob.—Imm.	.16	.15	.20	.25	.25	.14	.08	.15	—											
Rec. Ob.—Del.	.11	.12	.14	.19	.27	.12	.07	.11	.72	—										
Recog. Pictures	.33	.21	.31	.37	.42	.30	.29	.22	.20	.18	—									
SIP	.14	.06	.24	.23	.22	.21	.14	.12	.25	.26	.23	—								
Verbal	.90	.90	.53	.66	.46	.58	.57	.23	.17	.12	.30	.12	—							
Nonverbal Reas.	.58	.62	.90	.88	.57	.70	.66	.21	.25	.18	.38	.26	.67	—						
Spatial	.53	.52	.65	.62	.89	.90	.84	.23	.21	.21	.40	.24	.58	.71	—					
GCA	.77	.78	.79	.82	.73	.83	.78	.26	.24	.19	.41	.23	.86	.90	.87	—				
SNV	.60	.61	.83	.81	.79	.87	.81	.24	.25	.21	.42	.27	.68	.92	.92	.96	—			
Corrected Correlations[a]																				
GCA	.65	.67	.68	.74	.61	.74	.71	—	—	—	—	—	.68	.78	.71	—	—			
SNV	—	—	.69	.67	.63	.75	.71	—	—	—	—	—	—	—	—	—	—			
Basic Number	.47	.47	.60	.65	.47	.56	.50	.15	.18	.20	.32	.34	.52	.70	.57	.68	.69	—		
Spelling	.57	.47	.49	.58	.42	.45	.40	.29	.35	.22	.28	.35	.58	.60	.48	.63	.59	.57	—	
Word Reading	.64	.57	.50	.54	.46	.51	.48	.36	.27	.17	.34	.26	.67	.58	.54	.68	.61	.50	.84	—
Mean	49.6	50.2	48.6	48.8	50.1	50.4	50.5	50.3	50.9	51.4	49.8	51.4	99.3	97.4	99.9	98.8	98.6	98.9	98.7	99.3
SD	10.3	10.5	10.5	10.1	10.0	10.5	10.3	10.2	10.5	9.8	9.8	9.7	15.6	15.4	15.6	16.1	15.8	15.8	15.3	15.6

Note. N = 200 for all variables except Recall of Objects—Delayed, for which N = 189.
[a] Correlation of the subtest with the sum of scores on the other subtests making up the composite.

Table C.18. Intercorrelation of School-Age Subtests, Composites, and Achievement Tests by Age: 14:0–14:11

Variable	WDef	Sim	Mat	SQR	RDes	PC	PC(A)	RDig	RObI	RObD	RPic	SIP	Verb	NVR	Spat	GCA	SNV	BNS	Spel	WR
Similarities	.65	—																		
Matrices	.41	.38	—																	
S & Q Reas.	.57	.59	.57	—																
Rec. Designs	.38	.45	.43	.40	—															
Patt. Const.	.44	.46	.46	.54	.61	—														
Patt. Const. (Alt.)	.38	.36	.38	.43	.51	.88	—													
Rec. Digits	.31	.30	.34	.31	.23	.16	.05	—												
Rec. Ob.—Imm.	.14	.26	.17	.19	.28	.18	.14	.16	—											
Rec. Ob.—Del.	.13	.22	.08	.12	.18	.16	.11	.09	.69	—										
Recog. Pictures	.20	.31	.28	.27	.49	.31	.20	.25	.31	.29	—									
SIP	.20	.21	.23	.22	.17	.17	.06	.22	.23	.17	.20	—								
Verbal	.91	.91	.43	.63	.46	.50	.41	.33	.22	.20	.28	.22	—							
Nonverbal Reas.	.55	.54	.89	.88	.47	.57	.46	.37	.20	.12	.31	.26	.60	—						
Spatial	.46	.51	.50	.53	.89	.90	.78	.22	.25	.19	.45	.19	.54	.58	—					
GCA	.76	.77	.72	.81	.71	.77	.64	.36	.27	.20	.41	.26	.84	.86	.83	—				
SNV	.57	.59	.79	.80	.76	.82	.69	.33	.25	.17	.42	.25	.64	.89	.89	.95	—			
Corrected Correlations[a]																				
GCA	.64	.66	.58	.71	.59	.66	.54						.64	.67	.63	—	—			
SNV			.59	.62	.58	.67	.55									—	—			
Basic Number	.47	.46	.51	.62	.35	.54	.40	.30	.16	.18	.27	.25	.51	.64	.50	.65	.64	—		
Spelling	.49	.38	.42	.51	.23	.29	.20	.44	.21	.16	.26	.31	.48	.52	.29	.51	.46	.55	—	
Word Reading	.56	.47	.37	.46	.30	.39	.30	.35	.19	.16	.30	.26	.57	.46	.39	.56	.48	.51	.75	—
Mean	50.4	49.9	50.6	50.7	50.9	50.9	50.3	50.7	48.8	49.2	50.5	50.4	99.7	100.8	101.0	100.7	101.0	102.1	101.0	99.5
SD	9.9	9.6	10.5	10.2	9.7	10.0	8.7	10.6	9.9	10.0	8.8	9.8	14.7	15.5	15.0	15.2	15.1	14.7	15.0	14.7

Note. $N = 200$ for all variables except Recall of Objects—Delayed, for which $N = 187$.
[a]Correlation of the subtest with the sum of scores on the other subtests making up the composite.

Table C.19. Intercorrelation of School-Age Subtests, Composites, and Achievement Tests by Age: 15:0–15:11

Variable	WDef	Sim	Mat	SQR	RDes	PC	PC(A)	RDig	RObI	RObD	RPic	SIP	Verb	NVR	Spat	GCA	SNV	BNS	Spel	WR
Similarities	.69	—																		
Matrices	.45	.52	—																	
S & Q Reas.	.52	.52	.55	—																
Rec. Designs	.39	.49	.41	.43	—															
Patt. Const.	.39	.49	.48	.54	.55	—														
Patt. Const. (Alt.)	.37	.46	.46	.47	.51	.89	—													
Rec. Digits	.20	.16	.19	.22	.24	.24	.22	—												
Rec. Ob.–Imm.	.09	.12	.17	.13	.30	.21	.15	.29	—											
Rec. Ob.–Del.	-.01	.02	.10	.00	.24	.14	.10	.12	.74	—										
Recog. Pictures	.13	.19	.20	.20	.29	.26	.26	.11	.16	.11	—									
SIP	.10	.13	.03	.13	.10	.22	.15	.22	.00	.01	.09	—								
Verbal	.92	.92	.53	.57	.48	.48	.45	.20	.12	.01	.17	.12	—							
Nonverbal Reas.	.55	.59	.88	.88	.48	.57	.53	.23	.17	.06	.23	.09	.63	—						
Spatial	.44	.55	.50	.55	.87	.88	.80	.28	.29	.22	.31	.18	.54	.59	—					
GCA	.75	.81	.75	.78	.71	.75	.69	.27	.22	.11	.28	.16	.85	.87	.83	—				
SNV	.56	.64	.77	.80	.75	.82	.74	.28	.25	.15	.30	.15	.65	.89	.89	.95	—			
Corrected Correlations[a]																				
GCA	.63	.72	.62	.67	.58	.63	.59						.65	.70	.63	—				
SNV	—	—	.59	.63	.56	.65	.60						—	—	—	—	—			
Basic Number	.47	.44	.42	.61	.37	.46	.42	.30	.10	.00	.25	.23	.50	.59	.47	.61	.59	—		
Spelling	.50	.38	.28	.40	.27	.28	.31	.32	.07	-.04	.21	.27	.47	.39	.31	.46	.39	.50	—	
Word Reading	.60	.49	.42	.48	.43	.38	.40	.39	.13	.04	.24	.19	.59	.52	.46	.61	.54	.53	.79	—
Mean	50.7	50.7	50.2	49.9	50.9	50.1	49.4	50.2	50.2	50.4	49.5	49.6	100.6	99.7	100.3	100.3	100.0	101.5	100.1	100.1
SD	10.0	10.1	10.0	10.2	9.8	10.3	9.1	9.7	11.4	10.4	9.4	9.6	15.2	15.0	14.8	15.2	14.7	15.0	15.2	15.0

Note. N = 200 for all variables except Recall of Objects—Delayed, for which *N* = 187.
[a] Correlation of the subtest with the sum of scores on the other subtests making up the composite.

Table C.20. Intercorrelation of School-Age Subtests, Composites, and Achievement Tests by Age: 16:0–16:11

Variable	WDef	Sim	Mat	SQR	RDes	PC	PC(A)	RDig	RObI	RObD	RPic	SIP	Verb	NVR	Spat	GCA	SNV	BNS	Spel	WR
Similarities	.69	—																		
Matrices	.45	.52	—																	
S & Q Reas.	.67	.57	.56	—																
Rec. Designs	.48	.49	.46	.56	—															
Patt. Const.	.51	.54	.47	.67	.66	—														
Patt. Const. (Alt.)	.44	.49	.46	.63	.60	.89	—													
Rec. Digits	.42	.41	.27	.40	.28	.33	.33	—												
Rec. Ob.–Imm.	.20	.24	.26	.27	.32	.31	.31	.13	—											
Rec. Ob.–Del.	.18	.25	.32	.25	.34	.31	.31	.05	.74	—										
Recog. Pictures	.23	.17	.29	.32	.39	.25	.25	.10	.30	.31	—									
SIP	.22	.16	.20	.34	.21	.27	.24	.19	.23	.16	.15	—								
Verbal	.92	.92	.53	.67	.52	.57	.50	.45	.24	.23	.22	.20	—							
Nonverbal Reas.	.63	.61	.89	.88	.58	.64	.61	.38	.30	.32	.35	.30	.68	—						
Spatial	.54	.56	.51	.67	.91	.92	.82	.33	.35	.36	.35	.26	.60	.67	—					
GCA	.80	.80	.73	.84	.77	.81	.73	.44	.34	.34	.34	.29	.87	.89	.87	—				
SNV	.64	.64	.76	.85	.82	.86	.78	.39	.36	.37	.38	.30	.70	.91	.92	.96	—			
Corrected Correlations[a]																				
GCA	.70	.70	.60	.77	.66	.71	.65	—	—	—	—	—	.70	.75	.69	—	—			
SNV	—	—	.57	.72	.67	.72	.68	—	—	—	—	—	—	—	—	—	—			
Basic Number	.56	.52	.56	.62	.47	.54	.49	.38	.23	.16	.28	.28	.59	.66	.56	.69	.66	—		
Spelling	.59	.51	.41	.56	.36	.40	.35	.43	.19	.14	.15	.39	.60	.55	.42	.60	.53	.54	—	
Word Reading	.73	.64	.43	.60	.46	.50	.43	.49	.20	.17	.18	.23	.75	.58	.53	.71	.61	.49	.77	—
Mean	49.9	48.9	49.8	50.1	50.2	50.4	49.6	49.4	49.7	49.8	49.2	50.1	98.5	99.5	100.0	99.3	99.8	98.9	100.4	99.6
SD	10.8	10.3	10.5	10.1	10.3	10.9	9.0	10.2	9.5	9.5	9.0	10.0	16.0	15.2	16.3	16.4	15.9	15.6	15.4	15.3

Note. $N = 200$ for all variables except Recall of Objects—Delayed, for which $N = 190$.
[a]Correlation of the subtest with the sum of scores on the other subtests making up the composite.

Table C.21. Intercorrelation of School-Age Subtests, Composites, and Achievement Tests by Age: 17:0–17:11

Variable	WDef	Sim	Mat	SQR	RDes	PC	PC(A)	RDig	RObI	RObD	RPic	SIP	Verb	NVR	Spat	GCA	SNV	BNS	Spel	WR
Similarities	.62	—																		
Matrices	.38	.37	—																	
S & Q Reas.	.47	.48	.61	—																
Rec. Designs	.34	.41	.44	.45	—															
Patt. Const.	.38	.44	.51	.52	.58	—														
Patt. Const. (Alt.)	.32	.40	.48	.47	.46	.86	—													
Rec. Digits	.30	.21	.22	.22	.19	.16	.10	—												
Rec. Ob.—Imm.	.24	.24	.12	.18	.31	.11	.07	.24	—											
Rec. Ob.—Del.	.11	.12	.01	.06	.23	.09	.05	.11	.69	—										
Recog. Pictures	.32	.37	.16	.30	.35	.25	.18	.09	.37	.18	—									
SIP	.13	.17	.09	.17	.10	.05	.01	.15	.12	.03	.06	—								
Verbal	.90	.90	.42	.53	.41	.45	.40	.28	.26	.12	.38	.16	—							
Nonverbal Reas.	.48	.47	.89	.90	.49	.57	.53	.24	.17	.04	.26	.15	.53	—						
Spatial	.40	.48	.53	.54	.89	.89	.74	.20	.23	.18	.34	.08	.49	.60	—					
GCA	.71	.75	.74	.79	.72	.76	.66	.29	.27	.14	.39	.16	.81	.85	.83	—				
SNV	.49	.53	.80	.81	.77	.81	.71	.24	.22	.12	.33	.13	.57	.90	.89	.94	—			
Corrected Correlations[a]																				
GCA	.58	.61	.61	.68	.58	.64	.57	—	—	—	—	—	.57	.65	.62	—	—			
SNV	.58	—	.63	.64	.58	.66	.58	—	—	—	—	—	—	—	—	—	—			
Basic Number	.35	.38	.52	.64	.35	.44	.37	.22	.07	.04	.16	.17	.41	.65	.44	.60	.61	—		
Spelling	.57	.42	.33	.48	.24	.27	.22	.45	.15	.06	.21	.31	.55	.46	.29	.52	.42	.46	—	
Word Reading	.70	.51	.40	.44	.31	.36	.29	.43	.19	.06	.26	.22	.67	.47	.38	.61	.47	.45	.78	—
Mean	49.8	49.7	49.9	50.5	49.0	49.6	49.0	50.0	49.3	49.9	49.0	50.2	99.1	100.0	98.3	99.0	99.0	100.3	99.1	99.2
SD	10.2	10.5	10.0	10.1	9.9	9.7	8.9	9.6	10.0	9.4	8.6	10.0	15.4	15.2	14.8	14.9	14.8	14.3	15.2	14.9

Note. N = 200 for all variables except Recall of Objects—Delayed, for which N = 190.
[a]Correlation of the subtest with the sum of scores on the other subtests making up the composite.

Table C.22. Correlations of Preschool Subtests and Composites with School-Age Subtests, Composites, and Achievement Tests: Ages 5:0–5:11

School-Age Variable	Preschool Variable														
	VCom	NVoc	PSim	PC	PC(A)	Copy	ENC	MLLF	RDig	RObl	RObD	RPic	Verb	NV	GCA
Word Definitions	.55	.61	.35	.30	.35	.43	.58	.35	.47	.25	.21	.23	.64	.47	.65
Similarities	.60	.59	.33	.34	.39	.50	.61	.35	.49	.34	.26	.30	.65	.50	.69
Matrices	.33	.28	.31	.39	.43	.42	.45	.38	.21	.04	.09	.29	.33	.48	.50
Seq. & Quant. Reas.	.39	.35	.34	.34	.39	.49	.58	.39	.34	.18	.15	.27	.40	.50	.57
Recall of Designs	.32	.32	.37	.43	.45	.69	.46	.46	.24	.17	.12	.23	.35	.63	.58
Speed of Info. Processing	.37	.27	.28	.43	.34	.39	.46	.36	.16	.22	.12	.25	.35	.47	.50
Verbal Ability	.64	.66	.38	.35	.41	.51	.66	.39	.53	.32	.26	.29	.71	.53	.75
Nonverbal Reas. Ability	.42	.36	.38	.43	.48	.53	.59	.45	.32	.12	.14	.32	.42	.57	.62
Spatial Ability	.41	.38	.43	.84	.76	.67	.55	.58	.24	.23	.17	.33	.43	.82	.73
GCA	.60	.58	.48	.64	.66	.68	.73	.56	.45	.28	.23	.38	.64	.77	.85
Special Nonverbal	.48	.43	.45	.72	.69	.68	.65	.58	.32	.21	.18	.37	.49	.79	.77
Word Reading	.34	.39	.17	.15	.18	.24	.43	.22	.39	.08	.07	.10	.41	.24	.42

Note. $N = 200$ for all variables except Recall of Objects—Delayed, for which $N = 196$. See Tables C.6 and C.9 for means and standard deviations of all variables.

Table C.23. Correlations of Preschool Subtests and Composites with School-Age Subtests, Composites, and Achievement Tests: Ages 6:0–6:11

School-Age Variable	Preschool Variable														
	VCom	NVoc	PSim	PC	PC(A)	Copy	ENC	MLLF	RDig	RObI	RObD	RPic	Verb	NV	GCA
Word Definitions	.50	.57	.33	.36	.37	.41	.46	.37	.30	.31	.27	.23	.61	.47	.63
Similarities	.57	.57	.39	.31	.32	.34	.44	.37	.31	.28	.21	.25	.64	.44	.61
Matrices	.50	.34	.40	.51	.49	.47	.48	.43	.26	.31	.31	.41	.47	.60	.64
Seq. & Quant. Reas.	.57	.43	.46	.55	.58	.47	.65	.48	.29	.35	.29	.33	.56	.64	.74
Recall of Designs	.39	.32	.32	.56	.53	.59	.41	.44	.20	.27	.27	.39	.40	.63	.61
Speed of Info. Processing	.30	.22	.29	.37	.28	.20	.36	.24	.01	.28	.15	.24	.29	.37	.40
Verbal Ability	.61	.66	.41	.38	.40	.43	.52	.42	.35	.33	.28	.27	.72	.53	.71
Nonverbal Reas. Ability	.60	.43	.48	.59	.59	.52	.62	.50	.31	.36	.33	.41	.58	.69	.77
Spatial Ability	.42	.33	.39	.88	.81	.62	.48	.50	.26	.31	.30	.42	.42	.82	.74
GCA	.65	.56	.51	.74	.72	.63	.65	.56	.36	.40	.36	.44	.68	.81	.88
Special Nonverbal	.55	.41	.48	.81	.77	.62	.61	.55	.31	.37	.35	.45	.54	.83	.82
Basic Number Skills	.39	.37	.24	.36	.38	.38	.73	.30	.43	.29	.19	.30	.43	.42	.58
Spelling	.43	.28	.32	.37	.39	.38	.65	.30	.42	.27	.19	.34	.40	.46	.57
Word Reading	.44	.35	.29	.34	.39	.39	.70	.34	.48	.27	.17	.32	.44	.44	.59

Note. $N = 200$ for all variables except Recall of Objects—Delayed, for which $N = 182$. See Tables C.7 and C.10 for means and standard deviations of all variables.

Table C.24. Correlations of Preschool Subtests and Composites with School-Age Subtests, Composites, and Achievement Tests: Ages 7:0–7:11

School-Age Variable	Preschool Variable											
	NVoc	PSim	PC	PC(A)	Copy	ENC	MLLF	RDig	RObI	RObD	RPic	NV
Word Definitions	.54	.39	.42	.43	.35	.49	.36	.33	.29	.08	.27	.49
Similarities	.57	.36	.41	.43	.30	.52	.35	.41	.37	.15	.27	.45
Matrices	.33	.43	.50	.50	.44	.53	.40	.28	.25	.13	.39	.58
Seq. & Quant. Reas.	.37	.37	.51	.50	.42	.58	.42	.25	.25	.19	.29	.55
Recall of Designs	.31	.31	.50	.49	.46	.38	.36	.13	.22	.18	.33	.54
Speed of Info. Processing	.11	.10	.25	.25	.24	.27	.18	.07	.15	.06	.11	.25
Verbal Ability	.60	.40	.44	.46	.35	.54	.38	.40	.36	.13	.29	.50
Nonverbal Reas. Ability	.38	.45	.56	.56	.47	.61	.45	.29	.27	.17	.38	.63
Spatial Ability	.45	.41	.85	.78	.57	.50	.47	.22	.24	.17	.35	.77
GCA	.57	.50	.73	.71	.55	.66	.52	.36	.35	.19	.41	.75
Special Nonverbal	.46	.48	.78	.74	.58	.62	.52	.29	.29	.19	.41	.78
Basic Number Skills	.39	.36	.42	.41	.39	.70	.41	.31	.29	.16	.20	.49
Spelling	.34	.29	.32	.33	.42	.48	.38	.33	.27	.31	.20	.44
Word Reading	.39	.30	.37	.38	.43	.52	.40	.29	.31	.28	.17	.47

Note. $N = 200$ for all variables except Recall of Objects—Delayed, for which $N = 187$. See Tables C.8 and C.11 for means and standard deviations of all variables.

Appendix D

An Outline of the Rasch Model

This appendix describes item response theory in general and explains the application of the Rasch model to the DAS in particular.

An Overview of Item Response Theory Models

A model is a theoretical description of how something works. In psychological or educational measurement, a model describes how a test works or, in other words, how an examinee is likely to respond to the items. Predicting an examinee's responses is difficult. If the same questions are given to several hundred people, however, patterns in the responses emerge. The model attempts to explain these patterns.

All models that represent human behavior are imperfect at best. Although models may be useful in helping us to make general sense of people's test responses, no model will ever fit the data exactly; that is, no model can perfectly predict an examinee's performance. The goodness of fit of the model to the data must be assessed for each set of items and for each set of data.

This is not to say, however, that we must create new models to fit the tests. As Levy (1973) appositely stated, what we need are more tests related to theories rather than theories related to tests. The DAS is such a test. The developers of the DAS used the Rasch model of item response theory as the psychometric basis for all of the DAS subtests and achievement tests.

This model of item analysis and test scaling on which the DAS is based was first proposed by Georg Rasch (1960, 1966). After publishing a monograph in 1960, Rasch, a Danish statistician, lectured in the United States (Rasch, 1961) about his new method of analyzing test-item data. Wright (1968) further developed Rasch's work, created the first computer program for the new approach, and organized several training sessions (for example, Wright, 1970). The number of applications of Rasch's method grew quickly in the 1970s (Choppin, 1968; Forster & Ingebo, 1978; Lenke, 1970; Rentz & Bashaw, 1977; Woodcock, 1973), and it was soon applied to published tests (Connolly, Nachtman, & Pritchett, 1971; Koslin, Koslin,

Zeno, & Wainer, 1977; Woodcock, 1973, 1978). One of these tests was the *British Ability Scales* (Elliott et al., 1979). By 1980 this new field of measurement research had been named *item response theory* or IRT (Lord, 1980). Several comprehensive texts are now available, from basic (Baker, 1985; Hambleton, 1983; Warm, 1978) through intermediate (Allen & Yen, 1979; Hambleton & Swaminathan, 1985; Wright & Masters, 1982; Wright & Stone, 1979) to advanced treatments (Andersen, 1980; Hulin, Drasgow, & Parsons, 1983; Lord, 1980; Rasch, 1960).

The Theory

Item response theory assumes that one or more underlying characteristics or traits determine a person's observed responses to test items. Because these characteristics are not directly observable or measurable, they are termed *latent traits* (or, in the case of cognitive tests, *abilities*). An IRT model specifies an expected relationship between observable responses on a test and the unobservable traits or abilities that are assumed to underlie those responses. The trait or ability is a quantitative dimension on which both individuals and test items can be placed.

In theory, a person's position on the dimension should be independent of the items taken (if the items are reasonably appropriate in difficulty for the person). Also, the position of the items on the dimension should be the same for any sample of individuals who are given them: In other words, items should have the same scaled difficulty values relative to each other independent of the examinees' ability, age, sex, race, ethnicity, and socioeconomic status. If the difficulty value of a test item is not independent of such factors, that item will measure differently the ability of persons from different subgroups who take that item. This difference would result in biased ability measures. IRT models provide a means of identifying internal item biases of this type (see Chapter 10 for the way in which this analysis was applied to the DAS).

Finally, IRT models provide estimates of item difficulty and person ability that have equal-interval measurement characteristics. A given difference between two items or between two ability scores at any point on the measurement scale has the same interpretation.

Features of Item Response Theory Models

As Hambleton and Swaminathan (1985) point out, three important concepts form the basis of item response theory models: *dimensionality of the latent space, item characteristic curves,* and *local independence.*

Dimensionality

Dimensionality refers to the number of latent traits or abilities that underlie the performance of the people taking a test. Most IRT models assume that a single latent ability is sufficient to explain or account for individual differences in performance on a particular test. Models based on this assumption are called *unidimensional* models. Lord (1968) states that most tests are not strictly unidimensional, although some tests may reasonably approximate this characteristic. Various authors, such as Lord (1968) and Hambleton and Swaminathan (1985), suggest that factor analysis provides a useful method of assessing the unidimensionality of a test item. However, the correlations on which factor analyses are based are often attenuated by extremes of item difficulty. Therefore, factor analyses of items that vary considerably in difficulty are likely to yield equivocal results. Fortunately, a better statistical method of assessing unidimensionality has been developed, namely, goodness of fit to the model. Lumsden (1978) makes the point that if the unidimensionality requirement is met, the Rasch model will be realized.

In the following discussion of unidimensionality, the term *parameter* is used. A parameter is a numerical value in a statistical formula or mathematical model that represents a characteristic of the system. For example, in the formula used to draw a graph of the bell-shaped normal curve, numerical values for the mean and standard deviation are parameters of the normal curve. Item difficulty is a parameter in all IRT models and is of central importance because obviously it affects people's performance on tests.

For items to be unidimensional, a single item parameter (that is, item difficulty) should account for differences in the probability of examinees' responding correctly. By this definition, the Rasch model, which is often called the *one-parameter* model, can be characterized as a fully unidimensional model. With other IRT models, the introduction of additional parameters is necessary. In a two-parameter IRT model, the second parameter (in addition to the item-difficulty parameter) is item discrimination. In some tests, certain items discriminate better than others between high- and low-scoring persons, and the item-discrimination parameter accounts for this occurrence. Three-parameter IRT models introduce, in addition to item-difficulty and item-discrimination parameters, a third parameter (usually for guessing). Guessing parameters account for individuals' guessing the correct responses, as happens in multiple-choice tests.

By definition, the Rasch model is unidimensional for both persons and items, because it holds that the probability that a person will pass a test item is a function of only two variables—the ability of the person and the difficulty of the item. As with all test models, if the ability of the person is relatively high, the probability of that person's passing the item is also high. If the item is relatively difficult, the probability of the person's passing the item is low. This description of the basis of the Rasch model may seem unsurprising. It does indeed correspond very closely with the everyday assumptions of psychologists and others who administer tests to people. For example, if people do well or badly on a test, we say that they have either high or low ability. Also, if a person passes a number of items, we infer that the items are easy for that person, and if someone fails most of the items, we say that the items are hard for that person. The Rasch model merely formalizes these assumptions.

Although we commonly make these simple assumptions about ability and difficulty, we know that other factors also affect the probability of a person's success or failure on items. Fluctuations in health, motivation, and alertness may affect the performance of individuals. Furthermore, variation in the content of a test by the inclusion of items from somewhat differing cognitive domains may have different effects on the persons taking the test, according to their home, school, or cultural backgrounds. Such possibilities are not part of the formulation of the Rasch model, which is consequently a very simple model of human performance on ability tests.

For a test to exhibit unidimensionality, two conditions are necessary: (1) the item types must be specified so that, based on an educational or psychological inspection, the items form a unitary, unidimensional set; and (2) the items in the set must fulfill a statistical criterion of unidimensionality, namely, goodness of fit to the Rasch model. Both of these criteria—the psychological-educational and the statistical—are necessary conditions for unidimensionality, but neither is sufficient in itself.

In terms of content, the test constructor should be satisfied that all of the items are homogeneous and measure the "same thing." That is, the items must require the same combination of processes for the examinee to respond correctly, and the responses to any single item or to a group of items should not be qualitatively different from other items in the test. Word Reading is a good example of a unidimensional test. In such a test, each item consists of a printed word at which the child looks and to which the child orally responds. Clearly this task is complex: It involves many cognitive processes, including visual perception, search and retrieval from long-term verbal-memory stores, and verbal encoding of the response. Each process alone is complex, yet the test is unidimensional—each item broadly requires the operation of the same set of processes. The test constructor ensures that the items are as uniform as possible by deleting items that sample another process or area of knowledge, such as a foreign language. Having ensured through such psychological or educational judgment that the items compose a uniform set, the test constructor then needs to be satisfied on the statistical criterion.

The criterion of goodness of fit to the Rasch model will be discussed more extensively later in this Appendix. At this point, we need merely note that this criterion is a means of establishing that the items in a theoretically unidimensional test maintain their relative difficulty values across all ability groups of individuals for whom they are intended.

Item Characteristic Curves

An item characteristic curve (ICC) is a visual representation of the mathematical function which relates the probability of success on an item to the ability of persons taking the item, that ability being defined and measured by the test which contains the item. Different IRT models have different forms of ICCs. They are usually expressed as logistic functions in which the abilities of persons are measured in logarithmic units.

Examples of some common ICCs are given in Figure D.1. As ability (measured along the horizontal axis) increases, the probability of passing the item increases. Figure D.1(a) shows the logistic curves of two items which could fit the Rasch model: The two items differ in only one parameter, their difficulties. Item 1 is always easier than Item 2, whatever the ability of persons taking them. Figure D.1(b) shows two items which could fit a two-parameter model, for which item difficulty and item discrimination define the differences between the items. Figure D.1(c) shows the ICCs of two items which could fit a three-parameter model; the three item parameters in this case are item difficulty, item discrimination, and guessing. The curves in Figure D.1(a) are parallel at any horizontal level of the graph, whereas the curves in Figure D.1(b) and D.1(c) are not parallel. In Figure D.1(b), Item 2 has a steeper slope and, in traditional terms, would be considered a better discriminator than Item 1 between persons of high and low ability. This figure illustrates an unfortunate characteristic of item sets that contain items of differing discrimination. For two items, such as those shown in Figure D.1(b), that are fairly similar in average difficulty, the ICCs cross. As a result, Item 1 is easier than Item 2 for those persons with ability below X, and Item 1 is harder than Item 2 for persons with ability higher than X. In a fully unidimensional test, the ICCs cannot intersect because such a crossing of the curves would imply that the items will have different orderings of difficulty for persons of different ability.

The ability of persons is defined by the set of items whose ICCs we are considering. If the items themselves are not unidimensional (that is, the differences between them cannot be defined by only one parameter), then the abilities that those items are measuring cannot be unidimensional.

Local Independence

Local independence means that the probability of a person's responding correctly to a test item is not affected by his or her performance on any other item in the test. Because humans are changeable and learn from experience and practice, this property is unlikely to be strictly realized in many educational or psychological tests. Test constructors deal with this difficulty, however, by providing an adequate number of practice items at the beginning of a test, by arranging items in ascending order of difficulty, by inserting additional instructions at any point where a new complexity has been added to items, and by designing the test so that items are usually given in a fixed sequence. By such means, the practice effects from item to item are minimized and local independence maximized.

(a)

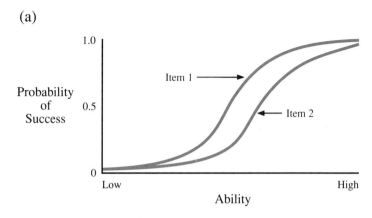

(b)

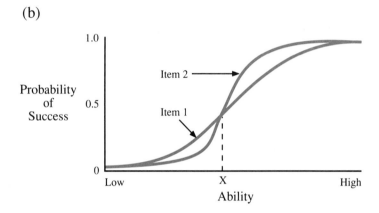

(c)

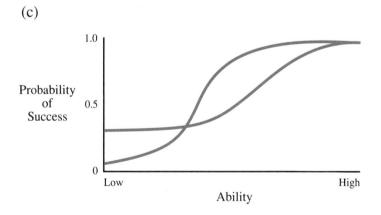

Figure D.1. Item Characteristic Curves for One-, Two-, and Three-Parameter Models

Mathematical Definition of the Rasch Model

The Rasch model holds that the probability of a person's passing an item depends solely on *the ability of that person and the difficulty of the item*. The ability of persons to solve a particular type of item can theoretically (if not practically) range from zero to infinitely great; similarly, the difficulty of the items can theoretically have a similar range. The model is concerned with defining dimensions upon which both person abilities and items lie.

If a person and an item are located at the same point on the dimension, then the person's odds of success on the item are even. Odds of success are commonly used in betting. Odds are the number of chances of success to one chance of failure or the number of chances of failure to one chance of success. Betting odds are defined as the probability of winning divided by the probability of losing, and the probability of success is defined as the odds of winning divided by the odds of winning plus one.

If a person's ability is at a higher point on the latent dimension than an item's difficulty, the odds are greater than even that the person will respond correctly. If ability is less than the difficulty of the item, the odds of success are less than even. This relationship is stated mathematically as

$$O_{ji} = \frac{A_j}{D_i}, \tag{D.1}$$

where O_{ji} is the odds of person j's responding correctly to item i, A_j is the ability of the person, and D_i is the difficulty of the item.

For purposes of this discussion, success is a score of 1 point, and failure, a score of 0 points on an item. This binary (right-or-wrong) outcome is the one used in many of the DAS subtests. Some subtests (Copying, Recall of Designs, Similarities, Pattern Construction, and Speed of Information Processing) utilize polychotomous scoring in which responses are graded on a scale of points, for example, 0–5 points. The basic model has been elaborated to apply to multipoint items by a procedure described by Wright and Masters (1982).

Equation D.1 expressed in terms of the probability (P_{ji}) of person j's passing item i is

$$P_{ji} = \frac{O_{ji}}{1 + O_{ji}} = \frac{A_j/D_i}{1 + (A_j/D_i)}, \tag{D.2}$$

This formulation of the Rasch model does not incorporate logarithms, yet certain presentations call the model a logistic model (Goldstein, 1979; Hambleton &

Swaminathan, 1985). The ability and difficulty values expressed above in the form of odds may sometimes be exceedingly large and can be transformed into logarithmic values, a more manageable form for computation. In logistic terms, Equation D.2 is

$$P_{ji} = \frac{e^{(a_j - d_i)}}{1 + e^{(a_j - d_i)}} \, , \tag{D.3}$$

where $a_j = \log(A_j)$, $d_i = \log(D_i)$, and a_j and d_i are natural logarithms to base e, where $e = 2.71828$. Consequently, $e^{(a_j - d_i)}$ is the antilogarithm of $(a_j - d_i)$ and is equal to A_j/D_i.

Equation D.3 is the most frequently presented expression of the Rasch model. Although Equation D.3 is in some ways a more convenient expression than Equation D.2, it is Equation D.2 which provides the most basic statement of the model. Equation D.2 presents the model in terms of a ratio-scale metric with an absolute zero and with equal-interval characteristics, whereas the logarithmic transformation in Equation D.3 preserves the equal-interval characteristics but removes the ratio-scale feature of an absolute zero.

Using the formulation in Equations D.1 and D.2, we may describe a particular person as doubling his or her ability over a period of time when that person has twice the odds of passing any item. Similarly, we can describe an item as twice as easy as another when all persons have twice the odds of passing it. We cannot make such statements about log abilities and log difficulties, the logistic terms of Equation D.3, unless we obtain antilogs.

In practice, the ability and difficulty values are estimated by a computer program. For the DAS, the main program used for this purpose was MSTEPS, written by Wright, Congdon, and Rossner (1987). The method and mathematical procedures for estimation are described by Wright and Masters (1982).[a] Further statistical and mathematical explanations of the estimation procedures can be found in the sources listed at the beginning of this Appendix.

---

[a]One of the central features of the MSTEPS program is its ability to scale polychotomous items. This feature was not used in the scaling of the DAS for the following reason. For polychotomous items, the MSTEPS program assigns a difficulty value to each **step** from one score level to the next higher one. This value can be considered a conditional difficulty: It represents the difficulty of advancing from one score level to the next, given that the person has already achieved the lower score level. As a result, a higher score level (for example, a score of 4 points on a Speed of Information Processing item) may be scaled as less difficult than a lower score level (such as a score of 2 points). Our interpretation of this outcome is that it takes less additional ability for an examinee who has earned a score of 3 points to earn a score of 4 points, than it does for an examinee who has earned a score of 1 point to earn a score of 2 points. Although this result is mathematically correct, it was not considered to be useful in the context of a difficulty scale, on which score points reflecting superior performance would be expected to be assigned higher difficulty values.

Tests of Goodness of Fit to the Model

Because the model is simple, we cannot expect it to be a perfect representation of how children actually perform when presented with test items. What we need to know is how far children's test responses deviate from this model. Relatively small deviations from the model indicate that the model provides a reasonable representation of test performance and that we can apply the advantages to our tests. We can develop tests that have reasonable economy. A test based on the Rasch model can provide flexible and accurate tailored testing procedures and useful features for interpreting scores.

With the model set and with data on children's test performances gathered, we can perform certain analyses that enable us to evaluate the extent to which children's actual performances on test items are consistent with this simple model. These analyses are tests of goodness of fit to the Rasch model. For ease of presentation, the dichotomous (pass–fail) type of test is discussed, although the method generalizes to polychotomous items (Wright & Masters, 1982).

When we give tests to a sample of children, we obtain a matrix of item scores. If each child is assigned a row and each item is assigned a column, the matrix will consist of a large number of scores of one or zero. With the Rasch model, the total score for an individual will contain all of the information needed to measure that individual's ability; moreover, the total score for an item (that is, the total number of correct, or 1-point, responses to that item) will contain all of the information needed to estimate the difficulty of that item.

From our matrix of ones and zeros, we can obtain the total scores for each person and for each item and use these to calculate the abilities of persons and the difficulties of the items. We can then insert these ability and difficulty estimates into the mathematical formulation of the model (see Equation D.3 above) to obtain an estimate of the probability that a person of a given level of ability will pass an item of a given level of difficulty. The discrepancies between observed and expected passes and failures on items are summed for all persons who took the items, and evaluated for statistical significance.

In technical terms, the standardized square of the residual is calculated for every response by a person to an item. These residuals are summed across persons to yield a fit statistic for each item. They can also be summed across all persons and all items to yield a fit statistic for the whole test. The residuals are weighted so that the responses made by persons for whom the item is relatively inappropriate (very easy or very difficult) have less influence on the magnitude of the item- and subtest-fit statistics. (For details, see Elliott [1983] and Wright & Masters [1982].)

Applications of the Rasch Model to the DAS

Division of Subtests into Item Sets

Items that have been administered and found to fit the Rasch model may be placed on a single, common scale. We may then give this set of scaled items to a new set of individuals to obtain an estimate of their ability to do the items. Alternatively, if the set of items is large, we may draw any subset of items from the larger set to form a test.

Because the item difficulties are on a common scale, we can obtain ability estimates for children who are given only a subset of the items and who respond correctly to a particular number of those items. These ability estimates are automatically equated because they relate to the same common scale as the items. This automatic equating is a great advantage of the Rasch model. Moreover, the Rasch method offers test constructors and us great flexibility in choosing subsets of items. By selecting the most appropriate items through the use of Starting and Decision Points (see Chapter 1), we can tailor the test to the child. These item sets, which are defined within each DAS subtest, are equated, and the ability estimates that they produce relate to a common scale.

The Unit of Measurement

In a measurement scale, the unit of measurement for persons (and for items) is usually defined by some characteristics of the items used for the measurement. For example, in measuring the weight of objects, we express the weights in grams or ounces or any other unit defined by a standard weight. We can transform an object's weight in one set of units to any other set of units of weight, by using a multiplicative constant.

The Rasch estimation procedures define a general unit of measurement, which may also be easily transformed into other units. This unit is generally known as a *logit*. In the MSTEPS program, the zero point on the logit scale is defined as the average of the item difficulties in a test. Equating this average with zero presents a slight problem for our usage because not only are logits expressed as decimal fractions, but also, easier items and persons of low ability are assigned negative values.

This inconvenience was avoided in the DAS ability scales: All item-difficulty and person-ability values are expressed as positive whole numbers. All logit values were multiplied by 10 and rounded to the nearest whole number. Thus, tenths, but not hundredths, of a logit define the scale values. Differences of hundredths of a logit between items or persons have little, if any, practical importance.

The transformation of item difficulties from logits to DAS ability values is

$$DIFF_{(DAS)} = 10[d_i + (1 - a_0)] \,, \tag{D.4}$$

and for person abilities,

$$ABIL_{(DAS)} = 10[a_r + (1 - a_0)] \,, \tag{D.5}$$

where $DIFF_{(DAS)}$ and $ABIL_{(DAS)}$ are, respectively, the transformed DAS difficulties of items and the transformed DAS abilities of persons with a raw score of r, expressed as integers; d_i are logit item difficulties; a_r are logit abilities; and a_0 is the estimated logit ability of persons with a raw score of 0 on the subtest. (Chapter 7 describes the procedure for estimating this logit ability.) Thus, a person who has a raw score of 0 on a subtest will be assigned an ability score of 10. The widest range of ability scores on any subtest is from 10 to 325 (on the Speed of Information Processing subtest).

The probability that a person of DAS ability $ABIL_j$ will pass an item of difficulty $DIFF_i$ is

$$P_{ji} = \frac{e^{[(ABIL_j - DIFF_i)/10]}}{1 + e^{[(ABIL_j - DIFF_i)/10]}} \tag{D.6}$$

The relationships among a person's ability, an item's difficulty, the probability of success, and the odds of success on items are illustrated in Table D.1 and Figure D.2. If the person's ability is higher than the difficulty of the item, the chances are good that the person will respond to the item correctly. On the other hand, if the person's ability is lower than the difficulty value of the item, the chances are that the person will fail the item. The probabilities in Table D.1 and Figure D.2 are calculated with Equation D.6, which is a slight modification of Equation D.3, and which accounts for the fact that DAS ability and difficulty units are logit values multiplied by 10.

Table D.1. Probability of a Correct Answer for Various
Combinations of Ability and Item Difficulty

Ability	Difficulty	Difference	Probability	Odds (For:Against)
100	40	60	.998	403:1
90	40	50	.993	148:1
90	50	40	.982	55:1
80	50	30	.953	20:1
80	60	20	.881	7:1
70	60	10	.731	3:1
70	70	0	.500	1:1 (Even)
60	70	−10	.269	1:3
60	80	−20	.119	1:7
50	80	−30	.047	1:20
50	90	−40	.018	1:55
40	90	−50	.007	1:148
40	100	−60	.002	1:403

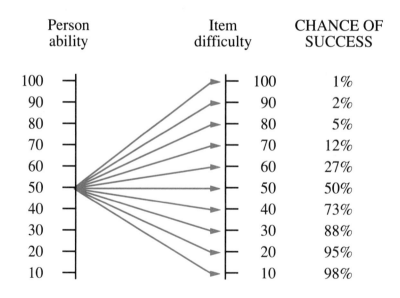

Person ability	Item difficulty	CHANCE OF SUCCESS
100	100	1%
90	90	2%
80	80	5%
70	70	12%
60	60	27%
50	50	50%
40	40	73%
30	30	88%
20	20	95%
10	10	98%

Figure D.2. The Relationship Between Person Ability
and Item Difficulty for a Person with a
DAS Ability of 50

Characteristics of Ability Scores

What do the ability scores actually mean, and how do we interpret them? The ability and difficulty values within a DAS scale have equal-interval measurement characteristics. That is, a given difference between two ability scores, or between an ability score and a difficulty value, has the same interpretation at any point on the measurement scale. An example from Figure D.2 clarifies this point. The figure shows the relationship between various item-difficulty values and the ability of a person with a DAS ability of 50. If an item is 30 points higher in difficulty than the ability of the person, that person has only a 5% chance of success on the item. Similarly, if the item is 30 points lower in difficulty than the ability of the person, that person has a 95% chance of success on the item. A person whose ability is at the same level as the difficulty level of the item has a 50% chance of passing that item. The relationship is the same for any given difference between ability and difficulty at any point on the latent-trait scale. For example, if the person's ability is 80, then that person has a 50% chance of success on an item whose difficulty is 80. That person has a 5% chance of success on an item with a difficulty value of 110 (that is, odds of 55:1 on failing the item).

We may also use the "Difference" column in Table D.1 as a means of interpreting the change in an individual's scores obtained on two occasions. For example, let us suppose that a child is tested on two occasions a year apart, and we observe a difference of 20 ability units between the two scores. We could interpret this change as indicating that the child had increased his or her odds of success seven times on any item in the scale. It would not matter if the child's ability had increased from 20 to 40 or from 93 to 113: The interpretation of the change in score is the same. This consistency of interpretation regardless of the location on the scale is what is meant by an equal-interval scale of measurement.

It is emphasized that the ability scores obtained on different DAS subtests are **not** directly comparable. For example, if a child obtains an ability estimate of 64 on the Matrices subtest, we cannot infer that his or her expected ability on any other subtest is 64. The ability values for the Matrices subtest apply only to the items in that subtest and to no other subtest. There are, of course, methods of comparing scores between subtests, but this comparing is not done by a simple, single comparison of the numerical values of the ability estimates on different subtests.

Summary

This Appendix has outlined the assumptions and features of the Rasch model. The advantages of the model for the test constructor include the statistical criteria it provides for the development of homogeneous, unidimensional, fair (unbiased), and reliable subtests. These aspects of the application of the model are referred to in Chapters 7, 8, and 10. For us, the major advantages of the Rasch model lie in the flexibility of the Starting and Decision Points, by which we can tailor the testing with maximum accuracy, and in the interpretability of the ability scores.

References

Ainscow, M., & Tweddle, D. A. (1979). *Preventing classroom failure: An objectives approach.* London: Wiley.

Allen, M. J., & Yen, W. M. (1979). *Introduction to measurement theory.* Monterey, CA: Brooks/Cole.

Alper, T., & White, O. (1971). The behavior description referral form: A tool for the school psychologist in the elementary school. *Journal of School Psychology, 9,* 177–181.

Anastasi, A. (1970). On the formation of psychological traits. *American Psychologist, 25,* 899–910.

Andersen, E. B. (1980). *Discrete statistical models with social science applications.* Amsterdam: North Holland.

Baker, F. B. (1985). *The basics of item response theory.* Portsmouth, NH: Heinemann.

Benton, A. L. (1974). *Benton Visual Retention Test* (rev. ed.). New York: The Psychological Corporation.

Blankenship, C. (1985). Using curriculum-based assessment data to make instructional decisions. *Exceptional Children, 52,* 233–238.

Blinkhorn, S. F. (1984). Review of the British Ability Scales. In P. Levy & H. Goldstein (Eds.), *Tests in education: A book of critical reviews.* London: Academic Press.

Brand, C. R., & Deary, I. J. (1982). Intelligence and "inspection time." In H. J. Eysenck (Ed.), *A model for intelligence.* New York: Springer–Verlag.

Bruner, J. S., Olver, R. R., & Greenfield, P. M. (Eds.). (1966). *Studies in cognitive growth.* London: Wiley.

Buckhalt, J. A., & Jensen, A. R. (1989). The British Ability Scales speed of information processing subtest: What does it measure? *British Journal of Educational Psychology, 59,* 100–107.

Burgemeister, B. B., Blum, L. H., & Lorge, I. (1972). *Columbia Mental Maturity Scale.* New York: The Psychological Corporation.

Burroughs, G. E. R. (1957). *Study of the vocabulary of young children.* Educational Monograph No. 1, University of Birmingham (England), Institute of Education. London: Oliver & Boyd.

Cameron, R. J. (1981). Curriculum development 1: Clarifying and planning curriculum objectives. *Remedial Education, 16,* 163–170.

Carroll, J. B. (1976). The nature of the reading process. In H. Singer & R. B. Ruddell (Eds.), *Theoretical models and processes of reading* (2nd ed.). Newark, DE: International Reading Association.

Carroll, J. B. (1982). The measurement of intelligence. In R. J. Sternberg (Ed.), *Handbook of human intelligence.* New York: Cambridge University Press.

Carroll, J. B., & Maxwell, S. E. (1979). Individual differences in cognitive abilities. *Annual Review of Psychology, 30,* 603–640.

Carrow-Woolfolk, E. (1985). *Test for Auditory Comprehension of Language—Revised.* Allen, TX: DLM Teaching Resources.

Cattell, R. B. (1971). *Abilities: Their structure, growth and action.* Boston: Houghton Mifflin.

Childs, R. (1984). [Review of the British Ability Scales]. In D. J. Keyser & R. C. Sweetland (Eds.), *Test critiques* (Vol. 1). Kansas City, MO: Test Corporation of America.

Choppin, B. (1968). An item bank using sample-free calibration. *Nature, 219,* 870–872.

Clark, H. H., & Chase, W. G. (1972). On the process of comparing sentences against pictures. *Cognitive Psychology, 3,* 472–517.

Connolly, A. J., Nachtman, W., & Pritchett, E. M. (1971). *Keymath: Diagnostic Arithmetic Test.* Circle Pines, MN: American Guidance Service.

Daniel, M. H. (1986, April). *Construct validity of two-dimensional and three-dimensional block design.* Paper presented at the annual convention of the National Asssociation of School Psychologists, Hollywood, FL.

Das, J. P., Kirby, J. R., & Jarman, R. F. (1975). Simultaneous and successive syntheses: An alternative model for cognitive abilities. *Psychological Bulletin, 82,* 87–103.

Das, J. P., Kirby, J. R., & Jarman, R. F. (1979). *Simultaneous and successive cognitive processes.* New York: Academic Press.

Deno, S. (1985). Curriculum-based measurement: The emerging alternative. *Exceptional Children, 52,* 219–232.

Dunn, L. M., & Dunn, L. M. (1981). *Peabody Picture Vocabulary Test—Revised.* Circle Pines, MN: American Guidance Service.

Ekstrom, R. B., French, J. W., & Harman, H. H. (1976). *Kit of Factor Referenced Cognitive Tests.* Princeton, NJ: Educational Testing Service.

Elliott, C. D. (1983). *British Ability Scales technical handbook (Manual 2).* Windsor, England: NFER-Nelson.

Elliott, C. D. (1986). The factorial structure and specificity of the British Ability Scales. *British Journal of Psychology, 77,* 175–185.

Elliott, C. D. (1989). Cognitive profiles of learning disabled children. *British Journal of Developmental Psychology, 7,* 171–178.

Elliott, C. D. (1990). *DAS administration and scoring manual.* San Antonio, TX: The Psychological Corporation.

Elliott, C. D., & Murray, D. J. (1977). The measurement of speed of problem solving and its relation to children's age and ability. *British Journal of Educational Psychology, 47,* 50–59.

Elliott, C. D., Murray, D. J., & Pearson, L. S. (1979). *British Ability Scales.* Windsor, England: National Foundation for Educational Research.

Elliott, C. D., Pearson, L. S., Daniel, M., & Ward, J. (1990). *The British Ability Scales: An historical and developmental perspective. II–Post-publication research and development.* Unpublished manuscript, University of Manchester (England), School of Education.

Elliott, C. D., & Tyler, S. (1986). British Ability Scales profiles of children with reading difficulties. *Educational and Child Psychology, 3,* 80–89.

Elliott, R. (1987). *Litigating intelligence: IQ tests, special education, and social science in the courtroom.* Dover, MA: Auburn House.

Embretson, S. (1985). [Review of The British Ability Scales]. In J. V. Mitchell, Jr. (Ed.), *The ninth mental measurements yearbook.* Lincoln, NE: Buros Institute of Mental Measurements.

Eysenck, H. J. (1967). Intelligence assessment: A theoretical and experimental approach. *British Journal of Educational Psychology, 37,* 81–96.

Eysenck, H. J. (1986). Inspection time and intelligence: A historical introduction. *Personality and Individual Differences, 7,* 603–607.

Flynn, J. R. (1984). The mean IQ of Americans: Massive gains 1932 to 1978. *Psychological Bulletin, 95,* 29–51.

Forster, F., & Ingebo, G. (1978). *Research on the Rasch measurement model* (Occasional Paper No. 13). Portland, OR: Portland Public Schools, Research and Evaluation Department.

Frearson, W., & Eysenck, H. J. (1986). Intelligence, reaction time (RT), and a new 'odd-man-out' RT paradigm. *Personality and Individual Differences, 7,* 807–817.

Frith, U. (1985). Beneath the surface of developmental dyslexia. In K.E. Patterson, J.C. Marshall, & M. Coltheart (Eds.), *Surface dyslexia: Neuropsychological and cognitive studies of phonological reading.* Hillsdale, NJ: Lawrence Erlbaum.

Furneaux, W. D. (1960). Intellectual abilities and problem-solving behaviour. In H. J. Eysenck (Ed.), *Handbook of abnormal psychology.* London: Pitman.

Gardner, H. (1983). *Frames of mind: The theory of multiple intelligences.* New York: Basic Books.

Gates, A. I. (1937). *A reading vocabulary for the primary grades.* New York: Columbia University Teachers' College.

Gentry, J.R. (1982). An analysis of developmental spelling in GNYS AT WRK. *The Reading Teacher, 36,* 192–200.

Gentry, J.R. (1984). Developmental aspects of learning to spell. *Academic Therapy, 20,* 11–19.

Gibson, E. J. (1969). *Principles of perceptual learning and development.* New York: Appleton–Century–Crofts.

Gickling, E. E., Shane, R. L., & Croskery, K. M. (1989). Developing math skills in low-achieving high school students through curriculum-based assessment. *School Psychology Review, 18,* 344–355.

Gillham, W. E. C. (1978). The failure of psychometrics. In W. E. C. Gillham (Ed.), *Reconstructing educational psychology.* London: Croom Helm.

Goldstein, H. (1979). Consequences of using the Rasch model for educational assessment. *British Educational Research Journal, 5,* 211–20.

Graham, F. K., & Kendall, B. S. (1960). *Memory-for-Designs Test.* Missoula, MT: Psychological Test Specialists.

Gresham, F. M. (1987). On the malleability of intelligence: Unnecessary assumptions, reification, and occlusion. *School Psychology Review, 15,* 245–255.

Guilford, J. P. (1967). *The nature of human intelligence.* New York: McGraw-Hill.

Hambleton, R. K. (Ed.). (1983). *Applications of item response theory.* Vancouver, BC: Educational Research Institute of British Columbia.

Hambleton, R. K., & Swaminathan, H. (1985). *Item response theory: Principles and applications.* Boston: Kluwer-Nijhoff.

Hargis, C. H. (1987). *Curriculum-based assessment: A primer.* Springfield, IL: Charles C. Thomas.

Hitch, G. J., Halliday, S., Schaafstal, A. M., & Schraagen, J. M. C. (1988). Visual working memory in young children. *Memory and Cognition, 16,* 120–132.

Horn, J. L. (1978). The nature and development of intellectual abilities. In R. T. Osborne, C. E. Noble, & N. Weyl (Eds.), *Human variation: The biopsychology of age, race, and sex.* New York: Academic Press.

Howell, K. W., & Morehead, M. K. (1987). *Curriculum-based evaluation for special and remedial education.* Columbus, OH: Charles Merrill.

Hulin, C. L., Drasgow, F., & Parsons, C. K. (1983). *Item response theory: Application to psychological measurement.* Homewood, IL: Dow-Jones-Irwin.

Hunt, E. (1980). Intelligence as an information-processing concept. *British Journal of Psychology, 71,* 449–474.

Hunt, E., Lunneborg, C., & Lewis, J. (1975). What does it mean to be high verbal? *Cognitive Psychology, 7,* 194–227.

Irwin, R. J. (1984). Inspection time and its relation to intelligence. *Intelligence, 8,* 47–65.

Jensen, A. R. (1970). Hierarchical theories of mental ability. In W. B. Dockrell (Ed.), *On intelligence: The Toronto symposium on intelligence, 1969.* London: Methuen.

Jensen, A. R. (1979). The nature of intelligence and its relation to learning. *Journal of Research and Development in Education, 12,* 79–95.

Jensen, A. R. (1980). *Bias in mental testing.* New York: The Free Press.

Jensen, A. R. (1982). Reaction time and psychometric *g*. In H. J. Eysenck (Ed.), *A model for intelligence*. New York: Springer-Verlag.

Jensen, A. R. (1987). Psychometric *g* as a focus of concerted research effort. *Intelligence, 11,* 193–198.

Jensen, A. R., & Munro, E. (1979). Reaction time, movement time, and intelligence. *Intelligence, 3,* 121–126.

Jensen, A. R., & Vernon, P. A. (1986). Jensen's reaction-time studies: A reply to Longstreth. *Intelligence, 10,* 153–179.

Joreskog, K. G., & Sorbom, D. (1986). *LISREL-VI: Analysis of linear structural relationships by maximum likelihood, instrumental variables, and least squares methods: User's Guide* (4th ed.). Mooresville, IN: Scientific Software.

Journal of Educational Psychology. (1921). *12,* 123–147, 195–216.

Kaufman, A. S. (1979). *Intelligent testing with the WISC-R*. New York: Wiley.

Kaufman, A. S., & Kaufman, N. L. (1983). *Kaufman Assessment Battery for Children*. Circle Pines, MN: American Guidance Service.

Kaufman, A. S., & Kaufman, N. L. (1985). *Kaufman Test of Educational Achievement*. Circle Pines, MN: American Guidance Service.

Kavale, K. A., & Forness, S. R. (1984). A meta-analysis of Wechsler scale profiles and recategorizations: Patterns or parodies? *Learning Disability Quarterly, 7,* 136–156.

Keir, G. (1949). The Progressive Matrices as applied to school children. *British Journal of Psychology, Statistical Section, 2,* 140–150.

Kohs, S. C. (1919). *The Kohs Block Design Test*. Chicago, IL: Stoelting.

Koslin, B., Koslin, S., Zeno, S., & Wainer, H. (1977). *The validity and reliability of the Degrees of Reading Power test*. Elmsford, NY: Touchstone Applied Science Associates.

Larson, G. E., Merritt, C. R., & Williams, S. E. (1988). Information processing and intelligence: Some implications of task complexity. *Intelligence, 12,* 131–147.

Larson, G. E., & Saccuzzo, D. P. (1989). Cognitive correlates of general intelligence: Toward a process theory of *g*. *Intelligence, 13,* 5–31.

Lenke, J. M. (1970, November). *The application of the Rasch model to achievement test data*. Paper presented at the meeting of the Northeastern Educational Research Association, Grossingers, NY.

Levy, P. (1973). On the relation between test theory and psychology. In P. Kline (Ed.), *New approaches in psychological measurement*. London: Wiley.

Lindley, R. H., Smith, W. R., & Thomas, T. J. (1988). The relationship between speed of information processing as measured by timed paper-and-pencil tests and psychometric intelligence. *Intelligence, 12,* 17–25.

Longstreth, L. E. (1984). Jensen's reaction-time investigations of intelligence: A critique. *Intelligence, 8,* 139–160.

Lord, F. M. (1968). An analysis of the Verbal Scholastic Aptitude Test using Birnbaum's three-parameter logistic model. *Educational and Psychological Measurement, 28,* 989–1020.

Lord, F. M. (1980). *Applications of item response theory to practical testing problems.* Hillsdale, NJ: Lawrence Erlbaum.

Lovitt, T. C. (1975). Applied behaviour analysis and learning disabilities: II. Specific research recommendations and suggestions for practitioners. *Journal of Learning Disabilities, 8,* 432–443.

Lumsden, J. (1978). Tests are perfectly reliable. *British Journal of Mathematical and Statistical Psychology, 31,* 19–26.

Madden, R., Gardner, E., Rudman, H., Karlsen, B., & Merwin, J. (1982). *Stanford Achievement Test—Special Edition for the Hearing Impaired.* Washington, DC: Gallaudet College.

Marshalek, B., Lohman, D. F., & Snow, R. E. (1983). The complexity continuum in the radex and hierarchical models of intelligence. *Intelligence, 7,* 107–128.

Matarazzo, J. D., Daniel, M. H., Prifitera, A., & Herman, D. O. (1988). Inter-subtest scatter in the WAIS-R standardization sample. *Journal of Clinical Psychology, 44,* 940–950.

McCarthy, D. (1972). *Manual for the McCarthy Scales of Children's Abilities.* New York: The Psychological Corporation.

McNally, J., & Murray, W. (1962). *Key words to literacy.* London: Schoolmaster.

Miles, T. R. (1951). On defining intelligence. *British Journal of Educational Psychology, 27,* 153–165.

Miller, G. A. (1976). Text comprehension skills and process models of text comprehension. In H. Singer & R. B. Ruddell (Eds.), *Theoretical models and processes of reading* (2nd ed.). Newark, DE: International Reading Association.

Mook, D. G. (1983). In defense of external invalidity. *American Psychologist, 38,* 379–387.

National Association of School Psychologists. (1988). Debate over usefulness of IQ. *Communiqué,* December, 4–7.

Nunnally, J. C. (1978). *Psychometric theory* (2nd ed.). New York: McGraw–Hill.

Olver, R. R., & Hornsby, J. R. (1966). On equivalence. In J. S. Bruner, R. R. Olver, & P. M. Greenfield (Eds.), *Studies in cognitive growth.* London: Wiley.

Otis, A. S., & Lennon, R. T. (1982). *Otis-Lennon School Ability Test.* New York: The Psychological Corporation.

Posner, M. I., & Mitchell, R. F. (1967). Chronometric analysis of classification. *Psychological Review, 74,* 392–409.

The Psychological Corporation. (1983). *Basic Achievement Skills Individual Screener.* New York: Author.

Rasch, G. (1960). *Probabilistic models for some intelligence and attainment tests.* Copenhagen: Danish Institute for Educational Research.

Rasch, G. (1961). On general laws and meaning of measurement in psychology. *Proceedings of the Fourth Berkeley Symposium on Mathematical Statistics and Probability, 4,* 321-33. Berkeley: University of California Press.

Rasch, G. (1966). An item analysis which takes individual differences into account. *British Journal of Mathematical and Statistical Psychology, 19,* 49-57.

Raven, J. C. (1958). *Standard Progressive Matrices.* London: H. K. Lewis.

Reitan, R. M. (1969). *Manual for administration of neuropsychological test batteries for adults and children.* Indianapolis, IN: Author.

Rentz, R. R., & Bashaw, W. L. (1977). The national reference scale for reading: An application of the Rasch model. *Journal of Educational Measurement, 14,* 161-179.

Reschly, D., Kicklighter, R., & McKee, P. (1988a). Recent placement litigation, part I, regular education grouping: Comparison of *Marshall* (1984, 1985) and *Hobson* (1967, 1969). *School Psychology Review, 17,* 9-21.

Reschly, D., Kicklighter, R., & McKee, P. (1988b). Recent placement litigation, part II, minority EMR overrepresentation: Comparison of *Larry P.* (1979, 1984, 1986) with *Marshall* (1984, 1985) and *S-1* (1986). *School Psychology Review, 17,* 22-38.

Reschly, D., Kicklighter, R., & McKee, P. (1988c). Recent placement litigation, part III: Analyses of differences in *Larry P., Marshall* and *S-1* and implications for future practices. *School Psychology Review, 17,* 39-50.

Resnick, L. B. (Ed.). (1976). *The nature of intelligence.* Hillsdale, NJ: Lawrence Erlbaum.

Roberts, R. D., Beh, H. C., & Stankov, L. (1988). Hick's law, competing-task performance and intelligence. *Intelligence, 12,* 111-130.

Samejima, F. (1977). A use of the information function in tailored testing. *Applied Psychological Measurement, 1,* 233-247.

SAS Institute Inc. (1985). *SAS User's Guide: Statistics Version 5 Edition.* Cary, NC: Author.

Sattler, J. (1988). *Assessment of children* (3rd ed.). San Diego, CA: Author.

Linking assessment to instructional interventions. (1986). *School Psychology Review, 15,* 317-374.

Curriculum-based assessment. (1989). *School Psychology Review, 18,* 299-370.

Scottish Council for Research in Education. (1967). *The Scottish standardisation of the Wechsler Intelligence Scale for Children.* London: University of London Press.

Shinn, M. R. (Ed.). (1989). *Curriculum-based measurement: Assessing special children.* New York: Guilford.

Shinn, M. R., Rosenfield, S., & Knutson, N. (1989). Curriculum-based assessment: A comparison of models. *School Psychology Review, 18,* 299-316.

Shrout, P., & Fleiss, J. (1979). Intraclass correlations: Uses in assessing rater reliability. *Psychological Bulletin, 86,* 420–428.

Siegel, E. (1972). Task analysis and effective teaching. *Journal of Learning Disabilities, 5,* 519–532.

Silverstein, A. B. (1976). Variance components in the subtests of the WISC-R. *Psychological Reports, 39,* 1109–1110.

Spearman, C. (1923). *The nature of "intelligence" and the principles of cognition.* London: Macmillan.

Spearman, C. (1927). *The abilities of man.* London: Macmillan.

Stankov, L. (1983). Attention and intelligence. *Journal of Educational Psychology, 75,* 471–490.

Stanovich, K. E. (1988). Science and learning disabilities. *Journal of Learning Disabilities, 21,* 210–214.

Sternberg, R. J. (1977). *Intelligence, information processing and analogical reasoning: The componential analysis of human abilities.* Hillsdale, NJ: Lawrence Erlbaum.

Sternberg, R. J. (1979). The nature of mental abilities. *American Psychologist, 34,* 214–230.

Sternberg, R. J. (1984). Toward a triarchic theory of human intelligence. *The Behavioral and Brain Sciences, 7,* 269–315.

Sternberg, R. J. (1985). *Beyond IQ: A triarchic theory of human intelligence.* New York: Cambridge University Press.

Sternberg, R. J., & Detterman, D. K. (1986). *What is intelligence? Contemporary viewpoints on its nature and definition.* Norwood, NJ: Ablex.

Sternberg, R. J., & Powell, J. S. (1982). Theories of intelligence. In R. J. Sternberg (Ed.), *Handbook of human intelligence.* New York: Cambridge University Press.

Sternberg, R. J., & Salter, W. (1982). Conceptions of intelligence. In R. J. Sternberg (Ed.), *Handbook of human intelligence.* New York: Cambridge University Press.

Thorndike, R. L., Hagen, E. P., & Sattler, J. M. (1986). *Guide for administering and scoring the Stanford-Binet Intelligence Scale: Fourth Edition.* Chicago, IL: Riverside Publishing.

Thurstone, L. L. (1938). *Primary mental abilities.* Chicago, IL: University of Chicago Press.

Tyler, S., & Elliott, C. D. (1988). Cognitive profiles of groups of poor readers and dyslexic children on the British Ability Scales. *British Journal of Psychology, 79,* 493–508.

U. S. Bureau of the Census. (1986). *Current population survey, October 1986* [machine-readable data file]. Washington, DC: U. S. Bureau of the Census (Producer/Distributor).

U. S. Bureau of the Census. (1988). *Current population survey, March 1988* [machine-readable data file]. Washington, DC: U. S. Bureau of the Census (Producer/Distributor).

U. S. Department of Education, Office for Civil Rights. (1978). *Elementary and secondary civil rights survey*. Washington, DC: U. S. Government Printing Office.

U. S. Department of Education, Office for Civil Rights. (1984). *Elementary and secondary civil rights survey*. Washington, DC: U. S. Government Printing Office.

U. S. Department of Education, Office of Special Education and Rehabilitative Services. (1986). *Eighth annual report to Congress on the implementation of the Education of the Handicapped Act*. Washington, DC: U. S. Government Printing Office.

Vernon, P. A. (1985). Individual differences in general cognitive ability. In L. C. Hartlage & C. F. Telzrow (Eds.), *The neuropsychology of individual differences: A developmental perspective*. New York: Plenum.

Vernon, P.E. (1948). Word counts of infant readers. In Scottish Council for Research in Education, *Studies in Reading—Volume I*. London: University of London Press.

Vernon, P. E. (1950). *The structure of human abilities*. London: Methuen.

Wallbrown, F. H., McLoughlin, C. S., Elliott, C. D., & Blaha, J. (1984). The factorial composition of the British Ability Scales for school-aged children. *Journal of Clinical Psychology, 40,* 278-290.

Warburton, F. W. (1970). The British Intelligence Scale. In W. B. Dockrell (Ed.), *On intelligence: The Toronto symposium on intelligence, 1969*. London: Methuen.

Warburton, F. W., Fitzpatrick, T. F., Ward, J., & Ritchie, M. (1970). Some problems in the construction of individual intelligence tests. In P. Mittler (Ed.), *The psychological assessment of mental and physical handicap*. London: Methuen.

Ward, J. (1972). The saga of Butch and Slim. *British Journal of Educational Psychology, 42,* 267-289.

Ward, J., & Elliott, C. D. (1990). *The British Ability Scales: An historical and developmental perspective. I—1965 to 1983*. Unpublished document, University of Manchester (England), School of Education.

Ward, J., & Fitzpatrick, T. F. (1970). The new British Intelligence Scale: Construction of logic items. *Research in Education, 4,* 1-23.

Ward, J., & Fitzpatrick, T. F. (1973). Characteristics of Matrices items. *Perceptual and Motor Skills, 36,* 987-993.

Warm, T. (1978). *Introduction to latent trait theory*. Oklahoma City, OK: United States Coast Guard.

Wechsler, D. (1939). *The measurement of adult intelligence*. Baltimore: Williams & Wilkins.

Wechsler, D. (1974). *Manual for the Wechsler Intelligence Scale for Children—Revised.* New York: The Psychological Corporation.

Wechsler, D. (1989). *Wechsler Preschool and Primary Scale of Intelligence—Revised.* San Antonio, TX: The Psychological Corporation.

White, O. R., & Liberty, K. A. (1976). Behavioral assessment and precise educational measurement. In N. G. Haring & R. L. Schiefelbusch (Eds.), *Teaching special children.* New York: McGraw-Hill.

Widaman, K. F., & Carlson, J. S. (1989). Procedural effects on performance on the Hick paradigm: Bias in reaction time and movement time parameters. *Intelligence, 13,* 63-85.

Woodcock, R. W. (1973). *Woodcock Reading Mastery Tests.* Circle Pines, MN: American Guidance Service.

Woodcock, R.W. (1978). *Development and standardization of the Woodcock-Johnson Psycho-Educational Battery.* Allen, TX: DLM Teaching Resources.

Woodcock, R. W. (1987). *Woodcock Reading Mastery Tests—Revised.* Circle Pines, MN: American Guidance Service.

Woodcock, R. W., & Johnson, M. B. (1977). *Woodcock-Johnson Psycho-Educational Battery.* Allen, TX: DLM Teaching Resources.

Woodcock, R. W., & Johnson, M. B. (1989). *Woodcock-Johnson Psycho-Educational Battery—Revised.* Allen, TX: DLM Teaching Resources.

Wright, B. D. (1968). Sample-free test calibration and person measurement. *Proceedings of the 1967 Invitational Conference on Testing Problems* (pp. 85-101). Princeton, NJ: Educational Testing Service.

Wright, B. D. (1970, April). *Mean value estimation.* Paper presented at the meeting of the American Educational Research Association (Pre-session Workshop), Minneapolis, MN.

Wright, B. D., Congdon, R. T., & Rossner, M. (1987). *MSTEPS: A Rasch program for ordered response categories.* Chicago, IL: University of Chicago, Department of Education.

Wright, B. D., & Masters, G. N. (1982). *Rating scale analysis.* Chicago, IL: MESA Press.

Wright, B. D., & Mead, R. J. (1976). *BICAL: Calibrating rating scales with the Rasch model* (Research Memorandum No. 23). Chicago, IL: University of Chicago, Statistical Laboratory, Department of Education.

Wright, B. D., & Stone, M. H. (1979). *Best test design.* Chicago, IL: MESA Press.

Wright, B. D., & Stone, M. H. (1985). [Review of The British Ability Scales]. In J. V. Mitchell, Jr. (Ed.), *The ninth mental measurements yearbook.* Lincoln, NE: Buros Institute of Mental Measurements.

Ysseldyke, J. E., & Salvia, J. (1974). Diagnostic-prescriptive teaching: Two models. *Exceptional Children, 41,* 181-185.